*The Particulars of Rapture*

# The Particulars of
# Rapture

*An Aesthetics of the Affects*

CHARLES ALTIERI

*Cornell University Press*

ITHACA AND LONDON

Permissions are to be found at the back of the book.

Copyright © 2003 by Cornell University

All rights reserved. Except for brief quotations in a review, this book, or parts thereof, must not be reproduced in any form without permission in writing from the publisher. For information, address Cornell University Press, Sage House, 512 East State Street, Ithaca, New York 14850.

First published 2003 by Cornell University Press
First printing, Cornell Paperbacks, 2003

Printed in the United States of America

Library of Congress Cataloging-in-Publication Data

Altieri, Charles.
    The particulars of rapture : an aesthetics of the affects / Charles Altieri.
        p. cm.
    Includes bibliographical references and index.
    ISBN 0-8014-4154-4 (alk. paper) — ISBN 0-8014-8843-5 (pbk. : alk. paper)
    1. Aesthetics—Psychological aspects.   2. Affect (Psychology)   I. Title.
BH301.P78 A48 2003
111'.85—dc22

                                                                2003019942

Cornell University Press strives to use environmentally responsible suppliers and materials to the fullest extent possible in the publishing of its books. Such materials include vegetable-based, low-VOC inks, and acid-free papers that are recycled, totally chlorine-free, or partly composed of nonwood fibers. For further information, visit our website at www.cornellpress.cornell.edu.

Cloth printing          10 9 8 7 6 5 4 3 2 1
Paperback printing      10 9 8 7 6 5 4 3 2 1

*To my colleagues at Berkeley—for their judicious indifference as well as their many kindnesses. They make it easy to write a book about mostly positive affects.*

# Contents

# Preface

This will probably be my last book, almost certainly my last effort to put together an extended abstract argument. So in working on this book I have also been dramatizing for myself how what I have been writing might be useful for my situation. How can one represent the range of feelings that go into seeing oneself doing something one cares about for probably the last time? Why is it so hard to eliminate that all-important "probably"? And, most important for my project, why is it oddly satisfying to be able to represent what is a sad state of affairs? Why is being able to say "this is probably the last" a way of making emotional alignments with reality and transmuting pain into something more than acceptance?

I cannot claim that this book answers these questions. But I hope it at least shows why they are interesting and provides the terms for making the questioning itself another form of satisfaction. I can claim that the stance of finality is an especially fruitful one for looking back and appreciating how friends, colleagues, and students have contributed to its taking the shape it has, and indeed to my taking the shapes that I have. John McGowan, Joshua Clover, and Charles Molesworth read the entire manuscript carefully, McGowan in lieu of the tennis that I had promised him. All three friends have long harbored hopes that they could improve my writing and in this case I think they did; certainly they sharpened the focus of my argument and clarified for me difficulties I had been trying to avoid, and helped me believe I had something worth saying. Several other friends performed crucial spot services. I tested my introduction with Henry Staten, my discussion of Martha Nussbaum with Richard Eldridge, Rei Terada, and Allen Dunn, my discussion of Richard Wollheim with Steven Arkonovitch, and my remarks on Joyce with John Bishop, all of whom managed to combine encouragement with sharp and useful criticism. My colleagues Paul Alpers, John Shoptaw, Anne-Lise François, Sam Otter, Kevis Goodman, Vicky Kahn, and Celeste Langan were marvelous at letting their fertile minds flow over the topics I obsessively posited to them. To Marjorie Perloff, Mei-Mei Berssenbrugge, Lyn Hejinian, Brenda Hillman, Jeanne Heuving, Miriam Nichols, and Tony Cascardi I want to express my thanks for years of engaging and fruitful conversation on this and related topics. And I cannot forget the intellectual and personal debt I have to my Berkeley students, especially Brian Glaser, Linda Voris, Craig Dworkin, Natalie Gerber, Lytle Shaw, Omri Moses, Paul Stasi, Charles Tung, Charles Sumner, Julie Carr, Jennifer Scappetone, and Jessica Fisher. Nor can I ignore the noble efforts of my colleague Michele Rabkin, Associate Director of the Consortium for the Arts at Berkeley, whose extraordinary competence freed me from administrative work and gave me time to write.

It has been a delight to work with Cornell University Press. Bernhard Kendler is that rare combination of intelligence, diligence, and trustworthiness that makes even the pains of editing and revising relatively pleasurable. And while not directly relevant to this book, it is directly relevant to the age question that my lovely daughter Laura has been living with me during the year I finally put everything together. She does not have my passion for abstraction, but she loves, and loves sharing, food and talk and travel, the things most desperately needed by those whose passion for philosophy is greater than their powers of analysis and exposition.

Finally I want to proclaim my love and gratitude for my wife, Carolyn Porter, whose great contribution to this book was her refusal to read it. That gesture kept the work at least partially in perspective and forced me constantly to confront crucial differences between writing about the affects and negotiating them in real time and real space. That the reality could be as satisfying as the writing was and is due largely to Carolyn, to whom I hope I never have to say the word "last."

CHARLES ALTIERI

*Berkeley, California*

*The Particulars of Rapture*

# I · The Arts as a Challenge to Dominant Philosophical Theories of the Affects

For a year I could not get him to talk about emotions; now people won't let me stop talking about them.

Monica Lewinsky

The physiologists who . . . have been so industriously exploring the functions of the brain, have limited their attempts at explanation to its cognitive and volitional performances. . . . But the *aesthetic* sphere of the mind, its longings, its pleasures, its pains, and its emotions, have been so ignored in all these researches that one is tempted to suppose . . . that they had either bestowed no thought upon the subject, or that they had found it so difficult to make distinct hypotheses, that the matter lay for them among the problems of the future, only to be taken up after the simple ones of the present should have been definitely solved.

William James, "What Is an Emotion?"

## I. The Aesthetic Approach versus the Cognitive

Lacking James's exquisite capacities for irony, I will have to begin in the confessional mode. This book originated as a reaction against dominant tendencies in my field of literary criticism. I had always hated criticism that preferred context to text and insisted on situating works in relation to historical forces and sociopolitical interests. But the imperative to work intensely on the affects came from recognizing that even criticism sharing my overall values seemed to me too eager to equate texts with the interpretive frameworks we could put around them. Criticism seemed so hungry for relevance that it could subordinate context to text only by attributing to the text some kind of moral wisdom or ethically enlightened attitude. I realized that I could not say this work misreads texts, and I would not promise a mode of reading that does not depend on some kind of interpretation. Yet I thought I could show

how most "ethical" readings tend to produce abstract substitutes for the text and so end up sharing with sociopolitical historicism a tendency to overread for "meaning" while underreading the specific modes of affective engagement presented by works of art. For my alternative I try to turn away from the inordinate faith in "interpretation" shared by critics in the arts who otherwise have very little in common. Instead I establish context by engaging philosophical discourses on the nature and significance of various affective dimensions of experience.

Theorists like Paul Griffith (16–17) and Richard Wollheim (*On the Emotions*, xii–xiii) warn us to be wary of assuming that there is any one preexisting general class like affect or emotion that can be defined in such a way as to include all of the cases one might want to consider if one is interested in varieties of what typically get grouped under terms like "emotion." Yet even to appreciate their warning I think we have to have some quite general understanding of a distinctive realm of experience that cannot be treated in the same way we treat either sensations or simple beliefs. So while I am quite willing to admit there will be problematic cases, I think we can use the term "affect" as our umbrella term.[1] This term provides a means of referring to the entire range of states that are bounded on one side by pure sensation and on the other by thoughts that have no visible or tangible impact on our bodies. Affects are immediate modes of sensual responsiveness to the world characterized by an accompanying imaginative dimension. Pain is usually a sensation; the assertion that someone else is in pain constitutes a proposition. But pain becomes an affect when it takes on a tinge of irritation with some particular situation that one wants to be otherwise or when it enters the domain of sadness by focusing on various kinds of loss.

Then one can go on to divide affects into four basic categories. Feelings are elemental affective states characterized by an imaginative engagement in the immediate processes of sensation. Moods are modes of feeling where the sense of subjectivity becomes diffuse and sensation merges into something close to atmosphere, something that seems to pervade an entire scene or situation. Emotions are affects involving the construction of attitudes that typically establish a particular cause and so situate the agent within a narrative and generate some kind of action or identification. Finally, passions are emotions within which we project significant stakes for the identity that they make possible. Particular details can elicit momentary sensations tinged with sadness. Those sensations can become aspects within a more general sense that one's world seems somewhat heavy and without pleasure. Or one might come to stage the sadness as produced by a particular memory or situation. Then sadness becomes an emotion, a means of representing one's situation and establishing values in relation to future actions. Finally sadness becomes a passion when it seems especially absorbing, as if one were compelled to make it a primary aspect of one's identity.

Armed with distinctions like these, I thought I could pursue a straightforward research project bringing to literary studies the best that philosophers had thought and said on the affects. However as I started to read these philosophers carefully, the situation got much more complicated, and much more interesting. I discovered in that discourse many of the same problems that in criticism had driven me to seek out the alternatives I thought I would find in working on the affects. Theorists of the emotions proved even more eager than literary critics are to stress cognitive and moral dimensions of the topic, in the process blinding themselves to phenomenological considerations that might help explain why we care about affects in the first place.[2] This realization provided a challenging opportunity, even though it would make for a much stranger book than I had planned. I became convinced that I could use the philosophical framework as a context for clarifying how we might engage the affective dimension of works of art and how we might articulate values for those works without collapsing them into either the ethical or the cognitive. But then I realized that I would have to use what the philosophers enabled me to see about the art against the philosophers. For the thick descriptions enabled by focusing on affects and relations among affects within works of art provided a very different image of both human activity and human investments than the ones shaping the philosophical work. I became fascinated by the degree to which using theoretical concerns about the affects to respond to the arts brought out an aesthetic dimension to our concern with the affects in all areas of our lives.[3]

This dissatisfaction with philosophy took two basic forms. First, my work in the arts made it impossible to accept what seemed to me the prevailing assumptions shaping the psychological descriptions provided by the once dominant cognitivist views of emotion (which I will soon engage). Patricia Greenspan, for example, identifies cognitivism as an emphasis on two basic "compounds—affective states of comfort and discomfort and evaluative propositions spelling out their intentional content" (4). I find the model of states of comfort and discomfort a very reductive way to look at elemental affects. And while I have to agree that evaluative propositions often play significant roles in how we cast emotions, it seems to me also that quite different versions of intentionality come into play, especially modes of intentionality connected to values like intensity and connectedness rather than to discursive propositions that evaluate possible actions.[4] Being moved takes many forms, some of which do not involve conceptual formulations of any kind, and there are many modes of expressive activity that call for various attunements not available when we think in terms of beliefs.[5]

For a while I thought I was going to revolutionize the study of emotions. Then it began to dawn on me that I was not the only one dissatisfied with cognitivism. Several significant criticisms had emerged. But while my ambition dimmed, my dissatisfaction seemed to increase. For even when philosophers provided substantial alternatives to the core cognitivist position, I found that they did not come much closer to the affective qualities that engaged me in the arts. These philosophers restored a sense of why specific feelings might matter and why expression can be a central value. However, in my view they still tended to assimilate affective states too quickly into models of reflective judgment that subordinated the phenomenology of the affects to the perspectives we bring to bear in orienting and in assessing actions.[6] To be adequate to our aesthetic experience of these affects, philosophy would have to pay considerably more attention to how aspects of our mental lives take on distinctive vividness for us and invite us to seek satisfaction simply in how that mental life finds means of expression. In effect, the arts inspire accounts that make affective experience not just something we understand, but something that we pursue as a fundamental value. And in articulating such possibilities the arts seem to require our developing a fairly tight connection between our aesthetic interests and what Baruch Spinoza elaborated as our conative drives.

Let me be more concrete. For the past three decades philosophers have been attempting to reverse a longstanding cultural bias that set irrational, seething emotions against the cool, analytic operations of reason. This work has made us aware of the many ways in which the emotions, if not all of the affects, complement reason by establishing salience and by constituting versions of value that ground private interests in shared cultural concerns. However, this work now seems to me to be fostering an intellectual culture where this new love affair between the passions and reason produces as part of love's blindness an inability to appreciate the differences that attracted them to one another in the first place. Most American philosophers and social theorists tend to dwell only on those aspects of our affective lives that complement reason. As a result we lose sight of both the danger in and the appeal of affective states that generate values resistant to reason's authority. And, even more important, we are coming to depend on concepts of agency that severely reduce the many channels of mental activity fundamental to subjective life, so that we end up honoring only a very limited range of values possible within affective experience.

I am of course generalizing about contemporary philosophy in a most unphilosophical way. But I see no alternative in this introduction to lumping within one philosophical attitude both the emphasis on adjudicating beliefs in traditional cognitivist accounts of the emotions and the more fluid treatments of judgment emerging in work critical of that position.[7] For my primary concern is simply that there are severe limitations to the fundamental model of mind informing how this work identifies particular affects and elaborates the possible values that such affects might have in our lives. And if recent philosophical work on the emotions has made my target less clear, it has also made it seem more urgent that I come close to hitting the mark. For we have to realize how difficult it is to develop philosophical positions sufficiently critical of cognitivist values, especially in an intellectual culture eager for a philosophy that can defend versions of realism sufficient to resist cultural relativism. And I hope we will also come to appreciate why it may be time to use the arts for exploring a quite different conceptual orientation toward affective experience.

Here I will base these explorations on two fundamental aspects of aesthetic experience. The first aspect is descriptive. I think the arts' insistence on exemplary concrete particularity provides a vital arena for developing working definitions for how we in modern Western society might best characterize various kinds of affects.[8] The second aspect is more abstract—concerned not with how we engage the world but with how we reflect upon the values involved in our various ways of experiencing the world. For I want to use aesthetic models to foreground conative experiences of affective states as ends in themselves, experiences quite at odds with the philosophical tendency to treat affects primarily as means for generating actions and attitudes. An aesthetic perspective invites us to ask what states, roles, identifications, and social bonds become possible by virtue of our efforts to dwell fully within these dispositions of energies and the modes of self-reflection they sustain. Rather than asking what we can know about the affects, or how they contribute to the work of knowing, we begin to ask who we can be by virtue of how we dispose our self-consciousness in relation to affective experience. How are we changed by what we feel, and by our adapting different ways of engaging what we feel? What needs get expressed, desires articulated, and modes of satisfaction elaborated because of how we engage ourselves in these processes, and because of how we see one another engaging in these processes?

This shift in focus can lead beyond the affects to more general questions about the roles in our lives of complexes of values that are very difficult for reason either to grasp or to assess. For the self-reflexive immediacy cultivated by an aesthetic perspective attunes us to values that are difficult to correlate with those that occupy traditional philosophical discourses. An aesthetic approach to the emotions can clarify different kinds of intensity, for example, but it cannot easily attach these states to moral terms. So, ultimately, an aesthetics of the affects also becomes a means of elaborating how there may be profoundly incommensurable perspectives on values that are nonetheless all necessary if we are to realize various aspects of our human potential. Ironically, this perspective then provides a challenge to the benign imperialism of philosophy's reaching out to the arts only so long as the arts turn out to sustain the hegemony of its modes of reflection. And by showing that the values that the arts sustain are not easily reconciled with those assessed by moral reason, we also challenge the current emphasis in the academy on the sociological and political dimensions of the arts. For that mode of questioning comes to seem only the flip, socially active side of the philosopher's narrow reduction of all expressive energies to concerns for how truths can be established. Both perspectives—the philosophical and the sociological—seem incapable of dealing adequately with the kinds of experiences and values made sharply articulate in how specific works of art structure reflexive consciousness.

## II. Five Topoi of Typical Contemporary Accounts of the Emotions

It is time to turn to examples. I want to illustrate what I have been claiming is the spirit of most contemporary philosophy on the affects so that a clearer picture emerges of how the arts may open significant alternative ways of reflecting on this topic. But when I make this turn I find that almost all the philosophical work I want to bring to bear is devoted exclusively to one particular kind of affect, the emotions. Little attention is paid to feelings and to moods because these affect types do not require forming beliefs and soliciting narrative accounts. So even the choice of examples marks a significant, and significantly limited, set of shared assumptions among those philosophers now taken seriously because of their work in this field. It remains the case that, philosophers being philosophers, this agreement on the topic to study is not matched by agreement on what the emotions involve. Yet I think I can establish a level of analysis where we can see that most contemporary philosophy on the emotions shares five basic topoi.[9] Then I will try to clarify what seem to me two basic limitations in this approach, limitations that have significant consequences for how discourse about the affects links to a range of practical concerns.

First, our philosophers would insist on characterizing the specific beliefs and desires that constitute the "intentional" component of the emotion. This move is absolutely central to contemporary thinking because it affords a sharp distinction between mere behavior and the presence of determinate and determinable emotions. If the physiology of feelings is primary, as in William James's theorizing about the affects, there is no clear way to identify the emotion or to understand what it involves for particular agents. We have to establish intentionality.[10] But once we locate an intention we can also identify the particular state as part of a narrative. We can describe how the emotion connects to what the agent thinks; we can specify its object or target; and we have a means of understanding how those beliefs are likely to orient the agent to particular actions. Suppose we see John acting out a barely suppressed rage as he observes his partner Jane "flirting" with their mutual friend Bill. We conclude that he is jealous because we assume that these physical signs are connected to specific beliefs about what Jane and Bill are doing.[11]

The second topos brings out one practical consequence of having formed an intentional perspective on the scene. For as intentions construct scenarios, they organize how attention is deployed, and they allow the subject to take in modes of information not likely to arise without the distinctive distribution of affective energies. Holding the beliefs he does, John finds himself disposed to watch Bill and Jane very carefully and to notice every sign that either confirms or disconfirms his suspicions. So we have a clear example of how emotion can be said to supplement reason and to provide evidence that enters into making judgments. But, as cognitivist philosophers tend to ignore, jealousy's relationship to "proof" can be a strange and disturbing one because this state not only generates information but also shapes how we go on to interpret its relevance. As *Othello* powerfully demonstrates, jealousy wants to become both the investigating force and the adjudicating one.

Affective intentions then are not just mental states. While we need intentions to specify what emotion someone is having, we often can see just from the state of someone's bodily expressions that the person is being moved by some cause. So a third topos emerges, consisting of the various ways that philosophers connect bodily states to intentions.[12] Cognitivists are especially wary on this point because they adamantly resist any Jamesian account of physical causality. Bodily states have to be rendered as accompanying and even complementing intentionality, but they cannot be cast as producing it. Whatever the specific theory of causality, all accounts of the emotion have to address how the specific state is manifested and interpreted by the agent. Jealously is an especially intriguing emotion in this regard because this physicality is almost always intense and often quite complex—no wonder that actors love to play jealous characters. Jealously involves the physical signs of rage, but usually in an abject manner or in a manner somehow fighting off that possibility of abjection. For jealousy can be as embarrassing as it is intense, with agents profoundly uneasy about being caught up in those very manifestations of passion. And that uneasiness spawns its own physical countermovements. The weaker one fears one is becoming because one shows the signs of jealousy, the greater the rage at the person held responsible, and the greater the need to conceal what so insistently seeks expression. It becomes difficult to know whether this emotion is best satisfied by inflicting pain on those who cause it or by escaping the embarrassment one comes to feel in entertaining it.

Jealousy is also an especially rich example of a fourth topos, one that introduces complex philosophical questions about the nature of agency. Because many emotions show themselves even when we try to conceal them, there is good reason to raise questions about dimensions of behavior that are passive or driven and those that are active or willed as expressions for which one wants to take responsibility. Several distinctions then become necessary. Emotions have different qualities depending on how closely they can be woven into the agent's own sense of active powers: Is the jealousy imposed or is it almost chosen or stylized as a way of accommodating oneself to a situation? Correspondingly we have to distinguish between expressions of emotion that may be seen as fundamentally symptomatic and those that are deliberately communicative. A person can reveal jealousy in his physical appearance even while denying it, or the person can intensify the physical gestures for deliberate effect on an interlocutor. Moreover, questions of agency seem bound up with concerns for the boundaries of individuation. With some emotions it makes sense to act as if they were distinctive features of an individual personality or of an individual response to situations. With others it can be a mistake to dwell too much on the individual because the emotion seems either painfully typical or ecstatically transpersonal. Part of the pressure on jealousy is our sense that even though we feel it so intensely, we know how utterly ordinary and predictable it is under the appropriate circumstances. We lose our distinctiveness as agents. Conversely, part of the joy we associate with love is a sense that we are not quite limited to our individual natures. Instead, we are somehow blessed by forces that extend beyond us and give us access to a select company of souls allowed this kind of experience.

My final topos emerges because no account of the emotions can be complete without addressing what Keith Oatley calls the roles the emotions play in "making action possible" (12). Traditional Western thinking stressed the danger of emotion's influence on action, since all the affects introduce irrational factors blurring judgment and subjecting us to all kinds of seduction. Contemporary theories, especially cognitivist ones, then have a substantial task facing them because they want to develop a very different practical story, with at least two important motifs. First, emotions influence action because they shape and reinforce appraisals. They establish salience among the details we observe and so organize situations in accord with specific values. (See for example Tangney and Fisher, 65). An initial angry reaction reorganizes how I perceive my situation. And it brings to bear an entire framework of values—negatively by recalling how much it matters to me that certain expectations or principles were violated by the object of my anger, and positively by producing specific projected satisfactions that I associate with justice and with revenge. And as I come to rely on these values, I also perforce strengthen the bonds I have to the social grammars that I learned when I established my ability to negotiate the culture I inhabit. Emotions generate actions because they bring into play learned scenarios and modes of appraisal that indicate what the likely outcome is of a particular self-representation. I do not have to do much figuring to understand where my jealousy is leading me.

The second motif shifts the focus from understanding how emotions influence actions to understanding how observers can modify the patterns of behavior governing individual lives. Here cognitivist theory provides an impressively tight case. Because emotions depend on beliefs and generate appraisals of how action might be possible, they involve a kind of reasoning. We can test the appraisals individuals make against what a more objective perspective might conclude if it were given this kind of person in this kind of situation. The observers have to be sensitive to individual differences, but they still might have cause to intervene if a person's emotional appraisals seem cognitively bizarre or strangely overwrought. For the fact that emotions shape salience is not always in our interest. The very fact that the emotions help us notice some things means they also are likely to blind us to other features of the situations.

So the more one can treat our motives in propositional form, the stronger the basis for intervening when we think the blindness is debilitating. We can point out discrepancies between the behavior and the agent's interpretation of it, or we can ask the agent to reflect on why the action pursued seems so different from how most other people experience the emotions in question.[13] Treating motivation as appraisal enables us to ask whether the emotion sorts events in ways that enable one to act in accord with his or her own best interests or potential. And if agents seem to be working at odds with those interests or potentials, we can try to clarify the apparent distance between what they seem to want and how they go about pursuing it. With jealousy, for example, cognitivist theorists would point out how we make two kinds of judgments. One asks if the interpretation of the person who has aroused our jealousy fit the facts of the case? And one asks if there are features of the subject's past experience that indicate he or she is prone to suspicion and hence ought to be aware of tendencies toward making errors in this regard? As the emotion plays itself out in action, it may provide ample materials for pointing out how much blindness comes with its insights.

## III. Representing the Affects: Adverbial versus Adjectival Treatments of Intentionality

Elaborating these topoi has been a major accomplishment for modern philosophy. But as with all major accomplishments, other features of the phenomena get pushed into the background or actively suppressed. In this case there are two conceptual victims, each of which can be revived by relying more intently than the philosophers do on examples drawn from aesthetic domains. The most obvious victim is the range of affects that do not take form as emotions. Because emotions are the aspects of our psyches most closely connected to action, or at least to the philosophy of action and hence to concerns about judgment, they draw the attention of almost all the influential philosophical discourse in this domain. In order to counteract this emphasis I will treat the emotions within an extended consideration of the roles that more elemental and fluid feelings play in our lives. Then we will be in a decent position also to address the second form of victimage, the reductive attitude toward affective agency that stems from emphasizing what we might call the belief-judgment nexus. I hope to complicate the understanding of agency that we bring to the topic of the affects by dwelling on those states and those values that get lost when we orient ourselves entirely to concerns about how beliefs are formed and actions motivated. In this section I will speak briefly on how the kinds of affects we emphasize make an enormous difference for how we construct the modes of intentionality fundamental in our theorizing; then in the next section I will take up the question of how we can bring different concerns for values to bear on our reflections about the affects.

If we insist on keeping feelings central in our discussion of the affects, then we make it possible to escape what now seems to me a vicious circle framing contemporary theory. The affects that matter for this theorizing are those shaped by beliefs and oriented toward action. These affects in turn reward a particular kind of description that gets as quickly as it can to the identifying beliefs. Those affects that do not fit this model get ruled out of court because they do not satisfy the philosopher's desire for clear and simple cases and because they do not seem to matter for the larger concerns about action and value shaping philosophical agendas. So there is no incentive to have theory address other, more fluid aspects of the affects, to dwell on how being moved can be a quite complex situation, or to concentrate on the internal dynamics by which feelings might alter emotions and modify intentionality. If we build outward from the feelings, on the other hand, we have to stress those aspects of our affective lives that emerge simply because of how consciousness is positioned in relation to experience, without necessarily turning to beliefs. Many affects have power in our lives because they emerge as immediate aspects of the kind of attention we pay to the world and to ourselves. And how we feel is often shaped less by belief per se than by how we experience the fit of various elements. Here works of art are instructive because so much depends on their internal dynamics, that is, on matters of structure and pacing and angle of perspective. Analogously, my jealousy can be fueled not so much by formulated belief as by how I attune myself to specific patterns of behavior in the other or to aspects of situations that bring my own recurrent fears and fantasies directly to bear. And my jealousy can be tormented or ambivalent because the representation I am giving fails to produce the fit among the details or among my own efforts to establish equilibrium that I want it to provide.

Most contemporary Anglo-American philosophy refuses to go beyond matters of belief to more complex affective states because it subscribes to what I call an "adjectival" perspective on the affects. Identifying affects in terms of beliefs tempts us to treat the emotions as if they were fixed objective states, and then to be content with standard adjectival terms like "jealous," or "sad," or "angry" when we describe the agent. There is very little sense of the agent as conflicted or even as attempting to develop a specific version of the emotion allowing satisfying self-representations on levels that go well beyond belief. Being hesitant in one's jealousy need not be just having weak beliefs; it can be a distinctive way of forming an emotional attitude that shapes how we treat other persons and find reinforcements for ourselves. Before criticizing this adjectival dispensation, however, one has to recognize its considerable power. Adjectives sort the world efficiently because they provide belief a stable network of assumptions. One can admit different ways of experiencing jealousy and yet still have common ground, something one could not have if one had to identify the relevant subtle affects each time. And the common ground allows us clear names for the shaping beliefs so that we then also have a clear story about the motives involved in actions. With the clear story comes the prospect of seeing quickly how we might modify the affective behavior by rational argument. Perhaps John's belief is ill formed: Jane is not even flirting. Or perhaps analyzing the jealousy will make certain forms of action seem overreactions.

Yet in matters of the psyche the promise of clarity can be a dangerous thing. For one is tempted to eliminate from one's description of affective states everything that does not align with this potential for explanation and for judgment. Sue Campbell makes a powerful distinction in this regard between accounts of action that treat selves as transparent, and hence as subsumed under the emotional categories, and those that value expressive processes because they appreciate how difficult it can be to be clear about the affective states influencing one's actions. In the latter case our concern is not with what makes a state a particular emotion but with how the affects modify the life of the subject. The adjective model gets in trouble when the beliefs become indefinite or complex or somehow imposed by the affect rather than in control of it. And emphasizing belief tends to blind us to the shaping force that specific details of perception, memory, or desire can exercise upon the psyche. Suppose one is not sure one is jealous but is sure there is some kind of persistent feeling affecting behavior. Or suppose someone takes a kind of pleasure in the pain that jealousy affords, perhaps because the signs of jealousy are accompanied by a feeling of authenticity based on the sense that so much pain must guarantee so much love. Beliefs still circulate through these feelings. But is not clear that the beliefs control the feelings. In fact the beliefs may be themselves influenced by the specific flow of feelings, so rather than helping us identify the emotion they become aspects of complex states that are quite difficult to characterize.

I suspect most cognitivists would admit that such affective states do occur. But for them such cases seem to lie beyond the ken of philosophy because there may be no clear way to characterize them and no way to treat them as representative. I have to respect that sense of limits, but respecting it only makes it the more important to also keep central for theory the perspective that the arts bring to such difficulties. Perhaps even if such complexity is not the norm, it does reveal structural conditions sufficiently basic that theory evades then at its peril. Where would any science be if it relegated itself to standard cases or to what is standard in perplexing cases? Even an adequate ontology of emotions seems to require our accepting Sue Campbell's claim that we cannot even name most of the emotions that matter to us. Many compelling affective states do not have names or are experienced as efforts to move among names to some more appropriate predicate.

Consequently when theory stresses present belief as already adequate for identifying the emotion, it makes two serious errors. The emphasis on adjective labels settles for a considerably less intricately contoured landscape of the mind than is in fact the case, with serious consequences for the values we can attribute to the affects. And the adjectival perspective ignores the values involved in bringing as much articulation as possible to what we seem to be feeling and to why we seem to care about such feeling. If we do not heed even the impulse for careful articulation of individual feelings, we deprive ourselves of basic resources that orient us toward hearing what matters to other people. Moreover, as Campbell points out, such inattention prevents us from developing political arguments showing how our institutions and cultural assumptions impose silences and blind spots affecting entire classes of people. Imagine a society in which the feelings of the homeless were as clearly recognized as the feelings of those who revel in running on beaches.

Clearly the stakes here go considerably beyond resisting the power of specific philosophical arguments. If I am right, we have to give our interests in expressive processes a much more central role in our psychology and ultimately in our understanding of ethics. Rather than dismiss what seems inchoate or indefinite, we may have to treat these qualities as fundamental features our affective lives are constantly negotiating. And that shift in focus substantially modifies our understanding of what other people need and how we can best relate to those needs. Rather than emphasize what it takes to understand their beliefs, we have to stress what is involved in attuning ourselves to their struggles for articulation, even if we cannot quite formulate these concerns in our disciplinary frameworks. Finally, for both our self-understanding and our relations with other people, we have to develop a conceptual structure enabling us to come to terms with the fact that there is often significant tension between some immediate aspects of responsiveness to the world—call them feelings—and some more synthetic construction bringing these feelings into harmony with beliefs and projections toward action. On the practical level this need will make it necessary to treat our terms for the emotions as representations that have to reconcile the resources of our media with an affective turbulence often insistent on its own immediate particularity. And when we turn to questions about values, we will have to accept a constant struggle between the clarity reasons bring and the performative qualities enabling individuals to elicit fresh transformations of our normative expectations.

In calling for this representational model I risk reinforcing those who prefer to identify the emotion with the belief and so ignore the pull that specific feelings exercise on our affective orientations. For it seems that I have to embrace the now almost universally rejected idea that we have to represent for ourselves deep psychological processes underlying surface phenomena. In order to account for this complexity, I will open the way to endless mystical claims about what lies on the other side of representation. It is much neater just to let the belief identify the emotion. Then there are no unspecifiable elements in our theorizing. But then there is also nothing inchoate in our affective lives, nothing putting pressure on the interpreter to reject certain renderings and to refine others. More important, there is no sense of value or satisfaction in recognizing that we have managed to find something close to adequate expression of complexes of feeling (nor is there an adequate sense of the frustrations that accompany failed efforts at aligning ourselves to our own affective intensities).

How, though, are we to avoid opening representational theory to endless hypotheses about what we do not see? Perhaps one can say that talk about representation becomes debilitating only when there is no clear evidence of how the representing term manages to fit with what it claims are the underlying forces it addresses. Clear debilitating cases arise in domains as disparate as Romantic metaphysics, where symbols are said to represent underlying spiritual realities, and identity politics, where individual traits are treated as representing unseen multitudes. But when we are dealing with the affects, on the other hand, we have at least two material features to which we can point as the sources of what we are trying to represent. We do not hypothesize something seeking expression but we witness agents trying to engage what seem powerful inchoate factors. We often confront publicly visible marks that bodies are undergoing particular experiences and that they are either satisfied or frustrated by the expressive process they are undertaking. So when agents change or modify views or just express discomfort, we have obvious concrete signs of whether or not the representation seems in touch with actual conditions.

Second, this relation to behavior also makes it possible to talk about representation without quite invoking the pictorial model basic to Enlightenment epistemic ideals. We are not picturing the feelings or making propositions about specific brain states. Rather this view of representation is fundamentally pragmatic. It is a matter of constantly characterizing and recharacterizing how various aspects of our accounts of experience do and do not seem to fit our behavioral states. We need representations to align elements and bring some relational focus to persisting dissatisfactions with the language available to the agent. There is no problem in recognizing that something resists representation; the problem lies in developing a language for that otherness without losing sight of what we can manage to express. Perhaps then we can supplement adjectival formulations of the affects by turning to Richard Moran's suggestion that we treat the affects along adverbial lines. Taken as adverbs, the affects are not states that agents enter but qualities of actions that agents produce in exercising their capacities as distinct subjects. On that basis we can shift from an epistemological model of representation to a quasi-political one. Even though we cannot hope to have our representative actually picture the range of phenomena for which it must stand, we can let the representation perform a range of functions that enable us to enter into communication about what in fact remains fluid and fleeting. The mark of expressive success is the psyche's willingness to keep the representative in office.

Clearly there can be a continuity between adjectival and adverbial modes of description, with different orientations necessary for different purposes. But reaching practical reconciliations can blind us to the deeper philosophical question of how we represent the agency whose affects we are trying to characterize. Therefore in this book I will spend a good deal of time insisting on strong differences between the versions of agency required for the adjectival and for the adverbial approaches. Kant will be my basic source for this distinction because he carefully establishes crucial differences between models of intentionality governed by the epistemic practices shaping cognitivist perspectives and models governed by the aesthetic concerns for expressive particularity that shape my remarks. One might even say that Kant virtually invented the aesthetic in order to establish a mode of judgment and related attitudes toward intentionality that were not trapped in Enlightenment fealties to the criteria-based, rule-governed practices governed by the understanding.

Kant had to show that there are two quite different modes of judgment that play central roles in human life. The first mode, the default mode, is practical or "determinative." Its task is to "think the particular under the universal" (18). Determinative judgments assign purposes. They place particulars within categories in ways that minimize tension between the particular and the various uses to which the mind assigns it. "Reflexive" judgments, on the other hand, have only the particular given to them. No universal is assigned. Rather than subsuming the individual under the universal, reflexive judgment extends the particular so that it can play the role of a universal. For example, where determinative judgment would conclude that Othello is jealous because his behavior is governed by particular traits, reflexive judgment can attend to Othello as bringing together a set of traits that in the future would have to be considered part of our model for what jealousy might be. Reflexive judgment allows a distinctive mode of exemplarity.[14]

Kant's term for this expressive particularity is "purposiveness without purpose." The relevant mode of intentionality is clearly directed by an intelligence and a will, but these do not seek discursive knowledge. Kant sees purposiveness as an intelligent causal force that cannot be subsumed under the languages we have for dealing with purposes. Instead purposiveness appears "as if" there were an underlying will, even though no such rule can be established. Purposiveness emerges when we cannot posit a will acting in terms of beliefs and projects, yet we can determine a forming power within the activity "only by deriving it from will" (65). Thus the concrete relational density within works of art seems clearly the product of intelligence and purpose. Yet our practical vocabularies do not provide adequate categories or criteria for understanding how this authorial intelligence is working. Why does a work labor so intensely to contrast this shade of red with a neighboring one? There is not likely to be a cogent practical answer unless we allow the work itself to establish the explanatory framework. That is why for Kant purposive authorship gives a rule to nature, for then we have to examine how nature is modified in order to appreciate what art works can compose.

I want to adapt Kant's sense of purposiveness for speaking about intentionality in affective states.[15] I think there is a tight fit between these concepts because in Kant purposiveness focuses on how the particulars establish intricate fits not easily thematized. Because we are talking about processes and not products, and life not art, we have to drop any strict Kantian notion of giving rules to nature or of establishing formal objects whose interrelationships clarify the values pursued by that purposiveness. Yet we still have a much richer way of talking about affective agency than we might if we stayed with a language of belief and the forms of rationality belief can sponsor. Imagine a situation where we see someone moved by certain feelings and acting in relation to them but we cannot attribute specific beliefs that seem to fit the situation. We can still grant purposiveness and try to construct an intentional stance for the agent to which we can respond. For we recognize that there is something active in the way the agent deals with what moves him, and we then try to project an overall intentionality for the process based on our cultural grammars for interpreting actions and psychological states. And because we have granted intentionality even if we cannot determine belief, we have some basic shareable principle through which we can seek further clarifications from the agent about what seems to be shaping the affective behavior. We enter the same kind of dialogue with the agent as we do with a work of art that engages us even though it does not allow us clear intellectual access to its ways of processing the world.[16]

A final reason for extending Kant's aesthetic psychology beyond his aesthetics is that he gives a superb practical focus to how we might go about understanding Spinoza's *conatus,* which will turn out to ground my most basic value claims. *Conatus* is a very general form of purposive orientation exercised by all living agents in their efforts to persist in their own being. Purposiveness seems to me a powerful way of identifying the dynamics of conative activity so that we can postulate satisfactions and interests that are not dependent on epistemic value stories. Kant helps us appreciate how intentionality can take complex forms resistant in their particularity to our standard interpretive categories. And Spinoza then helps us appreciate the satisfactions made possible by and within these intentional states. For his overall model of value is insistently anti-Cartesian. Intentionality is dynamic, seeking not just to know but to establish consciousness of certain powers as they orient us toward the world. I will devote most of chapter 4 to this aspect of

Spinoza, so for now I just want to issue promissory notes. Going from Kant's purposiveness to Spinoza's *conatus* enables us to establish overall accounts of how affective energies bring a range of satisfactions that can have very little to do with belief. How we inhabit our own inhabiting of the world proves at least as important as how we learn to form and judge beliefs about that world.

## IV. Values Mediated by Emotions versus Values within the States Emotions Make Possible

The other basic limitation that I want to elaborate will also lead to the importance of linking affects to conative energies, but it will follow a very different path. I want to shift the focus from describing affects to asking how theory can, and can not, appreciate the values we attribute to the roles that the affects play in our lives. I will begin by criticizing the degree to which contemporary philosophical discussions of the affects dwell on only those values that go into appraising the kinds of actions that the affects seem to sponsor or elicit. Philosophy seems to aim primarily at therapy by rational means, so it tends to treat human agents as if the only relevant orientations for self-reflection were cognitive. Reflection aims to clarify what practical interests the affects serve in relation to the beliefs that sponsor them, and it seeks to appraise their appropriateness for one or another "rational" version of admirable behavior. I hope instead to elaborate the kinds of satisfactions that the emotions offer because of how they modify consciousness and so serve as something more than instruments for selecting among possible goods and then motivating us to pursue them. Or, to put the same point another way, I hope to focus on those value outcomes that are related to the manner of our pursuing the emotions. The analogue with how we value works of art is a close one.

Jon Elster succinctly captures the therapeutic orientation basic to contemporary philosophy when he claims that if "emotions do not act like charms or enchantments but depend on beliefs," then "they are amenable to rational argument designed to change the beliefs" (56).[17] But a lot depends on how we interpret "amenable." There is a weak sense of the term that seems quite defensible. Where there are beliefs there must be the possibility of assessing the beliefs. But this leaves open the degree to which the beliefs are in fact the governing features of affective states, and hence the degree to which addressing them really has the possibility of modifying the behavior. So it is no wonder that those eager to keep reason allied with the affects emphasize those states where the beliefs easily and accurately identify the relevant disposition. More important, in order to make the beliefs effective there is a strong temptation to reduce our concerns about the affects to concerns about identifying them, rather than enjoying them or extending them into related possibilities for intensity. It comes to seem as if we have very little interest in what we are feeling apart from what will successfully guide specific actions. When identification is crucial, philosophy can offer a powerful model of how therapy might take place in relation to our beliefs. Philosophy can help us know ourselves because it can show what is there to be known. And it can provide clear models of appraising the beliefs. Those emotions are good or laudable which produce actions that can be approved in ethical or prudential or even virtue-based frameworks. All the rest is literature.

But literature must have its place. The literary brings to bear two basic dimensions of value usually ignored by philosophy in its focus on linking emotions to actions. At one pole, there is a range of states open to self-reflection that are too subtle or transient to have much to do with cognition or with rational appraisal. Such affects do not take the form of large dramatic emotions orienting us toward particular actions. Instead, these affects simply enliven our participation in moments as they pass, or they play out little dramas of attraction and repulsion toward the people with whom we come into contact. Consider again all the quick adjustments we make to erotic attractions we feel or recognize in others. These can be eminently enjoyable, but only so long as we recognize that letting them enter any plot is to overdetermine them and leave ourselves open to all sorts of embarrassments.

At the other pole, we encounter the problematic but provocative roles that the imagination plays in our affective lives. Cognitivist philosophy treats the imagination as a humble petitioner seeking direction and justification at the court of reason. But there are many self-dramatizing possibilities within affective life that tend to establish their own rewards and to be difficult to reconcile with efforts at rational assessment. On the simplest level, we have to recognize the importance of the efforts at expression that Campbell analyzes. There are theatrical dimensions involved in how we manifest our investments in certain emotions, and there are complex interpersonal adjustments to the affects that are shaped by projections about our audience. We could try to strip the affect of these accoutrements in order to assess its relation to possible actions, but that would blind us to how the effort at expression can itself be an action inviting our attention to just those apparently excessive elements.

When therapeutic ambitions abstract the affects from the person, they also reduce the action to motives that can be clearly stated, ignoring what is shown in how we represent and pursue those motives. And therapy too eager for rational assessment tends to treat all personal investments as if they were investments in the result of the action. Such thinking cannot honor the agent's second-order concerns for how the action might manifest distinctive individualizing traits. Nor can it bring to the foreground the shifting of roles that occurs as we imagine these manifestations being taken up by an audience. Phenomena like transference and countertransference are crucial indicators of a mobility and intricacy within the selves that our affects enable us to project.

If studying the affects teaches us anything, it is that we ought to be wary of all models of assessment that ignore how the affects open those processes of reasoning to theaters within which reason is not comfortable. How I envision others responding to my reasoning is not something that I can easily bring under the instruments for assessment that reason provides. Am I trying to appraise my jealousy because I want rational control of myself, or am I furthering the passion by other means since it thrives on my efforts to get it under control? And if I discuss the jealousy with a therapist, I have to be aware of the constant possibility that I may be engaging in a fantasy that I can thereby be more seductive because I am capable of such passion, or capable of controlling such passion with reason. Reason might force me to face these conditions, but at the risk of suppressing important aspects of them. Reason might even get us to eliminate the fantasies, but is it worth the cost?

## V. Two Versions of Expressivist Theory in Relation to These Values: The Hermeneutic and the Performative

In order to handle my concerns, I have to adopt a fundamentally expressivist view of affective agency: attention must be focused on how agents struggle to make their affects concretely manifest and on the values that can be claimed for such struggles. This domain of value considerations depends on how our expressive interests project and find satisfactions in particular states of consciousness and forms of social interaction. But having tried to clarify the importance of expressivist stances, I now cannot escape this introduction without confronting the fact that there are two fundamental poles of expressivist theory, each with quite different assumptions about agency and hence about the values and satisfactions that the affects afford. At one pole, expressivist theory borders on the same epistemic priorities driving cognitivist models of the emotions: we attend to expressive behavior in order to understand what motivates a person and shapes his or her particular values. At the other pole, expressivist theory is fundamentally aesthetic. Its most striking, if not always its most defensible, exemplar proves to be Nietzschean idealizations of a pure performativity as an end in itself. Such performativity is intensified by its ability to overcome all ties to what might be "known" about agents and might provide an interpretation of their behavior: expression is the absorption of what is other to the ego under the ego's stylizing powers. Theorizing will not get very far unless it recognizes these competing pulls and proposes some way of reconciling them. For theory has to flesh out the tensions indicating the complex roles that we ask the concept of expression to play, and it has to spell out the adjustments necessary if one is to carve for oneself some version of a middle ground.

Most expressivist theory tilts toward the epistemic because it retains a strong interest in how we know what we feel and what others are feeling.[18]

My basic example of this line of thinking will be the work of Sue Campbell, although I think we have to supplement her psychological emphases with Simon Blackburn's efforts to make expressivism basic to our understanding of ethical practices. Campbell makes inchoateness a fundamental feature of expressivist theory. For this inchoateness requires our shifting our attention from what we might believe to what imposes itself upon us as something we want to make articulate. Therefore expressive activity manifests a continual struggle between a sense of inchoateness and the forms of intelligibility provided by our social grammars. Expression provides representations for the inchoate. If I find myself acting aggressively toward people, I have a strong motive for attempting to sort out my feelings and make articulate what is bothering me. And if I can do that I can begin to take responsibility for the influence these feelings have on my behavior.

However, while these cases are obviously important, they by no means exhaust the motives we have for expressivity or the roles we can take in relation to our own expressive behavior. From a Nietzschean perspective, this epistemic view of expressive activity is extremely dangerous because it constantly threatens to replace what persons make with the concepts that the society produces to explain their behavior. What we can claim to know must be kept in constant tension with what we can claim to produce in relation to such knowledge. The self known becomes the third-person, the person interpretable in terms of objective frameworks. For full first-person existence, expression cannot be simply a process of revealing what explains my behavior. Fully personal values depend on maintaining a sharp distinction between naming one's feelings and coming to own them through the mark that one puts upon them. We have to look to the performative process in order to locate the force and quality of an agent's expressive energies.

It seems obvious that we need both Campbell's and Nietzsche's perspectives if we are to account for the full range of expressive activities. And it is hardly less obvious that we will always have troubles deciding which is the more appropriate stance in relation to particular situations. Given the current emphasis on epistemic aspects of expressive behavior, this book will emphasize the contrary case. I want to set performing one's affects against understanding one's affects, so that we recognize how even the process of understanding can sometimes become a matter of stylizing and personalizing. Taking this stance should help us recognize how on many occasions our affects actually participate in constituting values rather than simply embodying aspects of beliefs. And this stance will help us not only bring aesthetic discourse to bear but also show how the aesthetic provides significant models for existential values. By appropriating the notion of "ends in themselves" for the work of Nietzschean expression, I hope to show how modernist formalism also constitutes a substantial historical force modifying our understanding of ethical possibilities.

This turn to Nietzsche still leaves us with difficulties in clarifying when it makes sense to talk of ends in themselves. Either we rest in mystical claims about immediate states of awareness or we have to say why the ends can suffice in themselves. And then of course we are faced with giving an instrumental account of the very claim that these ends are not instrumental. But suppose we could argue that we have general instrumental interests in some particular states for which we cannot establish clear instrumental terms. Here the theory of affects and aesthetic theory can reinforce one another. Aesthetics shows what kinds of satisfactions are possible in modes of fit that emerge for particular moments of consciousness, so the theory of the affects can develop the psychological investments agents might have in just such moments. To the degree that expressivist theory attunes us to satisfactions that go beyond the cognitive, it joins aesthetics in celebrating the importance of how we find ourselves deploying our energies. It is quite important that I try to understand why I love someone or take pleasure in certain company. But it is even more important not to let the difficulties of understanding prevent my letting myself perform those states for myself to see what I become within the affects they allow. So the concept of end in itself need have no mysticism about it. It refers to those situations where the value for an agent resides simply in how affects immediately dispose the psyche to establish certain kinds of relations with objects, with other people, and with one's sense of one's own powers of agency.[19]

## VI. The Aesthetic and the Rational: A Brief Overview

Works of art help us test the boundaries of such states: At what point does pursuing ends in themselves transform us into heroes? at what point into monsters? And how do we tell the difference between those alternatives? I have no answer to such questions. But this book will insist that the theory of the affects has to understand how the questions arise and even to grapple in particular cases with the consequences of locating value in domains where cognitive measures have very little relevance. So I want now to introduce the kind of case that I think both haunts and justifies what is to come. Here we have to engage a situation where the aesthetic values involved clearly contrast with any instrumental analysis of the situation, yet have substantial appeal. For then we can get a clear grasp of why our emotional investments can not only conflict with reason but also sustain an expressivist defense for refusing to follow reason's ways. This defense would clarify what values inhere in the states that the emotions enable us to maintain and in the identities we can claim from the manner of our maintenance.

Jealousy generates good examples because the changes to the agent are so intense and visible. Suppose that someone were to take an aesthetic attitude toward his or her own jealousy—not simply as an observer of what being jealous involves but as an artist whose medium is one's own psyche. Most interpreters would find such reveling in jealousy at best a misjudgment, at worst lunacy. Critics commenting on *Othello* for example tend to assume cognitivist and therapeutic positions. Some see Othello's basic problem as his letting Iago get him to restrict the cognitive field in which he operates. Because Othello is seduced into admitting no competing information, he composes a world that continues to make sense for his overwrought psyche. Other critics accept this as a description of Othello's behavior, but insist that there must be some deep cause, some frustrated need for approval or terrifying encounter with Desdemona's less than idealizable sexuality that destabilizes him and opens the way for Iago's black magic. In either case, reading the play becomes an attempt to be sympathetic with Othello's jealousy without having to approve of his jealous actions or even of the exalted states that lead to these actions.

Suppose that, rather than judging how Othello goes wrong, we ask what might be of value in the experiences he has by virtue of his going wrong. What modes of intensity and what kinds of involvement with others become possible because he yields to his own inordinate demands? This shift in focus does not obscure the fact that Othello is trapped in tragic circumstances and increasingly comes to recognize just that. But rather than stress the sense of pathos seen from the outside, an aesthetic attitude will ask how we can flesh out what it must have meant to him to put the case performatively, "the pity of it, Iago, the pity of it." For it seems that his awareness of the tragedy he is enacting gives him access to ecstatic states completely lost in a moral or strictly action-oriented account of his situation. Othello does not simply murder Desdemona; he sacrifices her. And in that process he manages to develop an identity based on an amazingly intense awareness of what must be put at risk if one is to stay true to one's deepest sense of human possibility. Ultimately this intensity is magnified by the fact that he must still be accountable to the brute reality of what he has made of himself because of his pursuing his demands.

Yet the play is not at all content with stressing what Othello learns about reality as a set of limits or what the audience can learn through him. The play is not fundamentally epistemic or cognitive. There is much that we can learn from Othello and much that he should have learned about himself, but all this is a means to an end that takes us far beyond concerns for knowledge. Shakespeare's basic interest seems to have been the possibility of transforming what one can know into what one can sing—Verdi knew what made for great opera. The play stages jealousy as ultimately a possibility of making grandeur inseparable from bestiality, precisely because self-appraisal is so fundamental and so problematic a feature of erotic jealousy. On the one hand, jealousy ironically frees the lover to experience one of the most exalted realizations of what his passion involves; on the other, jealousy requires the lover to come to terms with his own powerlessness—even the most stable forms of proof can be utterly misleading. Desdemona's handkerchief ultimately becomes proof not of her infidelity but of how little he can control.

All this duality then makes possible a final affective intensity sustained by Othello's having to realize just how much distance there can be between the self who acts and the subsequent self who has to make an accurate assessment of how that action changed him. Othello's self-consciousness has no other life but to sound that difference. Therefore his final speeches resound with a sublime tension between the awareness of being reduced to a guilty thing and the expansive sense of how passion brought him to this impasse by for a short time letting him experience just how much the psyche can stake on being loved.

Despite my enthusiasm, or perhaps because of it, I cannot leave the example of Othello without also addressing the feature of his experience that resists my arguments. Few of us would choose to imitate Othello, so it is difficult to claim that the values realized by aesthetic attention to the text have any direct carryover into existential frameworks. One can praise the intensity of Othello's jealousy and the keen intelligence with which he faces his fate, but one cannot easily argue for anything exemplary for ordinary living in the extremities to which his passion drives him. Considered in practical terms, Othello would have been much better off if Iago had the interests of a philosopher-therapist.

I can think of two possible ways of pushing against this conclusion. The first is extreme, but it also brings out the tension between passion and practicality that may be fundamental to our topic. For one can argue that we have to be very careful in making negative judgments about Othello. It is possible that if one could actually participate in Othello's way of experiencing both love and justice, one just might choose these values as worth living for and dying for. It is difficult to imagine any more complete measure of love than one in which an agent both sacrifices the other and destroys himself in its name. And it is difficult to imagine a richer understanding of justice than one that so divides the self that its only recourse is self-destruction. Some ways of experiencing the world just might be worth dying for.

But I know of no such way that would be compelling in our intellectual culture. So I am forced to a second rationale better attuned to contemporary versions of practical judgment. Even if one doubts that readers might want to be Othello, or that Othello might want to be Othello, there remain other possible ways of warding off the imposition of rational judgments. There are states within being Othello that have compelling value for what they realize about love or about ultimate justice even if they are abstracted from any specific practical consequences within the play. The values reside in the capacities for focused feeling and thinking that the moments of aesthetic passion provide. This leaves room for practical judgment in deciding just how much these states are worth to us, so it does not fully challenge economic models of value. But such imagining can modify what counts as significant principles of assessment within these models. And once this possibility of identifying with passions begins to open up, it becomes likely that on some occasions agents will opt for values that do not make much sense by standard economic measures but still seem intelligible when we appreciate the identification.

Suppose, for example, we shift from Shakespeare's tragic world to Proust's melancholic comedy in order to consider Charles Swann's deliciously untherapeutic attitude toward his jealousy. For Swann, jealousy is emphatically not a disturbance or form of unpleasure leading him to pursue actions that might eliminate its cause or gain revenge on its objects. Instead, Swann seems to pursue jealousy, intensifying it and actively attempting to appreciate the intricate shifts in sensibility it creates for a love affair. Perhaps he even needs the jealousy in order to keep himself obsessed with Odette so that there can be passion across thick class lines. But the implications of his actions extend far beyond class lines. Suspicious of ordinary love talk as mere illusion dignifying biological impulses, Swann requires a theater for his erotic concerns that acknowledges how much they depend on the imagination while also preventing his making that fact the basis for cynicism about the entire process. Swann needs to know that the intensity of his love is made, not found, but he also wants to care about what the artifice makes possible. In his hands then, jealousy becomes an art form attuning him to every nuance in Odette's behavior. Were jealousy more subject to rationality, it would not be so able to intensify eros. Without jealousy's modes of producing salience, many of the details of their lives would remain inert, victims of rationality's high standards for significance. Conversely, caring for that very insignificance makes him continually aware of what one can gain when love provides release from habits of calculation fundamental for rational practical action. And his jealousy creates a theater for Odette because she can then perform delays and signs of affection to others that afford the two of them a highly detailed lover's world securing their intimacy. Jealous passion here does not overcome reason; it finesses reason so as to win for itself a more capacious immediacy.

Even this more habitable model, however, still risks bringing the aesthetic orientation too close to practical judgment without sufficiently addressing what must remain the tension between the two domains. The more I reflect on the limitations of epistemically driven attitudes toward the psyche, the more I am tempted to let the arts have the entire stage. It becomes increasingly difficult not to identify with prophets of the anti-epistemic like Nietzsche and Deleuze. But, as Nietzsche once put it, he who hovers long over an abyss had better be an eagle. And I am no eagle. So I have to find rapprochement with standard forms of rationality. To do that I have to admit that most of us are not Swann or even Odette, nor were we meant to be. But all of us can identify provisionally with Swann and Odette, as well as reflect upon what that identification might involve. And that possibility of identification seems to me all I need to make my case. For we need only show that our participation in works of art is capable of modifying how we register what seems forceful within the affects. We find ourselves invited to try out various attitudes toward valuing what we encounter, and, more important, we find some of those provisional identifications eliciting our own passionate investments and clarifying paths they might take beyond the work of art. That is what brings the aesthetic into the existential.

I suspect that few of us would want to eliminate all jealousy from our erotic lives—precisely because the jealousy binds us to the irrational features fundamental to appreciating what makes our erotic commitments different from our standard social ones. More generally, there are aspects of most emotions that we do not want to treat simply as instrumental vehicles helping us sort information and appraise possible paths of action. This is obviously the case in positive emotions like pride and joy and bravery. But there is also an aspect of negative emotions that calls for this aesthetic response. In my view one of the most civilizing of affective states is the capacity to cultivate a fine anger.[20] Anger is a state that has its own ripeness, its own rich satisfactions, so long as we do not let it slide over into resentment. To accomplish this we need a dose of irony mixed with the enjoyment of our own rectitude and the capacity to dwell in admittedly fictive modes of revenge. (If we lose the fictiveness, enslavement to resentment follows.) And if we accomplish this we manage to maintain our private judgments about harm done or wrongs committed while yielding to the polite acceptances that keep social life mildly harmonious.

I do not deny that many emotions are painful and so seen as impositions from which we want relief. Yet even there we often find value within the situation. Consider the example of mourning. Mourning is the kind of pain to which it is important that we yield. We have to resolve it (melancholia is to mourning what resentment is to anger), but we don't want to resolve it too quickly or base that resolution on concepts rather than on lingering over particular features of those we love until we feel we can adjust our feelings to the places they come to hold in memory. It may seem vulgar to speak of this kind of cultivation as "aesthetic." But that appearance may be the best evidence I can find for the importance of my appeal that we extend our uses of that term. We need "aesthetic" or some parallel term to indicate the various ways that appreciative attentions to particulars as concrete structures of relationships make us care about who we are and what we do.

## VII. Summary: Four Advantages of an Aesthetic Approach to the Affects

On the basis of these examples I want to risk repetition by being as explicit as possible on what I take to be the four basic advantages that I think follow from taking this aesthetic approach into theorizing about the affects. First, analogies with works of art can drastically alter how we develop a language for describing the affects. We learn to honor subtle differences in qualities of feeling and to see why they make a difference. Because these phenomena invite reasoning but do not easily yield to reason's authority, we also find ourselves adapting for psychology significant parallels with Kantian treatments of how art works take on distinctive powers. And attention to how art works integrate energies and develop resonance provides basic models for recognizing why affects take on important roles in our lives even though their internal dynamics do not quite fit causal languages or submit to reason's interpretive and evaluative categories. Second, attention to these dynamics requires our being willing to rely on various phenomenological strategies for developing theoretical frameworks. Cognitivist stances and more general epistemic orientations toward the affects are problematic not because they are wrong but because of how they imagine what might be involved in being right. By being content with standard emotions and simple paradigm scenarios, they trivialize the lives that become possible if we concern ourselves with the intricacies of affective states. So we have to turn to reflective stances that enable us to appreciate what makes particular affective experiences seem compelling. And to do that we have to be able to supplement talk of understanding with more dynamic concepts involving how we are moved to make identifications or respond to challenges or rest in admiration, or seek more articulate expressions of our own responses. On the most general level, attention to such qualities requires our privileging exemplification over explanation more than philosophers or social scientists find comfortable.

The third advantage is simply an extension of the second. Concentrating on the aesthetic aspect of our affects will have substantial implications for the ways we talk about values and about those aspects of human agency which underlie our attributions about value. Probably the weakest aspect of cognitive accounts of the affects is their treatment of the interests agents have in their own emotions. It becomes impossible to understand the kinds of satisfactions agents might seek. Cognitivist stances have to cast affective agency as primarily a process of seeking cognitive stability in relation to some disruption or surprise: How do I understand what is happening to me and how do I act so as to dispel the emotional turmoil? An aesthetic orientation will focus on how we actually have interests in qualities basic to the emotions and how we find satisfaction within the very modes of participation that consciousness allows and extends. Finally, all of these particular concerns should make it possible to appreciate why the arts have for the past two centuries consistently opposed themselves to the epistemic orientations basic to the modes of philosophy that became dominant in the Enlightenment. Clearly we cannot do without these epistemic values, but we can recognize the degree to which they dampen our involvement in affective dynamics and cover over fundamental tensions within our cultures' ways of dealing with values. Rather than assuming that there can be a single calculus for determining

among value claims, or even that there can be a single instrument like rationality for that process, the aesthetic attitude tries to show how a range of values can be intrinsic to the affective states one encounters. And that in turn
requires treating appraisal as a complex process that is likely to requite our
having to accept incommensurable positions as nonetheless appropriate under certain circumstances. We will have to call on people to express what is
involved in their particular way of constructing values, and we may have no
recourse but to adapt ourselves to their right to do just that, even if we are
dissatisfied with the results.

## VIII. Prospectus: An Outline of the Arguments to Follow

I have to remind myself, although probably not my audience, that the advantages I claim depend on making good on what here I offer only as assertions. In order to get beyond the level of assertion, my next two chapters will
concentrate on formulating a set of operating concepts that I think are necessary if we are to put philosophical discourse into significant dialogue with
the elaborating of affect in the visual and verbal arts. I hope to establish a
modest dialectic in which the concepts seem required by aspects of the works
that then take on power because we have the relevant terms to highlight what
the artist has achieved. If I manage the desired dialectic effect, I can also show
clearly why my approach is preferable to the tendency in contemporary criticism to rely on "response theories" in order to account for affective values.
Response theories locate the distinguishing features of the affects in the ways
that individual imaginations process the materials. But from my perspective
this line of thinking subordinates the work to the empirical self and so deprives the work of powers to modify agents or to reveal to them significant
affective states and configurations that were not part of the repertoires they
brought to the work. Therefore I will focus on the links works of art make
articulate between how representative agents are moved and how that being
moved positions consciousness to make certain kinds of observations and investments. These works then become experiments in how distributions of
psychological energies can realize and elaborate particular human powers.
The richer our conceptual language for the affects, the better position we are
in to identify what can be attributed to the work as an object capable of soliciting and structuring affective energies. And the more we can locate affect
in the working of the object, the better we can explain how the object itself
can take on social force by providing shareable and discussable models for
our emotional intensities.

Even to begin formulating a theoretical position open to the necessary
modifications, I have to offer conceptual means of distinguishing sensations,
feelings, moods, emotions, and passions. That enables us to see how the arts
elaborate the elemental building blocks isolated by our efforts at definition, es-

pecially with respect to characterizing the interfaces between sensation and feeling and between atmosphere and mood. Moreover, once we have these building blocks specified, we can engage more fully the range of questions about identification that seem to me basic to our inherited ways of thinking about the affects. How do we characterize the agent's responsibility or active presence and how do we distinguish it from his or her being passively possessed by those energies? How do we recognize pressures that build on the affects and how do we appreciate the processes by which those pressures are engaged or deflected or transformed? And, perhaps most important, how do we approach those situations where it seems that affective energies make problematic the very boundaries we normally use in speaking about identifications? How do we honor basic differences between those identifications that secure individual identities and those that invite the individual to transcend that individuality—either into some sublime impersonality or into modes of identification that are fundamentally roles within a shareable public sphere, perhaps even in the form of something like a willed absorption into the purely collective identities that can emerge at moments of crisis or intense pleasure?

Chapter 2 develops these concerns in relation to feelings and moods. It dwells on numerous examples of how art works model affective intentionality, and it tries to show how artists build on fissures and junctures that revised descriptive concepts help us locate. (There is also an extended appendix to this book attempting to show the various ways criticism of literature and visual art can focus on feelings.) In taking up these concerns I also begin trying to show what philosophy can learn from the very modes of articulation it helps us engage. When I turn in the third chapter to the emotions (and tangentially to the passions), I have to focus more intensely on limited examples because the stage has already been prepared by fine critical books, so the relevant experiences can be much more densely layered. For my theoretical framework, I engage at length with the perspective offered in Richard Wollheim's *On the Emotions.* Wollheim takes us well beyond cognitivism to an account of the emotions that restores to them their complex psychological reality. So he provides a superb set of terms for working out relations between what I call being moved, being positioned, and being invested as we form attitudes that give emotions external expression. But I argue that his model of psychological reality for the emotions is somewhat limited by his interest in aligning himself with Freudian concerns. In my view, we need somewhat different versions of how we construct the causes of emotions, how we understand attitudes as processes of adjustment and readjustment, how identifications can be established, and how second-order investments in the manner and the matter of the emotion get defined.

Many of my quarrels with Wollheim turn on the issue of how we can distinguish between those emotions that can be productively imaginative in the formation of attitudes and those that remain only imaginary and so dependent on underlying fantasies. I turn to two contrasting poems in order to explore some of the different economies possible in what Wollheim calls "the construction of emotion-attitudes." First I take up Matthew Arnold's "Isolation: To Marguerite," a poem where the attitude is pervaded by self-defensive fantasy. Considered historically, Arnold's poem matters because its limitations establish sharp contrasts with modernism's turn to feelings rather than emotions. Arnold's poem is a telling example of how the Victorian ego or Victorian imaginary desperately imposed self-congratulatory forms of identification on complex and disturbing feelings. The example is so telling in fact that it makes it easy to shift from a historical register to a theoretical one, where I can spell out the consequences of Wollheim's relying on the category of fantasy. "Isolation: To Marguerite" could be treated as a textbook illustration of the working of the Lacanian imaginary since the speaker even projects a dialogue with himself in order to have an "Other" to secure the identity he feels is slipping away. The poem, therefore, also can stand as a powerful example for all the skeptical theories like Sartre's that see the emotions as an imaginary evasion of responsibility for one's actual condition.

Then I turn to a second poem in order to raise the possibility of a theoretical path that acknowledges the role of fantasy in the construction of attitudes, but also develops by contrast other roles the imagination can play. I think the resources are there in Wollheim's model, but I can bring out their importance only by turning to a text that employs the figure of address quite differently from Arnold. So I have chosen Bishop Henry King's dense elegy for his wife, "The Exequy." Here the historical dimension risks undercutting my case because it reduces me to almost slavish imitation of T. S. Eliot's praise of the serious playfulness of metaphysical conceits. Yet I tell myself I should not be embarrassed by returning to Eliot in a context that sharpens our sense of his own grasp of the forces at play in our construction of emotion-attitudes. And making this move affords two theoretical advantages. We can look at therapeutic intelligence not shaped by our therapeutic culture. And we can see in exaggerated form the kind of work the imagination can do in pushing back against the temptations to flee into self-defensive fantasy. Arnold's speaker is always backing and filling, as if speech were continual evasion. King's speaker is always seeking metaphors that will enable him to bring into one framework quite diverse and painful registers of feeling. This capacity to synthesize in turn provides possibilities for weaving intricate identifications and shifting intentional perspectives into his overall stance. By keeping his focus on forms of address he can direct toward his wife, the speaker puts pressure on himself to live up to her projected scrutiny. Consequently, he finds it possible to adjust his sense of internal boundaries so that by the end the one mourned becomes almost inseparable from the passionate subjectivity of the mourner.

Obviously concerns with agency are, or ought to be, fundamental to almost any theoretical discussion of the affects. But there seem to me two aspects of this agency that are not sufficiently discussed, so I devote chapter 4 to establishing a context within which these questions can be fully explored. I begin by summarizing important work done by Richard Moran, who shifts attention from how we interpret emotions to how we give significant roles to the manner of acting by which they are made manifest. There is no better locus for dealing with how the affects constitute value, since many of our richest satisfactions occur when we manage to occupy states like delicacy in our expression of pity or pith in our expression of anger or convincing coldness in our negotiation of jealousy. Moran is terrific in showing how we make many of our judgments about works of art in terms of such manners of presentation rather than in terms of the adequacy of the beliefs involved or the work's responsiveness to appropriate ethical norms. I want to push his arguments further because I think we can use his treatment of manner to explain how we make first- and second-order investments in the affects.

However, we then also have to explain why we take such satisfaction in our manners of acting, even when the activities are not connected to ennobling categories like those emphasized in the study of virtue. What needs and drives make that satisfaction central for us? This is ultimately a question for science. But I doubt science will provide adequate answers until its search is shaped by speculative philosophy, so here I will pursue the speculative part. Chapter 4 will argue that Moran's arguments provide a strong reason to make the case for why Baruch Spinoza's treatment of conative energies ought to play a fundamental role in our theorizing. Where Descartes put Reason and its satisfactions, Spinoza put *conatus* and its realizations. Because a *conatus* fundamental to each living being "endeavors to persist in its own being" (Spinoza, 109), conative force manifests itself as resisting all those factors that can "annul" the sense of individual existence for itself. The affects then constitute the body's basic awareness of how its conative forces are deployed. For they are constantly registering the degree to which "the body's power of activity is increased or diminished, assisted or checked, together with the ideas of these affections" (104).[21]

Questions of satisfaction are inseparable from speculation on the interests being satisfied. I think Spinoza helps one avoid the basic contemporary models used to attribute basic interests to our behavior. Although he deeply values knowledge, he refuses to treat it as our most fundamental motive: there has to be an interest in how we pursue and adapt knowledge. Although he is concerned with the fulfillment of individual being, he is in my view rightly skeptical of the normative aspect of Aristotelian versions of such fulfillment. And although he then has to be radically individualist about the endorsing of values, he can help us avoid the versions of individualism posited by Nietzsche and by Deleuze, his most powerful misreaders. Spinoza can talk about proprial energies and the self's desire to feel its effectiveness in its environment without adding any notion that this feeling depends on manifesting power over others or on displacing the ego entirely into a world of events. I develop an argument that conative energies are generated not by one over-arching identity but by the various projections of identity that come with affective intensities. Then I try to demonstrate how this line of thinking might matter in a world beyond philosophy by turning to a series of poems by Robert Creeley. No poet I know has such an intimate grasp of the ways that conative energies push against objectifying forces and find small, persistent satisfactions in self-reflexive states. In Creeley the work lyric does becomes inseparable from the pleasure consciousness takes in its endless means of adjusting to what calls it into action.

My final two chapters return to the question of the kinds of values that become central if we take an aesthetic approach to the affects and push against the epistemic emphases fundamental to American philosophy. I begin by revisiting the issue of the relation between reason and passion, in part because I want to restore the traditional sense that there are serious tensions between the values pursued by each orientation. In attempting to treat the two as potential allies, contemporary philosophy risks simplifying both domains and leaving the emotions far too little power to disrupt and to delight. And, more important, this attempted alliance ignores the ways that affective forces constitute values and provide satisfactions in their own right. I will argue that it is not feasible to give reason authority in relation to these conflicts. Rather, we have to admit that reason and passion generate quite different kinds of value claims and have their own modes of assessment. There will be times when the affects produce just the modes of enhanced attention that reason needs and also guide reason toward possible modes of compassion or sensitive judgment. But I doubt we can establish any systematic way of giving reason hierarchy so that it becomes the arbiter in all such cases. There will also be occasions when the affects bring a salience that creates obstacles to reason (obsession is one mode of establishing salience), and there will be occasions when our interests in compassion completely contradict what reason dictates. How much pride is appropriate or how can we determine limits to compassion? It is not at all clear to me that in such cases we ought to follow whatever version of reason we trust. Instead I think the best we can do is embrace an overall expressivist position calling on us to be as explicit as we can in taking responsibility for the course we pursue. Then those who would judge us have to attempt to understand how our priorities seem to fit what we do, even if they do not ultimately agree with our decisions.

This position at least gives all the forces involved the opportunity of getting a hearing. And in some respects at least it strengthens the social fabric because agents have to find ways of articulating their priorities while audiences have to pursue the possibility of mutual recognition even when the recognition does not produce agreement. Moreover, we can make at least provisional distinctions between granting one another's affective priorities and demanding that we pursue common modes of reasoning for evaluating the actions that might follow from our passions. Those of our actions that impinge in serious ways on other people have to be regulated by what these people share or can share. And what we most clearly share is a capacity to produce reasons for assessing what might be in the common interest. However, it is crucial to insist that these judgments are judgments about actions, not judgments about how the psyche works or how people should prefer certain ends. We have to keep a free space for those affective investments that do not do harm to others or put serious strain on social resources. For these investments we do best to treat arguments about norms simply as ways of giving advice.

This line of reasoning brings me into almost total opposition with Martha Nussbaum's impressive *Upheavals of Thought*. Since there seems to me no way around that book, I have to go through it (in both senses). That will take an entire chapter. Nussbaum proposes a new version of cognitivist theory that can account for the complex aspects of intentionality on which I have been insisting, and she proposes that one can bring developmental psychology to bear in order to show how reason can remain the arbiter of normative principles for the emotions. In effect, the emotions involve us in the pursuit of eudaimonic goals, and Aristotelian reasoning holds out the promise of clarifying how the emotions best realize such goals. And if we are to appreciate fully how we make judgments about these eudaimonic goals, Nussbaum calls us to attend carefully to the modes of wisdom provided by narrative texts. Narrative is especially useful in clarifying what constitutes our richest models of human erotic love.

I quarrel with each of these assertions so that I can develop by contrast the expressivist approach to values that I think best suits the roles that the emotions play in our lives. On cognitivism, I argue that Nussbaum does not honor the full complexity of intentions because she keeps our reasoning faculties dominant and is insufficient on the roles feelings play. On normativity, I argue that she manifests in especially clear form the tendency of philosophy to seek control over the emotions by any means possible. Although her view of reason is quite different from the views held by most contemporary philosophers, that difference seems to encourage even more ambitious versions of philosophical imperialism. And on the uses of narrative fictions, I argue that she provides a contrast enabling me to test what an expressivist perspective can accomplish at linking literary theory to more general value concerns. In my view her reading of *Ulysses* ignores the complex relation that the author figure within the book has with the characters whom Nussbaum uses to embody normative ideals. Consequently she succumbs to a temptation endemic to philosophy, the temptation to sacrifice what is different about the way others imagine their lives in order to identify with and reinforce the opportunities for righteousness afforded by reason's power to construct abstract ethical norms.

After all this heat, I hope my concluding chapter can shed some light on how theory can honor these individual imaginings without surrendering the right to make practical judgments. The chapter takes up two basic ways of characterizing the kinds of values where judgment need not be based primarily on giving and heeding reasons. The first occupies most of my energies. I elaborate through literary examples three basic conative states that seem to me central to the specific value-investments stemming from affective engagements.

These states are intensity, involvedness, and plasticity, all of which prove very difficult to characterize or to defend within the languages used by philosophy to talk about values. But this difficulty need not entail the conclusion that the relevant values are irrational; nor does it justify the contrary conviction that those who pursue these states ought to feel themselves heroic rebels against disciplinary versions of rationality. It will suffice to clarify why current forms of philosophical reasoning are not likely to have terms for appreciating or for assessing what these states make available. So I try to show why and how someone might make intensity or plasticity a fundamental value consideration, or how one might be willing to risk the virtues of reason because of the sense of vitality and even of strange meaningfulness that these states pursue. And I try to flesh out modes of personal fulfillment that depend only on the qualities agents experience when they involve themselves directly in the concerns and struggles of other human beings.

Because relying only on conative states keeps questions of value too closely tied to processes of self-reflection, I eventually have to turn to a second aspect of this topic. I develop what I call a matrix of fundamental values that helps us link affective states to a quite general grammar shaping expectations about how agents attach themselves to the world and to other people. And then because I think this typology reaches out across cultures, I feel I can make a case against those who make strong claims about the roles that particular social constructions play in the constitution of these affective values.

Joyce's *Dubliners* offers an exemplary text because it takes as its situation the power of Dublin society to interpellate individuals into codified repetitions of the despair and the aggression that have to compensate for all the hopes the society destroys. But precisely because he so well understands how psyches get trapped, Joyce uses the last story of the volume to test how specific emotional complexes can open a way beyond the confines of the particular culture. Learning to attend with "generous irony" provides access to a level of identifications among agents that extends beyond church and nation and the bitterness they make inescapable.

## IX. On Being between Disciplines: Notes toward an Embarrassed Phenomenology

This process of summarizing the arguments to come leaves me painfully aware of how difficult it has been to convince myself I have done justice to my topics. Even now I am haunted by questions about audience and method that I have to address even though I am not at all sure I have adequate responses to them.

My envisioned audience is primarily those concerned professionally with philosophy and those who study the arts. But in what language can one address both, especially since it seems to me pretentious to claim that I can do genuine interdisciplinary work on the affects? I can borrow from other disciplines and be irritated by what I think are their limitations. However, I cannot claim to formulate positive assertions in a manner that will win for them a place in the appropriate disciplinary practices (although I do hope to influence someone who can make the appropriate disciplinary assertions). So where does this leave me? My first response is that I am not entirely without a disciplinary foundation, so there is some discursive universe in which the claims might be testable and even extendable. At the very least this book can be considered an effort to modify how we talk about literary works. Mapping kinds of affects may help critics specify distinguishing qualities of texts or clarify how different affective registers enter into tension with each other. And dwelling on immanent values may help us try modes of responsiveness to a range of art works that emphasize how history enters art rather than how art can be placed in historical contexts.

Analogously, I can hope that these arguments offer a way of seeing how art works can serve social interests without depending on the thematic allegorizing that now seems necessary for taking art as a serious human practice. Stressing the affects emphasizes modes of caring about the self and the world. It also creates opportunities for experiencing states like intensity, involvedness, and plasticity while encouraging us to reflect on who we become as we experience such states. Most important, my arguing as a critic may help bring vitality to the Romantic tradition's efforts to dramatize the limitations of epistemic orientations and to provide some countermeasures of what might count as significant ways to assess values. I come to that tradition through modernism's intricate efforts to make the nondiscursive and nonepistemic dimensions of art wield the same level of cultural force as did scientific and utilitarian argument. So now I hold out the hope that focusing on the affects can go a long way toward recuperating the impact of modernist ambitions for art without reviving modernism's ideological allegiances.

These modernist ambitions, however, make it impossible to be content with what my own discipline affords (despite its giving me Yeats to echo here). If one wants to make large claims about how the arts manifest not just values but principles for honoring values, one has to address a range of disciplines. So even if my goal were only to produce another in a long line of defenses of poetry, I would have to extend into areas where other disciplines have much better developed and more highly respected modes of analysis. Making these incursions is easiest in negative terms. Close attention to art works may provide convincing evidence that dealing with emotions in terms of standard adjectives cannot suffice to establish an empirical basis for making any psychological or sociological or even physiological arguments that will be adequate to the intricacies of human experience. So even if I cannot persuade philosophers I am right, I still may be able to indicate that they are wrong not to explore certain phenomena, especially those requiring us to take seriously claims about values that are simply not adjudicable within philosophy's traditional ways of making and assessing arguments. And I may indicate some of the pleasure and conceptual possibility that emerge if we base our thinking about the affects on what the arts can articulate.

Lest I close this introduction on too humble a note, I want also to point out that there is one methodological perspective within philosophy that I think is richly compatible with the reflective stance I want to take toward the arts, and hence which may give these arguments some hold within that discipline. I refer to the fundamental orientation established by phenomenology. I cannot imitate the systematic exploration of standpoints that one finds in Husserl or even in J. N. Mohanty's efforts to revive phenomenology. Nor can I share Husserl's transcendental ambitions to project phenomenology as an ultimate purifying of the structures of knowledge. But phenomenology also affords more practical examples. It provides a useful conceptual defense for being suspicious of explanation and for preferring careful descriptions of how consciousness actually engages the world in particular ways. And because it calls attention to the importance of saving the appearances, phenomenology insists that there has to be some kind of intuition or noncriterial judgment through which we register the possible rightness of our descriptions.

Put more formally, I see phenomenology as central to my project because it offers means of seeking generalization without relying on either induction or deduction. Descriptions become representative because they engage intuition and hence elicit agreement not only on how phenomena appear but also on what kind of significance might be attributed to the specific characterization. So the concept of "intuition" must do a good deal of work. But I don't think the basis for this work has to be mysterious or mystical. I take intuition to be a reflexive form of tacit knowledge, so its force is explainable simply in terms of the power of descriptions to elicit provisional identifications.[22]

Problematic as this model is for those who rely on more stable warrants for their truth claims, it is not difficult to find reasons for taking the associated risks. I offer two—one contrasting phenomenology to contemporary neuroscience and the other contrasting it to sociological interests in how states of mind can be seen as culturally constituted. First, most analytic and scientific work on the affects turns out to be painfully reductive because it is so eager to get to explanations or to therapeutic models that it is willing to sacrifice the textural qualities specific to how complex emotions engage us. The result is what I have called emotion by adjective, where it is difficult even to be sure that we are dealing with anything more than conventional signs used as shorthand for the very emotions experimentalists claim to be analyzing.

Applied neuroscience provides telling examples of what we lose when we ignore the phenomenological. Because of constraints on what experimenters can do with human subjects, most research on the affects proceeds by telling stories to subjects that seem obviously to evoke a standard emotion so that the scientists can map those areas of the brain that show increased activity. This however seems to me problematic on at least two fronts. First, it is not clear to what the subjects are responding. Using stories as stimuli leaves unexamined the possibility that the subjects within the experiments are not actually reporting on their own emotions but demonstrating that they know how to recognize standard rhetorical marks indicating that affective responses are called for. Second, just identifying the emotion one undergoes does not give an adequate rendering of human agency in these situations. We also need to trace second-order processes by which agents make or withhold investments and negotiate possible links to other affective complexes that may impinge. We do not just come upon emotions; we produce them and test them and enter into various degrees of ownership with them.

Wittgenstein provides a dazzlingly simple illustration of the point I am belaboring. In his *Remarks on Color* he insists on a sharp distinction between work that attempts to capture what seeing is like for those who can see and descriptions we give to the blind of "how the sighted behave." Most disciplinary work on the emotions seems to be addressing the blind: it characterizes behavior but it does not address what matters for agents within the behavior. There is good reason for that preference, since only the impersonal descriptions will stand as science. But there is not good reason for confusing what science can represent with what agents seem actually to feel or to care about in their feeling. Yet how can science not produce such confusion when its basic means of generalizing depend on the substituting brains for persons, or on abnormal psychology like the work of Adam Philips, which raises other kinds of representativeness questions)?[23] How can this science not reject surface complexity as mere obfuscation laid over core behavioral patterns? Phenomenology matters then because it seeks a very different kind of representativeness, one based on thinking's abilities to display complexity rather than its abilities to translate the experience into other languages that have experimental methods attached to them. Rather than explain or judge Swann's jealousy, the phenomenologist tries to bring attention to its distinctive energies and to show what possible uses such energies might have for the audience's own future projections of their affective capacities.

My second reason for taking the risk of identifying with phenomenology is that it seems to me the only way to defend my fundamentally ignoring contemporary interests in how affects and emotions are and have been culturally constituted (at least until I make a modest theoretical argument at the close of my final chapter). I have no doubt that there is obviously important work to be done on how historical and cultural differences influence our ways of forming, sorting, and evaluating affective phenomena. And I will try later to offer one way of showing how agents engage the social expectations involved in the scripts established by our cultural grammars for dealing with emotions. However, I have serious doubts that we have the intellectual resources now to deal well with cultural contexts, precisely because we do not yet have adequate frameworks either for describing affective conditions or for appreciating the kinds of investments people make in relation to those conditions. If standard adjectives provide our only map of emotional fields, then the only historical agents we will be dealing with are those whose lives can be summarized in those very frameworks. We will not have the imaginative ability to specify how agents adapt distinctive historical grammars for dealing with the complexity of affects or to appreciate the concerns about value that accompany them. Relying on standard adjectives for the affects will allow us to make large claims about cultural differences and to talk about how such difference are culturally constituted along lines that both organize and conceal specific group interests. But with only these rubrics, it will be impossible to capture how historical lives are intricately lived, intensely willed, and socially negotiated.[24] So before we start making historical claims, I think we have to spend considerable time specifying the range of qualities that make changes in human values worth studying.

# 2    *Engaging Affect in Painting and in Poetry*

Some mystic or other speaks of the intellect as standing in the same
relation to the soul as do the senses to the mind; and beyond a certain
border surely we come to a place where the ecstasy is not a whirl or a
madness of the senses, but a glow arising from the exact nature of the
perception.

> Ezra Pound, *The Spirit of Romance*

Poetry proves successfully, or fails to prove, that certain worlds of
thought and feeling are *possible*.

> T. S. Eliot, "Poetry and Propaganda"

## I. On Some Basic Difficulties in Dealing with Affect in the Arts

Richard Wollheim suggests that the success of cognitivism has left philosophy with the task of repsychologizing the emotions. By identifying intentionality with belief, the cognitivist tradition severely oversimplified the
psychological dynamics involved in affective life, so that it became difficult
to appreciate why the emotions have the power they do in our lives (*On the
Emotions*, 33). As should be obvious by now, I completely share Wollheim's
view of what is to be done. Yet I cannot just follow Wollheim's lead because
we have substantial differences that I will elaborate at length in the next chapter. Yet I need now to dwell briefly on three of these differences in order to
specify the rationale for this chapter. Wollheim speaks of repsychologizing
only the emotions, while I think the entire domain of affects requires this
process. While cognitivism severely narrowed discourse about the emotions,
it seemed to eliminate the need for any talk at all about other affects like feelings and moods because these were not shaped by belief and played less important roles in the transition from reflection to action. In fact, in philosophy

37

at least, the need now is not so much to repsychologize these other affects as to give them a psychology as if for the first time.

A second difference I have with Wollheim should help explain why this psychology of the affects seems now so minor a topic. When Wollheim speaks of repsychologizing, he has only one basic goal in mind—bringing our theory of emotions in line with the overall perspective provided by Freudian psychoanalysis. Psychologizing means showing how dimensions of imagination and fantasy enter our emotions and how they are constituted out of correspondences that overdetermine particular segments of our experience. Feelings cannot play much of a role within this process. Wollheim does address them, but primarily as elements whose significance depends on how they get interpreted within more comprehensive emotional attitudes. Feelings retain their force but lose their relevance for consciousness. Therefore I hope to show that attention to feelings as mediators of values in their own right can lead to modes of repsychologizing undreamt of in Wollheim's philosophy. At one pole, we can revive certain aspects of William James's thinking that stressed direct correspondences between how the world is sensed and how consciousness adapts to those sensations. From a Jamesian perspective, feelings require a subtle psychology because their main functions are simply to quicken consciousness and to attune it to the world. Feelings are situational not projective, and so not amenable to elaborate dramatic and autobiographical interpretations.[1] Yet, as Silvan Tomkins would put it, these situational qualities give us access to affective complexes much more varied and more supple than those Freud hypothesized. At the other pole, attention to feelings allows us a significant sense of how we come to make and to modify investments in received cultural practices. These practices both elicit and codify a wide range of possible investments in concrete experiences. Think of how we register nuance in dance or adapt to gestures in social life. Or psychological significance can emerge because of how inherited scripts are modified, for example when someone refuses to meet one's eyes or is overexuberant or surprisingly laconic about a triumph.

Once we decide that we must find a place in our philosophical psychology for these affects, we have to face the question of what will count as the relevant evidence and how we will test our interpretations of this evidence. Facing these demands requires my working through a third difference from Wollheim, this time "only" a methodological one. Wollheim is much more interested in the intricate examples afforded by the arts than most other philosophers, but he still prefers to take as his philosophical examples fairly simple practical situations. That will get him to the play of fantasy, but not, I think, to demands on psychological theory created by the range of complex states the affects can produce. To appreciate and interpret this aspect of psychology I think we do best to concentrate on examples provided by works of literary and visual art. These works test the reaches of intentionality and the suppleness of the kinds of judgment that may take place without the invoking of cri-

Caravaggio, *The Fortune Teller*. Louvre, Paris, France. Scala/Art Resource, NY.

teria and principles. And because these works make clear some of the variety and intensity available for affective states that do not fit our cultural grammar for emotions, they provide substantial opportunities for tracking the intricate adjustments that feelings invite from self-reflection as it attunes itself to our investments. Yet because the relevant states are fundamentally matters of immediate adjustment to situations rather than extended personal interpretations of those situations, these feelings provide significant opportunities to explore what agents can share in the affirmations they make about the world.

## II. Sensation, Feeling, and Interpretation in Caravaggio's *The Fortune Teller* and Titian's *Ecce Homo*

I will now turn to two Renaissance paintings that provide especially useful test cases because they offer striking engagements with my two basic concerns here—with how affective states cannot be confined to cognitivist frameworks and with how works of art can be said to offer distinctive ways of rendering those features that extend beyond those frameworks. In Caravaggio's *Fortune Teller* a sudden shift in how the young man experiences his own body sets in motion affective chains that seem to require his reshaping his own self-image and hence the identifications he can project. Titian's *Ecce Homo,* my second painting, follows just the opposite affective circuit. Here intense feeling comes into play not as the cause of the intentional state but as its consequence: we see the agent forced to express in his body what he cannot produce for his defeated self-consciousness. In both cases the art so positions reflection that it is only the objective properties of the work itself that seem capable of fully registering the pains and permissions created by the dramatic situation. Our task as critics is to elaborate in conceptual terms the force and possible significance of the expressive processes dramatized in the images and embodied in the painters' rendering of those images.

For Caravaggio the affective drama is located at the moment when physical sensation takes on psychological resonance, a moment of being moved that has clear analogues with the power that his painterly skills are projected as having on the spectator.[2] The young woman and the young man are obviously from different class backgrounds, her only power being the sexual suggestiveness of her touch. (It is impossible to say with certainty whether she is just reading his palm or making the explicit overture more pronounced in the Capitoline version of the same painting). Yet that simple touch seems enough to make an enormous difference for the young man, perhaps taking him beyond all the protections afforded by his youth and his social class and the ideas they sustain. Everything about the boy suggests power and self-enclosure. His cloak continues the curve of his body to keep his energies securely in his half of the painting. And the angle of his head, complemented by the depth-creating plume of his hat, extends his overall cockiness. But the eyes and the mouth and the small size of the head all seem to tell a somewhat different story, or to tell that he is leaving the realm where he has stories to tell. He may be entering a realm where only idealized visual powers have access to his transformed psyche.

Despite all the factors that should give the boy complete control over this scene, his eyes and mouth do not quite achieve the sense of uncomplicated presence suggested by all the other details of his appearance. Some kind of conversion is taking place. Perhaps it is a sexual awakening; perhaps it is a fear in relation to this woman's specific invitation, promising a version of the erotic for which he may not be prepared. Or perhaps he is shocked at his emerging disdain for everything that this woman has to offer, not unlike Christ in Caravaggio's *Doubting of Saint Thomas.* Whatever the cause, and it is crucial that we cannot know the cause even as we cannot doubt the effect, the woman's touch introduces visual lines of force disrupting his self-enclosure and providing an analogue for what we see happening to his eyes and to his mouth. The painting calls attention to a horizontal line of relationships extending from her long wrist and finger to his touched hand to the phallic sword, evocatively reaching out of his circular forms past the frontal plane of the painting.

Along that route we pass a gloved hand that could be out of Titian's portraits of young men.[3] But here the hand seems oddly remote and protected in relation to the other hand. Yet in its inertness it nonetheless provides a meeting point between the horizontal line of relationships and a vertical line linking the plume of his hat to the sword. Why have so inert an element so structurally important? The question virtually answers itself. This is the untouched hand (rendered in the Rome version as without any glove), the hand that is a residue of the dandy's protected self-confidence. Now this hand seems almost impotent, almost a relic of some other order of being. This hand is also for me an emblem of the entire domain of beliefs that the boy would have to rely on for discursive understanding of his situation. But what is actually happening is not occurring in this locale—literally or figuratively. What the boy registers about being moved becomes visible only in the implication that his body can no longer quite sustain the attitudes it could sustain before this encounter. So rather than locating intentionality in belief, this painting locates it in the boy's sudden sense that his powers to formulate beliefs about himself are sliding away into the hand and out to the sword. Where belief might be, the painting offers only this sense of beliefs now irreducibly inadequate. In order for his beliefs to hold, he would have to keep the woman in a subordinate position, visually subjected to the modes of design his body imposes. But Caravaggio has her occupy almost the same volume as he does, with almost the same structural relations among arms, shoulders, and head, despite her slight gesture and even slighter social position. The only substantial difference is that she is not enclosed by a cloak and so seems relatively attentive to what is happening to others. The power she can muster against him comes from her being much more experienced in the paths touch opens.

In many of Caravaggio's paintings feeling puts belief into crisis and in the process dramatizes powers of visual art to provide alternative perspectives on how agents are moved. When we enter a world for which our language is utterly inadequate, our only knowledge must be gathered from the kinds of information the painter provides. In Caravaggio's worlds, painting is necessary precisely because intentionality cannot be successfully understood in terms of the agent's beliefs. (Think of his David and his Judith and his doubting Thomas.) Yet Caravaggio's is by no means the only Renaissance mode of exploring through paint intentionalities that do not rely on conventional forms of attributing meaning and power. Titian's *Ecce Homo,* for example, emphasizes the priority of affective sensation over those forms of power by developing just the opposite implicit narrative from that of Caravaggio's painting.[4] Titian sees in the story of Christ's suffering the possibility of reorienting the thematics of incarnation in order to render psychologically the sense of powerlessness that the god must experience when he becomes man. So where Caravaggio represents his youth as undone by touch, Titian's Christ is so objectified by the mockery of his persecutors that he has only flesh as his expressive instrument. Titian's art is to give that flesh its own intentional presence by linking its expressive resources to his skills as a colorist.

Titian's title echoes and reinterprets the mocker's basic taunt—this person reduced to pathos cannot be god and so is merely human. At the core of that humanity is Christ's loneliness, defined by his being pushed into the foreground of the painting and rendered in the form of a large blocklike body. There are no other persons in the painting. And if there were, it would make no difference to Christ in this state. His eyes are closed and looking down, almost buried by his dark hair and beard. It seems as if he is so reduced by the cruelty of his mockers and by their inability to recognize him that he cannot muster the sense of self necessary to enter into eye contact. Once able to feel himself throbbing with all the powers of a god, Christ now cannot even enter the role of active human subject. All his self-consciousness seems absorbed into his defeated posture, with no prospect of communication with other human beings.

Yet Titian is not content with what Christ can believe or understand or bring to conscious expression. It seems that he wants to contact dimensions of Christ's sense of himself that continue to pervade his bodily consciousness. Perhaps the more the painting tries to sympathize with what Christ cannot say, the closer it can come to what he is actually feeling. Where Christ's face is hidden in shadow, his very broad chest and shoulder are bathed in light. And the light is delicately and elaborately painted in intricate modulations of skin tones. Perhaps then we have to see this chest and shoulder as embodying all of Christ's expressive needs, now deprived of language and capable of articulation only as these fine tonal intensities. The mind tormented by the judgments of the persecutors can remain human only by its pained withdrawal from the utterly embarrassed self. Yet the shame must out, even if only in the silent textures of these completely nonverbal feelings taking on the roles that we expect a face to perform. The ultimate irony of incarnation then consists in reversing the usual view of Christ as manifesting through his death and rebirth the power to rename the world whose law of universal death he has just overcome. In that view the right to call forth allegory is won by overcoming the essence of the empirical order. But Titian's Christ is not a founder of allegories. His full humanity resides in the discovery that even when he is silenced by the cruelty of others, his mortal body maintains its expressive power. The word made flesh must rely on the flesh as his word.[5] And while that may not be very encouraging theology, it sanctions a powerful painterly aesthetic. For only the kind of vision idealized through painting can be fully responsive to this particular expression of the psyche.

## III. Four Challenges in Developing Theory Adequate to These Examples

By dramatizing such dynamic relational fields, these paintings make demands on theory that obviously could not be met by the various discourses we examined when we were looking at how contemporary philosophers

Titian, *Ecce Homo*. National Gallery of Ireland.

would give an account of jealousy. What then will it take to bring our theorizing in accord with what these works make available for our participation and our reflection? Let me suggest four challenges that I think theory has to meet and that I will try to address in what follows. The most striking challenge emerges from the central role played in these works by the interface between sensation and feelings that modify the psyche but are too fluid to be handled by any discursive means or by the emotional typologies that sustain discourse in these domains. For then we have to recognize an enormous disproportion between the attention paid to those affects like full-scale dramatic emotions, for which we have verbal equivalents, and that paid to these more fluid moments that often also serve as fundamental elements within these emotions. And at the same time we have to recognize the inadequacy of the standard ways such feelings are treated. The characters in these paintings are not simply registering turbulence or reacting to shifts in how pleasure and pain are being experienced. At the least, we have to bring back into our picture William James's interest in how the brain can adjust itself to infinite gradations in affective awareness. Then we may be able to develop a vocabulary that will help us attune our theorizing to such intricacy.

Second, we need much more complex and supple terms for how agents try to make sense of their being moved. Once again cognitivist stances help make the problem clear. For it cannot suffice to equate the affect with the belief an agent has about it. We cannot assume that Caravaggio's youth has the feelings he does because he has a specific belief in relation to the disturbing force that the woman's hand presents. Knowing his beliefs might help provide a rough generic framework for what he feels, but it would not do much to help get at the specific qualities of how the affect modifies his state of mind. His response to her finger seems concerned not primarily with beliefs but with the quite concrete force of this touch, a concreteness sufficient to produce considerable anxiety about what he can believe. Affect threatens belief frameworks and the forms of self-assurance on which they rely and which they also sustain.[6]

How could the boy successfully identify what he is feeling? The short answer is that he would have to paint like Caravaggio. Lacking that option, he would have to begin with the recognition that while the force of the affect can be immediate, the psyche's responsiveness to this force is not likely to take the form of a straightforward process of testing hypotheses while keeping the phenomenon one is studying constant. Coming to self-reflexive terms with this affective situation requires admitting that one is trying to represent something not immediately accessible to the instruments one has available. There are likely to be significant tensions between the concrete conditions of being moved and the hypotheses or attitudes that the reflective spirit develops for interpreting them.[7] We need beliefs and attitudes if we are to give meaning to affective complexes. But we also need to recognize that powerful affects are not quite the kinds of phenomena we can represent by providing pictures that sustain propositions. For the subject is too much involved in the object and the object in the subject to allow for the distribution of parts necessary for epistemic judgments. Instead, we have to treat the agent's activity as a form of expression that links what the body reveals with what the manner of acting and reflecting attempts to make articulate. And

we have to accept that we cannot do a decent job of describing and interpreting what a person feels without attuning ourselves to what the expression seems to bring into intricate conjunction. We may have to formulate
terms for the expression, but we also have to be aware that there is likely to
be a significant gulf between what we can say and what we can see.[8]

The third challenge repeats what is by now a recurrent theme of my book.
Because we cannot successfully treat strong affects as if they were constituted
by beliefs, we have to develop much more complex models of intentionality
than we find in any contemporary philosophical approach to the affects.
Here again it is crucial to begin by developing an adequate concept of expression. For expression is not the subsuming of experience under belief but
a person's overt focusing of attention that seems to align consciousness with
the forces calling that attention into being. Thus while Christ in Titian's *Ecce
Homo* seems to have all beliefs beaten out of him, his body expresses his state
of pain because of how it both manifests certain signs and seems to dramatize his own self-reflexive identification with those behaviors. But what warrants our talking about self-reflection in this case? How do we distinguish
between a sense of Christ as symptomatically revealing his pain and Christ
as somehow self-reflexively offering this glimpse of himself as an effort to
make himself known, or, better, to make known his effort to make himself
known? Can there be a conceptual model for intentionality that enables us
to combine the concrete, nondiscursive awareness of his situation manifest
by Christ's body with the possibility of demonstrating that he somehow takes
responsibility for the state of the self he reveals to others?

The final challenge requires our taking up concerns about the modes of
evaluation we can bring to bear in such situations. The more complex and
supple we can make our sense of intentionality, the greater the need for bringing to bear a language of values that goes well beyond the one organized
around concerns for rational action. We have to be able to characterize the
kinds of satisfactions that come from the different manners in which we engage affective states, and we have to be able to say what is at stake in different qualities that expressive behavior can achieve or fail to achieve. And we
have to bring both sets of concerns to bear in relation to quite complex issues of identification. An agent can identify with expressive behavior by
bringing to bear any one of many identities, and there need be only partial
identification. The Christ who goes on to identify with how his body takes
over his pain and shame can be a very different Christ from the one who
identifies entirely with the character hidden in the shadows. And the problem facing Caravaggio's youth is precisely the kind of identification he can
establish with feelings that now make him differ from his prevailing sense of
himself.

So it will not suffice to treat the values involved in such identifications as
if they somehow involved a relation of parts to whole or discoveries of some
latent potential for unifying many identities. Identities can be unified—but

by a kind of explicit activity and not by the discovery of latent realities. But why does such unity matter? And how can it matter just to be satisfied that one has realized some particular aspect of an identity? Our language of value will require means of assessing how the expression positions the person in a web of social relations. We have to understand how concerns about identification create complex bonds with and dependencies on other persons (in ways that questions about belief do not). How can we characterize what is at stake in the agent's effort to elicit desire or attune an expression to the concerns and interests of a particular audience? And what qualities come to the foreground when agents resist the temptation to treat expression as primarily a means of seduction? What other modes of sociality can be organized around expressivist values?

## IV. A Vocabulary for the Affects (1): The Relation between Feeling and Sensation and the Need for Intricate Versions of Intentionality

The first step in meeting these challenges has to be developing a vocabulary enabling us to make rough distinctions among basic kinds of affect. For we need such distinctions to spell out the modes of intentionality that typically characterize these different states—in life as well as in art. Moreover we need an intricate vocabulary to be able to specify those arenas where we have to be silent because we cannot tell which conceptual and behavioral concepts are most appropriate or cannot be sure of their boundaries. Expressivist theory thrives on being able to indicate where we are prone to conflict and confusion and so where there is considerable pressure to identify with the work articulation can perform. And artists engage such boundary situations to test what they can make of the relevant expressive resources. Can they show why the difficulties arise, and can they use the problems to dramatize and intensify aspects of our affective lives that we usually simplify or suppress?

*Ecce Homo*, for example, gains much of its energy from the striking tension between all that the face denies and all that the chest displays. Here the immediacy of feeling clearly pushes against any interpretive structure that Christ might be capable of bringing to bear in his reflective circumstance. But being moved in this way also positions Titian's audience to appreciate in a radical form what it means to have a body, especially for a god to have a human body. One might even say that we are asked to recognize the power of painting precisely because it need not shy away from such complex boundary states. It can try to render a vision of what it might mean to be an incarnate god even though no words could possibly assume that burden. And it could ultimately make possible an identification with Christ precisely because it has the resources to push beyond the limitations of human language. Christ here is not simply an object of pathos. Exploring the boundaries of pathos may in fact be the basic challenge the painting poses. For as desperate as Christ is, there is a position suggested within the painting that can honor his desperation as itself a means of gaining a richer grasp of what it is he has to will in order to be an incarnate god. Christ seems so tormented by this conflict between the pains of self-consciousness and the florid expressiveness of the body that he is forced to come to terms with just what it means to be subjected to being human. The degradation of his being split by being mocked posits the challenge basic to his redemptive project.

But I am getting far in front of myself. Here I have to focus on elaborating the elemental vocabulary that will eventually help us flesh out more fully the kinds of examples artists provide. As I said in my introduction, "affect" provides my umbrella term, as it did for Silvan Tomkins, still for me the greatest theorist focused on this topic. "Affect" comprises the range of mental states where an agent's activity cannot be adequately handled in terms of either sensations or beliefs but requires attending to how he or she offers expressions of those states. Affects are ways of being moved that supplement sensation with at least a minimal degree of imaginative projection. Where pure sensation is at stake, we tend, as Keith Oatley suggests, to treat the state as "evoked by eliciting conditions that are physical rather than mental" (61). One is shivering because of the temperature, screaming because of the nail emerging from a shoe. But consider the difference between noticing a bird and noticing that the bird's way of running evokes a certain person or state of mind.[9] Sensations focus on how the world engages particular bodily responses, while affects call our attention to how those states take on significance for the imagination.

At the other pole, this presence of bodily activity distinguishes the affects from beliefs. Beliefs can attribute significance to such bodily states without keeping their focus on immediate appearance. Here we might think of the difference between attributing qualities to the bird's emergence and pursuing some argument about the bird, for example that it is a finch, not a hummingbird, or that it should be fed rather than chased away. In pursuing these arguments we may have to consider imaginative projections, but we try to eliminate their power. With feelings, on the other hand, we treat those projections as constitutive elements of the experience. Analogously, affects often involve reasoning, but we do not expect reasoning either to cause them or to direct them. Even when we get reason to control how we act, we may not be able to produce the same control of our affective relation to that action. I may bring myself not to hit someone with whom I am angry, but I may well stay angry and resentfully plot another form of revenge, now the more elaborate because my anger is mixed with shame and regret.

In order to map the various ways affects bring together sensation and imagination, I think we have to break the topic down into four paradigmatic modes, although we also have to grant that there will be myriad problem cases at the borders set by our categories. Here let me just state the basic distinctions that the next two chapters will elaborate. Feelings are elemental affective states characterized by an imaginative engagement in the immediate processes of sensation. Moods are modes of feeling where the sense of subjectivity becomes diffuse and sensation merges into something close to atmosphere, something that seems to pervade an entire scene or situation. Emotions are affects that involve the construction of attitudes that typically establish a particular cause and so situate the agent within a narrative. As a result, emotions typically generate some kind of action or identification. Finally, passions are emotions within which we project significant stakes for the identity that they make possible. In this chapter I will concentrate on feelings and moods, in the next on emotions. Passions will be only briefly discussed because I treat them as a particular orientation of emotion.

It is best to begin elaborating these distinctions by focusing on feelings. For feelings are basic building blocks for other affects, yet they have not been studied with anything like the care devoted to emotions. I think there are two reasons for this. Philosophers are leery of building any theoretical edifice on states that are so fluid, so often inarticulate, and so difficult to isolate from sensations.[10] And the philosophical discourses that we inherit on the feelings tend to one of two extremes, William James's emphasis on physicality, on the one hand, and, on the other, various essentially "Romantic" efforts (like Susanne Langer's) to make feeling attach us to values that cannot be adequately represented within the domain of concepts and interpretations.[11]

How then are we to establish an alternative perspective for dealing with feeling as a distinctive and significant concept? One might respond to that question by pointing out that there seem to be aspects of our concern with feelings that we do not usually bring to bear when we talk about sensations. We seem to exhaust our interest in sensations when we become aware of what they make present for us, simply as facts in our world. But our interests in the aspect of those sensations we treat as feelings often open into concerns with manner and quality and resonance. While we might "sense" certain refinements of a color, we are likely to speak of feelings involved when we get interested in the effects of the combination of this color with another one. Similarly we speak of feeling and not of sensation when we respond to how the color is applied with certain strokes or in certain densities or when one particular shade of color calls up related states, like the red of an imagined sunset or a remembered article of clothing. And finally, we invoke a notion of feeling to deal with our self-reflexive awareness of participating in particular processes or of moving between states. At one pole we use the notion of feeling to refer to what Richard Wollheim calls "the occurrent aspect of an emotion" that gives it an immediate presence: "Feeling . . . can stand to emotion as a mental state does to the emotion it serves" (*On the Emotions*, 119). At the other pole self-reflection engages specific sensations of transition, say, between degrees of intensity or connectedness.[12] For stronger examples, we

could turn to James's great work on the feelings embodied in our preposi-
tions and other transitional features of language. And we often rely on feelings to measure how time is unfolding relative to interests we project into it.
Consider the differences in our senses of time when we are feeling angry or
hungry or elated.

Because feelings are so elemental yet so woven into the life of consciousness, they seem to provide our most basic motive for metaphor. Metaphor
promises to honor both how consciousness finds itself embodied and how it
has the power to elaborate upon what sensation provides. Think of how readily we apply standard metaphors to states like feeling hungry or feeling angry. The path to art may begin here. So too does a path to a certain
temptation for philosophy and for literary criticism, a path worth the attention of anyone who wants to appreciate why feelings matter and how philosophy can easily get into trouble explaining that significance. (And once
philosophy gets into such trouble, it becomes much easier to ignore the role
of feelings than to retool our conceptual instruments.) Because feelings seem
continuous with the senses but not reducible to them, they promise a concrete grounding for acts of imagination. Feelings become affects when they
introduce *asness* into the core of sensation. It should come as no surprise then
that this concrete grounding is readily idealized as establishing a rich connection between the mind and the processes or forces generating our sensations.

Susanne Langer, for example, proposes that we "think of feeling as a phase
of vital process itself under special conditions, instead of as a new substan-
tive element produced by such a process." Her own metaphor for this state
both illustrates and honors the ways that feelings take on significance for us:
she suggests that we can grasp how feeling might be a phase of this vital
process by comparing it to "the incandescence of a heated wire." Feeling then
becomes "a condition of the wire itself and not an added entity" (*Feeling and
Form*, 151). When we respond as the wire does, we do not seek interpretations and evaluations that we bring to the event from the outside. Rather we
experience immediate modifications based on the specific qualities of our engagement in what we sense. Think of how Caravaggio's young man directly
feels the fortune-teller's finger engaging his own imaginary identity. And the
shoulder of Titian's Christ seems almost literally incandescent in its registering his shame and impotence. In both cases, the sensual takes fire for consciousness without ever losing its frightening and exhilarating particularity.
The self brought into activity here is not the self living in plots and plans but
the self called into acute awareness of how its own immediate processes are
charged with a significance going beyond that immediacy.

Powerful as Langer's example is, however, it seems to me as distracting as
it is enabling for our purposes. Langer's ultimate concerns are ontological.
She wants to show how we can imagine thinking as an extension of feeling
and feeling as an extension of responsiveness to natural process. Without

feeling we are condemned to a world of purely epistemic practices. This does not seem wrong to me today, but it is not quite appropriate to our culture's central concerns. The blocking force for contemporary thinking about the affects is not positivism but cognitivism, and cognitivism must be opposed by a richer psychology, not a richer ontology. Caravaggio and Titian then have a lot to teach us. Their paintings help us see how the immediacy of feeling manages to pervade sensation with the capacity to engage the imagination and so to modify our sense of our own psychological powers. These works render feelings as the point of intersection where what would otherwise merely appear and then disappear takes on a different mode of existence—now a part of the mind's framing of relationships that condition the impact of further sensations. Feelings become the vehicle by which the psyche finds itself invested in these appearances—either because of the qualities that they take on or because of the agent's modified grasp of its own relation to these qualities. Feeling activates or quickens the objects of sensation and in the process elicits a momentary intentionality concerned less with interpreting itself than with expanding or refining its mode of participation in the unfolding possibilities.

## V. Modernist Art and the Separation of Feelings from Emotions

My own interest in the psychology of feeling stems from the efforts by modernist poets to set the feelings against the emotions. So I am going to turn briefly to that cultural moment in the hope that this will intensify the importance of such distinctions. Almost all the major modernist painters and writers saw themselves as facing two basic, interrelated problems. They confronted an intellectual culture increasingly dominated by positivist perspectives, so they needed means of acknowledging the force of these perspectives while also repudiating them for new forms of spiritual work that imagination might perform. And they thought they had to oppose dominant cultural attitudes that seemed to gain their authority by relying on conventional "rhetorical" postures. Class and privilege cloaked themselves in the assertion of noble emotions and exaggerated powers of sensibility. But if the artists could treat feelings as if they were separate from emotions, they could develop aspects of the affects not so easily contaminated by these social identifications.[13] The emotions then seemed beyond repair. They were too contaminated by centuries of association with rhetoric. And the very fact that emotions invoked explanatory plots made them seem irreducibly self-theatricalizing. The feelings, on the other hand, could be honored for a subtlety and fluidity impossible to stage within socially approved abstractions. When feelings did involve intentionality, they contoured the imagination to the sensation and not the sensation to gesture and posture and belief. So an art devoted to the feelings seemed capable of a leanness, an honesty, and a concreteness that might actually challenge the positivist spirit almost on its own grounds.

I tell an elaborate version of this story in my *Painterly Abstraction in Modernist American Poetry*. Here I want to isolate from that story materials that will help briefly to illustrate two fundamental qualities that I think enable feelings to take on imaginative significance. First, the modernists were fascinated by those moments when imagination seemed continuous with sensation so that a sense of significance could emerge that did not seem to derive from discursive processes. In effect, they managed to capture the sense of charged surface basic to our Renaissance examples while isolating the intentionality involved from any specific dramatic context. Feeling itself becomes a dynamic force conferring significance without relying on ideological baggage.

Consider the example of Kasimir Malevich. He wrote endless prose devoted to the observation that feeling opens within sensation an "additional element" called "non-objective sensation." Then he complicated the issue by claiming that this "non-objective sensation" is at the core of what constitutes objectivity. How is this link possible? I think it occurs because feeling marks the conjunction of psychological and natural energies: it charges the world of sensations with internal relations without structuring those relations in any plot or argument. And then the awareness of these relations as relations becomes something like a higher-order sensation—hence the ideal of "non-objective sensation." These relations among relations reinforce the possibility that art can be so expressive in its particularity that it need not lean on allegory for a sense of its significance.

The result is an astonishing synthesis of heightened intimacy and abstract reach. For, on one level, psychological life is involvement in these strange and intricate balances among delicately poised shapes, reinforced by quick leaps among related color tones. But the balances cannot be treated simply as momentary states. They suggest, at the least, that there is a power in the psyche to attune itself to elemental forces. The awareness of abstract relatedness depends on and extends the constant perceptual adjustments we make as we feel what color, line, and rhythm can create. This awareness may not justify Malevich in asserting that his art demonstrates "the falsity of the world of will and idea" (Chipp, 342).[14] Yet it is true that neither will nor idea seems sufficiently supple or sufficiently concrete to interpret what is happening at the very core of sensation.

Feelings take on a second aspect of significance for Malevich because they have to provide an alternative to the modes of thinking and of valuing that do sustain this world of will and idea. If we are to be fully responsive to the values that circulate through and around the paintings, we cannot approach them through intentional states based on the development and testing of beliefs. I have already insisted on this motif, but abstract art provides an important concrete justification for complementing the play of feeling with a parallel flexibility of mind. This flexibility does not preclude using the relevant experiences to sustain or test beliefs. But such uses become possible only if we first let our intentional states contour to the concrete relations the works foreground. Like Mondrian, Malevich wants us to experience subjectivity as if it too were an elemental building block of our world, a synthetic function of the relations on the canvas rather than an independent locus of meaning and value. By displacing the subject of will and idea, the work invites a version of intentionality that can experience value as itself a condition of how these relations take on vivid presence.

Other works inspired by this early modernism offer even more radical redistributions of intentional energies. One might invoke surrealism. But for my purposes kinetic sculpture has proved most inventive in elaborating strange modes of intentionality required to participate in elemental relations between sense and affect. Traditionally art elicits sensations that it codes in particular ways. We see red paint but treat it as the surface of a barn or a boat; we see a set of lines but treat them as outlining either a represented form or an abstract one. Art provides a metaphoric path giving meaning to the linking of sensation to feeling. Most kinetic sculpture refuses to provide this path, at least in any determinable way. We see only a material object moved by some force that can be overt, like a motor, or hidden, as when magnetism provides the dynamic energies. Yet we know this is art and so supposed to do something significant. Therefore because the scene seems stripped of intention and purpose, we have to attribute expressive force to the most elemental of factors. We find ourselves having intense affective relations that remain very close to the activity of our senses, indeed almost identifiable with them. When Takis allows white balls to stand suspended over upturned magnets, we find ourselves literally feeling the tension between gravity and magnetism,[15] as if our bodies partially inhabited some alternative site. Or when we encounter his work *Signals* with long steel fibers delicately vibrating although there is no visible force acting upon them, we feel strange conjunctions between pure proprioceptive states and a rush of imaginative projections. The particular rhythm and reach of the vibrations become something more than an analogue for the psyche, something closer to a self-reflexive awareness of our inherent capacity to be moved in pure harmony with sensation.

In my view, this is repsychologizing with a vengeance. The objective forces take on a haunting *asness* that allows us to envision ourselves as desiring mechanisms closely attuned to the flow of pure force. Yet even to attempt turning these delicate parallels into the language of beliefs is to destroy the very domain of possibilities they make inviting. Perhaps our beliefs have very little to do with what attunes us to this matter that refuses quite to be only matter. However close we come to pure sensation, the psyche seems incapable of not finding itself in the object, as if it invited us to invest in the object's materiality many of the energies that we typically dispose differently in more content-ridden situations. Imagine those magnets as versions of the fortune-teller's finger, now simplified to its most elemental relational force.

## VI. A Vocabulary for the Affects (2): The Significance of Mood

Another possible example of the folding of feeling into sensation might be the work music does in movies like the original *Planet of the Apes.* Such music must correlate with the plot by helping sensation modulate into affect, yet it has to keep from being absorbed into the stabilities of belief or else it becomes merely programmatic. In *Planet of the Apes,* music is especially important because there are long scenes where the humans are exploring the planet. For the exploration to continue and suspense to build, it is crucial that nothing happen. But something has to seem to be happening at every moment in an American movie, so the filmmaker called on music to supplement the quest. And his composer responded beautifully. The music is as bare as the environment, but also as probing in its skittery intensities as are the cautious spirits of the adventurers. In addition, the music manages simultaneously to keep us at a distance from the explorers and to give a sense of moment-by-moment anxiety that something might change. We find the questers remaining mysterious wanderers in an expansive alien environment, but we also have a sense we are attached to their inner lives. More important, this attachment to their inner lives is not quite psychological: it is more elemental and more otherworldly than that. So we cannot quite treat the music as the expression of subjective feeling. The music is not continuous with the situation of any one agent, but plays among the agents while keeping a distance that invites us to treat the framework as the determining source of the affects and not any agent's psychology. Nor is there any clear object to which the music is matched, as it might be to a storm or a flood or even a particular scene emphasizing human affections. Rather, the music matters primarily because it elaborates an overall atmosphere affecting every particular in the movie and pervading everyone's psyche.

All these qualities tempt me to call this mood music of a very high order, fit to provide a transition to the second mode of affect—the phenomena of mood in general. However, this move immediately requires qualifications, although the qualifications in turn show us something important about what artists can make of the elements foregrounded in moods. The music we have been considering is much more active in its particular effects than is most pure mood music. Perhaps we have to say that the music for *Planet of the Apes* seems to occupy a strange interface where feeling is abstracted and mood particularized. Such is the fluidity of affect, and such is the genius of art in dealing with that fluidity. And moods seem to me especially susceptible to such purposive manipulation, for reasons we are about to explore. On this topic philosophy will prove a rather bland yet helpful companion. When we reflect on mood, almost all the interesting cases are those in which artists explore the most generalized possible means of locating *asness* within pure sensation.

All the philosophical instruments seem to agree that both feelings and moods differ from other kinds of affects in their pure absorption in the present and in their corresponding lack of concern for how an agent is oriented toward action or evaluation or commitment. Both feelings and moods need not be woven into belief, and so have to be interpreted in terms of the sensations that they inhabit, as if they brought sense to the threshold of psychological interest and psychological interest to the modalities of sense. Yet within these similarities there are two striking differences. Moods depart from feelings in how they engage objects and in how they construct intentionality.[16] Moods tend to be encompassing. They do not attach to specific objects but pervade situations—hence the link to atmosphere (and hence Richard Wollheim's lovely term "permeant" for them [*On the Emotions*, 76]). In moods the affects seem continuous with some overall state of the subject. But the continuity is insistently not one for which we can provide a narrative, perhaps because moods seem total and so have no beginning and ending, only extension and duration and evanescence. One is not gloomy or melancholic or anxious or exuberant primarily in relation to some segment of a scene. Moods are synthetic and imperialistic, absorbing details rather than conforming to their specific appearances.

Second, because moods are so pervasive, they elicit a mode of intentionality in which the subjectivity of the individual subject is not very important. We certainly feel ourselves involved as subjects, but we do not organize the scenes in terms of our specific interests or perspectives as subjects. Rather subjectivity floats, modulating between a sense of one's own participation and a sense of being taken up into states of mind that any subject might enter because the states of mind seem to exist independently of practical perspectives. Moods entirely lack the shaping of desire by practical beliefs that seems central to many emotions. Instead of orienting agents toward actions, moods seem to pervade agency and absorb it into something vaguely transpersonal. When we experience moods, they do not seem aspects of transitions between sensation and investment or between desire and action. Instead they seem complete conditions in their own right, in principle capable of absorbing agency for extended periods of time.

Because of all these traits, mood seems incompatible with the moralized, action-oriented views of the affects now in fashion among philosophers and perhaps in the culture as a whole. Moods do not involve judgment, and they have very little to do with desires for self-expression and for approval by others. Consequently, philosophers pay very little attention to them. Yet this indifference to action and to the ego-formations actions depend upon has proven very attractive to artists and to writers. How could they not be fascinated by states that seem to evade meaning and practical judgment, yet have the power to redistribute what seems to matter about the psyche? How could they not be fascinated by glimpses of what our psychological lives might be if we were able to step partially free of our bondage to our imaginary subjective identities?

Mood offers us a thin but evocative sense of how we might find at the core of subjective states conditions we share completely with other agents, as if the psyche could be said to dwell in its own version of atmospheric landscapes. And even though moods render subjectivity passive, the passivity is often embraced by the agent as the means of letting oneself go. Mood produces overall affective coherence, and as such attracts subjects to make identifications with its insistent but ungraspable totality. So when we yield to certain moods, we submit ourselves to a strange yet often compelling doubleness. One aspect of consciousness looks at the self from the outside, often becoming appalled at how the agent has surrendered himself or herself to a situation in which the ego renounces its active powers. Yet from within the identification with the mood such reflective judgments seem almost irrelevant and vulgar because they fail to comprehend the immense psychological expansiveness that the mood affords.[17]

Martin Heidegger is a striking exception to my claims that philosophers have by and large ignored the significance of mood. Heidegger's dense and rich discussion of this topic is noteworthy in its own right because it offers the only twentieth-century philosophical account I know that tries not just to describe mood but to appreciate how certain values might seem important because of where moods position us. But I am even more interested in the contrast that Heidegger's account enables us to draw between his own existential values and the quite different perspectives artists develop as they let their imaginations dwell on what the affective logic of mood seems to afford those who participate in its power. The contrast will help us appreciate why these artists might find it so important to explore not just particular moods but the structures of consciousness that moods exemplify. And it might help us appreciate how their products can make a difference in our own imaginative pursuits.

Heidegger's basic statement on mood will seem somewhat forbidding, at least in English translation, but we should be able quickly to see its relevance:

> Even if Dasein is "assured" in its belief about its "whither," or if, in rational enlightenment, it supposes itself to know about its "whence," all this counts for nothing as against the phenomenal facts of the case: for the mood brings Dasein before the "that-it-is" of its "there" which, as such, stares it in the face with the inexorability of an enigma. (175)

"Dasein" is Heidegger's term for the structure of individual consciousness aware of its contingent situation and yet seeking to exercise its capacities for care. Mood matters in our thinking about Dasein because it presents subjectivity at its most contingent. Even when we can describe the "whences" and the "whithers" that matter to us, mood makes us aware that there are various, irreducible frameworks that may dictate how particular modes of caring constitute both the facts and our relation to those facts. Mood makes utterly visible the self's thrownness into existence because mood is felt as intensely personal, yet it seems not to depend on the subject's practical orientations. Mood composes enigmatic states where the subject is not in control of what seems most intensely subjective about a situation. When I am gloomy or ecstatic, those affective frameworks seem to precede and to color the "that is" directing my propositions. Yet the states themselves seem to offer none of the objectivity that would allow propositions about them, not even propositions about what elicits the feelings involved. Moods come from nowhere and exist nowhere, yet they can have a power over subjects stronger even than the power of ideas.[18]

Such talk makes ready sense in our culture because we are so familiar with the state of depression. But Heidegger helps us keep the concept of mood more general, more phenomenologically oriented, and less reducible to serotonin levels. And he explains how troubling mood can be for certain kinds of ethical consciousness. Mood turns out to conflict with everything kept in focus by questions of "whence" and "whither." Its subjectivity takes place before the empirical subject gets defined, and so it is a threat to all those values that depend on our taking responsibility for contingency and establishing individual commitments. Heidegger calls the appeal of mood an "evasive turning away" from those aspects of the self that attempt to make articulate the "there-is" of its "that" (175). Why go through all the trouble of coming to terms with our own mortality when our affective lives can float in the indeterminate expansiveness of affective agency celebrated in Tennyson's "Lotus-Eaters"?

Heidegger's most influential confrontation with this evasiveness takes place in his brilliant and influential account of anxiety. The mood of anxiety is ethically important for Heidegger because it reveals the severe spiritual blindness that occurs when a culture tries to reduce this mood to specific emotional theaters shaped by the concept of fear. Epistemic culture constantly tries to convert anxiety into fear, reducing the primordial to the practical and in the process reinforcing the psyche's faith that there is an unequivocal concept for each motivating state of mind. Fear enables belief to formulate a target and a plan. And fear allows the individual subject a clear role as the one who has to act by working through indeterminacy to an organized plot, shaped by a logic of cause and consequence. Yet there are substantial dangers that producing this plot may create a false sense of coherence and blind us to the groundlessness of our specific investments.

More important, treating situations as if they were shaped by the affect of fear narrows the subject's field of concerns to what can be dealt with in the

practical present. Anxiety attunes us to aspects of situations that fear sup-
presses or sublimates. And in the process it elicits a very different sense of
subjective agency. For anxiety is like fear in its shaking of the subject's initial sense of security. But anxiety does not produce a single object one can
engage and thus work through to a renewed sense of self. Rather than finding itself defined by the need to act, the anxious self finds itself deprived of
just such worlds. It is unable to articulate what might determine the roles in
which it can invest. There emerges "the nothing of the world" constituting
a present situation with which the agent "does not have any involvement
whatsoever," except for the mercilessness of its quest for involvement (393).
The subject is trapped in an endless awareness of the gulf between its desires
and any objective conditions that might justify them.

Anxiety is the foundation of existential heroism. For it reveals our contingency by forcing us to encounter subjectively the world's indifference toward subjective desire. But if we simply yield to anxious moods, we only
theatricalize that contingent finitude without taking responsibility for it.
Therefore Heidegger wants anxiety to play a double, quasi-dialectical role.
Its negative function is to free consciousness of any illusion that it can find
the meanings it desires in either objective structures of the world or its own
practical abilities. Anxiety dramatizes the emptiness that each subject must
take into itself as the challenge to give meaning to its own mortality. But then
this negative function has to be itself grasped in its limitations. Anxiety reveals a power of spirit that can find positive uses for this lack of grounded-
ness. Faced with the lack of external determinants, subjectivity can embrace
its own contingency and identify with its particular modes of caring. The
question of right and wrong becomes much less important than the question
whether the subject is indifferent or engaged.

## VII. From Atmosphere to Mood: Munch as a Transformation of Pissarro

Now my own little quasi-dialectic has to take one more twist. It seems to
me that Heidegger's existential stance requires his repeating on an ethical
level a basic move that he criticizes on a practical one. He shows how reducing anxiety to fear creates a limited and overconfident practical subject.
But is there ultimately much difference between that reduction and the effect
of reabsorbing contingency into the engaged self-reflexiveness of the existential subject? Is it really the case that the subject can find itself through the
anxiety that mood creates? Heidegger is careful not to give his ethical subject the same clear pragmatic focus that fear allows the practical subject. Yet
Heidegger's subject seems to win a kind of spiritual certainty, at least insofar as subjectivity gets realigned with commitment. Once we no longer evade
our finitude, there seems to be a remainder or residue left over from our anx-

ieties. What begins as an analysis of mood quickly loses sight of the affect involved and concentrates instead on the ontology of subjectivity. As being possessed slides into being capable of existential choice, Heidegger seems to ignore perhaps the most fundamental feature of anxiety—that the corollary of objectlessness may also involve at its core a condition of subjectlessness. The contingency we feel may emerge not because we realize the essence of subjectivity, but because we cannot attach to a plausible version of subjective agency. Perhaps mood demonstrates an irreducible tension between how we might come to consciousness and the imaginary constructs we need in order to take responsibility for that consciousness.

As is all too often the case, the pursuit of ethical ideals here sustains the suppression of phenomenological intricacy. But tracing this temptation also helps us see one important way in which the modernist artists and writers differed from the various philosophical stances current at the time. Artists and writers in the generation before Heidegger's cultural moment were so eager for alternatives to the oppressive idealizations in what passed as ethical discourse in their societies that they turned eagerly to mood as perhaps the one sanctuary in the psyche where talk of ethics could not penetrate. In effect they asked whether any promise of authenticity makes it worth surrendering the enigmatic and transpersonal dimensions that moods afford us. And they wanted to explore the resources consciousness might discover were it to hover over not quite objects in roles that do not quite establish subjects. Therefore, I want to spend a little time exploring three variations on the logic of mood developed by these artists. Each variation seems to me important in its own right as an example of how an intentional structure can provide distinctive connections to the world and satisfactions for the psyche. But I am also interested in how we might project historical links among these variations. For then we see how the articulation of particular affective states makes it possible for related stances to take on urgency—in part as realizations of paths not taken and in part as responses to pressures that emerge as agents discover limitations in the investments they make in any one type of affective condition.[19]

Mood became an especially attractive affect because it had strong affinities with impressionist interests in rendering the atmospheric effects pervading particular scenes. Atmosphere offers much the same overall tonality and dispersed subjectivity we find in moods, and it frees affects from demands that they attach to concerns for character and for action. But it proved difficult to be content with the naturalizing of subjective agency created by an emphasis on atmosphere. So a second generation of artists tried a variety of ways to psychologize atmosphere by stressing its affinities to psychological states that had the same pervasive power yet did not smoothly correlate with the natural world. At one pole (which I will not engage) we find Whistler's aestheticizing of mood; at the other, a quasi-Heideggerian exploration of how mood can so position the subject that its anxieties come to pervade the very atmosphere that was once a means of escaping concern with just such anxieties. These painters had the visual resources not to need heroic subjects to focus their stances toward anxiety. Finally in the work of a third and fourth generation there emerged the possibility that one might address these anxieties by treating atmosphere as something entirely constructed rather than as something discovered. Atmosphere then would prove inseparable from the powers of the artist's medium. And the logic of mood might apply to the modes of imaginative life made possible by the states of mind the artist could make continuous with the work that medium performed. Color and line might have the same totalizing force that impressionists found in light and movement. But because the elements were inseparable from the life of the psyche, there would not need to be any alienating difference between the artist's making and the states of mind the work offered as distinctive sites of feeling.

I am not trying to retell the story of modern painting. I am interested only in basic elements that trace a partial history of mood within modernism. For example, as I turn to Monet's *Impression Sunrise* (1864), the painting that inspired the name "Impressionism" and that still provides a striking example of impressionist values, I will be concerned only with how small and undramatic human presences become in this work. We do get enough detail to infer that these presences are fishermen. But we certainly learn nothing about how they fish or how they might express their affective relationship to their labor. The relevant agency here is not that of those who are represented, but the painterly skill and intelligence that distributes the fishing boat into the play of elements constituting the emergence of morning colors and tones. Impressionism was a radical movement not only because it changed our understanding of seeing but also because it changed our investments in the kinds of affective human presences painting both rendered and addressed. Agency became much less dramatically centered, much more intricately distributed into the appearances taken by surrounding environments. And that required our learning to appreciate the kinds of affects best suited to this way of distributing visual energies.

In my view Camille Pissarro provides the richest examples of just how these impressionist investments can be articulated and appreciated. For Monet and Renoir seem entirely seduced by their new technology. Art could realize what gave moments their intensity as adventures in light and color. Indeed these adventures could be seen as replacing dramas based on human events by purely visual dramas allowing the spirit to dwell in the present tense, despite the loss of so much of its self-idealizing heritage. Pissarro, on the other hand, seems to want something more, something better attuned not just to seeing, but also to the forms of desire that might be deployed by virtue of our desire to dwell in the present. So he never quite lets vision as such take priority. There is almost always something about the whole of the painting, about the synthesis of visual features, that reaches beyond the moment to

Camille Pissarro, *The Garden of the Tuileries in Winter*. New Orleans Museum of Art.

make manifest how a psyche might be able to participate affectively in the overall visual field. Grasping a sense of the whole might be as important in viewing a landscape as in engaging a classical dramatic situation.

Monet seems to have become excited over specific sections of a painting where tones suddenly fused or color won small victories over the logic of shape and structure. But in Pissarro's best work such absorption in particulars would seem somewhat vulgar or reactionary, as if the artist were seduced by the position of the individual subject rather than set free to identify with the capacity of overall atmospheric effects to stretch and to realign our affective priorities and even our sense of the boundaries of personal identity. Sensation is not the source of intensity. Rather intensity emerges as we recognize how the experience of wholeness ceases to be merely abstract and takes on almost material form as a presence within the figured landscape. Sense seems somewhat abstracted, but the abstracting mind manages to strip itself of all practical investments so that it can regard itself primarily as the site for realizing and appreciating this capacity for expansive sensation. Atmosphere almost takes on the comprehensive objectlessness of mood, while the responding agency has to refine and spread itself in order to attune to this fluid totality.[20] In effect, the viewers are invited to suspend the quest for local intensities so that they can try out identifications with the fluid yet comprehensive sensibility composed by the painting. And the more successful that suspension, the richer the sense that awareness of this encompassing atmosphere has an intensely transpersonal dimension. Attempting to take in the entire scene aligns desire entirely with conditions of viewing and shows how that viewing is likely to be fundamentally alike for all of us who make the necessary effort.

Even Pissarro's atmosphere does not offer the full realization of the features of intentionality mood can provide us. Atmosphere can engage us affectively because it shares many of the attributes of mood, but we do not quite encounter a sense within the scene of the intensely psychologized totality that for Heidegger gives a shape to subjectivity before the agent can take responsibility for his or her situation. This is not to say that Pissarro's implied viewer is without this sense of enigmatic affective totality constituting the precondition for self-awareness. It is to say that Pissarro's implied viewer is not personally responsible for or in conflict with the demands that the totality imposes, so we do not feel the mood as necessarily implicating the concerns that the subject has about its own place in the world. There is little anxiety in Pissarro and thus little demand for struggling to understand how one's own agency is implicated in and constrained by the atmosphere.

This may be only to say that Pissarro remains an impressionist while Heidegger's version of the subject is shaped largely by the models of agency developed in expressionist art. But I took so long in saying it because I want to make visible how closely allied an expressionist disposition is to the impressionist one. In order to work out the concrete affinities I will turn to Edvard Munch's *Street Musicians* (1905?), a great work that concentrates on a moment where atmosphere seems to be transforming itself into mood. The painting then allows us to see how both the differences and the similarities between the two dispositions can do significant affective work.

Munch's painting shows that he has learned a great deal from impressionist uses of light and sky to establish an overall structure of tonalities. But where Pissarro revels in the degree to which affect can be freed of the burden of psychology, and hence of emotions that keep the needs of the subject in the foreground, Munch will not let the landscape stand on its own. For him there can be no independent "that-it-is" of its "there." While a cool limpid atmosphere pervades the scene and gives a sense of presence to the pervasive stone, these material qualities are not sufficient to explain this scene's effects. Something intensely psychological seems inseparable from the street's appearing as it does here. We know that the painting is responding to features of this scene that are far in excess of what can be pictured. So the viewer has to project into the scene in order to find ways of taking up attitudes toward the landscape.

Yet there is no dramatic center for this psychology. In fact the images seem intended to dispel just such centers while inviting us to identify with some

Edvard Munch, *Street Musicians*. Zurich Kunsthaus.

unnameable sense of urgency and loss that pervades the atmosphere. The subjectivity expressed here is in the grip of forces not at all accessible to self-consciousness. And for that very reason self-consciousness must dominate the scene. We do not ask what is being painted but what is happening to the painter and to his personages (who could never aspire to being "characters"). To feel what this painting seems to present, we cannot impose dramatic emotion but have to surrender to that pervasive uncertainty, as if that might also be an index of what it means to be a subject in Munch's world.

The painting is quite large. The general scene is a city street rendered in cold pale tones that match the sky. Everything seems drained. At just above the middle of the painting there is a band of musicians stretched across the single street forming a bold vertical shape through the painting. Seen from what seems the immense distance of the painter's location, the musicians have no individualizing traits. They could almost be black notations in a Cy Twombly painting. Closer to the foreground some distinct faces appear, presumably as passersby. But when we examine their features, they too seem to collapse into the same lack of distinctiveness we saw in the musicians. They all dwell in this place without quite inhabiting it.

Even the music seems to have no active force on any of the auditors. Existence remains frighteningly visual, with all human activity flattened into the landscape onto which the humans seem almost pasted, the musicians much more played upon than playing.

The subjectivity here is distributed much as in Pissarro, so that any identity we attribute is simply derived from a projection of what it would require for affective consciousness to take in the scene as a whole. But now to take in the scene is to feel oneself painfully distanced from the natural and social worlds that it represents. What pervades the scene is ultimately not something primarily visual, not something that can be attributed to the play of air and light and reflection. Perhaps Munch is rendering visually what it feels like to be within the world while being aware that whatever might establish value lies outside that world or somehow tauntingly on its margin. Perhaps he is expressing a sense of the world that about ten years later Wittgenstein would put this way:

> If there is any value that does have value, it must lie outside the whole sphere of what happens and is the case. For all that happens and is the case is accidental. For what makes it non-accidental cannot lie *within* the world, since if it did it would itself be accidental.
> It must lie outside the world.
> And so it is impossible for there to be propositions of ethics.
>
> (*Tractatus*, 6.41–6.42)

The worlds of the happy and the unhappy man must wax and wane as a whole precisely because such values seem frames for the world of fact rather than phenomena operating within that world. Analogously, Munch's represented agents seem aware that there is something beyond the world they perceive, but in this case they know that only by their inability to engage fully in the situation where they find themselves. Their affective state seems pervaded by a sense of a totality that lacks any distinguishing marks of happiness or unhappiness, even though the agents would prefer even unhappiness to this anomie.

Why do I call this sense of disaffection a mood? One reason is its continuity with impressionist atmosphere. But the more important reason is the fact that the very lack of distinguishing traits among the citizens here pushes a viewer to ascribe some total condition that pervades the scene. And we need to hypothesize mood because of the distinctive ways that the painting as painting works to create affect in the viewer. Again the lack of any dramatic center proves decisive. The strongest affective operator here is not anything the painting portrays but the sense of scale that it projects as an immense waiting, a sense of space disturbing for those who do not need this scale for whatever actions they in fact perform. Just visually taking in the entire scene requires considerable stretching of neck and eye. Yet that is not the only form of labor required. The physical stretching is paralleled by a sense that we are engaging a psychological limit along with a visual one. By attempting to bring all these details and shifts in atmospheric tonality within one overall response to the painting, we seem ourselves to have explored the entire territory and found nothing that was not painfully accidental, yet utterly determined. We cannot name what keeps everyone within this affective framework, but we know that they are all caught in the same circumstance. And we need no names in order to be possessed by the way the physical atmosphere comes to seem continuous with the sense of pervasive discomfort linking us to the agents in their uneasy passivity. The painting has to spread itself out if it is simultaneously to express and to encompass how limited the world is for these people. Here there is no dreaming of existentialist alternatives; there is only this shared minimal subjectivity made taut and painfully self-aware by the effort to take in how this world "waxes and wane as a whole" (*Tractatus*, 6.43).

## VIII. From Mood to Painterly Abstraction and the Work of Art as Exemplary Agent: Kandinsky, Rothko, and Smithson

Mood in Munch (and in Heidegger) offers a strange paradox. The very factors that distance intentionality from the empirical subject also haunt that subject with its relative impotence. Abstracting from the self provides a sense of the whole, but this wholeness is disturbingly incomplete because there is no clear connection between affect and action, or even between affect and specific structures of care. Mood absorbs agency rather than helping it orient its energies toward the practical world. But for the two generations of artists following Munch, that absorption seemed a very attractive alternative to what the world was becoming, especially when it could be so intimately linked with the painter's weaving of intricate atmospheric relationships into the texture of the mood. So they tried to establish positive aspects of these abstracting tendencies by emphasizing how creativity itself might find a powerful analogue in the affective dispositions mood provides. The ability of mood to overwhelm personal psychology might be taken as something to cultivate, especially if one could imagine a kind of feeling or sense of inner life whose reality one experienced when one managed that suspension of ego. Rather than being haunted by the weakening of will and idea, mood might help define how the psyche might find liberation in its proximity to totalizing atmospheric effects. And the evanescence of mood might so successfully evade reality that one could imagine a work of art constituting its own atmosphere. The overall tonalities fascinating the artist could have more to do with musical form than with landscape. Analogously, the ability to manipulate the elements of tonality in expressive ways might be seen as a process of the spirit reaching out to express directly what language cannot capture. Art did not need to content itself with registering how alienated faces drift away from social scenes; it could directly present as relational fields the elemental spiritual realities that society distorted and repressed.

All of these transformations depend on envisioning the practical world as more a source of blindness than of spiritual satisfaction. For then alienation is a form of homecoming, so long as there can be means of expression for how that distance affords its own psychological intensities. Or, to put the same point another way, the more it seems feasible to treat the empirical subject as bound to the world of will and idea, the greater the temptation to seeks means of characterizing alternative possibilities of agency. Mood becomes heuristic. And "realist" desires to dramatize consciousness aligning itself with the actual world come to seem traps for the spirit, limiting it to appearances that block out the underlying rhythms and forces shaping and structuring relations among these objects. Thus Oskar Kokoschka in 1912 would dream of surrendering "our closed personalities, so full of tension" in order to begin feeling his soul as "a reverberation of the universe" (Chipp, 172).

Also writing in 1912, Wassily Kandinsky gave this new perspective its then definitive formulation (in terms oddly sensitive to the painful states that an artist like Munch could develop by emphasizing scale):

> The eye which is directed at one point (be it form or content) cannot possibly survey a large plane. The inattentive eye, roaming over the surface, surveys this large plane or one part of it, but is caught by the external dissimilarities and loses itself in contradictions. . . .

> Anarchy is planfulness and order which are not produced by an external and ultimately failing force, but are created by *the feeling of the good*. Here too limits are set. However they must be designated as *inner* and they must replace the outer limits. . . . Contemporary art, which in this sense is to be correctly designated as anarchistic, reflects not only the spiritual standpoint which has already been won, but it embodies the spiritual which is ripe for disclosure as a materializing force. (Chipp, 160)

I am not sure how to translate Kandinsky's formulation into discursive terms that will stand up as argument. But I think it is clear how the logic of mood underlies this sense of a materializing spirituality because the life of that spirit consists in its power to render compositional effects. Here the emphasis falls on two distinctive aspects of intentionality. First, art had to reveal powers of abstraction that could free the psyche from the processes of forming and testing specific beliefs. This required elaborating a new vocabulary of concrete elements capable of demonstrating internal powers no longer felt when consciousness tied itself to the world of determined objects and practical purposes. Art could not be content either with the eye narrowly focused on a single scene or with the eye wandering all over the place, buffeted by contradictions it could not resolve. This meant locating eye's affective content in material properties and relations not yet conscripted for social networking.

Art had to go back to the subtleties of atmosphere and the fluid yet psychologically charged sensations established by artists like Pissarro and Munch.

But the new art could not look primarily to the past. It had to develop fresh conceptual frameworks valuing the sensations and relations that abstraction put on center stage. Otherwise an art without reference might collapse into pure design or arbitrary individual expression. This is where the second new aspect of intentionality would enter. In the place of dramatically organized feelings, visual art would turn to alternative models for how one could plausibly talk about these atmospheric relations as truly manifesting the life of spirit. One standard response to this challenge was to call attention to how the elements of painting might be conceived as notes within a musical structure. Then art might have a synthetic force that paralleled harmony in music. And that model of synthesis also stressed the way spirit was inseparable from matter: spirit was not a way of reaching beyond sense to abstract meaning so much as a way of dwelling within the sensible so as to appreciate fully the qualities of mind making the sensible itself a world of complex relations. Thus we find Hans Hofmann celebrating the subtle adjustments painters make between physical and psychological domains by speaking of "the symphonic animation of the picture plane" (Chipp, 540). Art becomes animation by virtue of a materialization so radical that only spirit seems an adequate concept for the intensity and subtlety of the fields of energy transfer dynamizing the work's surface.

While he, too, often relied on musical analogues, Kandinsky was not content with such straightforward comparisons. He insisted that the painterly intentionality leading us to develop these analogues take on a second-order dimension enabling him to treat the painting as a mode of disposing the will. And in so doing he prepared a useful framework for understanding how a later generation of painters, preeminently Mark Rothko, came to imagine that there were still major developments to be explored within the affective dispensations opened by modernist abstraction.

In essence Kandinsky's "feeling of the good" is a fantasy of being god-like. Just as God rests at the end of creation and finds it good, the painter rests after his painting by securing it as a feeling for the good. This goodness does not involve any particular judgment about segments of the painting. Rather it is a second order judgment of the painting as a whole. He can link the overall effects of musical structure with a kind of inner need within the painting. The feeling for the good then combines a sense of responsibility with a sense of deep satisfaction.

Were there a specific goal for these energies beyond the work, spirit would be consumed by efforts to be satisfied by external objects. And then the artist would be back in a world where the only requirement was to mediate culturally established values rather than to create fresh links to the universe. But Kandinsky is careful to distinguish the feeling for the good from feelings involved with particular goods. This enables him to focus attention on the state of the subject rather than on properties of the object. And on that basis he can link the feeling for the good with what he called the painting's capacity to establish "inner resonances" (159) more capacious and intensive than anything we can attribute to the immediate attunements of physical and psychological planes. The painter and the viewer do not simply judge whether particulars realize some kind of goodness. Rather they seek satisfaction in an overall pervasive goodness created by a close fit between what the work makes visible and what seems to have elicited it in the first place. Satisfaction here is an affirmation of the resonance as fully sounding the spirit it makes present. Feeling in the art Kandinsky idealizes is not for specific sensations but for what we might have to call the "meta-sensation" of judging that the overall framework one inhabits fully satisfies the spirit's need to find material expression. Feeling becomes the source of willed identifications with specific organizations of energies for their own sake.

I have to hope that pictures will speak more clearly than my words do. So I will very briefly turn to two contrasting readings of Kandinsky's feeling of the good—first by Mark Rothko, who extends Kandinsky's efforts to conceive painting in musical terms, then by Robert Smithson, who reverses the entire development of modernism by returning mood to its grounds in atmosphere—but now atmosphere can be taken literally rather than figuratively. These two modern artists then can be seen as further transformations of Munch's transformation of Pissarro. But where Munch stresses the psychology of mood, we might say that the modernists emphasize how that psychology opens into fresh perspectives on the very elements constituting what psyches are likely to share as they participate in whatever gives the paintings their distinctive identities. The work becomes the agent, and its relations among elements become literal examples of possible intentional states the psyche can take on once practical orientations can be suspended.

In Rothko the painter himself cannot be treated primarily as a craftsperson mediating the life of spirit. Rothko wants us to envision the painter as literally transformed by the site he composes. Much of this power resides in the way that the relations among colors seem to fold back into the radical presence of color made utterly and actively material by being given its dynamic inner life. The individual color tones do not dance or engage in complex balances. Instead they verge on a point where all the differences collapse or blend into a single substance that hovers within the painting, perhaps constituting the source of the particular light it radiates. The painting's agency then just is the complex process of giving a body to spirit. We feel our psyches released into something like a materialized version of the totality mood takes on as what brings together a range of diverse feeling-sensations. But we do not stop with this quality of release. There is also a strong sense that in the release we also find a place for spirit to dwell.

To participate in a Rothko is also to let ourselves feel what might be involved in becoming absorbed within the painting. Abstraction ceases to be a matter only of how the surface of painting deploys visual forces and controls dynamic balances. Abstraction becomes access to a particular kind of substance and a particular disposition in relation to that substance. That relation, I think, is a distinctive kind of second-order willing. Nothing else will explain how such intense freedom seems inseparable from being grounded within so much expansive pleasure. We feel spirit not only because of the painting's dynamic energies but also because of the qualities of rest it affords when we experience ourselves fully yielding agency to it. We become introspective not by thinking about the painting, or thinking about ourselves viewing the painting, but by thinking about what it might be like literally to take on the mode of existence that these color relations make utterly and mysteriously material. Rothko makes atmospheres that stay atmospheres because they are no longer in any way attached to the weather.

Yet the form of agency that Rothko affords does depend, often painfully, on another kind of weather. The painting offers itself as an alternative site where there need be no irritable reaching after fact and reason: viewers can find relief from the anxieties that haunt the empirical ego. But there remains a sharp and disturbing difference between the world inside the painting and the world we enter when we turn from it. Promises of relief from the anxieties of being an existential subject make us especially vulnerable to those moments when paint is just paint and spirit fails to make itself manifest. So Rothko felt he had to find a visual means of getting beyond the alternation of transcendence and despair apparently built into his idealized version of what particular paintings might accomplish. And he did so, at least for the moment, in his brilliant work constructing a memorial chapel on the grounds of the De Menil Museum in Houston. There he decided to make a composition consisting of several canvases in different combinations of brooding purples and blacks, all open to changing outdoor light. The result is a substantial modification of the ontology we have been tracing. The individual canvases retain and even deepen his sense of how color can provide a dwelling place for the psyche. But now the painting is not the only source of mood. Mood becomes intimately linked with the actual world. So the substantializing and totalizing aspects of mood enter into dialogue with the sensations produced in relation to a very different register of totality. Mood is forced to open itself to process, and process is engaged through the encompassing dispositions that mood establishes. Identification then goes in two directions at once—into the inner depths of these mournful colors, and into the enduring forces whose ways of returning bring the vitality of change to the starkness of these brooding surfaces. Exaltation and mourning become part of the day's cycle and not just elements in human dramas. And totality is not just an idea; it is the demand to encompass the relation of canvas to context.

By emphasizing Rothko's chapel I think we can see that it is in some respects not a large leap from his aesthetic concerns to the treatment of atmosphere and mood explored by Robert Smithson's *Spiral Jetty*, although Smithson's aesthetic commitments are utterly different from Rothko's. Smithson can be said to close the circle opened by Pissarro. For he once again cast art as inseparable from an appreciation of how spirit is distributed within the atmospheric aspects of natural scenes. Atmosphere matters because of how it embodies in radical physical form the insubstantial and pervasive affective totality that mood produces. But in *Spiral Jetty* the atmospheric effects are not illusory but actual: we are asked to attend to how nature itself takes on dispositions in relation to a specific phenomenon. So Smithson brings to a new level the modernist ideal that the work be a reality in itself to be assessed by how it actually modifies those surroundings. Now art must be brought out of the museum and the gallery, those asylums where works wait for critics to pronounce them "curable or incurable," so that it may take "direct account of the elements as they exist day by day apart from representation" (Smithson, 154–55).

To make good on my claims I have to turn to Smithson's own account of the genesis of *Spiral Jetty*. For he tells us he realized that at the Great Salt Lake one could encounter a version of the sublime that erased all differences between artifact and heightened sensation. The eye's encounter with the expanse of lake and stone and sand made it seem that "no ideas, no concepts, no systems, no structures, no abstractions could hold themselves together in the actuality of that evidence" (Smithson, 146). A viewer experiences in heightened form the awareness of sensation becoming a field of fluid relations that first inspired impressionist painting and later shaped one course for how noniconic painters viewed their relation to their own compositional activity: "Solid and liquid lost themselves in each other. It was as if the mainland oscillated with waves and pulsations, and the lake remained still" (Smithson, 146). Matter fuses into motion and motion into matter. And pervading all these metamorphoses there emerges an abiding stillness that I think has close parallels to Kandinsky's feeling of the good. But Smithson's version of a will inseparable from a sense of immanent totality demands that one focus attention on the work's power to subsume the ego in relation to this totality. As consciousness finds affinities with the stillness pervading lake and stone and sand, its version of totality takes the form of "the *alogos*" undermining "the *logos*" (147). The feeling of the good proves identical with the rapture of being released from the hold of closed personality:

> Chemically speaking, our blood is analogous in composition to the primordial seas. Following the spiral steps we return to our origins, back to some pulpy protoplasm, a floating eye adrift in an antediluvian ocean. On the slopes of Rozel Point I closed my eyes, and the sun burned crimson through the lids. I opened them and the Great Salt Lake was bleeding scarlet streaks. . . . My eyes

became combustion chambers churning orbs of blood blazing by the light of the sun. All was enveloped in a flaming chromosphere. I thought of Jackson Pollock's *Eyes in the Heat*. . . . Swirling within the incandescence of solar energy were sprays of blood. . . . Perception was heaving, the stomach turning, I was on a geologic fault that groaned within me. (148)

For me there are two especially striking moments in this passage. First, despite his denigration of painting, Smithson at his most intense thinks not of nature but of Pollock's art. This is partially because Pollock is an obvious rival. But I think he also turns to Pollock because there is no richer example that he might use to show how all of the resources of the cultured mind here take on something like a material presence within the work. Thus where Pollock's eyes in the heat remain figures attempting to bridge the distance between the artist's actual world and the mythic realms he wants to enter, Smithson's eyes literally become the heat. These eyes are directly attuned to the ego's decomposition and recomposition into congeries of floating atmospheric elements.

Second, at the end of this passage, what had been a drama of sensual surfaces undergoes a surprisingly quiet transformation into a more permanent, more substantial parallel between psyche and landscape: "I was on a geologic fault that groaned within me" (148). This equation manages to attune itself to a totality pervading the entire modulation of affects while simultaneously reattaching the entire experience to Emersonian projections of the American ego. Only now the figure for that totalizing ego is not the transparent eyeball but the hollowed-out cavities of the psyche's own irreducible propensities to participate in the undoing of the logics that seem to sustain it. And here feeling's way of pervading sensation takes on a rich affective resonance. As sensation, the groan expresses terror before the inevitable dissolution of substantial structures. But at the core of such sensation the metaphoric register of groaning takes on a concrete existence where we hear, or more accurately where we almost become, the possibility of new birth because of how our energies now flow between landscape and psyche. Where Pissarro absorbs mood into a depicted landscape, here subjectivity comes to life because of how the actual atmosphere becomes a living presence framing and transforming what now counts as art.

I cannot leave this chapter without acknowledging my awareness that what art history gives, it also takes away. Despite Smithson's clever trumping of Pollock, history tells us that it is Pollock who has gained the upper hand. There are many reasons for this ascendancy—not the least of which is that for all his boldness as an artist Pollock never took the risks that Rothko or Smithson did in taking on forms of intentionality that challenged the hegemony of the ego. Pollock wanted to keep all the painterly forces that made it possible to escape the empirical ego, but primarily so that he could then enlist those forces in the pursuit of a sublime version of that ego. So mood remained suspect because it provided a means of avoiding existential responsibility. Indeed mood became for him primarily a feature of the quasi-representational Picasso-influenced paintings from which he tried to escape. With his drip paintings he could dramatize a willingness to embrace that existential responsibility. In these works there is very little sense of the painting discovering properties of color relations or objective spiritual states that make demands on the painter to enter that reality. Instead, the whole is insistently a series of existential choices, endlessly variable and so referring constantly to the artist's terrifying freedom to make changes and recompose overall structures. For Pollock no other reality mediated through art could compete with the drama of giving the self a concrete existence by focusing on how it might perform itself in relation to a chosen medium.

Our contemporary art world seems more closely attuned to Pollock than it is to Rothko and to Smithson, perhaps because these are times when it is important to fight for the ego against those affective states that dissolve subjectivity into various kinds of totality. But while granting this, we also might keep in sight the image of Pollock the aggressive drunk willing to go to absurd lengths to fight for his sense of what that ego entails. Then we will at least recognize how valuable it can be to have strong alternative versions of intentionality.

# 3  *Interpreting Emotions*

> All colours, all sounds, all forms . . . evoke indefinable and yet precise
> emotions, or, as I prefer to think, call down among us certain disem-
> bodied powers whose footsteps over our hearts we call emotions; . . .
> the more perfect [the work] is, and the more various and numerous
> the elements that have flowed into its perfection, the more powerful
> will be the emotion, the power, the god it calls among us.
> W. B. Yeats, "The Symbolism of Poetry"

## I. Introduction: How Emotions Differ from Feelings

Our interpretive perspective has to change dramatically when we shift
from the topic of feelings and moods to concerns about how we experience
emotions and passions.[1] With the emotions and the passions there is no escaping the empirical ego. Emotions differ from feelings primarily because
they are modes of affect in which the ego has to position itself as a psychological unit in relation to the conditions that move it. Feelings quicken and
animate the psyche, while emotions involve it in caring about how it will engage certain states of affairs over time. We adjust to feelings or we let them
direct our attention toward some quite particular momentary satisfactions.
With emotions, the imagination not only participates in what it engages but
also functions synthetically. When we identify a state as an emotion, our
imaginations represent feelings as components within larger complexes, with
the complexes usually taking the form of attitudes developed to deal with
dramatic situations.

I am overwhelmed by the theoretical work that has been done on the emotions. So in this chapter I am even going to pretend that I can adequately survey the various stances that have been taken or assess the various claims that
have been made for their nature and significance. Rather I am going to rely

on Richard Wollheim's *On the Emotions* for a core account of the philosophical issues.[2] Then rather than provide a survey of types of emotion, an
endless task, I will concentrate on elaborate readings of two poems which
raise the philosophical and social issues most interesting to me in relation to
this topic. I will treat Matthew Arnold's "Isolation to Marguerite" as an example of fundamentally symptomatic or passive constructions of an attitude
that relies on imaginary energies to conceal from himself what subsequent
observers are likely to observe. This example is interesting in itself for the
remarkable mobility of our powers of self-deception. And it is especially interesting for those who are concerned with why Modernists became suspicious of the framing of attitudes characteristic of emotions, preferring instead
the more fluid and less self-staging possibilities of dwelling on feelings. Then
in contrast I will spend considerable time on a seventeenth-century poem,
Bishop Henry King's "The Exequy," an elegy for his wife. This poem seems
to me to take every opportunity to stylize standard emotions and defeat the
sense of self-importance that these standard emotions typically create. So I
will treat the poem as illustrating how agents can develop distinctive ways of
forming the attitudes that sustain emotion. King's poem provides a telling
example of why an adjectival approach to emotions is severely limited, and,
correspondingly, how an adverbial approach concerned with the manner of
one's actions can activate our imaginative resources.

## II. Recasting Richard Wollheim's "Characteristic History of an Emotion": On Being Moved, Being Positioned, and Being Invested

My exposition of Wollheim's position may be somewhat tedious, since I
try to render the core of Wollheim's arguments without the charm of his
voice or the bite of his examples. Yet the tedium should prove worth enduring because even in condensed form the arguments afford by far the
strongest analysis of what is wrong with cognitivism and what it will take
to strike out in new directions. Even more important, the perspective he establishes proves much more amenable to the arts than other current views
do, a condition which in turn allows me to rely even more heavily on the
arts as evidence supporting my efforts to make adjustments in Wollheim's
framework. Finally, engaging Wollheim is crucial to my project because I
strongly disagree with his efforts to bring psychoanalytic thinking to bear
on the topic.[3] I hope to show that one can preserve the psychological intricacy of emotions while relying simply on how intentionality is formed and
identities pursued.

Wollheim is not the kind of philosopher one can just cite or raid for particular ideas. He is so careful and so precise that each claim is carefully embedded in several others. So I have to produce at least a minimal overall
representation of how his book is structured; then I can take up those specific

aspects of his case that I want to elaborate or contest. I begin then with what Wollheim calls the "characteristic history of an emotion":

> (one) we have a desire:
> (two) this desire is satisfied or is frustrated, or it is in prospect of being one or the other: alternatively we merely believe one of these things of it:
> (three) we trace the satisfaction or frustration, real or merely believed-in, actual or prospective, to some thing or some fact, which we regard as having precipitated it:
> (four) an attitude develops on our part to this precipitating factor:
> (five) this attitude will generally be either positive—that is, tinged with pleasure—or negative—that is tinged with unpleasure—though sometimes it may be neutral. And it will generally be positive if it originates in satisfaction, and negative if it originates in frustration, but this is not exceptionless:
> (six) the attitude persists:
> (seven) the emotion, as it now is, manifests itself in a number of mental states, and it generates a variety of dispositions:
> (eight) the emotion tends to find expression in behavior:
> and
> (nine) it is highly likely that the mental dispositions that the emotions generate will include desires, and, if this is so, and if we possess the necessary worldly information, the emotion may generate action, but only indirectly. "Indirectly," for what directly generates action, here as elsewhere, is the motivating conjunction of desire and instrumental belief. (15–16)

Like the cognitivists', Wollheim's story culminates in an account of how emotions influence the actions we perform. But for Wollheim the influence must be indirect, and that makes all the difference. If we want emotions to have a direct influence on actions, we have to equate them with beliefs or with desires, and then we lose their distinctive psychological qualities. Emotions become instruments directed by some primary mental process. If however we keep the three arenas separate, we can have this simple and elegant division of roles: "If belief maps the world and desire targets it, emotion tints or colors it; it enlivens it or darkens it as the case may be" (15). And if emotion is to color the world, imagination must serve as both its palette and its brushwork. For emotion's colorings cannot take place in accord with the same mechanisms that govern desires and beliefs, yet the colorings must be able to have an influence on desire and belief if emotions are to modify actions at all. In order to make the necessary connections Wollheim shows how we construct emotions by developing attitudes that give a shape to the frustration or the satisfaction of desire.[4] In establishing that shape, usually in narrative form, we organize correspondences producing an affectively charged imaginative environment.

It would take too long to address each of Wollheim's nine elements. Therefore I will impose on his "characteristic history" my own general framework, since then we can readily see how his analyses help flesh out responses to the three fundamental questions I employed in discussing how feeling functioned in Caravaggio and in Titian. First, we have to establish what is involved in being moved or thinking we have been moved by some aspect of experience. What factors constitute the sense that we are responding affectively to particular conditions? Second, we have to characterize how persons turn being moved into an active way of situating themselves and so taking up a position in the world. How do agents give expressive shapes that personalize being moved and make articulate what it enables for them? Finally, a full account of the emotion has to spell out the possible values that take form because of that expressive activity.[5] We have to examine what differences it makes for the agent that he or she adopts the particular mode of expression that is pursued. Why does it matter that I express my anger by tight control rather than by losing my temper? What sense of myself does that sustain for me and what connections (and disconnections) does it establish in relation to the other person? Then there are also possible second-order concerns about the modes of public responsibility that one takes on by that mode of expression. How we express emotions brings to bear elaborate concerns about both identification and misidentification. For our expressions often take the form of endorsements or of the explicit taking of responsibility for what one feels—"Í know I am angry and I want everyone else to know how I feel about this person." Correspondingly, we are also likely to find significant patterns of self-defense and ironic distance. I repudiate the anger even as I manifest obvious signs of it. So it can often be a delicate matter to decide on the degree of self-possession the expression offers.

In Wollheim's history of an emotion, being moved involves two distinct steps. There is a concrete process of having to adapt to the satisfaction or frustration of desire, real or imagined. And there is the need for some kind of representation or retrospective construction of that being moved so that it seems part of a causal sequence. From these two features he draws several important corollaries. Emotions cannot be desires because they involve us in handling the consequences of desires. (Jealousy is not an expression of desire but a response to frustrations of desire.) And emotions cannot be beliefs because of the particular way we are moved—our need is not to make judgments about desires but to accommodate ourselves to a particular state that brings the desires into play. This particularity proves crucial because Wollheim can then cogently insist that emotions have their origin in psychological and not epistemic contexts. Satisfaction and frustration are not amenable to the general reasoning that brings beliefs to bear but require quite specific self-reflexive adjustments. Consequently the satisfaction and frustration involved in emotions put into play associations and condensations whose logic is not susceptible to the instruments we use to adjudicate beliefs.

Wollheim is so careful to show how being moved to emotions is different from forming beliefs and desires because he wants to emphasize the distinctive mode of situating the self which the emotions make possible. Having an emotion is inseparable from constructing attitudes. For it is the forming of attitudes that enables us to come to terms with the consequences of being satisfied or being frustrated by changes that take place in our lives. Attitudes transform the experiences of satisfaction and frustration by turning them outward, and so they help the agent locate what brought about the experience (76–77).[6] We identify emotions not in terms of beliefs but in terms of the specific ways that we are led to connect this outward turn with characterizations about how the psyche is engaged. Hence our use of terms like jealousy, anger, and wonder that involve overall imaginative stances, not just specific beliefs. Until we produce an attitude, the initiating frustration or satisfaction of desire lacks all definition. I could be frustrated because I am jealous of another or anxious about myself or even worried about the person over whom I am tempted to be jealous. When the attitude is established, it fixes a "precipitating factor" that gives the emotion a causal shape in relation to the situation. And in reaching back to the originating condition, attitudes also channel thoughts toward a self-interpretation of how that precipitating factor shapes one's situation in the present.[7] One perceives or imagines the cause now as specifically something that calls forth jealousy. And one is in a position to develop desires in relation to the resulting narrative so that the desires may in turn indirectly influence one's actions.

At the core of this transformation of immediate frustration or satisfaction, Wollheim attributes to the developing attitude the power to organize a range of "correspondences." These correspondences create complex relations forming something like an affective field of particulars that together establish the figurative colorings giving a tonality to the agent's affective world. Correspondences reflect the power of the object of the emotion to distribute an inner state over an objective situation (80). When anger takes hold, for example, it almost makes sense to speak literally about seeing red. Many of the objects of one's environment no longer seem independent entities but take on qualities consistent with the emotion and give a body to the attitude. Analogously, correspondences bring various aspects of the psyche into closer relationships with each other. For jealousy to emerge as an attitude charged with emotion, I have to locate my desire specifically in relation to some object and I have to read several of my own reactions like my anxiety and my anger and my obsession with particular details as all correspondences manifesting the significance of that precipitating cause. If imagination alters the correspondences, it also alters either the intensity of the emotion or its overall identity.

Probably the best way to use Wollheim's framework is to envision the construction of attitudes as occupying a continuum from simple gestures to quite complex efforts to represent the self in particular ways. Then we can account for the differences between these poles by bringing to bear a concept of expressive activity. Where most theorists of expression use that concept as a means of developing connections between manifest content and inner causation of some kind. Wollheim limits the concept so that it applies simply to how the agent manages to personalize the forming of an attitude. Expression is not specifying what the emotion is but forming an active stake in what the correspondences produce. Until we develop an attitude, the affects make us "hostages to the moment" (82) with its changing demands. But once the attitude is formed and the related correspondences are established, it is at least possible to proceed as if our emotion "derives from how we are, and from how we perceive the world, and ultimately from the history that we have led" (82). What is expressed is not need and desire per se, but the relation the person maintains toward the attitude being developed.

Expression then is the process by which this sense of personal activity becomes articulate about itself. Unlike our typical versions of causality, expression is "a causal relation that appears to be unconstrained by initial conditions" (137). Because there is no initial constraint indicating a determining cause, expression puts the focus on "how the emotion seems to us." Cause has to be located in how the person elaborates a situation, not in the situation itself (as a behaviorist would have it). The cause is the agent's bringing to bear a particular life history as he or she composes correspondences and links a projected cause to a single interpretive stance. And by connecting the self so intimately to the interpretive framework, Wollheim can clearly distinguish expression from statements of belief and of desire, a distinction that then also shifts the kinds of criteria that become appropriate in engaging what the agent proposes. Drawing on his work in the aesthetics of painting, Wollheim can show that expression does not simply refer to an emotion but also embodies what is being referred to (*Painting as an Art*, 80–89). Paintings are not just pictures of events that have emotional impact. Rather they are composed surfaces that actually give physical presence to certain affective states. In *On the Emotions* Wollheim offers the example of an expression of shame because it links the material signs indicating the emotion, like a blush or a shriek, with a pervasive psychological texturing of the situation (139). Identifying the emotion is a matter not of locating a specific belief but of attending to how the person seems to produce and elaborate the "initial conditions." We are expressive when our active agency radiates outward through the correspondences that the attitude enables.

I find useful here Nelson Goodman's suggestion that works of art metaphorically possess the qualities that they express (87). For this formulation emphasizes what we might call the literalness of the expressive properties. Agents cannot just point to these properties, for example by asserting a description of themselves as sad. They also have to reveal that sadness as an aspect of their behavior, and, for Wollheim but not for Goodman, there has to be a clear sense that the agent's own investments are manifest in that behavior.[8] Then it becomes obvious that some of these expressions will embody quite conventional attitudes and investments. Here the interpreter can rely on cultural grammars and not have to worry much about causes that go beyond the immediate precipitating factor. But the more elaborate the articulation, or the more difficult it is to read in conventional terms, the greater the pressure on the interpreter to connect the immediate precipitating factor to specific expressive desires and to the individual's overall desires and dispositions.

Finally, Wollheim's account of expressive activity makes possible an important claim about the kinds of investments that come into existence through the attitude. When we are dealing with belief and desire, we usually engage values that are "logically prior" to the judgments we formulate. We proceed as if we knew what values shaped our concerns so that the important issues become working out how these values can be realized in particular situations. And because we know the ends involved, we can speak cogently of beliefs and desires being satisfied (130). But with attitudes there is no clear way to talk about satisfaction.

Attitudes develop values that are "logically posterior" to the emotion, so that there are no clear expectations to be satisfied. That is an important way in which emotions differ from beliefs and desires. With beliefs and desires one can identify the value without reference to the emotion: the belief proclaiming envy presupposes goodness; the belief supporting indignation presupposes justice. But if the emotion shapes the value, the value depends on the attitude, and hence on investments that the person brings to the attitude.

Because the value established for emotions depends on the attitude, there cannot be any determinate conceptual framework and hence no grounds for making "rational" judgments. Instead, we have to appreciate the constitutive role that the personal investment introduces. The only adequate way to understand the values that attitudes produce is to trace the agent's expressive activity.[9] We understand why the attitude is connected to specific values when we appreciate how the internal relation among thoughts, feelings, wishes, and fantasies gives rise to desire. The relevant desires can take any of three forms, all of which then indirectly influence our actions: "We can observe that the desire may be directed (one) towards the object of the emotion, advancing or retarding it, (two) towards the consequences of the object of the emotion, maximizing or minimizing them, or (three) toward the emotion itself, reinforcing or attenuating it" (133).

## III. Some Reservations about Wollheim's Theory: His Emphasis on Fantasy and Hence His Preference for the Imaginary Rather Than the Imaginative

Wollheim takes us a long way toward an adequate analysis of how agents negotiate affective turbulence. His discussion accounts for how we produce images of precipitating factors so that we can give them psychological significance in our accounts of being moved; it allows us to explain how we organize sets of correspondences enabling the emotion to color entire segments of our world; it therefore indicates how emotions have a density and complexity that cannot be relegated simply to beliefs; and it provides the basis for attributing passivity and activity to the ways we respond to being moved. But before I can approach particular works of art I need to modify Wollheim's position in three ways—in relation to his model of how emotions emerge, in relation to his relying on frameworks that stress psychoanalytic methods of interpretation, and in relation to the difficulties of adequately defining active expressive agency from within this psychoanalytic orientation.

Wollheim's model of how emotions emerge gives us a clear account of what it is to be moved, and it provides a dynamic structure clarifying how we experience states that invite our attributing beliefs and intentions but do not seem to depend on them. Perhaps more important, relying on terms as general as "satisfaction of desire" and "frustration of desire" enables Wollheim to bring a wide variety of cases under a single conceptual framework. Yet in my view, speaking of "satisfaction" and "frustration" invites equivocation among quite different kinds of desires and so promotes a misleading uniformity in the treatment of emotions.

Wollheim's model fits those cases where quite specific desires precede the emotion and play a part in causing it. But there are other situations where the desires that preexist the emotion are very general, like those for happiness or companionship or the satisfaction of conative interests. When the desires are specific, it usually makes sense to give a concrete causal account of the emotion: this person frustrated my desires by getting the job I wanted and so I need to develop an attitude like envy or anger or jealousy. But when the desires are more general, a causal account is more difficult, largely because we need to supplement the general desire with some additional mental act, some judgment that itself is instrumental in determining what aspect of the desire is relevant and what counts as satisfaction. These emotions, at least, are not behavioral adjustments but specific choices within what can be quite complex psychological states, as in the poems I will soon discuss.

States such as wonder, love, and sympathy seem less dependent on specific preexisting desires than on quite general interests in being moved or finding value in our lives. These states do not so much derive from desire as play roles within a process of developing what we then experience as desires. The causes of love or wonder or sympathy have more to do with appraisals and what inspires them than with reactions and what enables us to adjust to them. So it seems necessary to admit that some of our most basic satisfactions occur in relation to desires that follow or accompany emotion rather than precede it.[10]

Caravaggio's *The Calling of Matthew,* for example, presents a case in which we would lose the force of the manifest emotion if we had to translate it into a response to either satisfaction or frustration.[11] Caravaggio's dramatic point is that Matthew is directly moved by the presence of Christ and of Peter in ways that he cannot quite read as either satisfaction or frustration. (One could call this state either satisfaction or dissatisfaction about the lack of definition, but that only indicates how ill-defined the general terms are.) Matthew is asked to focus not on himself but on the pull exerted by these figures, a pull that Caravaggio works hard to keep enigmatic.[12] (The two figures blend visually into one, out of which Christ's pointing finger emerges, and both figures are dressed as peasants sharply contrasted to the dandies comprising Matthew's world.) Caravaggio is also careful to base many of the lines of force in the painting on the work that hands do—I think because he wants to keep the focus of emotion quite concretely on this being pulled beyond a world where one's own satisfactions and frustrations can provide an adequate compass. Matthew cannot know whether he is satisfied or frustrated; he can only know that this is a call he has to heed, with the hope that in so doing he will find the most responsive attitude.

I am not sure how important my reservations are. They do seem to me to help ward off what we might call premature causal accounts of emotions and so help us keep theory committed to clearing the way for dwelling on the phenomenology of specific emotions. And they make me wonder about the wisdom in Wollheim's efforts to provide both a general causal account of why we develop emotions and a specific, retroactive account of the "precipitating factor" produced as we formulate an attitude. In one case, the drive producing the emotion is causal; in the other, it is established hermeneutically. When we pursue both, we end up with each having to war against the other. Will our account of satisfaction and dissatisfaction be a concrete causal one or a reflective reconstructed hermeneutic one open to the many possible meanings "satisfaction" and "dissatisfaction" can take on?

This tension between the causal and hermeneutic probably pervades Wollheim's account because it is very difficult to escape in even most the sophisticated efforts to bring psychoanalytic frameworks to bear on the theory of the emotions. Far be it from me on this occasion to enter into a full-scale critique of psychoanalysis. But one has to notice the price Wollheim pays for his fealties—primarily because psychologizing the emotions becomes in effect the study of fantasy and its causes rather than the study of imagination and its uses. That price is most evident, and most practically consequential, when in his concluding chapter Wollheim turns to extended discussions of two moral virtues—guilt and shame.

Wollheim's emphases are somewhat disconcerting because he deals almost exclusively with those moral virtues that are shaped by experiences with authority figures when one is young. Shame and guilt typically develop out of early experiences and "never altogether lose the characteristics of that phase in personal development at which they originate" (152). But even if one grants the influence of such figures, I do not think this is an exhaustive list of affectively based moral virtues. A causal relation to authority figures is not obviously the case, for example, with civic pride or with forms of public compassion, where what grounds the emotion are figures in one's present tense or even projections of future possibilities.[13]

One explanation for Wollheim's choice of moral virtues is the book's tendency as it proceeds to be more comfortable with "malformed emotions" than with emotions that are not primarily defensive formations. Wollheim defines malformed emotions as those in which a person is "unable to tolerate the subsequent experience of satisfaction or frustration" (82) in relation to desire and so activates a defense against the anxiety. Consequently "in the case of a malformed emotion, phantasy takes the place that is occupied, in the case of a normally formed emotion, by an attitude" (89) and the expressive registers that it organizes.[14] In contrast, emotions are not malformed when the development of an attitude is projective rather than defensive. Then the imagination helps us respond to reality rather than escape into daydream. In fact where the emotions are well formed, the imagination not only constructs an attitude but keeps the attitude in active dialogue with factors whose existence and control do not depend solely on imagination. Imagination gives these attitudes existence in real time, where they take on the power to modify the agent's continuing relation to the world beyond the imagination (see p. 90).

But ultimately Wollheim's claims for the powers of imagination give way to those centered on the specific roles that fantasy plays—that is with the role of the imaginary rather the imagination. It is fantasy that for him accounts for emotional depth. Whether the emotions are well formed or malformed, "the final constituent of emotion, or that which gives emotion its depth" is "phantasy, and its cognate, the wish" (140). Fantasies project illusory satisfactions of desire, establish a self-defense mechanism designed to ward off anxiety by removing its causes from mind, and thicken or recontextualize emotions by associating elements of the attitude with internalized figures (like mother and father) (140–42). The depth of fantasy comes from the fact that "on the bottom level phantasy . . . represents desire by bringing before the mind in a particularly vivid form the object of desire" (140).

Once fantasy becomes central in his account, so too does an insistence on causal factors in our interpretations of emotions. In his introductory analyses Wollheim is careful to keep emotion and expression separate from the modes of causality that come into play when we speak about belief and about desire. But explaining fantasy requires our positing causal factors that extend beyond the specific experience of satisfaction and frustration—hence the significance of psychoanalysis. For when we engage fantasy at its most powerful, we encounter the direct presence of imaginary figures from the past now having a strong influence on how the attitude gets organized. Jealousy for example is greatly intensified by the presence of nurturing and betraying imaginary figures deriving from childhood.

Consequently narrative becomes for Wollheim the central framework within which to understand why our attitudes take form and why they come to matter for us. Fantasy gives emotions depth by anchoring them in the traumatic features shaping individual life histories. Elaborating these histories takes us a long way from the modes of narrative called for by cognitivist theory. Wollheim wants us to approach narrative as Freud did, that is by reading through the manifest content to expose its resources for occluding reality and sustaining fantasy (143–46). Narratives provide the slots into which fantasy figures its figures.

Obviously one cannot accuse Wollheim of not appreciating the full range of the imagination's activities. But perhaps one can argue that he has an inadequate framework for correlating the imaginative activity to which he is so sensitive in works of art with his psychoanalytic model for dealing with the emotions. After all, Wollheim has always been uncomfortable with the normative generalization and the implicit self-congratulation that seem fundamental to philosophical ethics. So he simply ignores the kind of thinking we find in virtue ethics or in Christine Korsgaard's neo-Kantianism, thinking that ties our emotional commitments to specific desires about pursuing and maintaining identities.[15] And he seems so intensely embattled with cognitivists that he does not entertain the ideals of educated moral sensibility that philosophers such as Martha Nussbaum see fostered by the arts. Perhaps because even an enlightened cognitivism seems to ignore what is to him most psychologically interesting about the emotions, Wollheim in reaction concentrates only on those features of ethics that can be treated in terms of imaginary projections and so relegated entirely to psychoanalysis.

I am speculating of course and may well be wrong. But we cannot ignore the degree to which Wollheim seems unconcerned with those aspects of ethics where judgment plays a positive role and pride solicits moral identifications that may have very little to do with the kinds of fantasy that support psychoanalytic speculation. Wollheim's disdain certainly saves him from putting too much faith in our reasoning processes. But it also creates two serious problems. In so fully bypassing cognitivist values, Wollheim also blinds himself to the arenas where developmental scenarios may be less important than the struggles agents pursue to make moral sense of their actions, to pursue ideals, and to honor commitments to being reasonable. And by giving developmentally formed fantasies so huge a role to play, Wollheim ends up with a view of morality (and indeed of affective agency in general) that can never allow moral action to be an end in itself. The assertion of ethical value must be analyzed for the fantasies underlying it.

The irony here is worth remarking. In his zeal for a psychology much richer than anything cognitivism can bring to bear, Wollheim ends up developing a mode of interpretation that leads him to another version of cognitivism's epistemic commitments. His cause and effect is not the cause and effect of cognitivist theory. Wollheim does not base his theorizing on how emotions produce knowledge or are influenced by it. And when he interprets causality he is not interested in the fundamentally efficient cause that belief constitutes. How the emotion is defined is to him much less important than why it has the affective charge that it does. Yet these departures from cognitivism serve only to develop an even more limiting version of the epistemic. At least a reliance on belief honors the judgments individuals make. By replacing belief with fantasy as the force shaping our values, Wollheim ends up shifting from the pursuit of efficient causes to the pursuit of something very close to final causes, even as he recognizes how difficult it is to make definitive judgments about these causes. He is fascinated by issues of depth that take him to imaginative sites and modes of intensity that cognitivism cannot approach. But his only means of developing a language for depth is to characterize underlying fantasies and interpret the effects they produce. And because he then has to interpret the fantasy rather than focus on actual situations, he has little interest in how moral values might emerge within the phenomenological texture of our activities. The observer has to seek out preconscious and unconscious "grades of consciousness" (143–46) in the agent's life history because only there can one find the appropriate causal nexus. Psychologizing the emotions turns out to require shifting our attention from what agents do with emotions to what causal forces demand of them.

My third objection to Wollheim is of a piece with my second because at stake in his causal account is the question of what forms of agency we can attribute to the expression of emotions. Wollheim is quite careful to insist that the relevant form of agency is expressive. Agents do not merely observe their emotional states and describe them from a distance. Their identities are worked out in the attitudes they compose. But while Wollheim draws very useful links between the formation of attitudes and the work imagination does in projecting objects and in forming correspondences, he seems to me not to follow up with an adequate account of the kinds of expressive work that may be called for in order to reflect on that imaginative activity or to endorse or will it. There is in Wollheim no fascination with the inchoate, and hence no sense of expression as an achievement or a source of insight (in contrast to Campbell). This may be because for Wollheim it is not the agent but the one in the analyst's position who comes to understand what expression reveals. And for him the relevant understanding consists in being able to explain dispositions rather than in showing how one can align one's will with the terms one brings to bear as self-clarification. He recognizes no theoretical demand to deal with what might be significantly indeterminate or needing work in the agent's relation to the present situation. Instead all the interpreter's energy goes into clarifying relations to past events and figures who recur in the present fantasy.

If we are to have a plausible alternative we have to be able to resist Wollheim's tendency to link the active dimension of expressivity with fantasy. And the best way I know to do that is to give some content to the distinction between the imaginative and the imaginary toward which I have been gesturing. Wollheim makes a useful beginning with his seductively straightforward distinction between active and passive aspects of affective agency. As we construct an attitude we shift from the passivity of feeling satisfaction or frustration to the active role of composing a stance for the self: "When we respond to something toward which we have not formed an emotion, our response can readily be wayward" (82).[16] But for me difficulties arise when Wollheim goes on to provide a context for such responses. He argues that once we form the emotion, "our response derives from how we are, and from how we perceive the world, and ultimately from the history we have led" (82). Just identifying a precipitating factor is for him a sufficient reason for taking oneself as active agent, "even if it does not strike us as this" (82). And then there is a clear link to the concept of expression: where there is activity within the forming of an attitude there is expressive behavior. Expression is not a matter of what the agent wills within the expression but of the very fact that the agent is concretely present as manifesting particular aspects of a life history, whatever the degree of self-consciousness the agent can bring to bear.

This scheme is very effective in clearing the way for psychoanalysis. Wollheim can proceed on the basis of a clean distinction between the passive state of being satisfied or dissatisfied and the active production of expressive significance. He does not need an idealist-tinged story of what the mind or will add to make the expression itself active in some spiritual sense. Just illustrating how we need the agent's presence in order to specify how the expression works suffices to explain why it is reasonable to locate the source of those meanings in a developmental history. And a thin account of expression allows fantasy a central role in accounting for specific meanings because there is no distinction in theory among different vehicles for making present the force of an individual's investments.

But we also then lose the capacity to make central in our accounts significant differences between kinds of expression, especially differences between those that we have to consider symptomatic and those that constitute significant achievements in taking responsibility for one's particular investments and commitments. In order to do that, I think we have to set the fantasy dimension of attitudes against other uses of imaginative powers. So I will call the alternative a "dialectical" relation to the formation of attitudes as means of expression. Agents engage in the dialectical formation of attitudes when they bring the imagination to bear in seeking modes of articulation enabling them to place their wills and their understanding in accord with their affective condition. For example, I may want to engage my jealousy so that I understand it better and have at the least the opportunity of directing where it might lead me. As the basis of this dialectical process we have to be able to specify qualities of self-consciousness that might allow complex interactions between our passive and our more active relations to being moved.[17] Then we can show how as we develop some attitudes we can also articulate why we eventually find them satisfying for the sense of identity they allow or for the relations they make possible with other people. In such cases a typical scenario involves first realizing that our initial projections provide inadequate responses to what they help us discover is folded into what we are feeling. Then that feeling of insufficiency motivates us to make explicit what begins as inchoate, or perhaps as fantasy-driven, until we find that we can make visible an active investment in the version of the self that the attitude affords. Constructing attitudes need not be a single act but often involves a constant process of revision.

If we are to take these processes of revision seriously, we probably have to turn to ways of dealing with expressivity elaborated within Hegelian traditions, although that need not require our embracing idealist conclusions.[18] Suppose for example that my initial jealous rage begins to seem inadequate because I recognize my own complicity in the other's disaffection. Or imagine that while I am not content with a given expression of anger, I still insist upon my expression as a means of indicating that I care about how I was insulted. In cases like these, we are dealing with the powers the agent has to bring imagination to bear by modifying states that in retrospect seem too much given to the imaginary. The expressive component calls attention to what one can do as an active being—not just shape correspondences but develop judgments and modifications sponsored by and altering what counts as significant emotion.

Then we can add a second level to this process. Suppose that I not only want to show how I understand my being moved but also want to make the attitude the active shaping of a position in the world through which I can take responsibility for my emotions. Then the sense of being an active agent does not stem simply from giving an interpretation to my being moved. Rather activity depends on manifesting a second-order relation to what my attitude makes manifest. I am active because I endorse particular features of my attitude as articulating values I think important, perhaps even central to an identity that matters to me. And I am active because I am bringing to bear a more capacious sense of the person engaged in the attitude—not by offering further evidence of how my fantasies are shaped but by demonstrating how I can go about caring about my relationship with the other person.

I am already presupposing the possibility that Wollheim can help us move from a concern for how attitudes position us in the world to a focus on their roles in determining our commitments. Let me now just indicate three overlapping ways that a revised notion of expression allows us to represent such investments. The first is grammatical, the second modal, and the third dialogical. Each of the three establishes a possible way of attributing depth to the attitude and hence of specifying values involved in the agent's activity.[19] And each provides a domain where we can identify how investments go wrong by sustaining imaginary identifications and trapping agents within problematic social frameworks.

By "grammatical" I refer to those aspects of attitudes that come to us as part of our cultural framework. Most of our attitudes take their shape from scenarios we learn when we learn how to use language in a particular culture. We absorb not only what the signs of sadness or anger are but also what counts as a serious expression of taking responsibility for such emotions. We do not have to imitate the scenario exactly. We can modify it while alluding to it, and in the process we can call attention to what we hope is distinctive in our own construction of the situation. By refusing to show any of the signs typically attributed to the standard roles involved in expressing emotions, I can theatrically distance myself from them. My hope is that I then distinguish the jealousy as under my control, and I make visible the very sense of responsibility that this emotion usually undermines. One's life history can become a factor that helps explain how these responses play out. Yet for this expressivist perspective, that history is less important as an explanatory context than as a set of elements that the agents want to make significant in their expressive engagement with a situation. Life history does not explain my action, but I use my action to engage patterns that characterize my life history. For if I know myself at all, I will have to confront within my expressive behavior the possibility that I am merely once again seeking control. And that may lead me to attempt being more impulsive or more generous.

Modal aspects of expressive investments are quite similar to these grammatical ones. They too call attention to concrete aspects of the behavior sponsored by an attitude. But here the emphasis lies less on large-scale self-staging than on quite particular qualities of the agent's manner of acting that become aspects of the attitude. And here we emphatically produce an expressivity that is not a matter of interpreting our experiences for what they might "mean" to an observer. Modal qualities reflect what kind of person the agent becomes in the very process of engaging the affective state. Even if we cannot quite attribute "meanings" to the activity, it matters enormously how carefully one listens to others or scrutinizes situations or holds oneself in check or how intensely one lets oneself participate in the energies that attitudes organize. And degrees of ambivalence or hesitation become crucial expressive registers.[20]

Finally, by insisting on dialogical aspects of expression I want to address one final problem in Wollheim's account. His version of affective agency seems to admit only two basic roles. There is the agent who forms attitudes as means of negotiating with his or her own psychological states. Then there has to be a character (possibly the same person) who takes on the task of analyst. This character tries to interpret what lies beneath the fantasies by reading against the narrative and so exposing what it works to conceal. Agents produce fantasies because of patterns of need and desire shaped by family dramas. Analysts then seek evidence for the continuing force of those dramas. They want to discover how the subject enters into complex webs of substitutions that preserve the shadowy presence of those figures from the past who have been most influential in shaping the agent's sense of possible identity. One feels moral guilt because one can achieve approval for oneself only by going through the detour of pleasing some figure of authority.

But this obsession with figures from the past seems to blind Wollheim to the importance that figures in our present life have in influencing how attitudes get formed and responsibilities both asserted and evaded. Even fantasy itself has a significant social dimension. Agents do not develop fantasies simply as vehicles for repressed or problematic features of their development. They also project relationships to imagined audiences and in the process fantasize audience figures whom they expect to bestow certain meanings of forms of approval on the emotional behavior they exhibit. Fantasy projects imaginary figures who can confer desired identities. So by speaking of dialogical investments in our attitudes, I want to call attention to the strategic roles our imagining plays in our actually constructing paths for real world situations. Then rather than casting our primary imaginary relations in terms of authority figures whom we imitate or try to kill off, we can dwell instead on what roles and identities our various projections make possible for us. It matters less what our figures "mean" than how they position us as capable of achieving certain goals or states or identifications.

I am speaking very abstractly because I am trying to negotiate my own dilemma. I want to bring out the price Wollheim pays for ignoring Jacques Lacan's recasting of the Freudian models on which he relies. But at the same time I don't want to embrace the Lacanian position except as suggestive about the theatrical, audience-based aspects of our self-projections. I exercise this caution in part because I simply do not understand Lacan sufficiently to feel I can identify with his overall perspective. And I think Wollheim is even less sympathetic to Lacan, so I want to be able to cast the issue in terms that meet Wollheim at a site where there might be some intellectual exchange. More important, I want to honor the fact that there are many sociologists who have worked concretely on the issue of how audiences shape our values. Lacan is not the only thinker for whom the imaginary is fostered by the pursuit of projected identifications. But at the same time, if we ignore the Hegelian underpinnings of Lacan's specific arguments about why we are dependent on these projections, as the sociologists do, I think we miss the

basic reasons why subjectivity seems always dependent on imaginary projection.[21] The crucial question is not how to avoid the imaginary but how to
align it with other, more public and more testable aspects of our imaginative
powers.

So I propose taking the imagination of an audience as a fundamental feature of the construction of attitudes, as basic as the expansive coloring effect
of the constructed correspondences. Insofar as identity is at stake at all in
the construction of an attitude, that construction will include a projection
about audience. Such projections are especially important in our second-
order investments in our attitudes because they determine both our efforts to
take responsibility and our needs to secure ironic distances. Yet the projection need not always involve fantasy, although it does always involve the
imaginative elaboration of possible worlds. At times, the worlds we construct
will even help us resist purely fantasized identifications because they can put
pressure on us to specify whom we are addressing and why we take that audience as central to the attitude. The richer our appreciation of the persons
we are addressing, the fuller our sense of what will and will not count as
significant in the expressive activity we produce.

## IV. Emotion as the Forming of Attitudes: Matthew Arnold's "Isolation: To Marguerite" and Imaginary Identity

Even I am getting impatient for some extended concrete examples. So now
I have to face directly how this chapter can contribute to the two basic tasks
I have set myself—to clarify what theorizing about the emotions can bring
to the arts and to show how the arts so engaged challenge us to modify our
governing concepts about the emotions. I need the two poems I have chosen
because I want to be able to compare different ways that the background of
Wollheim's theorizing helps us interpret how texts enable us to contrast the
imaginative and the imaginary in the construction and adjustment of attitudes. Moreover, setting these lyric examples against each other will test the
range of readings made possible by Wollheim's terms—for their capacity to
enhance our appreciation of the texts and for their capacity to illustrate why
the texts remain relevant now in their particularity.

I choose lyrics for both examples because in testing the value of Wollheim's
perspective, we can also be pushing against the grain of contemporary philosophical discourse. There almost all efforts to connect theoretical formulations about the emotions to literature concentrate on the novel—not
surprisingly, since novels emphasize reading actions in contexts and so emphasize modes of interpretation that are consistent with cognitivist assumptions.[22] I want instead to emphasize intimate psychological processes of
forming and endorsing attitudes (or failing to endorse them), and I want
qualities like intensity and force to be in the foreground. Lyric provides a
medium that helps us resist the rush to moral judgment by minimizing con-

text and focusing attention on who the agent becomes by virtue of the disposition of consciousness rather than by virtue of actions. In the process it tends also to dramatize how that consciousness positions itself in relation to the imagined presence of second persons. Lyric tests the full repertoire proposed by specific theories of the emotions, and it enables us to exemplify the work the imagination can do in all our attitude construction.

Matthew Arnold's "Isolation: To Marguerite" may seem an odd selection, given the range of possibilities available. Yet I know of no better way to have one work address several aspects of the arguments I have been making. Let me count the ways, since each of the themes we track through the poem can serve as a topos through which to discuss how emotions develop and what they make available for the psyche.

1. Arnold's poem offers an extended and intimate process of constructing and modifying an attitude under the pressure of multiple precipitating factors. Being moved here seems at first a simple case of frustration over rejected love.[23] But as the attitude develops, the sense of precipitating force also shifts somewhat—from a concern with the lost love to a need to recompose the shattered ego of the failed lover.

2. The poem makes clear how important it is to see the attitude not simply as a momentary construction but as a process of working through conflicting needs and projections. Arnold's poem offers in its constructing of attitudes an immanent projection of how certain kinds of intentionality do and do not take hold in the world.

3. As we trace that process of attitude-formation, we see some of the powerful roles that can be played by the forming of correspondences—for their content as metaphoric elaborations of the emotion and for the sensuous qualities that bind the affects to this particular imaginative understanding. Tracing correspondences provides a path from sensations to feelings to their roles in the larger frameworks emotions provide.

4. "Isolation: To Marguerite" helps us appreciate how complex the expressive process can become. The poem not only establishes an attitude but also seeks to produce desired identities through the qualities of self-consciousness that the attitude makes possible. As the poem unfolds, it calls attention to the intricate interplay between what the speaker deliberately makes articulate and the more symptomatic expression revealed in behaviors that the speaker seems not to control.

5. The work of expression here is tightly bound to the presence of second-order interests involving how the agent endorses the emotion and connects it to the forming of identities.

6. The poem also establishes the importance of how the speaker projects an audience for his expressive activity. How he sees himself is continually modified by how he imagines making an impression on an internalized observer.

7. The concern with audience highlights the ways in which the forming of at-

titudes takes place against a background of paradigm scenarios that agents and interpreters bring to bear in the forming and assessing of attitudes. Assessment then has both a cognitive and a performative dimension. We want to know whether the agent's beliefs match the facts, and we want to know whether the investment put into the attitude correlates with the energies that seem to be motivating the expressive process.

8. Arnold's poem invites us to rely on the grammatical framework that scenarios provide in order to stress the manner as well as the matter of the attitude-forming process. Qualities like perspicacity, sensitivity, scope, and even inventiveness can be as central to our understanding of agents as any explicit self-interpretation the speaker offers.

9. The telos or implicit goal of the agent's attitude is not preparation for an action but the establishing of a frame of mind, sense of identity, and possibility of self-enjoyment that can negotiate what was involved in his being moved.

10. The particular drama offered by Arnold's poem creates an interesting test for theory in relation to our assessing the emotions because the better we understand how benighted this speaker is, the more we are tempted to respond with sympathy rather than disdain. Understanding that orientation has to be part of our theory of the emotions because it confronts us with the strange routes to value that are fundamental to affective experience. Suspicious readings can sustain considerable empathy.

11. Finally, I am fascinated by how this poem embodies everything that the modernists hated about Victorian efforts to stage their own nobility in terms of the lucidity they could bring to bear on their experiences.[24] After we pay close attention to this poem's blend of self-absorption and self-deception, we will be well positioned to appreciate why the modernists turned away from the synthetic and self-reflexive aspects of emotions. In their place, these writers and artists emphasized the more immediate qualities of feelings, and they replaced argument and narrative as synthetic processes with modes of organization less susceptible to the manipulations of the imaginary. I recognize that this sense of historical watershed can be little more than a footnote to this account. Yet I think it sharpens our appreciation of skeptics like Sartre who distrust all emotions as acts of bad faith. And at the same time it makes clear what tests the formation of an emotional attitude would have to survive in order to get beyond our suspicions and win our admiration.

This is the poem:

> We were apart; yet, day by day
> I bade my heart more constant be.
> I bade it keep the world away,
> And grow a home for only thee.
> Nor fear'd but that thy love likewise grew,
> Like mine, each day, more tried, more true.

The fault was grave! I might have known,
What far too soon, alas, I learn'd.
The heart can bind itself alone,
And faith may oft be unreturn'd.
Self-sway'd our feelings ebb and swell—
Thou lov'st no more:—Farewell! Farewell!

Farewell!—and thou, thou lonely heart,
Which never yet without remorse
Even for a moment didst depart
From thy remote and spheréd course
To haunt the place where passions reign—
Back to thy solitude again!

Back! with the conscious thrill of shame
Which Luna felt, that summer night,
Flash through her pure immortal frame,
When she forsook the starry height
To hang over Endymion's sleep
Upon the pine-grown Latmian steep.

Yet she, chaste queen, had never proved
How vain a thing is mortal love,
Wandering in heaven, far removed.
But thou hast long had place to prove
This truth—to prove and make thine own:
Thou hast been, shall be, art, alone.

Or, if not quite alone, yet they
Which touch thee are unmating things—
Ocean and clouds and night and day:
Lorn autumns and triumphant springs:
And life and others' joy and pain,
And love, if love, of happier men.

Of happier men—for they, at least,
Have dream'd two human hearts might blend
In one, and were through faith released
From isolation without end
Prolong'd, nor knew, although not less
Alone than thou, their loneliness.

(61)

We cannot summarize this attitude by any one label—if we could there would have been little point in writing the poem. Instead, we have to concentrate on the particular process by which the forming of an attitude simultaneously interprets and wards off the speaker's pain at having been rejected by his beloved. This process has its own particular way of gathering and dispersing intensity as the attitude weaves together incompatible sets of investments. And it reveals the degree to which the pain is not simply a precipitating cause from the past but also a constant factor in shaping what seems livable in the present—even if the consequence is a pervasive pattern of self-deception. Arnold's speaker shifts perspective, using his reactions to failed love as a ground for casting himself as winning a heroically lucid acceptance of a loneliness at the heart of things. Yet to the observer this victory is a hollow one because we come to realize how thoroughly his efforts are driven by a need to shore up an ego shattered by its failure in love.[25]

The poem's opening lines indicate the pressure on the agent to develop just such a complex attitude. The situation of addressing the lady puts everything on a theatrical basis. The speaker has to handle the pain of losing her, and he has to develop a voice he can present to her without (fully) betraying how devastated he is. Neither task is easy, especially given what the opening shows about his disposition. His idea of loving is inseparable from his idea of duty ("I bade my heart more constant be"), and his understanding of the woman leaves rather a lot to be desired, since he assumes she should act in the same way he does. It is not surprising then that the remembered "we" quickly modulates into this needy "I" in dialogue mostly with itself. By the second stanza this self-absorption seems capable of establishing a firm resolution simply by accepting the end of the affair and regretting that he did not anticipate that inevitability. But then there emerges the first instance of what becomes the poem's characteristic structuring device. The speaker introduces the third stanza by repeating the final words of the second, as if he could not quite yet identify with the attitude he is constructing. Something remains inchoate or ignored, so the pain will not yield to the representation imposed upon it, and the speaker cannot fully endorse his own efforts at closure. Instead, he has to change his mode of address to confront the self who let himself fall in love. It turns out that he has lost considerably more than her love. He has lost his image of his own power, and a simple farewell will not reestablish that. He has to recompose a self-image on the basis of what may be the only material he has for that task—his relation to his own solitude. And for that task he needs the more elaborate correspondences provided by metaphors that shift his attention from memory and description to the testing of ways of framing his own identity. When he turns away from the lady, he looks to an orbiting star in order to link his loneliness to the fundamental structures encompassing the real—as if what the eye sees could represent what he hopes his mind can accomplish.

The poem's structure both emphasizes and comments upon this shift in the speaker's efforts to reestablish an identity shattered by his being rejected. The last three stanzas push in just the opposite direction from the first three as he tries to provide what he could not find in his initial efforts to accept his solitude. Where the first stanzas grow increasingly narrow in their sense of that solitude, the last three try to handle the loneliness by giving it some general significance. In stanza 5, the first stanza of this triad, the movement to generalization goes directly to a devastatingly simple and clear conclusion: "Thou hast been, shall be, art, alone." But we then immediately see that this character cannot abide such clarity. He quickly modifies the situation, attempting to soften the law by ennobling himself for recognizing it. He seeks to identify with all those who can live as unmating things acknowledging this law of solitude. Then he tries his boldest move. If he can accurately generalize about love's vanity, and if other people continue to pursue love, then he is much better off than they are. The role of enlightened hero is saved for the person who sees through all this illusion.

My students find this final self-congratulatory move appalling. But, older and lonelier, I want to keep sympathy for the speaker even while recognizing just how deeply self-deluding this bid for an ennobling lucidity is. The best way I know to keep judgment and sympathy in balance is to return to the concept of expression, particularly to the ways that expressions can implicate both active and passive aspects of agency. We might locate these two conditions by relying on the grammatical fact that the notion "expression of" admits both a subjective and an objective genitive. As an expression of the subject, an attitude can make visible and plausible why the agent is invested in a particular emotion. As an expression of some objective condition, the attitude can seem to reveal symptomatic factors that have control over the agent without his quite recognizing what is happening.

In Arnold's poem, the speaker's considerable abilities emerge most fully in the elaborate case he makes for his own preferred view of his situation. He not only weaves intricate correspondences but also controls their expansion and contraction in order to provide the affective fuel he needs to transfer the loss of love into the triumph of self-love. Yet at the core of his realized expression we find imaginary projections only tangentially connected to the actual world. There is a painful gap between the identity that the speaker thinks he is successfully composing and the one his activity actually reveals. In fact, he is addressing three audiences—he responds to the woman; he talks to himself in an effort to clarify his situation; and he pleads his case to some ideal figure in relation to the threat she constitutes for his ego. This last mode of address has the effect of reinforcing the second, directing his imaginative capacities into a self-defensive projection positing his failure as a mark of nobility rather than of his ineptitude. Self-possession turns out to be self-evasion. And considerable force of will cannot hold off the pathos of his endorsing and accepting responsibility for a stance ironically exposing the shaky grounds on which that will has to stand.

Yet I remain sympathetic to the speaker because the particulars of the expressive process make his projections both understandable and engaging. Notice how the fourth stanza brings these subjective and objective aspects of expressiveness into close and, I think, touching proximity. Structurally this stanza occupies the center of the poem. It is framed by the opposition between the two three-stanza units, but it has no positive role to play in developing the contrasts between specificity and generality. The stanza does, however, play a brilliant negative role. Here we have the speaker freed from his compulsion to generate self-defensive arguments. He essentially lets himself go, yielding to what is released when he turns to Luna for correspondences with the realization that he now has to go back to his solitude. In this moment between his various rationalizations, the speaker allows himself an interlude of intense feeling that also establishes the lyrical expansiveness basic to the speaker's psychology.

The result is a momentarily undefended participation in Luna's "conscious thrill of shame," lovingly elaborated by the dallying syntax and elaborate sonority taken on for the moment by Arnold's poetry. We know enough about this speaker to be surprised by the intricate intimacy of this identification. But we also know enough about him to understand why he might let himself go on this topic. He needs an idealized analogue for his sense of having sacrificed his nobility and his lucidity to try out the messy domain of human love. And the lyrical expansiveness of this correspondence also facilitates his connecting to another, deeper level of shame for which he cannot take responsibility. This level of shame stems not from his yielding to passion but from his fear that in defeat he has lost the sense of power that would enable him to identify with the gods in the first place. So we begin to recognize here that the attitude he is constructing is "to double-duty bound." He wants to see his pain as noble, and he has to reconstitute an identity strong enough to compensate for having let himself become powerless before someone who then took advantage of her power to reject him. Arnold's speaker needs to interpret his failure, and he needs through that interpretation to become the person he could imagine before this rejection threatened his entire ego structure. At the floating center of the poem we find an analogue for the speaker's ultimate inability to get a structural hold on his situation.

Given this floating lyricism at its core, it is not surprising that the poem's speaker keeps turning back on himself. The uneasiness that led him to revise his initial "farewell" only intensifies as he labors to save his dignity. After what must seem to him the all too bleak direct statement about loneliness that concludes the fifth stanza (and that seems a reasonable conclusion for the poem), the speaker again turns to self-revision as his means of generating each of the last two stanzas. The opening of the sixth stanza cannot manage a complete revision—the previous absolute statement is too imposing. But there emerges some room for adjustment, as if the speaker were desperately seeking some breathing space for the imagination. In reaction to the utterly negative realization of his loneliness in all tenses, the speaker seems eager to open some possibility of community, even if it has to be only with "unmating things—Oceans and clouds and night and day: / Lorn autumns and triumphant springs."

Then a strange twist occurs, revealing how much disturbance this gesture too seems unable to resolve. The speaker manages to fold lovers who dream "two human hearts might blend" into his list of unmating things. This may be a sign of how reluctant he is to give up on that human ideal. For this speaker, however, or for this great a disappointment, that sense of possible companionship proves far too weak a compensation. His ego needs a more absolute loneliness so that he can be a truly distinctive hero. Introducing these lovers enables him to turn on them in a final contrast between their mere dreaming and his learning from his suffering a certain kind of integrity. Now his suffering can become a lesson enabling him to endorse his loneliness as a mode of heroic identity. Making that commitment even frees him to think he occupies the ontological condition of those truly unmating things that constitute nature's grand forces. He dreams of a heroic lucidity ultimately recognized as such by his community. But he enacts only the pathos of his need for this dream.

For our purposes the most interesting feature of this poem is the way that the work of self-examination ultimately merges with the blindness of fantasy. For Arnold makes clear how hard the imagination has to work for the attitude it constructs to match the intensities his agent feels. And he shows how the speaker's identity depends on keeping the cognitive and the projective in close conjunction. Here the speaker makes a plausible case about the limitations of yielding to love and the satisfactions of accepting one's own loneliness. Yet his heroizing of his own lucidity also serves as a means of concealing from himself why he needs that heroic role and what he has to ignore in order to rely on it. In fact, he cannot quite accept loneliness. He must continue to elaborate a fantasy that he can win the respect of audience figures by the nobility of the gestures establishing himself as the one who knows, indeed as the only one who can bear what is known. Ironically, that delusion can only deepen his actual loneliness because he has to keep shoring up a value that only he can see himself as honoring.

This speaker would have to be judged by cognitivists as irrational and, I suspect, by Wollheim as trapped in fantasies that malform his emotions. Both would be right. But neither would quite capture the force of what this expressive process makes available for an audience. For neither perspective offers us a theoretical framework for talking about the specific qualities that come to the fore through the effort of articulating attitudes and the relations to audiences that this articulation can involve. In the case of Arnold's poem, we find ourselves having to deal with the speaker's inventiveness (in the service of self-delusion, but still impressive), as well as the blend of sensuality and sweetness that comes through when his correspondences begin to wander from his argumentative control. More important, we find it difficult to escape the affective force of this speaker's vulnerability, painfully evident in the lengths to which he goes in order to defend himself from its consequences.

Noticing the roles that such qualities play is only half of the theorist's task. It is also necessary to develop contexts for explaining why these qualities can take on vividness sufficient to make us care about the person they character- ize. A large part of this answer will have to deal with how human beings are shaped by their cultures to be responsive to various aspects of human activity. But there is also an important structural feature that our analysis enables us to carry over as a theoretical category. The speaker's projection of a desired audience serves not only to display his own needs in a highly theatrical fash- ion but also to create a distinctive relation to actual audiences. For the fact that we all experience this sense of address as an aspect of our own expression makes us sensitive to the roles it plays in how others develop attitudes.

If we notice how Arnold makes these expectations a dramatic feature of his poem, I think we can also recognize something central to our affective lives. At first we are aware primarily of how disturbing his need for an audi- ence becomes as he is forced to expose increasing levels of his underlying fan- tasy structure. But eventually we also have to take up this question of possible sympathy with his dilemma. I think the sympathy stems largely from the fact that his own need for an audience puts those who hear his address in the po- sition of feeling that they somehow have to complete the conversational cir- cuit. Because the speaker narrows the process of call and response to his own needs for self-defense, he makes that structure seem painfully incomplete, and that seduces us into wanting to provide the desired audience.[26] How- ever, we could not see ourselves as the desired audience if we simply judged or analyzed what we are seeing. The presentation of emotions for an audi- ence invites the audience to respond to the situation as it is expressed rather than as it is described. We want to give the speaker the knowledge he lacks in his idealizing a loneliness he dreads. For we recognize his pathos and the inventiveness he exercises in order to avoid facing that pathos. So because our grasp of him is more accurate than his own grasp is, there is a tempta- tion to try offering him the possibility of developing a relation to himself that will not prove embarrassing either for its weakness or for its compensatory overconfidence. We are sufficiently moved that we have to construct our own attitudes, and we want to be able to endorse them by thinking of how they might give us access to his underlying situation. In that process, I hasten to add, we find ourselves motivated by states that do not translate easily into a language of satisfaction or frustration.[27]

## V. Metaphoric Play and Imaginative Expressivity: Bishop Henry King's "Exequy"

My second poem may seem an even odder choice because I go back to the seventeenth century for Henry King's "The Exequy," an elegy for his wife. For the reader eager for twentieth-century examples of how poetry engages the affects I can point to several of my essays.[28] Here I want a poem that has no interest in narrative, so that all of its attention is on the building of an attitude in relation to an utterly generic situation.[29] More important, I simply know no richer exploration of how one can harness and adapt to reality the temptations to the imaginary that are fundamental to strong emotions. King shares with Arnold a concern for the dynamics of address, but for him address keeps the attitude formation focused on an intimate and demanding test of whether he is worthy of the wife he praises. I think it is ultimately her continual dialogical presence in his imagination that accounts for the poem's refusal quite to concede to the temptations of self-pity fundamental to the mourning situation.

Let me begin with a catalogue of what our theoretical concerns help us appreciate in this poem. This catalogue can be somewhat shorter than the one I proposed for "Isolation: For Marguerite."

1. Again we see how crucial it is to treat the formation of attitudes as a process within which the terms shift and adjustments are continually being explored. Where Arnold's poem changes its sense of the precipitating cause in order to accommodate the demands of an imaginary sense of the speaker's desired dignity, King's poem tries to transform the pulls of the imaginary back into workable means of establishing connection with his wife. We would seriously undervalue this poem if we took its precipitating cause to be only grief. The cause involves a passion to understand how his particular grief helps him appreciate what his love has been and can be.

2. In what may be too much the spirit of T. S. Eliot, I hope to show how King uses metaphysical conceits to offer elaborate versions of what Wollheim calls correspondences. In his poem the correspondences elaborated by the emerging attitude not only flesh out the emotional timbre of the situation but also provide a vehicle for stabilizing and mobilizing what would otherwise be disruptive excess energies. Elaborate metaphors keep on parallel tracks materials that otherwise would flee into the buried lives that haunt Arnold's poems. Without the metaphors, grief might dissipate into various repressive mechanisms, from within which it would return only in refusals to accept the reality of his situation. And correspondence here thrives in part because of King's end-stopped couplets. We know the rhymes are coming, so they provide a framework of repetitions that in turn allows the poem to range over diverse figurative contexts. More important, the rhymes build into the experience a continual sense of repetition as inseparable from renewal, with the tightness of fit an apt practical emblem for the force of the bond between husband and wife. This mode of embodying fit is of course unique to poetry, but it reminds us of how many frameworks operate as correspondences simply because of how they structure information, whatever the content may be. Think for example of memories of places or the roles popular songs play in our lives.

3. As I have already mentioned, King's poem shares with Arnold's an em-

phasis on how fantasies of address bring intensity and direction to attitudes. But where address enables Arnold to melodramatize his solitude, address calls King out of the selves into which he is tempted to regress. Address keeps vital the importance of the "not I" in situations easily swallowed up into the priorities of the "I" in pain. Here the address keeps present for him the question "Who can I be for her as I play my roles in the projected dialogue?" That question too, of course, can be a screen licensing all sorts of fantasy. But it also gives him compelling reasons to keep his imaginings and his expressive behavior respectful of the constraints of the practical order.

4. Tone plays a crucial role in the work done by the poem's self-consciousness about modes of address. Tone at times proves the dominant feature of an attitude. And that provides one important reason why we cannot equate an emotion with the beliefs involved. The emotion consists in how the beliefs get engaged by intentional states.

5. I know no poem as insistent as King's on the constant pressure of second-order assessment and endorsement. The poem virtually defines love as that force which makes the self want to be able to see its choices as valuable because of the relation they sustain with another person. Viewed this way, or, better, experienced this way, love prepares a context of address that has strong claims to survive beyond death because of how it continues to influence the most intimate levels of self-reflection.

6. Another way of making the same point is to call attention to what constitutes the agent's satisfaction when he does finally form an attitude enabling him to rest. Satisfaction is clearly not in an action, but in the developing of a state of mind that is inseparable from a relationship to another person. The poem's ultimate concern is with being able to hear all its pain and playfulness as plausible means of maintaining an active connection with what she might have wished. And even though there is no concern for specific resolving actions, the final state of awareness promises to influence all of his actions because it modifies his fundamental sense of his own identity.

7. In its interpretation of the elegy, King's poem is less interested in winning sympathy from an audience than in giving the audience the possibility of admiring what love can become under such circumstances. In our culture it sounds pompous to think of giving others opportunities for admiring what we do. Yet I know no other way to characterize the strange sense that this speaker knows he is being overheard and takes that fact as an important challenge to treat his grief in an exemplary fashion. He is not concerned primarily to represent what he actually feels so that he can take responsibility for it. Instead, he seems to want to be able to test the degree to which he can idealize a possible attitude that he, and through him we, can then try to imitate. The ideal is not a fantasy, as we usually employ that term. Rather, the work offers an attitude constructed in part as a process of honoring the call that comes when one seeks visibility before a responding public. This framework affects not only how the speaker presents himself but also how an audience is invited to engage that expressive activity. The audience is not expected to

be satisfied because it can attribute truth to the attitude. It is expected to treat the attitude as inviting it to try on something it can consider a better self, a self worthy of what can be possible because of where the structure of concern can lead the imagination. Ultimately King invites us to see that a crucial aspect of our investments in society stems from our pleasure at being able to imagine the entire social unit endorsing such expectations and shaping itself around the likely consequences.

"The Exequy" is too long to cite in its entirely, so I will select some passages and offer running commentary on how the attitude takes form. This is the opening:

> Accept, thou Shrine of my Dead Saint,
> Instead of dirges, this Complaint;
> And for sweet flowres to crown thy Hearse,
> Receive a strew of weeping verse
> From thy griev'd friend, whome Thou might'st see
> Quite melted into Teares for Thee.
>
> Deare Losse! since thy untimely fate
> My task hath beene to meditate
> On Thee, on Thee; Thou art the Book,
> The Library whereon I look,
> Though almost blind. For Thee, lov'd Clay
> I Languish out, not Live the Day.
> Using no other Exercise
> But what I practise with mine Eyes;
> By which wett glasses I find out
> How lazily Time creepes about
> To one that mournes; This, only This,
> My Exercise and bus'nes is:
> So I compute the weary howres
> With Sighes dissolved into Showres.
>
> (68–69)

As with Arnold, there is an early shift in the mode of address—here not from the other to the self, but from the opening highly public language to an intensely private one in the second stanza. Each voice produces a distinctive set of correspondences. The public voice has to deal with the actual tomb, transforming it into a site for paying homage. And it has to define itself through an oppressive haze of self-consciousness about his impotence. The correspondences developed in this mode insist on her pervasive presence but at the cost of his remoteness from the rest of his world. Under this public burden, the self appears only in the third person as the grieving friend. For this state, for this attitude, the tears do not make his pain visible but make him seem invisible to her because he is nothing but tears. Already the effort to address her has forced two painful realizations from him, both I think quite powerful—that even the grief of deep love can seem so destructive to agency that one feels one can only see the self from the outside, and that pure grief has only limited expressive value because it becomes abstracted from any particular personal agency.

Each of these feelings immediately exerts complex pressure on the speaker. The attitude he must form has to resist this passivity, and it has to allow some second-order stage by which the speaker can manifest his distinctive possession of his grief. As his first effort at such possession, the speaker switches to the intimate tone of "Dear loss," an expression that captures both his need for intimacy and the absence he finds in the psychological place in which he has been accustomed to find that intimacy. But this expression also provides him a new way to cast his grief. He can resume what has been a familiar conversational role, and he can begin to experience his own feelings in a way that might allow him to bring them into some kind of order without imposing a repressive silence that wards off pain. That proves no easy task. Grief has a tendency to dissipate into local intensities like particular memories or fears or senses of absence. And while these correspondences cannot be surrendered, they make it impossible to restore to memory her full hold on him or to grasp again why she can be the entire library on which he looks.

We have to recognize the pressure of these multiple feelings if we are fully to appreciate what the metaphysical style brings to the conditions of elegy (as well as what poetry can bring to the theory of emotion). This style's dazzlingly quick and intricate figures honor these diverse feelings while creating a site in which they can come together. And the coming together allows for rich transitions between three aspects of the grieving—the painful sense of the deadness of the world where he sees only blankness and loss, the range of memories standing in contrast to that blankness, and the effort to make the grief itself a means of affirming and of better understanding the love that is its cause.

As the speaker shifts from a public voice to a more intimate one, he paradoxically puts himself in a position where the resources of this ornate style prove especially desirable. With the relaxation into intimacy, feelings emerge that are more various and less under control. But this shift of voice makes him more aware of his powers of agency.

In the second stanza it is he who risks blindness, not she. And it is he who has now to get beyond the dominating figure of the monument in order to work out correspondences for these multiple feelings. So he has the second stanza enact a series of quick associations, sharp in their intelligence but without abiding substance unless the poet can bring them into significant connections without destroying their individual differences. (The speaker's job has close parallels to the work that the couplets do.) She appears in at least three guises—"Dear Loss," "the Library whereon I look," and "lov'd Clay." The better he can keep all three in conjunction, the richer the powers of recognition he manages to develop. For in this stanza he is the one to whom the poem gives eyes. Although he is almost blind and cannot yet directly see her as his library, he can navigate by his tears. Crying in fact becomes the means of metaphysical union, translating feeling into a kind of seeing and establishing for him an exercise and a business that link him to the various ways she continues to call him to her. The exercise of crying forces him to register each weary hour, and that in turn establishes for him the business of being a kind of accountant.

Our speaker also has much more complex computing to do, computing whose instrument almost has to be poetry. All this exercise brings memory into play, and the figures of tears and blindness and weather conditions all return with a more intense and more painful personal charge. As these memories threaten to absorb his present, the poem forcefully poses the challenge of whether he can mourn with all his intelligence. To do that he has to bring everything that pulls him into the past back into a present that he can make something other than a space of despair filled with the alienating repetition of feelings for which there is no distinctive future tense:

> Nor wonder if my time goe thus
> Backward and most praeposterous;
> Thou hast Benighted mee, Thy sett
> This Eve of blacknes did begett,
> Who wast my Day, (though overcast
> Before thou hadst thy Noon-tide past;
> And I remember must in teares
> Thou scarce hadst seene so many yeeres
> As Day tells howrss. By thy cleere Sun
> My Love and Fortune first did run
> But Thou wil never more appear
> Folded within my Hemispheare,
> Since both thy Light and Motion
> Like a fledd Starr is fall'n and gone;
> And 'twixt mee and my Soule's deare wish
> The earth now interposed is,
> Which such a straunge Ecclipse doth make
> As ne're was read in Almanake.
>
> (69)

Losing her as the light of his day pushes him back into memory, presented here as a cross of compulsion and involvement. For a moment the poem dispels the clouds and restores her in all her powers to serve as his sun. Even his speaking becomes suffused with second-person expressions reveling in her presence that another part of his mind knows will soon bring much more pain than pleasure. This light is so intense in its momentary emergence that its loss demands a figure considerably stronger than the simple setting in of night. To address this, King develops one of the great conceits in English poetry. What blocks the sun is not night but earth. The actual grave produces a figurative eclipse—a blockage of light that is not part of normal natural processes but betokens all sorts of accompanying horrors—the greatest of which is the terrifying literalness of this elaborate figure. The expansiveness of imagination finds all too accurate a home in the facts of her situation.

The more elaborate King's expression of grief, the more pressing becomes a standard problem in literary theory. How can we trust a grief that leaves space for so much playful intelligence? How intensely can we empathize with the mourning of someone who has the imaginative energy and bravura to develop these attention-grabbing figures? Were this a contemporary poem, I would be complaining that the wife's death seems an excuse for the poet to demonstrate his skills. Yet I suspect King wants us to ask questions like these as a means of putting pressure on his style. For the resources of the style are for him inseparable from the library she afforded him and the apparent qualities of discourse that must have characterized their love. The full play of language is what they once shared, so it is strikingly appropriate that he call upon that now as a continuing of her heritage. And here he certainly needs that playful intelligence because that trait may be the only possible means of taking completely seriously both the power of earth and the perspectival mobility necessary to win from that darkness a continuing appreciation of her legacy. The figure of the eclipse honors the power of earth and hence of death while also preserving his own sense of the strangeness and singularity and continuing vitality of this loss. This honesty then also allows the poem to return to the figures of darkness and blindness that it has been elaborating, as if the process of writing could bring sufficient force to keep its own imaginative space open for hope and for desire. Even recognizing the cosmic indifference embodied in the eclipse is not sufficient to suppress this particular effort to keep love alive.

After a slight lightening of tone in which the speaker imagines bargaining with his wife to get her to return, he finds himself facing the full realization that he simply will never see her again. That realization instantly generates the poem's most intense moment. In what has to be seen as a writerly instance of the very logic of ultimate redemption to which the poem alludes, the poet offers this description of what their lives will be like after the judgment's refining fire compensates for all this pain:

> . . . That fitt of Fire
> Once off, our Bodyes shall aspire
> To our Soules blisse; then wee shall rise
> And view ourselves with cleerer eyes
> In that calme Region where no Night
> Can hide us from each other's sight.
> (70)

Here there is none of the brio we found in the treatment of the eclipse. But the passage depends perhaps even more on the poet's sense of what his writerly activity enables. The poet can speak with utter plainness because he is relying on a dense set of correspondences set up earlier in the poem. All of the parallels between the psyche's blindnesses and nature's darkness now get reconfigured simply by the image of what the lovers would bring to "each other's sight."

Criticism pales before the task of explaining why this simple reference to their mutual seeing proves so forceful and so much an intensifying of the very idea of clarity, as if the poem too had its refining fires. There is no difficulty in interpreting the passage, but there is considerable difficulty in explaining why it has the charge it does. That charge has something to do with the way that the clarity of the language matches the clarity it attributes to their visions of each other. In addition, I think we have to see second-order factors playing a substantial role here, the more so because they are only implicit and not allowed to upstage the seeing. Perhaps that is the point. Nothing could upstage this seeing, yet all of the poem's art exists to have these details take on precise echoes of what has gone before. So it is almost as if the speaker recognizes how this particular sight fits the context prepared for it, and the recognition suffices for an utterly complete endorsement that would be trivialized by efforts to make it explicit.

Now the speaker's suffering has produced a vision of what makes it all worthwhile. But what if the vision is at best momentary, to be instantly replaced by the recognition that she will never return? Facing this concern forces the speaker to change his addressée. He turns immediately to the fact that earth now possesses her, and for the short term he can do nothing about that. He can, however, modify his way of thinking about loss. I think he realizes that no single image will resolve this pain or even frame it so that he can will the grief and not seek release from it into states like self-pity. If he is fully to accept the necessity of his grief, he has to put this present situation in context. He has to pursue a more abstract (but also more elemental) process of coming to terms with the rhythms of blindness and sight, approach and loss, that now govern his experience. While there are no answers that might end or alter the process, there are different ways of contextualizing or committing oneself to it. Therefore he tries negotiating with earth rather than condemning the blindness it imposes. That process requires him to think of earth itself as instrument rather than as a final resting place. On that basis he can identify his own interests with the divine concern that this trustee nourish and attend to what seems worthy of God's own investments:

> For thou must Auditt on thy trust
> Each Grane and Atome of this Dust,
> As thou wilt answere Him that leant
> Not gave thee, my deare Monument.
>
> (70)

Immediately after this recasting of the poem's opening frustration before her monument, the poem arrives at a simple two-line stanza that enables a resolving turn, based less on any reaching beyond the processes of his reflection than on a fresh appreciation of where these processes have been leading him. The process of valuing and the process of attuning himself to what drives his grief turn out to be identical:

> So close the ground and 'bout hir shade
> Black Curtaines draw; My Bride is lay'd.
>
> Sleep on (my Love!) in thy cold bed,
> Never to be disquieted!
> My last Good-Night! Thou wilt not wake
> Till I Thy Fate shall overtake;
> Till age or grief or sicknes must
> Marry my Body to all that Dust
> It so much loves; and fill the roome
> My heart keepes empty in Thy Tomb.
> Stay for mee there: I will not faile
> To meet Thee in that hollow vale.
> And think not much of my delay;
> I am already on the way,
> And follow Thee with all the speed
> Desire can make or Sorrowes breed.
> Each Minute is a short Degree,
> And ev'ry Howre a stepp toward Thee.
>
> (71)

Here we find significant news for a theory of the emotions because everything depends on achieving and maintaining this particular tone. The isolated couplet assenting to her burial occurs exactly two-thirds of the way into the poem. Enough lyric time has passed for the speaker to be able to frame this finality. Then, with her place fixed, he has to find a mode of address capable of granting that she is dead without giving up on the specificity and intimacy of his love. So he manages to treat her being buried with the same tone that he might use in thinking of her asleep in their bed. In fact it becomes difficult to tell whether sleep is a metaphor for her dying or her dying a literal sleep that his love turns back into a metaphor. Yet that hovering between alternatives proves crucial because it enables him to keep the dead body and the loved person in a close affinity very hard to realize. And by doing that he can extend the going-to-bed metaphor to include his own apparent dallying before he joins her. His own desire to die can be experienced on this intimate casual level because metaphor so elaborately knits fields of correspondences. The correspondences in turn produce the power once again to anchor emotion in plain speech, but this time in speech that is responsive to the power of time.

The last passage cited also begins to work out an important transformation of the dominant motifs in the first two-thirds of the poem. There figures of darkness and of light made the eye the fundamental medium of their exchange. Now tone becomes the crucial medium, bringing into play other figures for bodily awareness less vulnerable to cycles of light and dark. The emotion now centers in the heart and gathers into the expressive force of his beating pulse. The concluding two stanzas bring us to this state by at first reacting to her power to impose shame and grief, then recognizing that these prove to be dialectical states that enable him to bring all his playful intelligence to bear on this climactic experience of their bond:

> 'Tis true, with shame and grief I yeild,
> Thou, like the vann, first took'st the Field,
> And gotten hast the Victory
> In thus adventuring to dy
> Before Mee, whose more yeeres might crave
> A just praecedence in the Grave.
> But hark! My Pulse like a soft Drum
> Beates my Approach, Tells Thee I come
> And, slowe howe're my Marches bee,
> I shall at last sitt downe by Thee.
> The thought of this bids mee goe on,
> And wait my dissolution
> With Hope and Comfort. Deare, (forgive
> The Crime) I am content to live
> Divided, but with half a Heart,
> Till wee shall meet and Never part.
>
> (71–72)

The first six lines sound a playfully formal note. Even though his age should have earned him the victory of dying first, he has to grant the victory to her. He must acknowledge shame and grief, but shame and grief displaced from his being a survivor to his being defeated on a battlefield he envisions them constructing. Then the fact that they can have this playfulness between them allows him to extend the figure of the battlefield, this time to offer the poem's most intimate rendering of their connection. The poem now has progressed from the eyes that bind them to the fealties of the heart to the urgencies of the pulse. So awareness of his pulse is not the heightened sense of self created by sexual desire. Pulse here is the expression of his being persistently and pervasively intent upon the goal of joining her in death. This thought allows him to await his dissolution with hope and comfort because it shows that the most fundamental laws of his being in fact tie him to his desire and direct him toward the shared world he has been fantasizing.

But why then this strange appeal to her that she forgive him for this crime of continuing to live? Why must potential irony and demanding leaps characterize even this last stage in forming his attitude? Part of the answer involves his guilt both at surviving and now at accommodating to his surviving. He has to take responsibility for where his construction of this attitude has left him. By asking for her forgiveness he keeps their dialogue primary. He recognizes his situation because he has to be responsible to his feelings for how she will see him. Then he offers another clever and convincing leap in logic. The fact that he knows she recognizes his worries manifests the scope of their intimacy and makes it plausible for him to assert that they do complete one heart. So even if he submits to living out his life, the reluctance he continues to feel will also be the evidence that he lives as only half the heart he now sees that they can share. In this union he can affirm his waiting. This affirmation does not nullify his pain; the pain is inseparable from the pulse that traps him in time. But his suffering is qualitatively refigured because he can see it as helping to establish what now becomes a life of waiting that they have in common. If he can do so well with only half a heart, the chances are pretty good that when they do meet again they will never be separated.

## VI. What My Argument Cannot Handle, or How I Learned to Avoid Taxonomy

It is all too clear that what I have offered here cannot suffice as an overall theory of the emotions. Even by piggybacking on Wollheim (an image that may redeem this chapter), I cannot get beyond showing how we can read selected poems closely by dealing with them as processes of forming attitudes that give shape to our affective experience. I console myself that this may help us dwell a little more on phenomenological complexity and make us a little less trusting of the available conceptual schemes. And in my more optimistic moments I hope that the approach taken here will prove suggestive for those engaged with the larger theoretical concerns central to philosophical discourse on the emotions.

But just to be respectable I think I have to take up two of the most visible omissions in these readings in the hope I can strengthen their status as examples that both challenge and reward theoretical discourse.

First, I have provided no account of how the expressions of emotions become legible as efforts to communicate with other people, or as elements eliciting and helping to produce narrative forms for our own actions. Analogously, my expressivist focus has restricted me to talking about audience only from the point of view of the agent's emotion. I have paid scant attention to how theory might engage questions of assessing interpretations of the complex attitudes involved. Audiences enter my account only as imagined figures in relation to whom agents formulate their own versions of why affective states are significant.

Here I will not offer suggestions on those topics. I will, however, take the time to argue that the emphasis I have developed might afford a timely shift in priorities. Almost all the influential conceptual work on the emotions emphasizes the position of audience and judge: theorists care much more about how we interpret than about how the projection of interpreters affects our expressive activity. Within cognitivist traditions all the emphasis is put on judgment. Because this stance emphasizes how a person is positioned to perform actions, its theory is primarily concerned with how observers can understand and judge motives. Value gets located in the ways that people become interpreters of actions rather than performers of passions. Similarly, when expressivists like Campbell and Taylor turn to questions of value, their psychology forces them to switch from the value within the agent's actions to the truths about the selves the agent discovers. So I rely on lyrics, and hence on how lyric speakers are affected by imagined audiences, because these works are focused almost entirely on the kinds of satisfactions that are available for agents simply because of the qualities of consciousness they bring to what they are feeling. From this perspective one can argue that emotions have the importance we see them having in people's lives because they compose the arenas in which we most intensely talk to ourselves about our intensities. That is the domain within which we explore what identifications and bonds might emerge from how we handle being moved.

The second omission may seem even more damning. I don't even address ways of providing classifications among emotions or otherwise honoring the structural differences between factive and epistemic emotions, or self-oriented and other-oriented emotions. My only defense is to confess that I simply have nothing of interest to say about the constituents of specific emotions or ways of cataloguing them. Then I can go on to explain a theoretical commitment that conveniently justifies my incapacity. I can imagine on some occasion arguing that we still have much to learn from the specific analyses and taxonomic connections developed by classical philosophers like Descartes, Vives, and Hume. But in our culture the more pressing need is to argue against the taxonomic instinct in all its forms. For there is a strong temptation once we have named an emotion to ignore the agents who manifest it. What we know about the emotion suffices to tell us what the agent is probably experiencing. All that matters then about the agent is how his or her formative beliefs shaping the emotion are or are not adequate to the situation. And then it is not a large step to assert that all that matters about the emotion is the place it has in the operations of a particular culture. For, as I argued in my first chapter, this approach is fundamentally *adjectival*. Emotions provide ways of labeling states that agents enter and of characterizing behavior that stems from entering those states, so long as narrative provides the relevant contextual pegs for the analyst to place within the prearranged patterns.

Theorists often manage partial escapes from the conceptual logic imposed on them by their commitments. So I exaggerate the practical consequences of adjectival thinking, but not to an enormous degree. And the exaggeration serves the very useful purpose of dramatizing the need for an alternative that might modify how we take up these overall conceptual commitments. I think the necessary move is to explore where we can go by thinking of emotions in adverbial rather than in adjectival terms. Then emotions become first of all modifiers of how people act rather than of states people enter. Emotions are not entities but attributes of attitudes being formed by agents in ways that modify desire and hence indirectly modify actions. The more we stress the modifications, the less central taxonomy becomes. We still need a grammar of expectations, but it becomes crucial not to substitute the grammar for concrete expressive activity and the modes of self-consciousness it brings into social life.

# 4 Why Manner Matters: Expression and Conative Value

That will be one of the grandeurs of immortality. There will be no space and consequently the only commerce between spirits will be by their intelligence of each other—while we in this world merely comprehend each other by different degrees—the higher the degree of good so higher is our Love and friendship. . . . Now the reason I do not feel at the present moment so far from you is that I remember your Ways and Manners and actions; I know your manner of thinking, your manner of feeling; I know what shape your joy or your sorrow would take; I know the manner of your walking, standing, sauntering, sitting down, laughing, punning, and every action so truly that you seem near to me. You will remember me in the same manner.

John Keats to George and Georgiana Keats, January 1819

Let us liberate ourselves from the notion that our body is constituted by the form that makes it an objective for the observation and manipulation of an outside observer. Let us dissolve the conceptual crust that takes hold of it as a subsistent substance. . . . Let us cease to identify it [the body] with the grammatical notion of a subject or the juridical notion of a subject of decisions and initiatives. . . .

Movements do not get launched by an agent against masses of inertia: we move in an environment of air currents, rustling trees. . . . These movements have not only extension; they surge and ebb in intensity. They are vehement, raging, prying, incandescent, tender, cloying, ardent, lascivious. It is by its irritability, its fear, its rage, its languor, its exuberance that an octopus in the ocean, a rabbit caught in our headlights, . . . become visible to us. Our movements become irritable with the insistent whine of a mosquito, fearful before the fury of a hornet whose nest we have disturbed. . . .

Our ethics, from Socrates, whose physical ugliness Nietzsche noted and made much of, to John Rawls, has not known what to make of physical splendor. Our ethics, which has built up so extensive a vocabulary, has not given the name of virtue to the compulsion of a man to acquire the strong and proportioned musculature of bulls and elk, the compulsion of a woman to move with the grace of a panther.

Alphonso Lingis, "Bestiality"

## I. The Relation of Manner to Expression: Subjective and Objective Genitives

I hope the reader is as struck as I am by the fact that there are so few highly regarded contemporary philosophical or critical accounts that share Keats's concern for the manner of acting embodied in the expression of emotions like joy and sorrow. In my preceding chapter I tried to establish building blocks for thinking about expressive activity that will allow us to characterize how manner might become central in our attention to what people do in relation to being moved. Now I want to address questions about the values that can emerge when we fully commit ourselves to this shift in focus. So I will concentrate on showing how an insistently adverbial model for dealing with the full range of our affective experiences can modify some overall assumptions about the interests agents have in such activity.

This concentration will prove much too cowed by contemporary analytic philosophy to take on the tone or the convictions of my second epigraph. I offer that only as a melancholy emblem of where I wish my theorizing about manner could ultimately lead. But I fear the most I can hope from the arguments to follow is that they afford some conceptual breathing room within a stifling intellectual climate. Cognitivist theorists subordinate how we act in expressing our formation of an attitude to how our beliefs bring about actions. And while expressivist theory does foreground the agent's activity, most theorists in this vein treat the expressive activity as important for how it constitutes or reveals meanings rather than for how it directly displays significant qualities of agency. Sue Campbell, for example, presents the goal of expression as the development of increasingly adequate representations of what we are actually feeling and why we might be having such feelings.[1] And now with the burgeoning of cultural studies, expression seems best understood in relation to how various cultural traits and contradictions get articulated in and through our actions.[2]

To carry out my project I have to begin by developing my claims about the adverbial and so specifying what is involved in focusing on manner rather than on belief or meaning. Rather than speaking about an emotion of anger, we might speak of an expression as an angry one or as the display of particular qualities of anger. In these cases, our focus is less on what agents believe about what moves them than on how they perform who they become by virtue of the attitude they have been constructing. A hermeneutic sense of "express" gives way to a dramatic one, or better to a dramatistic one.

Whether the source of the anger is obvious or obscure, our concern shifts to what agents make of their own relations to such sources as they forge a particular stance that gives the emotion a practical presence.

If I can elaborate this perspective, I can then show how foregrounding dramatistic aspects of our affective experience provides a richer appreciation of the satisfactions available from such experience than we could develop by focusing on how beliefs are formed and deployed. Considered dramatistically, expressions matter for what they do rather than for what they reveal. Or, at the least, our efforts to understand causes have to be correlated with careful attention to how agents deploy imagination and adapt the resources society gives for taking on particular identities and reaching mutual understanding. Ultimately, manner matters because it leads us to give concerns for how we realize certain states priority over concerns about how we make judgments. Stressing realization calls attention to how we make investments in the carrying out of expressive acts. And this emphasis helps explain a range of possible identifications that prove important to us even though they have very little to do with the domains of morality or of prudential interests.[3]

Obviously not all of our emotional experiences invite this attention to manner (although the lack of such concern can itself be a significant feature of the manner in which a person acts). The easily labeled emotions often do not display any distinctive concern for qualities in the expression, and they often have very little to do with the agent's concerns about identity.[4] But there are many quite various occasions when it cannot suffice to treat an agent's development of an attitude as if it were a standard cultural gesture. Some expressions establish distinctive qualities to actions even when we are quite unaware that we are acting with particular sensitivity or attention or rudeness or volatility. Other expressions seem to intend the activity to be recognized as a special responsiveness to another person or situation. Think of the immense difference between someone who regularly explodes in anger and someone normally considered meek who finds himself getting angry and deliberately lets himself go in order to modify how someone sees him (or how he is entitled to see himself). Then there are standard cases of relying on the manner of an expression specifically to create responding attitudes in others—for example when our display of emotion manages to calm another down or to induce trust or produce an overall atmosphere charged with tension.

These examples indicate that our attending to manner can provide richer terms than contemporary philosophy seems to possess for clarifying how our enacting of attitudes engages us in gorgeously intricate possibilities for developing and modifying identifications. Our first-order expressive activities establish significant features by which other people can recognize and engage us. Second-order investments in the manner of those activities then allow us to bring to bear concepts of will that quickly become problematic when we are concerned with the status of beliefs. By dealing with manner we take willing as making particular kinds of second-order identifications in order to assume immanent responsibility for what we make of our expressive energies. Think for example of the force of a wink or the power of emphatically leaving things unsaid or emphasizing the labor of making something as articulate as possible. Very simple second-order endorsements suffice to express our very strong investments in particular ways of acting. Indeed they do so in a manner that at least partially bypasses the infinite regress of willing to will, ad nauseam. This immanent willing need not depend on self-reflexive decisions. Rather such willing suggests that many of our most telling definitions of ourselves take place when there is no explicit reasoning we give for our actions. And when we do give reasons, an emphasis on manner does not separate concerns for the logic of the reasoning from an overall concern for the commitment to reflection that the reasoning brings to bear.

In order to establish a path from elemental concerns for manner to questions about value, I will begin by attending carefully to Richard Moran's essay "The Expression of Feeling in Imagination." Moran's primary concern is to provide an alternative to mimetic accounts of art so that he can remind analytic aesthetics of how and why the authorial energies within the work demand interpretive attention. Yet I think the account is sufficiently rich, and the critique of epistemic assumptions sufficiently telling, to warrant an effort to use this analysis as a means of speculating on what I have to call the ontology of expressive behavior. From Moran we can elaborate how we make second-order investments in our own specific ways of engaging experience. So after I spell out the relevant arguments I will turn to how Moran's work helps us appreciate what is at stake in the delicate yet powerful versions of second-order investments elaborated in Robert Creeley's lyric poetry. Then to establish a speculative framework suggesting why these investments matter to us I will turn to Baruch Spinoza's account of conative activity. Even though Spinoza's assumptions and methods differ substantially from contemporary practices, I think his discussion of conativity helps us develop a version of expressivist values that does not entail the forms of individualism established by Hegelian and Nietzschean misreadings of his position. Finally I will demonstrate how Spinoza gives us access to particular kinds of satisfactions and identifications by turning to what I will call Wallace Stevens's exponential poetics. Stevens's fluid second-order states bring the values of manner into the most elemental forms of identification, in the process elaborating a simple yet powerful set of grammatical resources for making these values articulate.

## II. Richard Moran on Fictionality and How That Helps Us Understand Issues of Manner in All Expressive Activity

Although he is very highly respected by his peers, Richard Moran seems to have had no impact at all on critics in the arts. The reason is not hard to find.

He is a superb philosopher who refuses to trumpet large claims, but instead works very carefully to show how there might be specific ways of avoiding insuperable problems within the still dominant epistemic ways of dealing with psychological issues. Most of his early work dealt with the limitations of the belief model for the theory of action, since our most elemental decisions cannot be based on reasoning in accord with propositional criteria. We have to take up positions so that specific sets of criteria become relevant, and the taking of these positions cannot itself be determined by criteria.[5] The more recent essay with which I will be dealing takes its departure from the critique of another aspect of epistemic thinking—the difficulty of capturing the force of affective intensities within fictions if one insists that fictions are only make-believe worlds. Moran does not posit an alternative notion of fictionality. Rather he challenges the entire model of fictionality as a primary framework for discussing the role of feelings established within literary texts. In doing this Moran is careful not to reach beyond the arts, so I suspect he would be much more cautious than I will be in extending his work to how we invest in the affects within our more quotidian experiences. I find the temptation irresistible because he so powerfully locates why manner is central to expressivity and why we cannot appreciate that expressivity if we are concerned primarily with the beliefs shaping the emotion. Moreover, I think Moran makes it possible to produce some rapprochement between the analytic tradition and the intensely speculative work of Gilles Deleuze, in my view the greatest contemporary thinker on expressive values. For Moran's thinking seems to me entirely compatible with the Deleuzian view that humans are primarily animals with a large stake in having ourselves and the world take on vivid intensities as modes of becoming.[6]

Because Moran is very careful and wants us to change our overall perspective on issues of fictionality, I will have to trace his argument in detail. This argument begins by isolating and challenging the fascination in contemporary American aesthetics with the question why we have strong emotional reactions to persons and situations that we know to be fictional. I suspect that very few literary critics have been engaged by this issue. Yet for philosophers working with epistemic assumptions, this seems a troubling situation: if our emotions are shaped by our beliefs, then we ought to have strong emotions only for those objects that we believe really exist. If we do not have that belief, how can we muster real emotion? To answer this question we have to rely on strategies like those elaborated in Kendall Walton's influential *Mimesis as Make-Believe*. Walton solves the problem of fictionality with a single stroke. We can have real emotions for fictional objects because these objects invite us to make believe that the world they occupy is a real one. Fictions engage us in games where we have learned to assume attitudes that take propositions about the fictive world as "true-in-the fiction" or "fictionally true" (76). Hence we can become really afraid in a horror movie, but only because we pretend that this world momentarily constitutes our reality. And as we look at ourselves pretending, we actually observe how we would feel if the situation were true.[7]

Given the prevailing assumptions, Walton's solution certainly seems a workable one. But, Moran asks, should we be content with the form of the question Walton sets out to answer? Perhaps we need to rely on ideas of make-believe only to hold onto the primacy of belief-based modes of analysis. Perhaps the sharp dichotomy between fictive and real is not the most appropriate framework for dealing with the aspects of imaginative life basic to our affective experiences. So Moran asks us to step for a moment outside of such philosophical commitments. Are our practical lives in fact so resistant to fictionality? Do our "real world" emotions depend on testing for truth conditions? And why make fictionality so central a concern for our reflection on art? Artists make fictional worlds, but that making is very much part of our "real" world. So emphasizing fictionality may severely distort our relations to those immediate qualities of the text expressing authorial investments.

These concerns lead Moran to concentrate on two specific problems within Walton's argument. First, while fictionality can make a difference to some emotions, "our paradigms of ordinary emotions exhibit a great deal of variety in this respect" (79). We have all sorts of emotions in the "real" world that are fundamentally constructs of imagination—think of the work memory and desire do. Perhaps, Moran suggests, "most of the suffering and satisfaction in life takes place either *prior* to the expected events that are supposed to deliver the real goods, or after the fact, savored in remembrance or sticking in one's craw" (79).

Moran's second point is even stronger. Walton's position allows only a very limited view of what authorial composition can establish for the audience. Because it becomes so important to make the experience seem real or be treatable as occurring in a make-believe real world, the only aspects of the authorial activity that Walton can honor are those that produce vividness and convincingness for the reality of the imagined world. But then what can we make of other features of the text that are directly expressive of authorial investments or explore what particular stylistic experiments make available? Such features often actually hinder our taking the imagined world as if it were consistent with the practical world we typically negotiate. For they emphasize qualities of the making—either as performance or as the expression of emotions and interests in relation to the fictive structures. Yet Walton is bound by his convictions to treat "'the conspicuous brushstrokes on the surface of Van Gogh's *Starry Night*'" as factors that inhibit "psychological participation" by an audience (82). And, as Moran points out, Walton would have to rewrite Shakespeare's dense language in order to enhance the audience's ability to make believe that the world of the work can be a real one.[8]

It may take a philosopher's arrogance to be as blunt as Walton is in building generalizations on such limited taste. Yet his position has substantial affinities with perspectives we find in even the most "sophisticated" literary criticism. Consider how often eagerness to develop clear representational relations between text and actual historical situations leads to an impatient distrust of the author's investments in style and structure. In fact, style and structure become interesting for such criticism only when the critic can show how the artifice tries to escape "real history" and so then can treat the activity as part of the history it is trying to escape. One might then think of deconstructive criticism as a way to recuperate this active intervening. Certainly it is devoted to aspects of artifice highly suspect in more overtly "political" and "historical" criticism. Yet deconstruction's interest in textuality and artifice seems to me to stem from its continuing to see the practical world in epistemic terms. The play of artifice and the emphasis on distinctive expressive traits matter primarily because they create aporias within practices based on establishing knowledge. Deconstruction then differs from Walton's position only by making the inverse claim within an assumed epistemic framework. Rather than stress make-believe, deconstruction stresses the undoing of possibilities for belief. The two stances completely share an inability to treat the artifice as directly engaging powerful participatory energies from the audience.

Recognizing these affinities should make it clear why Moran tries to change the entire framework by which we think about how an audience's feelings get deployed within fictions. He wants us to see that relying on notions of make-believe is a compensatory strategy for negotiating the fact that epistemic orientations simply cannot provide positive terms for imaginative activity because they cannot adapt to the manners of acting that expressions embody. Rather than begin with a sharp distinction based on real-world beliefs and make-believe adjustments, Moran proposes that we ask how our feelings for what fictions offer might be continuous with analogous uses of our imagination in the real world.

Take the issue of vividness as a test case. Moran argues that Walton was right to stress vividness, wrong to locate it in the logic of make-believe. Walton's sense of vividness requires his insisting that any artifice that does not play a role "in the construction of any fictional truths must detract from" the "coherence of the fictional world depicted" and hence from possible emotional engagement in that world (Walton, 82). Vividness must be something that influences belief in the status of a fiction, not something that foregrounds distinctive qualities as direct claims on our attention and our interest. Consequently Walton's theory reduces the artist to the role of purveying vividness as a means of seducing audiences into successful make-believe the artist as director of American blockbuster films. All of the artist's relevant craft goes into enabling an audience to treat the imaginary as if it were real. And all of the audience's energies are seen as observing how they might feel were they to participate in that reality. By analogy, all that would matter in our emotions would be the vividness (or salience) they brought to our beliefs and the propositions that embody them. Expressive intensity would have to be seen as an effort to call attention to some feature of the beliefs involved. The manner of expression would have no significance either as a demonstration of specific qualities within an attitude or as a means of eliciting responses from an audience. Therefore an emphasis on the imaginary denies us access to how expressions can have imaginative force. We arrive where Wollheim does although we take a very different route.

The more clearly we see how narrow vividness becomes within frameworks like Walton's, the better prepared we are to appreciate the kinds of values that come to the fore when we shift our attention to what can be made present in how we perform expressive acts.[9] Where Walton finds van Gogh's style a distraction, Moran can insist: "The very expressive qualities that disrupt any sense of a fictional world are in fact central for our psychological participation with artworks" (83). "We know that *Starry Night* would not really be more emotionally engaging if Van Gogh had calmed down and left out all of that overwrought brush work" (83). Artists and writers are concerned with much more than giving vividness to the appearance of a fictional world. We have to see the vividness produced by artifice as something other than an instrumental quality in the service of eliciting particular beliefs. The vividness is simply a manifestation of value in such circumstances because it becomes an index of the author's capacity to give expressive definition to particular qualities of attention and care. And this vividness resists the entire mimetic model of fiction because it foregrounds "elements that are often impossible to imagine as part of any fictional world" (84). Speaking of Macbeth's speeches, Moran notes that features like "the rhythm of the relentless piling up of image upon image" become "directly productive of feeling on the part of the audience, and not through their role" in elaborating a make-believe reality (85). We might add that from this perspective Rothko's making manner the actual substance of art simply foregrounds an ontology perhaps implicit in much of our aesthetic experience.

III. Three Modifications of Moran That Clarify How We Can Use His Work on Fiction to Talk about the Affects in General

Unfortunately we cannot simply use Moran's arguments as the basis for an alternative account of our responsiveness to fictions or of the roles manner plays in expressive activity. There are three interrelated aspects of his position that need some rethinking before I attempt that more general case. First, we have to notice that Moran's focus is much more on how audiences respond to authors and characters than on how the one doing the expressing reaches any kind of satisfaction in the expression. Given my concerns, I will have to adjust his case to emphasize instead how the manner of the imagining displayed by author and character expresses their affective states. Second, I have to be careful to qualify the claims I am making for vividness. I do not want to say that the vividness of our manner of acting determines its value. That claim might make Hannibal Lector happy, but it will not advance philosophy. However, I do want to say that insofar as we concentrate on how an expression establishes value for affective states, vividness does become a primary consideration. (There well might be overriding concerns when we think about acting in relation to the affective state.) Even if the action is evil, its vividness of expression might explain why it satisfies the agent and why the agent might be able to appeal to an audience to honor the identifications that the action secures.

The third aspect subsumes the others. Moran makes no distinctions between the vividness of authorial engagement and the vividness achieved by particular characters. Yet on the face of it, it seems that the author has a quite different relation to the audience than the work's characters do. The author is not within the fiction. He or she occupies a position in the real world, however modified it may be as the fiction unfolds. So once the foregrounding of that role is admitted at all (something Walton refuses to grant), we almost have to take the manner of acting as a direct engagement with the audience. Here Moran's case makes obvious sense. A character's speeches made within the fiction, on the other hand, do not have any urgency or distinctive manner until they are contextualized within a world real only in imagination. This situation forces Moran to go to great trouble explaining how we can treat the character's expressive activity as parallel to the author's activity. But that argument seems to me somewhat strained, and I doubt it is necessary. For it is much simpler to treat the character's speaking simply as an element within the author's made world. It is the author's made world that directly intersects our world. Macbeth's speeches engage me directly because I envision Shakespeare intending them to have that effect. I do not make believe they are having that effect but I participate imaginatively in a situation where their role is to have that effect.[10]

Now I think the way is clear to attempt adapting Moran's arguments about fictions to my concerns with emphasizing the manner displayed in all forms of expressive activity. Precisely because he shows that authors function as elements of our actual world, he provides terms for dealing with those forms of authoring within that world that negotiate practical situations. We cannot appreciate the range and subtlety of affective life in general if we keep assuming that all of the energies that go into expressive behavior are devoted either to teasing out some inner reality or to coming to richer representations of it. Instead the expressions often seek simply to make their manner matter because of the vivid presentations they afford and because of the identifications that this vividness allows. The manner is the authorial or dramatic agent's way of making its presence felt because of how the activity engages a particular situation.

Consider for example what we engage when we take Shakespeare's writing as directly manifesting certain traits of the character Macbeth. We could go on to interpret the traits as elements within some thematic allegory. But in so far as we deal with them as a manner of acting, we are responding directly to how Macbeth engages the world under certain conditions of intensity. The vividness is not an invitation to interpretation, but a manifestation of actual processes fundamental to his being Macbeth. And responding to Macbeth then is not simply a matter of finding a way to take his beliefs as continuous with our world. Rather, the response has to be a positioning of ourselves so that we can both participate in and react cogently to what his mode of speaking makes vivid. We do not read through the vividness but take the vividness as itself his (and on another level the work's) claim to have a hold upon us. We may go on to interpret why these particular forms of expression absorb his energies, but then we are in a very different practice where we are not engaging Macbeth but resisting the immediacy of his presence so that we can put it within a conceptual frame. There may be good reasons for that. Moran's news is that there also may be good reasons not to rely on interpretation, or not to forget the vividness that led us to seek out the interpretation in the first place.

Responding to such vividness requires more than appreciating what agents are expressing. It also requires modifying substantially how we envision our roles as interpreters. Indeed one of the basic problems with cognitivist orientations is that they value only those attributes in an audience that enable us to develop and process beliefs. Moran suggests a very different set of powers necessary for our being able to attune ourselves to vividness and compose for it frameworks that honor its specific expressivity. Not surprisingly, the imagination becomes a central player. For me this proves very useful because in the previous chapter I could do little more than assert a substantial difference between the modes of imagination that go into the construction of attitudes and the imaginary projections that enable the attitude to make investments in substitute realities. Now Moran helps us flesh out how "the imaginative" (86) plays significant roles not available when we lapse into the imaginary. And he does so in a way that differs sharply from the way roles are attributed to imagination in Romantic theory and in much of the hermeneutic thinking that emerged out of that tradition (although his perspective is quite Keatsian). Imagination need not pursue Romantic projects like seeing beneath appearances or developing symbolic registers for our experiences. Rather its most basic role is simply to keep salient details vital and to project means of composing these details into overall attitudes that carry expressive significance. Imagination, in other words, is the aspect of our mental life responsible for registering vividness and synthesizing the particular energies producing that vividness. Imagination is our way of opening ourselves to being affected. And it is our way of exploring how we can adapt to the forces that create that vividness without impatiently turning vivid particulars into instances—or expressions into the stuff of propositions. Imagination can be our means of escape from hermeneutic views of expression into performative ones.

More important, imagination may have the power to alter the very structure of self-consciousness in ways that completely escape cognitivist theory. Moran works this possibility out by taking on the positioning of the subject that seems necessary in Walton's account of how the emotions work in fiction. Walton argues that "[p]art of what is imagined" must have "a content referring to oneself" (87): I imagine not only Macbeth's fear but my own relation to this fear as I translate between fictive and real worlds. For without that additional reference to the self one could not explain the degrees of vividness by which the figure of Macbeth comes into one's imagination (88). And because readers must be constantly aware that they are involved in make-believe, they then always see their own state as the vehicle by which all other emotional states take on reality. That I am imagining Macbeth's self-loathing makes it possible for me to give him reality in my make-believe world.

But are we in fact always so much at the center of our emotions or responses to emotions, especially those that depend on the work of projective imagination? Must imagination be so closely bound to the forms of self-consciousness fundamental to belief? Or might we be able to distinguish different kinds of imagining that involve different kinds of resources and different modes of intentionality? Some representations, for example, take on vividness not because I add another belief about myself, but because my mind is provoked "to do various things (relating, contrasting, calling up thoughts)" (89). The vividness is not part of the content of what is imagined, as if it depended on a thought that could be adjusted for varying degrees of intensity. Rather vividness comes from the manner of my imagining in relation to what provokes it. Vividness stems usually not from thoughts about Macbeth, but from what happens as an audience engages Macbeth's way of expressing his thoughts. Consequently the imagining ego often occupies a position very different from the one Walton postulates. For Walton the projection of beliefs about the fiction casts the agent as occupying a clearly established point of view, as if he or she assumed a position making it possible to see the projected events. But when we treat the vividness as produced by offering provocations for the mind, we need not postulate the agent's specific awareness of its own situated existence. What is perceived need not be seen from the point of view of an observer whose location can be mapped. As Moran puts it, "The point is that to imagine something visually is not the same thing as to imagine seeing it" (92).

If these observations are right, we have to acknowledge that it is an oversimplification to treat our participating in art works on the model of vision. We do much better to treat the visual as one of several manners of imagining, each with different possible locations for the empirical ego. Moran points out that even painters sensitive to the visual often take advantage of these modal possibilities. Artists like van Gogh and Cézanne, and even Raphael, are much less concerned with where the painter stands, or where the viewer is projected as standing, than with how their chosen mode of seeing brings out particular qualities within the visual field. Van Gogh is not very helpful in enabling me to make believe I am taking up an imaginary position in a field of flowers. Instead he makes me experience a visual intensity based on a direct sense of the energies circulating through that field. And when I am so engaged, the fact that it is I who am so engaged is relevant only for outside observers; the "I" is not a necessary location for the literally ecstatic condition of vision involved. Self-consciousness itself can dissolve into the intensities and intricacies by which manner comes to matter. I need not see myself take on van Gogh's imaginative stance; I need only engage in the affective possibilities that his way of seeing makes possible. "I" can appear as simply an extension of that process, if "I" appears at all.

## IV. Three General Claims Based on Moran

Going on so long about a particular essay leaves me in the position of an unlucky gambler. I have to raise the stakes in order to recoup my initial investment. So I will try to justify all this discourse by using Moran's arguments as the basis for three quite general claims—one involving his general critique of mimetic ways of understanding affective experience, one extending the treatment of the ego's position in these experiences, and one postulating what our stakes are in our expressive activity so that we can appreciate more fully the satisfactions concerns with manner make possible.

In establishing the first of these claims I want to push harder than Moran does on how strange it is that contemporary American philosophy takes issues of the rationality of emotion as its fundamental concern when addressing the topic of affect in the arts. Moran is content to offer a very strong critical analysis of this view, then to suggest a positive alternative addressing only aesthetic examples. But I am led to reconsider even Wollheim's work on the role of attitudes because of the degree to which it seems shaped by epistemic concerns. On the face of it, this is an odd claim because Wollheim shows how the attitudes we construct for emotions cannot be reduced to propositional versions of belief. But he casts attitudes as performing much the same role as beliefs. They synthesize details and provide a single overall intentional structure by which to understand our actions. His attitudes are bodiless, and hence mannerless. They organize how we feel, but they do not sufficiently serve as means of exploring and adjusting to what the feeling involves. In the previous chapter, I tried to demonstrate how important these processes are. Now I can use Moran to explain that importance. It is the qualities of our activity that allow them to elicit identifications and make us care that this is the mode of expression we are carrying out.

Wollheim seems to me right that we feel emotions because we have to deal with something like satisfaction or frustration or, as I prefer, with some way of being moved. However, we usually do not proceed directly from being moved to formulating an overall imaginative construction by which we can identify what we are feeling. Our manners of activity enter at two basic levels. First there are processes that emerge as we work toward an attitude we can trust. My initial reactions to being moved by what becomes jealousy may reveal my inability to control myself or my tendency to exercise so much control that repression generates ancillary behaviors like irascibility with colleagues and friends. And even as I formulate the attitude there will be important distinguishing qualities involving how I process information, what fantasies gain degrees of influence on my projections, and how I comport myself in relation to other people. The manner of my forming the attitude then can become more significant for me than the attitude at which I arrive, even if it proves a complicated and subtle one. One might even say that *Hamlet* is in large part the dramatization of someone so engaged in the manner of his reactions that he holds off forming any one attitude with which he can entirely identify. Poor Ophelia expects him to declare himself as a lover, but all she gets are his ways of deferring any such defining attitude.

Then there are processes that accompany the formulated attitude and constitute fundamental building blocks within it. Since Shakespeare seems to be directing my discourse, let me shift the focus from *Hamlet* to *Romeo and Juliet* and *Antony and Cleopatra*. In both plays, characters at very different stations of life find themselves not only falling in love, but being often surprised by what they find themselves doing because they regard themselves as being in love. For Romeo and Juliet the processes involve mostly coming to realize how their verbal powers keep intensifying what they mean to each other. Our most positive emotions have the force they do because the vivid ways of acting that accompany them usually reinforce our investments in them. In *Antony and Cleopatra* the stakes are even higher because these characters understand what happens when love begins to fail and we change the kind and intensity of investments we can make in our attitudes. So they have to attempt to live up to their language even when they cannot quite believe themselves or each other. The comedy and the tragedy of adult love may be this sense that the more difficult it is quite to trust the attitude we are formulating, the greater the demands on us to act as believers.

The comedy and tragedy of writing theory is that it has to descend from such examples to a far more practical orientation. For me this means once again observing how sharply this concern with doings contrasts with cognitivist emphases on the beliefs shaping the emotions. And pursuing that contrast seriously changes not only what we emphasize about the agent, but also how we position those persons attempting to respond to the agent. Adapting to expressive behavior cannot be only a matter of finding how to make the beliefs compatible with rationality. We also have to learn to recognize and to appreciate what the particular activity makes visible about the person's relation to the specific situation. That is why the relevant normative background for understanding affects cannot consist primarily in criteria for assessing the rationality or irrationality of beliefs. Instead we depend on a much more complex cultural literacy that provides rough terms enabling us to converse about whether or not particular expressions have effective force. And our sense of the force of the expressions will often be most engaged when that cultural background proves not quite immediately effective. Rather than simply adapting to the codes that the expression invokes, we find ourselves having to adjust to its power of vividly maintaining its partial inappropriateness and hence its significant specificity.

The second reason why Moran is so important for me derives from his treatment of self-consciousness. I think he enables us to say that we need not stress belief in our account of the emotions because there are many occasions when the conceptual position necessary for formulating beliefs is not given and is not important to the phenomenology of the experience. In other words, what Moran says about visual perspectives holds also for interpretive ones. Many affects take form not because we hold a specific belief but because we attune ourselves to some event or position established by another subject. And many emotions do not project a distinctive position for the role of rational observer and judge. Wonder is not a condition that depends on belief, or even that can be justified in terms of beliefs. And various kinds of sympathy or senses of solidarity occur not because of beliefs but because of immediate recognitions and attunements.

On the basis of such cases, I think we have to postulate more direct and more flexible affinities between the psyche and what moves it than philosophers like Walton can grant. We can express emotions without committing ourselves to beliefs, and we can respond to other people's affective states without consciously interpreting them and testing our hypotheses. In the cases of van Gogh and Cézanne, the vividness and expressive force derive from a manifest sensibility but not necessarily from a positioned self-reflexive ego (at least within the visual scene). And responding to their vividness is a matter less of understanding their beliefs than of participating in specific deployments of visual energies, deployments that we can take up without worrying about their relation to where we stand actually and figuratively as viewers. There might be very good reason to bring the ego into play as a consequence of such experiences, for example in various forms of second-order investments endorsing this as a mode of seeing one wants to pursue. But those second-order features are not necessary to sharing in the vividness. And their very possibility may depend on a first-order experience in which the position of the self is not given. This sudden sense of finding oneself vividly aware, but not cogently positioned, offers strong incentives for trying to understand how one might then formulate a position for the self capable of incorporating phenomena for which one has no belief categories.

Modernist artists intent on purely visual phenomena afford obvious and strong examples of this flexibility in how we produce and respond to vivid aspects of experience. But I want to turn back to the Renaissance for examples that take on social substance even though the visual field does not conform to any central perspective occupied by an ego formulating a self-conscious attitude. Consider for a moment the challenge of painting the return of the prodigal son. This experience becomes most intense for both father and son when they both register a change in their lives that makes the perspectives they habitually occupy a hindrance to what they must realize. And what they must realize cannot depend primarily on belief because the relation they forge cannot be even close to what their preceding experiences allow them to project. The father must experience a forgiveness whose intensity can not be premeditated. And the son must feel the moment of reconciliation as a profound combination of renunciation and recovery. Guercino registers all these factors by making his version of the reconciliation a flurry of hands and arms that creates a distinctive overall shape for the two persons. Neither quite father nor son, the agents simply are whatever this realization of coming to hold one another allows them to take as the persons they now want to be. The agents give up individual visual perspective so they can feel what the audience sees—that the mutual reaching of hands and the encompassing quality of embracing arms create for the moment a subject absorbed in touch and what touch mediates.

Representing the holy family may well present artists with even greater challenges in composing emotions not quite contained by the agent's particular beliefs. Instead, the bonds must come from qualities more fundamental to their being as a family. Clearly what makes them feel themselves as a holy family cannot be primarily a belief that they are the holy family. Nor can the determining consideration quite be their ability to stand back and form an attitude enabling them to acknowledge all the virtues that they have. Rather what makes them the paradigmatic family is that they experience their subjectivity almost entirely in terms of feelings for the family unit. Other families are likely to have similar experiences some of the time. But these families will also constantly experience the pull of seeing the world from the point of view of separate subjects who then have to work their way by reasoning back to this sense of collectivity. The holy family is distinctive because the sense of separateness is never not balanced by their awareness of their relation to each other. Or so it seems in the way Giorgione's great small *Holy Family* in the National Gallery in Washington, D.C., stages the manner of their relationship to each other. The audience is not asked to participate in any specific drama undergone by an individual. Rather the vivid life of the painting consists in the governing rhythms that define the whole as something like the feelings families can have for their collective being.

Giorgione, *The Holy Family*. National Gallery of Art, Washington, D.C.

Giorgione sets the stage by having the entire family echo in visual structure the shape of an arch that constitutes the central form in the background. Within that rather bold framing effect, the painting goes on to establish intricate lines of force uniting the three persons in several registers, most dramatically by rendering the Christ child in terms of Cézannian *passage* linking Mary's body and Joseph's. The child literally folds the parents into a fluid unit. Analogously, feelings organized by a sense of scale come to play a central role in establishing this distinctive identity. By giving the world of the painting so little space, Giorgione does not allow any one person to stand out and to become a single organizing vision for the whole. The agents and the audience both feel the pressure that the frame exerts so that we see active agency in the painting as deriving from the family unit as a whole. Moreover, the force of scale seems to me to distance the viewer's interpretive intelligence. This is not high allegory; it is domestic space charged by all the intricate adjustments necessary to keep that space a domain in which intellectual justifications are not necessary. All we need to know about this family is given in the attitudes they display as they adjust toward one another's bodily forms. Their holiness consists in the vivid intensity of those adjustments, so that visual lines of force define states of mutual responsiveness that go deeper than beliefs. And our access to holiness here depends not on what we believe but on our capacity to identify with these people simply in terms of what they make manifest. Their relation to divinity resides in their commitments, not in their opinions.

Finally, I want to supplement Moran by making as explicit as possible what I see as the stakes in emphasizing manner as my means of calling attention to basic values and satisfactions within expressive activity. The best way I can elaborate this claim is to return to the distinction between approaches to the emotions that treat them adjectivally, as modifiers of our beliefs, and those that treat them adverbially, as modifiers of activities through which we understand expressivity. Then we can use this distinction to specify the kinds of identification allowed by an emphasis on manner. Ultimately, we will be able to return to the original question Moran posed because treating the idea of fictionality itself in adverbial terms helps us appreciate why fictions can become so important to us.

For most practical purposes it suffices to give an adjectival account of expression. I see the behavior as manifesting a belief that brings with it an identifiable attitude toward some object. Both my anger and my sadness are possible attitudes for negotiating the belief that my friend Bill has done me wrong. However, such accounts will be thin on psychological reality, and they will reduce concerns about value to how the attitude leads to action. This perspective does not afford a means of honoring specific qualities in the expression that take on vividness; nor can it comfortably handle the ways that sadness and anger might be mixed in the agent's expressive response to the situation. (The mixture may be not just a balancing of the beliefs but also a complicated embodiment of confusions and tensions underlying the beliefs.) If we want a means of addressing these features—this specificity of manner and this complexity of response—I think we have to turn to an adverbial approach. This approach not only affords a fuller description of agency than an adjectival one but also facilitates richer value stories for what the agent makes articulate.[11]

When we consider emotions adverbially we consider them as direct modifications of activities by the subject. For what becomes vivid is not our idea about the emotion but our sense of what goes into expressing the emotion. From this perspective the most important feature of the expression is not its possible reference to feelings or its struggle to bring articulation to inchoate feelings. The expression has force because of the qualities it exhibits as features of the forming of an attitude. Manner matters because it puts the emphasis on concrete vividness as the locus of significance for the activity. Consequently, when we register the emotion adverbially we adjust how we project identities—about our own emotions or about agents whom we observe. We are responding not to how beliefs shape the person's world but to who the person becomes as he or she manifests the working out of attitudes in relation to that world. (The attitudes will usually involve beliefs, but what matters is the cast they are given by expressive activity—Wollheim's account of emotions leads to a performative view of expressivity.)

Because it makes states of the agent so fundamental, this adverbial approach also helps us clarify the kinds of values that bring satisfaction within these affective states. Concerns about manner clearly open the way for the range of second-order endorsements and self-assessments that are fundamental for any sophisticated emotional life. For examples we need only recall our discussion of Arnold's Marguerite poem and King's elegy. In both cases, our primary concern was with how, as the speakers formed attitudes, they also made manifest particular qualities basic to their negotiating their worlds. The relevant values are limited because we have only their verbal performances, not their full presence as agents. But that verbal behavior is enough to make clear why we have to respond not only to what they believe but also to what makes their believing important as behavior. We have to project ourselves imaginatively into what creates the vividness and gives it the possible power to modify its environment. The expression asks of us not that we offer an interpretation of it but that we adjust to its specificity. If we seek only explanations for actions, we tend to ignore everything that might give such particular expressions distinctive vividness and force.

Analogously, if we treat fictions only in terms of belief we miss the range of motives and qualities that might be expressed in how the fiction is presented. While Walton and his fellow philosophers have to locate fictionality in the object, an adverbial approach helps us emphasize what it involves for the subject.[12] And then we have a clear rationale for treating the entire work not as a construal but as a presentation directly engaging real emotions in fictional worlds. We would still have to acknowledge that on many occasions the agents' adverbial relation to fictionality is simply a matter of an imaginary contract inviting readers to flesh out the make-believe world the writer's craft projects. In such cases fictionality can elicit affects, but the quality of fictionality is not a significant feature of the specific affects that get developed. The situation gets more challenging when we turn to writers for whom fictionality is not simply a contractual state but an inescapable feature of how we produce and respond to affective intensities. Then we cannot stop with identifying the fiction as a fiction; we have to deal with the specific manner that an agent develops in expressing affective states organized in relation to concerns about this fictionality.

Take for example Flaubert's *Madame Bovary*. There fictionality is central to the formation of attitudes at every level of the book—from the nature of Emma's fantasies to Flaubert's own complex relations to her. So we cannot simply enter a make-believe world as if it were real; nor can we treat emotions as direct responses to how the imagination is invited to construe this imaginary world. The emotions we engage in relation to the author and to the characters themselves involve coming to terms with various manners of dealing with fictionality. Correspondingly, fictionality is less a definable attribute of the text than a constant demand for certain kinds of self-consciousness. And the self-consciousness cannot just be abstract. It does not suffice to say "I know that persons get caught up in a web of fictions." The important concern is how the agents employ that inescapable fictional dimension. Emma Bovary's romantic life begins as an enslavement to romance fantasies that bring ridiculous but deeply satisfying resonance to her sexual dalliances. By the time she has her last affair, she has become a master of manipulating the fictions so that she can deliberately stage her erotic life and make her knowledge of that staging part of her pleasure. Where her first affair was consummated in bright sunshine that belied her own ignorance of how she was being manipulated, her final one has its most intense realization in the curtained compartment of a taxi where she controls what her young lover experiences.

There is no doubt that Emma's investment in her fictions dooms her to eventual suicide. But the novel is not content to judge her. One of its basic aims is just to make vivid how her fantasies provide a way of coping with mid-nineteenth-century social conditions in rural France. In fact, one could argue that Flaubert is judging that society, not judging Emma, since even the hope for a decent life requires attempting to evade the structures that eventually triumph over her. But to stop with any form of judgment is to miss what is probably most fundamental to Flaubert's authorial attitude. He wants to foreground the ways that a sense of fictionality shapes his own stance as a writer. This stance cannot be shaped by a clear contractual relationship to the reader because that relation would require his adapting the bourgeois values that he skewers within the novel. And entering a contract would presume that he knows what he feels about himself and his characters so that he can stand back from the novel. But Flaubert saw his writing as itself an ongoing passion, continually modified on the one hand by his sense of this subject, on the other by how he felt himself changing as he engaged the world he was composing. Instead of proposing a contract, he could only dramatize his own difficult but exhilarating problem: How could he judge Emma when he found her the most engaging creature in her social world? But if he concentrated on her powers, how could he then keep himself from being just another of her conquests who would then have to surrender some of the lucidity that writing made possible?

The entire novel can be seen as an adverbial expansion of Flaubert's writerly situation as he vacillates between sympathy and contempt for Emma as well as pride and despair in relation to his own engagement with her. When Flaubert said "Emma Bovary c'est moi," he was not just stating a fact. Rather he was calling attention to a process of finding himself seduced by the imaginary life of another person while also having to keep that seductive power in perspective, if only because the perspective adds the *frisson* of degradation to the identification. In this regard, *Madame Bovary* does not ask us only to bring real concerns to its fictional world. It makes writing itself the construction of an intricate attitude expressing in its shifting sympathies the affective intensities created by attempting to correlate his own fiction making with his understanding of Emma's. Flaubert's novel does not just render a world with Emma in it; it also explores what it means to find oneself caring about a world that one also finds almost unbearably ridiculous.

The novel then cannot be read as a picture of Emma's life or even of Flaubert's construction of an attitude. It is the literal embodiment of the manner of working out that attitude. Ultimately, Emma makes vivid how fictions pervade the real. And *Madame Bovary* as a whole constitutes a challenge in the real world that we come to terms with a pervasive distrust of the very sense of excess that gives the affective life so intense a hold upon us. Only by engaging this play of disgust and excess, of identification and efforts to maintain ironic withdrawal, can we appreciate why Flaubert makes the identifications he does. Only by working to understand those identifications can we appreciate why Flaubert's heirs found it extremely difficult to return to the conventions allowing them to embrace fictions as make-believe worlds. They had to make visible their own identifications with Flaubert's sense of what authorship involves, and so they found themselves following a path that continues to separate modernism in the arts from mainstream philosophy.

## V. From Passive to Active: Second-Order Identification and the Positing of Value within Emotional Experience

Suppose philosophy were to explore how it might develop at least some affinities with those modernist enterprises. It could do worse than to recognize how this emphasis on self-reflexive manner offers a means of characterizing why our expressive activities become central values for us. For then we can clearly distance ourselves from both the instrumental perspectives brought to bear by cognitivist perspectives and the versions of expressivism fostered by Wollheim and by Campbell. Any value story we tell about the emotions will have to be grounded in some concrete aspect of our activities. But not every story has to be based on the roles judgment plays in generating actions or modifying knowledge.

According to Wollheim, we value emotions because they enable us to reenact the fantasy structures fundamental to our deepest investments. For Campbell, value resides in the power of our expressions to identify and help us address underlying needs and conflicts. But I think Wollheim maintains too much distance between psychology and phenomenology, so that for him all the value is in the projection, none in the specific realization made possible by single expressive acts. And Campbell tends to collapse phenomenology into hermeneutics, so that another mode of self-reflexive judgment becomes far more important than the range of satisfactions one might have in the particular affective states.

The basic challenge I face then is finding a way to bring a language of values into more intimate contact with the phenomenological qualities displayed as we enact the forming of attitudes. I think one can do that by emphasizing our second-order awareness of our own manners of forming and enacting attitudes. That emphasis in turn allows what I hope are new perspectives on two concrete philosophical questions. I will try to show how attention to manner provides a fresh means of dealing with the distinction between active and passive relations to emotions. And I will spell out ways of linking second-order evaluations to concerns for identity and identification so that we understand one of the deepest sources of our satisfactions in how we pursue our affective lives. On the simplest level, there are substantial satisfactions simply in recognizing how our usual senses of ourselves can change when we are intensely engaged in developing emotional attitudes. And, on more complex levels, by making manner the focus of our interests we can develop rich accounts of how we build into our expressions significant investments in taking responsibility for the persons we become because of the attitudes we pursue.

It seems as if it should be relatively simple to distinguish passive responses to emotions from active ones. Arnold's self-deceiving speaker seems to have a significantly different relation to his emotions than does Bishop King's speaker as he makes his mourning into a means of reconnecting to his wife. More generally, there appear to be important differences between those agents whose activity seems shaped by forces we attribute directly to emotional turbulence and those who seem to ride the emotion as if it were a wave both requiring and encouraging distinctive personalizing traits. Yet it proves very difficult to establish any consistent distinctions that do not cause conceptual troubles. Many emotions seem to combine a sense that the agent is partially overcome by some condition and a sense that some active responsibility seems possible. And more comprehensive philosophical solutions seem far too abstract to do anything more than indicate how we might speculate about ultimate possibilities of emotional agency, apart from the muddles that emerge when we deal with particular cases.

Baruch Spinoza offers a telling example. He presents probably the strongest and most striking philosophical distinction we have between the poles of activity and passivity, perhaps because he was so acute a critic of how emotions foster imaginary worlds. This is the first proposition of book 3 of his *Ethics,* the book devoted to the emotions: "Our mind is in some instances active and in other instances passive. In so far as it has adequate ideas it is necessarily active; and in so far as it has inadequate ideas it is necessarily passive" (104). Having an adequate idea means aligning oneself with an adequate cause, a cause whose effect can be perceived as directly emerging from it. An inadequate or partial cause, on the other hand, is one "whose effect cannot be understood through the said cause alone." So we are active "when from our nature there follows . . . something that can be clearly and distinctly understood through our nature alone." We are passive "when something takes place in us, or follows from our nature, of which we are only the partial cause" (104).[13]

Spinoza's formulation certainly helps us make distinctions among the levels of cognitive awareness that go into different attitudes. Consider the difference between immediate anger insistent only on a proximate cause and a realization that some person one has to deal with is deeply flawed and likely always to act in a way that will warrant an angry response. Or consider reflecting on the anger in a way that makes us realize how it stems from our own inadequacies rather than the world's. Or, finally, consider the difference between being moved by sexual desire and approaching the world as if it could sustain an intellectual love of god that would enable us to affirm entirely how reason renders everything in relation to necessary causes. For Spinoza this intellectual love is the richest form of active spirit because it aligns our wills to the limited place we occupy within this nexus of causal relations.

But when we see where his distinction between active and passive is leading, I think we have to draw back because his model will not fit contemporary contexts.[14] Many of us are less comfortable than Spinoza in talking about the affects in terms of knowable causes (although we are not uncomfortable speculating on neurological causes), and we find it difficult to distinguish consistently between responding only to contingent appearances and adapting ourselves to necessity or to our true "natures."[15] More important, Spinoza's rationalism requires sharp value dichotomies between passivity and activity that do not seem quite congruent with what we care about in specific emotional experiences. If passivity is rendered in cognitive terms, it will always be something to avoid or to judge negatively. Yet passivity as an aspect of an attitude might prove very important precisely because it allows us to dwell in affective states until their power begins to rival reason's authority. Being able to yield to the emotion so that we do not entirely control it seems fundamental to appreciating its force and even to expressing those aspects of ourselves not activated in the search for causes. And subordinating our needs to distinguish ourselves or to find explanatory reasons may afford us deeper recognitions of what we are undergoing. So it should not be surprising that various ideals of wise passiveness or finding our peace in god's will pervade religious thinking.

Ronald de Sousa's subtle analysis of these issues leads to this reasonable assessment:

> For three reasons, emotions as a class of mental states undermine the dichotomy
> between the active and the passive. First, the mode of their rationality is neither

simply epistemic nor simply strategic. Second, our assumptions about responsibility for our emotions support neither of the simple opposing views. And third, their role as frames for other states gives them a determining role in choice but makes them too deeply rooted to be simply chosen. (319)

But even if we accept de Sousa's arguments, we are left with the fact that the old model provided important distinctions that we still have to make in some form. So we have to ask what conceptual scheme will allow us to separate those emotions and attitudes which seem for the most part imposed on the agent and those where some kind of active control is present. And we have to worry whether we can speak of control or even mastery of emotions without defining that control in rationalist terms as an understanding of necessity, or for that matter as any kind of comprehensive understanding.

Focusing on manner may provide the shift in conceptual background that we need. This orientation enables us to make practical distinctions between passive and active states without bringing in any language about understanding. And it helps us recognize how there can be complex interplays between the poles. We attribute activity and passivity simply as descriptions of how agents dispose themselves toward being moved. In most passive responses, agents rest content with quite conventional attitudes that immediately provide ways of attuning themselves to situations—not always bad states to inhabit. Active responses, in contrast, are those where the self-conscious ego plays a foregrounded role in shaping the attitude and controlling the manner by which the attitude gets enacted.

Seen this way, the distinction between passive and active loses all of the normative force it has traditionally exerted. If we are to restore that force on a different basis, we have to show how our ways of expressing the relevant attitudes sustain or fail to sustain a range of second-order investments. Our judgments have initially to bracket concerns about what agents understand in order to explore the degree to which agents treat the expression as an articulation of their capacities to give values to their situations. Even the most blind passion can sustain a second-order investment: "I know I am madly jealous but I cannot give up on my passion until some revenge is realized." But not every second-order investment will stand up to subsequent analysis without producing shame or guilt. And on many occasions we in retrospect explicitly disavow the endorsements we made under such emotions—sometimes because our understanding changes, but other times because we simply do not want to identify with the way we acted, even if our specific understanding of the cause of the emotion has not changed. We tend to use expressions like "that was not me" or "I promise to be different in the future."

If we are to rely on second-order states, we have to establish a means of distinguishing between these problematic endorsements and those producing identifications we continue to embrace. The first step is to find a different terminology for the fundamental opposition between emotions that control us and emotions we more or less control. I propose we handle this by distinguishing between emotions we find we can endorse as significant for our senses of ourselves and those we find embarrassing or threatening to those senses. We make quite different kinds of endorsements, ranging from what Silvan Tomkins stresses as interest in our interests to the full-fledged taking of responsibility by identifying entirely with one's anger or one's pride or one's sorrow. But these endorsements all seem to me to share a manifest caring that extends to the identities made possible because of what the first-order activity provides. Simple interests in our interests manifest a minimal identification that establishes our having particular cares and investments. The case gets more complex when that caring extends to how these investments reflect our qualities as agents. The most elaborate of these endorsements involves the self-conscious taking of responsibility for how we act in relation to what we feel. The expression of responsibility indicates that the agent accepts being in this state and basing the action on a particular account of his or her investments. And this taking of responsibility binds the agent to responding to public judgments about the manner in which the emotions get expressed.

In my view, the most important value emotions afford consists in the kinds of identification they allow. But we still have to distinguish identifications that seem appropriate from those that seem symptomatic (and hence part of the force of the emotion, rather than of the agent's engagement with the emotion). I equate symptomatic identification with attitudes that Spinoza would consider passive. These attitudes are such that they either cannot carry significant second-order valuations (except as choices to be conventional) or quickly fail when an observer tries to match the terms projected with the actual qualities performed in the expressive activity. For the first kind think of those emotions that we treat in terms analogous to those we use to describe ourselves when we are drunk or seriously distracted. (For Sartre this form of identification was the norm.) We acknowledge the activity but we claim that in various ways we were not ourselves at the time. It is more difficult to provide a formula for deciding when identifications are made but prove faulty. But one rough measure consists in what I call "retrospective observation." Attitudes successfully bear identifications when their expression persuades a competent observer that there was sufficient self-control to establish accurate self-reflexive investments.[16] We cannot provide strict criteria for making such judgments. But talk of explicit criteria seems to me inappropriate for most concerns about identification. The important issue is not clear principles for assessing behaviors but reliable means of establishing modes of conversation eliciting from agents further efforts at self-description. Recall J. L. Austin's famous quip that the only way to prove that someone in an asylum is not the famous personage he claims to be is to ask him to try being that person in a range of circumstances.

## VI. Robert Creeley's Poetry as the Drama of Second-Order Performative Value

Soon I will have a good deal more to say about identification as a second-order process. But before I do that I want to bring into the discussion some literary examples, in particular some lyrics by Robert Creeley. For I want to demonstrate how complex and subtle identification can be, and I want to dramatize as fully as I can how many of the second-order processes that go into identifications can bear substantial investments without requiring us to project ideas about character onto them or test specific beliefs. We can find intense satisfaction in identifications that rely simply on the manner of our acting and the articulate positioning of reflexive consciousness. And if that is so, we may have to adopt much more flexible notions of identity than philosophers are accustomed to use. In particular, attending to Creeley will provide a vital challenge to the impressive philosophical work on identification by Howard Kamler to which we will soon turn.

In his introduction to his volume of poetry *Words,* Creeley made explicit how intently he sought alternatives to traditional notions of character and self-knowledge:

> Things continue, but my sense is that I have at best, simply taken place with that fact. . . . So it is that what I feel, in the world, is the one thing I know myself to be, for that instant. I will never know myself otherwise. Intentions are the variability of all these feelings, moments of that possibility. How can I ever assume that they come to this or that substance? (*Quick Graph,* 261)

But such prose takes on its full resonance only in relation to the poetry that sponsors it. My first example of this poetry presents Creeley at his most minimalist, where the distinction between activity and passivity seems as crucial as it is ineffable. This is all of Creeley's "The Souvenir":

> Passing into the wilderness of twisted trees,
> below the goats and sheep look up at us,
> as we climb the hill for our picnic
> years ago.
>
> (*Collected Poems,* 197)

By introducing temporal contrasts the last line turns the visual scene into a memory and in so doing charges that scene with second-order implications. On the most fundamental level, we have to ask why the speaker defers that information. Moran can help here: deferral makes the physical perspective

Creeley occupies less important than his specific investment in the scene. Because "years ago" flows so fluidly out of what seems a present tense, the poem invites us to treat this speaker as someone obsessed by this memory. (Notice how the poem also suspends its syntax so that modifications get resolved only in the third line when the poet settles on the cause of his obsession.) Yet this is not just any obsession. The poem's tautness defines the speaker as both trapped by this memory and willing to recall it in its purest, most tormenting form. Because the speaker seems to will that this scene persist in his memory, he occupies the position of the goats and sheep, literally and figuratively fixated on what recedes from their world.

Creeley's brilliance consists in his tying the pathos of the situation so closely to the specific manner in which its elements unfold. And by doing that he brings to the foreground two significant second-order features of this experience. On the dramatic level, the poem provides a compelling example of why we have to be able to distinguish mastering emotion from being mastered by it. The only possible identification for this speaker is with the structural roles played by the goats and the sheep. In his world as in theirs, the only action possible is observation, and the only affect possible is frustrated distance from unrealized possibilities. And the compression of the poem makes this condition seem utterly inescapable, as if the poet had encountered the fundamental necessities of unresolved longing. No wonder the identifications involved can be as understated as they are absolute.

Yet if we deal with this poem only as a dramatic event, we ignore the second-order possibilities given by its status as a carefully wrought artifact. On the level of artifact, all of the devices that heighten the pathos seem to be capable of taking on other affective registers. For the sequence presents not only a memory but a specific and highly self-conscious way of dealing with this memory as well as with those it might represent. And as a deliberately written work the text brings to bear quite different identifications than does the scene that is rendered. The poet's second-order identification is not with the sheep and the goats but with what he manages to achieve by this specific manipulation of the resources of language. Here the relevant first-order states become every gesture that intensifies and sharpens the dramatic rendering, especially the crafting of beautifully balanced syntactic and sound units. (Creeley's making the concluding short phrase seem equal in weight to the longer lines is an especially impressive achievement.) The artifice is not just the exercise of craft at its finest. It is also a manner of coming to terms with the very idea of the kinds of loss that bind us to the sheep and the goats. But by his manner of enacting the attitude the poet constructs a quite different set of identifications. The poem calls attention to its accomplishment in negotiating such awareness with none of the self-pity we find in Arnold's quite similar situation. Perhaps only an identification with this bare sense of structural relations will allow coming to terms with both the necessity of loss and the necessity of obsession without softening or evading either.

Creeley's "Joy" deals with almost the same affective phenomena, but this time with more pronounced emphasis put on the second-order identification between the poet and the work the poem does:

> I could look at
> an empty hole for hours
> thinking it will
> get something in it,
>
> will collect
> things. There is
> an infinite emptiness
> placed there.
>
> (350)

Here feeling oneself coming to satisfaction as a subject does not demand any particular narrative or image of one's character; nor does it rely upon what might be considered any kind of uplifting vision. It requires only managing to appreciate the difference between being the one placed and having the intentional force to control the placement process.[17] Initially the poem presents thinking as a separate order of being from that of the empty hole. Thinking observes from the point of view of the "I," casting the hole by contrast as a figure of need and enforced passivity. But the slight shift to "There is" seems to me to bring with it a substantial change in affective possibilities. The poem moves from the subjunctive and the subjective to an impersonal or transpersonal figure of transparency. So the speaking consciousness need not just project into the world correlates of its own emptiness. Instead, its own activities can be aligned with space rather than time, so that the emptiness is not just received but realized as a certain kind of accomplishment. Emptiness is given its force by an intentional presence now becoming fully aware of the roles it can play.

Creeley's linking lineation with breath units defines just what kind of an affective accomplishment placement is. Placement becomes a fundamental means of lyric concentration. Almost every line ends with a pronounced incompleteness, hovering between a predicate expression and some possible object. We have to take the pauses as marks of anxiety, each expressing an urgency to see emptiness somehow filled and each frustrated by a beyond to the order of things that produces the feeling of emptiness. But negotiating emptiness here also dramatizes on the most intimate levels how it might feel to experience the kinds of satisfactions that occur when intentional dispositions hook onto what they seek. Each suspended emptiness stages possibilities for a sense of arrival—not as large dramatic realization, but as simple intensifying of the mind's apparently finding places for its energies. Forming beliefs and images proves far less important than tracking how the poet as desiring animal continually reorients the dispositions enabling him to inform desire with consciousness without displacing it into interpretations about desire.[18] The basic ambition driving the poems is not for the self to gather itself in heroic expressive acts, but for it to feel itself able to make all the turns and twists necessary to stay connected with where thought and speech might lead it.

As should be obvious, I could look at Creeley for hours. But I will confine myself to one more example, this time attending to what may be Creeley's most intense rendering of second-order investments that manage to escape the projection of idealized self-images. "The Figures" is very much in the spirit of Moran's essay because it explores the degree to which the writing of poetry can also be an act of will in the real world. The reality consists in how the resources of "so" absorb the self within the matter of manner:

> The stillness
> of the wood,
> the figures formed
>
> by hands so still
> they touched it
> to be one
>
> hand holding one
> hand, faces
> without eyes,
>
> bodies of wooden
> stone, so still
> they will not move
>
> from that quiet
> action ever
> again. Did the man
>
> who made them find
> a like quiet? In
> the act of making them
>
> it must have been
> so still he heard the wood
> and felt it with his hands
>
> moving into
> the forms
> he has given to them,
>
> one by singular
> one, so quiet,
> so still.
>
> (245; cf. 371)

Because utter simplicity is so central to this poem's figuring of satisfaction, extensive critical commentary would be more of a violation than it ordinarily is. Therefore I will only indicate what I take the structure to be and explore briefly how the final lines expand the possibilities for identification implicit in the grammar of "so." The poem progresses through three states of awareness—first of the wooden figures themselves, then of how the maker might have found "a like quiet," and finally of how the poet himself can take on a version of the maker's state. Correspondingly, the opening "so's" serve primarily as adverbial intensifiers evoking for the stillness a sense of its power to compel attention. When attention shifts to the maker, "so" takes on the additional force of mapping the equivalences by which the artist feels his way into the forms he has composed. Now it seems as if the adverbial qualities indicated by "so" take on a psychological force drawing the poet into the artist as the artist is drawn into his own creation, encountering it as an extension of his own charged body. Imaginative motion literally composes the stillness within which the artist hears the wood and appreciates what form can make out of temporal contingency.

In the last stanza, the speaker identifies completely with the artist. The shift in focus is subtly but clearly marked by the way a third aspect of "so" now seems to hover over the scene. This is the "so" of "so be it," the ultimate expression of will aligned with what the world makes available. Will need not represent itself to itself in the figure of some graspable human identity. Willing too becomes part of the play of forces and causes organized within this particular manifestation of caring. The manner of the artist's making elicits this mode of reflection. And making the mode of reflection articulate proves sufficiently powerful to sustain an act of affirmation apparently aligning the artist to a form of thinking suddenly taking on force for him. The speaker avows a responsibility that is not to any abstract principle but simply to the particular attunement he manages to realize. The particularity of the event may prove to be precisely what it takes to make intelligible differences in how the speaker goes on to pursue his own art. It certainly raises the possibility of producing a more powerful identification than any idea about art or about himself that the speaker is likely to develop.

## VII. On Howard Kamler's *Identification and Character,* or Why Identification Need Not Be Bound to Ideal Egos

In this chapter I first proposed a case for describing emotions in terms of how they adverbially modify agency. Then we took up the question of what kinds of satisfactions we might find within these adverbial states. The richest of these satisfactions turn out to involve the second-order identifications we can make because of who we see ourselves becoming in those states. Now I want to clarify what I see involved in this identification process. How can we carry over into philosophy the senses of value that pervade the second-order states Creeley makes so compelling? Can we find conceptual means of resisting the tendency to see identification as the bringing to our manners of acting cogent and compelling images of ourselves as single coherent characters? Can we speak meaningfully about identification and still focus on multiple identities, divided up among a variety of manners that taken together constitute a life? These questions circulate around the need to clarify how much latitude we can give the concept of identification before it no longer provides significant information linking what we observe to enduring traits we associate with character and with responsibility.

Howard Kamler's *Identification and Character: A Book on Psychological Development* can take us a long way toward answering these questions.[19] Kamler provides very useful terms for clarifying just how identification takes place. And he proves even more helpful because of his manifest struggles to reconcile a Nietzschean view of identification with some kind of grounding that enables the identifications to be judged and applied. I want to use his terms to suggest that we do not need the notion of character basic to his account because identification can remain a flexible process linked to the manner of our actions.

Kamler argues that if we are to understand identification we have to begin with a sharp distinction between our experiencing a state and our identifying with it. Identifying requires two activities—self-reflexively attempting to own our behavior and finding a way to attribute the behavior to what makes us distinctive characters. Moreover, the attribution cannot be only a matter of recognizing how some trait fits with what one postulates is one's character. Identification is in part a constitutive "psychological process of internalizing features of the world." The features are not aspects of identity until they become internalized and so part of what we refer to when we refer to ourselves as selves (21).

In making this case Kamler walks a thin wire. On the one hand he offers strong arguments that identification presents us with a version of the self that has to be seen as made rather than as found.[20] But then he has to find a means of showing why specific identifications take hold and others do not—no easy task. Not surprisingly he handles the first part of this case better than he does the second. Kamler argues that the very process of making identifications shows how we need not base our sense of self on some fundamentally given substance. Rather than speak of "self" at all and risk substantializing subjectivity, he prefers to speak about how we establish and recognize a sense of "who-ness" for individuals:

> It is about a choosing of how to be, a choosing of which traits to identify as oneself. A person sees traits in the world that he would like to have as his own. As an identifier he chooses them to be part of who he is. And in that special kind of identificatory choosing, he succeeds in actually having these traits constitute his character. In choosing these traits he takes psychological ownership of them. (22–23)

Identification is a matter of being willing to take responsibility for the identities so constituted. But if we are always making selves rather than discovering them, how then do we know there is any identity at all that informs our identifications? In response to this question Kamler relies heavily on the second-order quality of owning or disowning what the manner of our expressions makes present. Then he can argue that while we cannot locate a particular substantial self, we can locate positing specific characteristic manners of acting that keep our identifications from seeming to be creations out of the void. If the formation of character takes place as second-order activity, our identificatory choices have a supporting context. These choices are constantly called for by our need to take up a stance toward our own intensities and the relations they establish with the world. Referring to our histories of producing identifications provides a measure of which decisions we go on to make are likely to be in our best interest.

I think we do not have to be so eager to find principles of continuity. Despite all his resistance to substantializing the self, Kamler seems to me ultimately to rely on an insufficiently flexible notion of identification. He postulates only two basic ways that agents establish values for themselves—"brute valuations" and "ultimate valuations." Brute valuations are the means by which individuals set the terms for what will count as value. And ultimate valuations bring to bear on choices a sense of the agent's own ideal character: "In choosing to embody certain valued traits as one's character—in choosing them as standards by which one wants to live and grade his life—a person chooses those traits as having a kind of perfection about them. . . . In choosing about character one just is positing a trait as having *total value* for himself" (179). Our "character evaluations" then become "of ultimate value" because "they define the standards for what we see as good." Hence "only through their creation can goodness in life ever be part of a person's experience" (181).

Now, however, the idea of character is providing just the sense of substance that Kamler claims to reject. One refers to one's ideal character as a kind of criterion for deciding what standards will count for our evaluations. I do not see why such criteria have to play a central role in the identification process. Identification need have no reference point beyond the specific mode of activity toward which one takes a second-order attitude. For identification is not a process of comparing states to see which ones actually belong to me. It is more like a process of extending the self by deciding that this mode of activity engages me to take responsibility for it because of who I become during the time I am engaged in it. We can surprise ourselves by finding particular manners of acting eliciting a second-order evaluation based simply on how we feel ourselves modified by the occasion, no matter what our vision of character. This is not to say that we do not make the kinds of identifications Kamler describes. Nonetheless I do want to argue that we do not have to take the idealizing step he proposes simply in order to develop identifications. Some of the time we identify because we are choosing against what we think our character is—say by suddenly realizing that we want to attach ourselves to some standard set of cultural expectations. I might decide that I was wrong in attempting to teach a certain way and instead take on practices that my colleagues exemplify. Or I might observe myself restraining anger for purely practical reasons and find myself wanting to retain that mode of acting. Or I might find myself deeply moved by some work of art and decide that I want to explore the possibilities of that attitude by committing myself to a particular course of study or changing my habits.

Character is involved in such choices, but not as their source. Experiences of value are almost as likely to modify character as a sense of character is likely to shape what counts as significant value. By ignoring this, Kamler misses two important theoretical possibilities afforded by an emphasis on second-order investments. First, because the object of our investment is concrete, we often do not rely on any explicit criteria in order to identify with certain states that we consider valuable. Identification need not depend on classical forms of judgment. We can endorse a state and treat it as continuous with our sense of self simply because of the satisfactions that emerge as we carry out an activity. Even when the endorsement becomes the taking of responsibility, we need not derive the responsibility from specific criteria. It is enough that we find ourselves wanting to be represented by our caring about a particular state and the social relations it entails. There are, of course, also situations where we do rely on something like principle, situations where we base taking responsibility on an overall reflection about our most important goals and what it takes to pursue them. But the very importance of such situations indicates how rare they are and how often we rely on quite different modes of identification.

The second theoretical possibility follows closely. Because we make identifications in such various ways, we have to maintain a flexible notion of how we make investments in our emotional states. As we saw in speaking about responsibility, there are occasions when we have to take identification in the most comprehensive sense: our sense of character must include in a loosely hierarchical order the full range of our investments and the basic principles on which we make evaluations. But most of the time we are free to cultivate various identities without worrying very much about how they can be integrated (so long as the lack of integration does not become debilitating). In such cases we are not establishing ultimate values; we are simply attaching our sense of identity to particular ways of acting or responding to others. I rarely have to link my identities as professor with my identities as an aging athlete with my identities as a member of civic organizations. Most of my activities can be seen as simply exploring where these various selves lead me and testing what becomes valuable because of those explorations. In fact, it seems to me somewhat pathologically narcissistic to demand that there be one single character persisting through all these identifications. Clearly there will be continuities, but they will be more like shifting family resemblances than well-defined structures. Analogously, most of our actual investments in identities do not form definable units within specifiable structures. Rather, they emerge as loose webs of connections that depend on circumstance and need. We are free to explore our emotions while letting our sense of character take on various forms and intensities.

## VIII. Spinoza's *Conatus* and the Ontology of Manner

Now I face a problem similar to the one I attributed to Kamler. By being so loose about identification I may have cheapened the concept and deprived it of any capacity to explain commitments. So I have to address the question of whether there can be an overview that brings my emphasis on manner into conjunction with a feasible notion of how human beings make and weigh investments, especially the second-order investments that constitute identification. My initial temptation was to deny that we need or can find such a basic and encompassing theoretical perspective. But suppose we loosen the standard so that the overview is not something we have to defend on empirical grounds, but something that provides speculative guidance by clarifying how various claims from agents might fit together in a way that constitutes plausible representations of typical experiences. I think I can meet this demand by turning now to Spinoza's treatment of conative energies because his thinking provides the best framework I can find for bringing the various concerns of this chapter together.[21] Spinoza shows why an emphasis on manner makes a concern for realization fundamental to human behavior; he provides a powerful way for characterizing what is at stake in expressive activity; and he lucidly establishes identification as the basic source of the satisfactions we find in our affective states.[22] Finally, because Spinoza's thinking is constantly focused on the nature and quality of satisfactions (and frustrations) resulting from the conative directedness of our emotional lives, he takes us beyond description to a concern for the teleological principles giving purpose to expressive behavior and the flexible identifications we make through it.

If we are to bring a Spinozan framework to bear on our reflections about manner, we have to review briefly Spinoza's efforts to place expressive activity and processes of identification within a comprehensive and dynamic framework sharply opposed to Cartesian thinking. Descartes notoriously separated extended substance from thinking substance, so that what mattered was to get right the forms of certitude distinctive to our mental lives. Spinoza saw that the Cartesian model locked us into a static duality: mind's empirical role was to mirror extended substance, and its sense of its own activity apart from matter led directly to a world of abstract principles. Either the mind provided pictures of facts or it pursued its own powers in endless self-reflexivity. Spinoza wanted to put the dynamic energies of the mind within the actual world. Just as the mind is the idea of the body, not an idea about the body, thinking itself could seek to be the mind of the world in its becoming, not a mind seeking to represent the world.[23] Therefore Spinoza did not idealize description, but concentrated on the modes of identification that become possible when one sees one's world in coherent causal terms.

To defend these changes Spinoza had to develop an alternative to Descartes's fundamental separation of the world into two substances, extended matter and the power of thought. So he recast ontology in terms of only one substance. Then all differences become matters of how attributes of substance take modal form:

> Matter is everywhere the same, and there are no distinct parts in it except inso-far as we conceive matter as modified in various ways. Then its parts are distinct, not really but only modally. For example, we conceive water to be divisible and to have separate parts in so far as it is water, but not in so far as it is material substance. (42)

Acts of mind become themselves modes of substance (not representations of substance) because they give it vivid manifest qualities. Value inheres in how particulars are composed: "Particular things are nothing but affections of the attributes of God; that is, modes wherein the attributes of God find expression in a determined and determinate way" (49). As Deleuze would later emphasize, Spinoza gives us a world in which expression is not only a psychological activity but the fundamental force in the emergence of all being.

I would love Spinoza just for the alternative to epistemic thinking that this ontology provides. But his perspective also makes at least three contributions to our appreciating the satisfactions and identifications we produce within our affective lives. First, in Spinoza articulation, and hence realization, is a central value as an end in itself. The more vividly we spell out what constitutes a modal state, the more fully we participate in the unfolding of substance. For Descartes, the ultimate work of mind is securing representations of extended substance or of the mind's own powers. For Spinoza, realization is more important than representation because aspects of the world are continually emerging. And we best engage them by treating them as unfoldings of possibility that seek articulation. We need reason and causal explanations. But such intellectual work is not aimed simply at picturing the world. Rather it is aimed at loving the world because of the structures of determinate passionate relationships in which we come to see ourselves participating. Explanation itself is charged with affect and with second-order possibilities of appreciating how one positions oneself in such activity—hence the ultimate importance of the intellectual love of God. Just as the mind is the idea of the body, dynamic reason is the immanent idea of the world. And all our efforts at articulation contribute to this fundamentally immanent sense of powers giving our world its reflective intensities.

Spinoza's second contribution is more concrete. Because he is so concerned with realization as a dynamic process, he pays considerable attention to the kinds of satisfaction individuals gain by performing expressive acts; so he thickens what we can claim about identifications. In fact his entire psychology turns on such satisfactions. For he postulates as "the essence of each thing," not just of each person, a *conatus* that "as far as it can, and as far as it is in itself, . . . endeavors to persist in its own being" (109). Negatively, each individual is driven by the effort to resist all the factors "that can annul" the sense of individual existence for itself. Positively, the conative aspect of a being is most visible in a being's affective states. For it is the affects that constitute the body's basic awareness of how its conative forces are deployed. The affects are constantly registering the degree to which "the body's power of activity is increased or diminished, assisted or checked, together with the ideas of these affections" (104). If we consider the conatus in terms of passive relations to external causes, we see that pain is "what diminishes or checks man's power of activity" and hence what registers "the passive transition to a state of lesser perfection" (126). Pleasure, on the other hand, is the experience of an increase of activity and hence of "the passive transition of the mind to a state of greater perfection" (111). Given this primacy of desire, Spinoza adds, "We do not endeavor, will, seek after, or desire because we judge a thing to be good. On the contrary we judge a thing to be good because we endeavor, will, seek after, or desire it" (110).

Pleasure then is both exhilarating and dangerous. We feel ourselves capable of composing the spaces through which our desire moves, and we feel capable of pursuing what seems to us good. But we need reflection in order to determine which of these movements are in fact in accord with our nature and which imposed upon us. Because there is no escaping our conative processes, there have to be different qualitative ways of distinguishing among them. Otherwise there could be no way of setting the active against the passive, and no way of developing idealized possibilities for these conative energies. In other words, Spinoza needs to build into these conative processes a possibility for the exercise of some kind of judgment, yet he also has to avoid Cartesian and Kantian visions of judgment as having third-person force. For Spinoza the principle of judgment cannot come from the outside—cannot come as Law imposed by some other based in rationality or authority. There have to be possibilities of judgment that are immanent features of our conative affects.

Spinoza finds the appropriate principle by postulating a conatus distinctive to the mind: "The mind endeavors to think only of the things that affirm its power of activity" (136). I think the result provides the basis for a very appealing speculative view of how second-order identification can work as a feature of our affective lives:

> Man knows himself only through the affections of his body and their ideas. . . . When therefore it happens that the mind can regard its own self, by that very fact it is assumed to pass to a state of greater perfection, that is, . . . to be affected with pleasure and the more so the more distinctly it is able to imagine itself and its power of activity. (136)

Mind expands the space through which the body moves in its efforts at perfection. At one pole this expansion takes place because the imagination fosters images we reach out to desire;[24] at the other pole, it takes place by the work of active intellect bringing the body into the realm of determining causes. Identification is not just naming a process one's own. It is also testing how conative energies can be maintained and extended when we bring second-order considerations to bear on the spaces opened by our manners of acting. Some identifications prove problematic because they trap conative energies in contradictions or prevent them from reaching through the range actually available. If I want to foreground a specific emotion I feel as fundamental to me, I could find myself unable to identify with contrary ones that are in fact more central to my basic orientation. Or I could reduce my identity to its ugliest or angriest components. Other identifications enable conative energies to push out into entire fields of possible satisfactions. Think of what happens when one takes on a professional identity or moves to a new place or tries out a new path for understanding one's own investments. Or, more concretely, imagine coming to a richer understanding of how one typically assumes jealous attitudes and performs the actions these generate. The better one understands the causes, the richer one's sense of the density and scope of what one realizes has to be confronted. All of those affective investments become available for affective reconfigurations, either as possible willed identifications or as possible sources of panic—am I really motivated by such banal or ugly considerations?

Because he can keep satisfaction specific and avoid a need for recognitions in the symbolic order afforded by social relations, Spinoza can also make a third contribution to my case. He substantially modifies how we can view the individual interests at stake in our expressions in a way far more telling than his heirs' versions of conative interests. From Hegel and Nietzsche to philosophers like Solomon and Kamler, it has been a standard practice to equate conative desires with something close to a personal will to power.[25] After all, how can one know that one has achieved any kind of significant individuality if one cannot measure it in terms of how it is reflected in the subordination that it imposes on other people? To be a strong individual one must differ assertively from other persons, and for the difference to matter as identification it has to allow the person to be recognized in that difference. But for Spinoza individuation is not dependent on recognition by others. He is in no way an idealist for whom being depends on ideas about being or individuation on treating the self as a "character." Rather, for him, individuation is a matter of how a body positions itself in relation to a combination of causes and possibilities. Individuation is not a construction but a fact of how contexts take form. Ideas may facilitate those individuating positions and even extend them, but the position is a position of the body registered as such by the mind. The conative drive does not depend on some independent structure of recognitions provided by the mind. And the affect is in the condition of striving, which includes striving for articulation. So even if we fail to achieve articulation for others, the struggle to get clear on one's feelings can in itself provide significant satisfaction.

Spinoza uses this emphasis on processes rather than substances to ground this distinctive treatment of individuation:

> We thus see how a composite individual can be affected in many ways and yet preserve its nature. Now hitherto we have conceived an individual thing composed solely of bodies distinguished from one another only by motion-and-rest and speed of movement. . . . If we now conceive another individual thing composed of several individual things of different natures, we shall find that this can be affected in many other ways while still preserving its nature. . . . Now if we go on to conceive a third kind of individual thing composed of this second kind, we shall find that it can be affected in many other ways without any change in its form. If we thus continue to infinity, we shall readily conceive the whole of nature as one individual, whose parts—that is all the constituent bodies—vary in infinite ways without any change in the individual as a whole. (76)

I do not want to continue to infinity. But I do think we can rely on this way of thinking to minimize the degree to which an emphasis on conative expressivity entails a will to power specifiable in terms of character and recognition. Seen as aspects of processes, the conative drives need not be connected directly to projections about specifiable persons or even ideal egos.[26] Conativity can reside in specific individual states that seek their own perfection. There will remain many perspectives in which it matters that we attend to how agents express those conative investments. But we do not have to interpret the state in relation to the activity of a single will, with its needs to protect its own power.

In most cases expression is a matter of articulating traits, not of articulating anything as abstract as an individual person. Even the second-order identifications do not have to focus on any one constant notion of self. As I argued in relation to Kamler and can demonstrate better now, when we make identifications we are usually not involved in pursuing particular ideas about the self but seek the satisfactions available in realizing what we can develop from a particular state or practice. My interest in tennis is very important to me, but I think it has very little to do with what we might call my will to be an individual character. The basic individuation is specific to the identifications I can make with how I am playing at any given moment. My interest in teaching is more connected to my sense of character, but still the major emphasis is on how in that teaching I make articulate certain passions and through that come to inhabit the space, real and imaginary, that the teaching affords me. One can always take a more abstract view and interpret the individuation in terms of character, but that perspective does not get any closer to essential truths about how character operates within those particular practices. The abstract view simply establishes a broader context, which in turn provides some advantages and some disadvantages in appreciating how investments are pursued.

## IX. Wallace Stevens: Conative Intensities and the Pleasures of an "Exponential" Poetics

Because I am concerned primarily with how we speculate on our satisfactions, it seems to me appropriate to close with Wallace Stevens's version of these identification processes. He does not directly evoke Spinoza, although with his interest in all things genealogical in relation to his Dutch ancestry he might be very pleased with the identification. (That Spinoza was Jewish might have made Stevens uncomfortable, but that puts us in another story.). Like Spinoza, Stevens realizes on the most concrete level how we can imagine forms of satisfaction and identification in the manner of our affective lives without having to submit these satisfactions then to ideas about our character or place them in social struggles for overt recognition. So Spinoza's range of conative intensities becomes for Stevens the pleasures possible when we let an "exponential" poetics serve as the vehicle by which the poet speaks for the lives of other people. Not only does Stevens provide a psychology of second-order investments that shows how little questions of "self" need to enter the picture, but his notion of the exponential also shows how second-order affective states make possible a complex range of intricate and intimate satisfactions.

Let me pick up Stevens's career in the mid 1930s as he tried to understand how his imagination might possibly make a difference in a world desperately in need of political change. While he recognized that need, he also quickly and painfully realized that his own talent for luscious abstraction turned into banal rhetoric when he attached it to specific political agendas. So he had to find a way of convincing himself, and perhaps his audience (or of convincing his audience and perhaps himself), that there was another level of imaginative activity addressing not our beliefs but our orientation toward belief. Rather than project any single practical ideals or forms of heroism, poetry might explore how we can continue to believe in the very idea of idealization. However, that exploration could be worth pursuing only if the process of idealization could be rendered at so intimate a level that it shaped our most fundamental affective states. Poetry had to empty itself of the idea of the poet as expressive hero in order to locate a site of identifications fundamental to the very processes of common life and hence to what we might recognize in one another:

> The validity of the poet as a figure of the prestige to which he is entitled, is wholly a matter of this, that he adds to life that without which life cannot be lived, or is not worth living, or is without savor, or in any case, would be altogether different from what it is today. Poetry is a passion not a habit. This passion nourishes itself on reality. Imagination has no source except in reality, and ceases to have any value when it departs from reality. Here is a fundamental principle about the imagination; It does not create except as it transforms. There is nothing that exists exclusively by reason of the imagination, or that does not exist in some form in reality. Thus reality = the imagination, and the imagination = reality. Imagination gives, but gives in relation. (*Letters of Wallace Stevens,* 364)

Stevens wrote this in a 1936 letter. At about the same time, he was working on *The Man with a Blue Guitar* in order to make concrete this radical break from the then prevailing ideas of imagination. Stevens would have nothing to do with the views that imagination realizes a distinctive content, symbolically charged with visionary meanings or composed to produce moral effects. For him the imagination could affect our values not by altering what we see but by modifying how the relations we forge with experience come to carry value for us. Correspondingly, he was experimenting with how poetry could replace an emphasis on the character informing expressive acts by turning instead to an emphasis on the satisfactions afforded our conative interests by the situations that engage them. Perhaps the poet's temptations toward solipsism could then be reconciled with our deepest concerns for sociality because the poetry could become sufficiently abstract to define intimate levels of relational feelings we share with each other even when we pursue quite diverse content. And perhaps the poet might find specific linguistic resources for bringing to the foreground how these second-order feelings within writing might intricately color the world without displacing it into metaphor.

The first step would be to replace an emphasis on the poet as heroic sensibility with attention to the relational play of a casual guitar:

> The man bent over his guitar,
> A shearsman of sorts. The day was green.
>
> They said, "You have blue guitar,
> You do not play things as they are."
>
> The man replied, "Things as they are
> Are changed upon the blue guitar."

> And they said then, "But play you must,
> A tune beyond us, yet ourselves,
>
> A tune upon the blue guitar
> Of things exactly as they are."
>
> > (*Collected Poems*, 165)

Rather than establish the significance of the guitar player by dramatically placing him in a situation, Stevens identifies with the improvisational mode characterizing his music. Satisfaction is not a matter of realizing plans or expressing character. Satisfaction is at once more intimately conative and more fluidly relational. The player has to locate his affective interests in the very forces establishing his sense of power. His identity in relation to these forces depends on his managing, on the one hand, to register what his instrument makes possible and, on the other, to articulate his efforts to attune himself to the needs and the demands of his audience. The poem's "meaning" becomes its reflection through thirty-three sections on how its moods and modes correlate the "composing of senses of the guitar" (*Collected Poems*, 68) to the audience's need to appreciate what it brings to things becoming as they are. And the most important of these senses of the guitar turns out to be what the poet manages to establish as the self-reflexive capacities brought into play by the almost magical linguistic operator "as." Just this simple passage offers a powerful contrast between the epistemic "as" governed by descriptive ideals and the modal "as" acknowledging and celebrating the modifications subjects bring in giving the world the status of reality for them. This second "as" links the flux of appearance to the constant permutations feelings bring, and it establishes a relation term through which we can formulate second-order appreciations of the differences these feelings make.[27] The poem fleshes out what can be involved in identifying with the movements of the guitar as a mode of reflection.

For Stevens's full virtuoso playing on the "as" we have to go directly to the poem's climactic section, which focuses on the intricate tasks that the "as" performs in such balancing acts. Here "as" brings into play the conative force of our elemental and intimate feelings for how we make adjustments to specific situations. *As* these feelings explore ideas for possible intensity, they also make possible identifications specifying who we become *as* we reflect on where those ideas position our sensibilities:

> I am a native in this world
> And think in it as a native thinks,
>
> Gesu, not a native of mind,
> Thinking the thoughts I call my own,
>
> Native, a native in the world
> And like a native think in it.

It could not be a mind, the wave
In which the watery grasses flow

And yet are fixed as a photograph,
The wind in which the dead leaves blow.

Here I inhale profounder strength
And as I am, I speak and move

And things are as I think they are
And say they are on the blue guitar.
(*Collected Poems,* 180)

The initial positioning here is tonally quite complex. The speaker repeats the claim to be a native so many times that we cannot but wonder what anxieties drive him. To insist on being a native is probably to expose oneself as an immigrant or an exile terrified that one's "I" is "merely a shadow" (169) before a world that exceeds it. The desire to be a native seems then to stem from a strong sense of being alienated from substance, and hence to be constantly fighting a fear of death. The poem's task is to make adjustments that grant the impossibility of achieving traditional ideals of becoming native while still affording grounds for making long-standing identifications. Being native has to become the process of constant adjustment to shifting conditions that is exemplified in the final two stanzas. We cannot stop asking where "here" is. But we also have to learn that an adequate answer to the question can no longer hold out the old promises of identity. "Here" has initially to be defined negatively. "Here" is the place for sensibility won by reflecting on one's distance from all that cannot be mind. When we make that adjustment, or, better, *as* we make that adjustment, we become capable of recognizing that the only enduring native site is the fact of our mortality. Yet through that negative we also encounter the possibility of a "profounder strength." The identifications we can make will depend on how we bring "as I am" to things "as I think they are and say they are on the blue guitar." If we can do this, we can understand being a native from the inside, that is, from the modal role of inhabiting the world as natives might. Being a native is not an attribute linked to place, not an echo of William Carlos Williams, but an attribute basic to a particular sense of intimacy. This intimacy is best captured by poetry when it makes the reader's acts of self-definition part of the very process of taking a place in place. Ultimately, that stationing of the reader then introduces second-order possibilities for affirming that which makes us accept such limitations.

I find the "as" so satisfying a resource for working out identifications because it not only indicates the importance of manner but also enables us to register the degrees of intensity made possible by second-order conative identifications with how we speak and think. It would take Stevens some years to work out this implication, but when he did he offered the bold idea of treating the entire process of poetic self-reflection as an exponential one, a description that I think would have deeply pleased Spinoza:

> The major abstraction is the idea of man
> And major man is its exponent, abler
> In the abstract than in his singular.
>                         (*Collected Poems,* 388)[28]

Major man is our fiction of our own fullest self-satisfactions. And because those satisfactions must include an idea of themselves, major man is abler in the abstract than in his singular. The good news is that for major man that abstract is also inseparable from singularity, most pronouncedly as the vehicle for identifications that do not require reaching beyond our thinking processes to shadowy images of selves we think we are or want to become. Poetry need not build up idealizing notions of its subject matter because it can put all its energies into how this individual expounding takes place. Rather than build make-believe worlds, poets need be concerned only with the making of a "vivid transparence" (*Collected Poems,* 380) that quickens our appreciation of what our relations to the world make possible. Exponential poetics does not depend on metaphors that propose interpretations for events or desires; rather it focuses attention on specific intensities and related senses of empowerment that the poem makes available for an engaged reading. The abstraction necessary for a philosophical poetry exists not in the ideas but in the scope of the direct thinking by which the exponential stance engages its subject. And because the magnification of intensities depends on simple expoundings, our senses of empowerment come with an inescapable social horizon. We are bound to each other through the qualities of expounding that our language can produce.

It is relatively easy to speculate on the exponential force of "as" as a second-order operator. As we become aware that our sensibilities are disposed in a certain way, that awareness feeds back into the sensibility and makes possible more intense endorsements or willings of the person one is in fact becoming. But it is much more difficult to make lyric poetry actually demonstrate this process in motion while refusing to allow itself the forms of intensity produced by dramatic illusions. In my view Stevens most fully realizes these possibilities in the following passage from "Examination of the Hero in a Time of War." And in doing that he offers a powerful demonstration of how feeling can establish evaluative identifications that bypass the entire edifice of argument. Notice especially how the progressive use of "as if" deploys conative sensibility:

> It is not an image. It is a feeling.
> There is no image of the hero.

There is a feeling as definition.
How could there be an image, an outline,
A design, a marble soiled by pigeons?
The hero is a feeling, a man seen
As if the eye was an emotion,
As if in seeing we saw our feeling
In the object seen and saved that mystic
Against the sight, the penetrating,
Pure eye. Instead of allegory,
We have and are the man, capable
Of his brave quickenings, the human
Accelerations that seem inhuman.[29]
(*Collected Poems*, 278–79)

The drama here is all in how we are led through different stages of thinking. Initially we are presented with sharp contrasts. After the feeling is separated from the image, a second contrast seems also to place on the feeling the burden of reconstituting those images once able to sustain the idea of heroism. Then the contrast makes the notion of image seem so remote that it must be entertained as a negative hypothetical. Perhaps the more abstract the reflection needed to maintain the idea of image, the more concrete the alternative becomes. So the poem considers itself freed to turn directly to the most proprioceptive of feelings. These feelings attach to the hero by virtue of their being engaged in the self's processes of thinking. Both the content and the form of the "as if" constructions require first seeing our seeing as itself a charged activity, then recognizing that we can work through to significant second-order feelings by refusing to let sight be consumed by its objects. Second-order feelings place the object within the frame afforded by the subject.

With feeling so abstracted, and thereby made so concretely a part of the activity of seeing, the poet can propose a clear alternative to allegory, and perhaps to a range of epistemic assumptions. Where allegory is necessary to give significance to objects of sight, the concluding lines here can locate the significant idealization simply in self-reflection on what the hypothetical emotions have brought to bear within the poem. Now the entire mode of apprehending the poem becomes a demonstration of what it claims about the hero. We can look beyond images to the feelings that we bring to them, and we can find in the quickening that occurs as we look precisely the expansiveness and sense of possible lives that make heroism possible. While the poem cannot prove that heroes exist now, it does provide self-reflexive processes helping us recognize in ourselves desires and needs which will not let us accept any lesser state. This form of heroism does not rely on assumptions about character. It depends on just the opposite set of possibilities. It depends on recognizing and on willing the fluidity of individuation and hence of identification. Heroism lives because the poet's instrument can give immediate and shareable content to large abstractions like "capable," and "human" by locating them in the quickenings that they elicit. It is these quickenings that give us the richest possible modes of identification as individuals and as social beings whose conative intensities prove here entirely shareable.

# 5 Emotions, Values, and the Claims of Reason, Part 1: Martha Nussbaum's *Upheavals of Thought and the Limits of Normative Theory*

> In short the geography of the world as seen by the emotions has two salient features: uncontrolled movement, and differences of height and depth. Think again of Proust's description of Charlus. The world of Charlus in love is compared to a landscape full of mountains and valleys, produced as if by "geological upheavals of thought"; and this differentiated landscape is contrasted with the "uniform plain of his previous unattached life where no idea stood out as urgent or salient, no evaluation jutted up above any other." . . . His new world of twisted jealous and towering love is a more agitated world, alive as it is at every moment to small movements of thought and action in a person whom he in no way controls (and who is, besides, especially inscrutable and unreliable). And yet the narrator tells us this is a world "enriched"—and enriched *by the agitation itself*. This normative conclusion remains to be examined.
>
> Martha Nussbaum, *Upheavals of Thought*

## I. Passion and Reason: A Plea for Reviving Traditional Tensions

Almost everyone who deals conceptually with the emotions has eventually to face the question of how our capacities for rationality can be correlated with our affective intensities. For our emotions to matter they have to create substantial turbulence in our lives. But for them to establish values with which we can make substantial identifications, it seems as if we have to find mental powers that enable us to control such turbulence and adapt it to the goals that shape our considered hopes for the future. Faced with that need, we seem to have only two basic options for explaining how reason enters the picture, although the options seem capable of almost infinite variation. We can assume some version of the Stoic attitude that preserves the authority and power of reason by demonstrating how the emotions are unruly and untrustworthy and how by contrast reason's capacity for self-analysis earns it hegemony. Reason deserves to drag the emotions behind as unwilling but ultimately compliant captives. These emotions deserve their fate because they are irresponsible. They take their values from fantasies where imaginary projection overvalues particulars, shapes practical interests to fit these partial projections rather than pursuing objective means of judgment, and prefers the satisfactions of the moment to the weighing of the present in relation to long-term interests and probable outcomes.

The other alternative is somehow to forge an alliance between the emotions and our rational powers along the lines pursued by contemporary cognitivism. This perspective aligns emotion with judgment rather than with fantasy since the beliefs shaping the emotions are at core beliefs about particular values. And since the emotions sustain such judgments, they are potential allies paralleling reason's ability to clarify assessments and to weigh alternatives Correspondingly, reason needs the emotions if it is to be saved from its own tendencies to rely entirely on analytic processes that in themselves cannot produce compelling ends but only specify what each alternative might involve. Examples of this logic abound, ranging from the Neoplatonic vision of the passions serving as passageways to the deeper mysteries of self-reflexive spirit to Adam Smith's treatment of the sentiments as establishing ways of knowing and of caring that instrumental reason seems bent on destroying. Speaking for the cognitivist orientation in our culture, Martha Nussbaum offers an elegant summary of why this view has ongoing appeal: "Seeing the emotions as forms of evaluative thought shows us that questions about their role in a good human life are part and parcel of a general inquiry into a good human life," an inquiry best pursued by "a liberal brand of Aristotelianism or with a flexible virtue-oriented type of Kantianism" (*Upheavals of Thought*, 11, 12).

Neither alternative, however, seems to me fully responsive to the intricacies of emotional life. The first position—let us call it the "rationalist perspective" (which carries over into Enlightenment ideals of lucid instrumental reason)—seems to provide no positive terms for those aspects of the emotions that sponsor modes of attention and of concern basic to our overall welfare. On the other hand, the second perspective—let us call it the "teleological perspective"—seems to minimize drastically the problems we encounter in making assessments of our emotions. Many of the values we project and enjoy are very difficult to correlate with the forms of generalization that reason requires if it is to take public responsibility for its judgments. If Nietzsche is at all right that emotions not only create values but become ends in themselves, then we have to grant the possibility that these ends will not seek the sanction of reason and indeed will often bind us to satisfactions that reason wants to judge in negative terms.

Perhaps reason can be brought to recognize that states like pride and anger have value for individuals because of the qualities of intensity and focus that they make available. But even then reason will not be able to assess the manner and matter in which these attitudes are displayed in relation to the agent's long-term interests or in relation to public welfare. How much pride is good for a person or a society? When does anger become so dangerous as to outweigh the sense of power it gives an individual? What comparisons can we make in order to draw necessary evaluative contrasts or to get agents to revalue their investments? And in the public sphere how do we decide whether to honor our compassion for a criminal or to yield to a public clamor for exemplary severe punishment? Our answers to these questions depend in part upon how we reason, but also upon how we are disposed to admit what counts as a reason.[1] And what constitutes disposition is in part a matter of cultural background, in part a matter of how our affective states position us in the world in relation to these concerns. That affective positioning in turn is in part a matter of biology and context, in part a matter of the degree to which we find ourselves fully engaged in and by certain attitudes. So I think the best we can do is recognize the inevitability of conflict, admit that there are incommensurable modes of assessing values involved, and hope that recognizing the incommensurable will lead agents to attempt to clarify for others why they make commitments that run counter to the other's priorities.[2] In such situations it may be rational to admit our need to depend on expressive processes for appreciating and negotiating our differences about values.

Ironically the rationalist and the teleological perspective agree that persons are somehow defective if they do not yield to the rational capacities that might be brought to bear on the emotions. But where the one envisions reason as having to control the emotion by suppressing it, the other treats reason as helping to clarify what may be good in what the emotions cast as urgent and desirable. I find neither option tolerable. For there seems to me no plausible way to show that reason should consistently have either form of authority over the affects. In fact, when philosophers give reason central roles to play in relation to the emotions, they also perforce give their own discipline and the psychological dispositions it cultivates substantial authority in shaping how we go about making the relevant judgments. So it is not surprising, but ought to remain noteworthy, that, seen from the outside at least, professional philosophers seem to secure these privileges for reason by sanitizing emotions and by underplaying what attracts us in those very features that prove problematic for rational analysis.

Philosophers are obviously not unaware of these problems.[3] But their grappling with them tends to take the form of efforts to readjust and recombine the two frameworks I have been outlining. Therefore, I think it is time to pursue the possibility of a third overall perspective for dealing with the values that the emotions project and pursue. Rather than concentrate on how we might produce a supplementary power that can make various kinds of judgments about the emotions, I want to dwell on the immanent forces within the emotions that constitute particular states as values. Therefore I propose in this chapter and the next to test the degree to which we can establish this third perspective by emphasizing conative models of value and by elaborating the expressive registers that dramatize what agents make of their investments in conativity, at times by struggling against the dictates of reason.

I cannot not begin by engaging Martha Nussbaum's recent *Upheavals of Thought*. This book seems to me the most extended and most lucid engagement we have with these issues. And those virtues also help make it an ideal text for exploring the limitations philosophers encounter when they work only in terms of the two prevailing perspectives. My next chapter will then take on the positive task of identifying specific kinds of values whose force for us does not depend on reason but emerges as an extension of conative interests and the emotion complexes that give these interests scope, focus, and social resonance. After proposing the relevant descriptions, I hope to indicate how we can pursue and assess emotion-based values by relying on operations that are for the most part internal to affective life.[4] Where norms are at stake in such cases, they emerge not from specific concepts but from exemplary scenes and agents that people can put together and modify in many different ways.[5]

In many respects my arguments will flirt with anachronism. For I hope to persuade my readers that we have to make at least a partial return to the once dominant story of passive and unruly passions intensely resistant to reason's authority. Cognitivism's failed efforts to escape that story seem ironically to force the old oppositions back upon us, at least in those situations where belief is not the primary motivator. For if beliefs are clearly not the driving force for our investments, we have to look to the full range of intentional states that motivate us, and we have to acknowledge how important imaginary or fantasy states are in that process. And then the more we have to honor the force and urgency driving this imaginary dimension, the sharper our realization that reason becomes problematic, although it often proves the more powerful need because of that problematic status. There emerges a deep gulf between what is turbulent within the emotions and what can produce shared deliberative assessments of where they might lead us.

Yet it seems that we have learned too much about what is positive in the emotions to be content with the inherited ways of dealing with this opposition, especially since these traditions vest authority in the powers of reason. I see little alternative, then, but to let aesthetics shape our view of how to handle the conflict between the two domains. There we find a long history of resisting the claims of reason in both the guises we have been considering—as an imperious judge and as Greeks bearing gifts. So we have substantial models for developing an essentially Manichean stance on the relation between reason and passion: reason and passion have to be accorded their distinctive domains—separate and equal. There will often be conflict, and much of the conflict will involve incommensurate perspectives because there is no secure shareable warrant for insisting to the agent that the conclusions of such reasoning outweigh the importance to him or her of being modified in the particular ways that the emotion affords. It is perfectly feasible to say to someone, "This passion is excessive or irrelevant from the point of view of reason, but given the likelihood that no substantial harm will be done to others, I am going to persist in it because of the sense of power it confers or because of the relations it enables me to develop with my social environment."

What then becomes of reason's conventional primacy in such matters? I have no interest in denying the central roles that various forms of reasoning do play and ought to play in our lives. My interest is only in showing that reason is not a constitutive dimension of the valuing that takes place in relation to many emotions and affective states, nor need it be the arbiter when values clash. That requires my turning to other aspects of the psyche for an account of why the values become significant for us in the first place. But recognizing the limits of reason's authority for individuals does not preclude granting it substantial regulatory authority in relation to social questions. For then our point of reference is not the psychology of emotions but the demands posed by the fact that we share a world with other people and need mutually accepted means of negotiating with them. Reason continues to matter because it has the power of spelling out articulate practices of assessment through which persons might carry out conversations on the importance of certain ends as well as on the fit between those ends and the means pursued to realize them. Even though reason cannot compel us to accept those disciplinary processes, society can compel us to do so when our emotions threaten to do substantial harm or to impose serious injustices on those with less power to pursue their projections. And our own interests can compel us to accept rational modes of assessment because those modes provide something like the default position making it possible for us to maintain identities—for ourselves and for others—as agents concerned with ethical considerations.

Yet we also have to recognize that there are other, more ethos-based, ways of establishing these identities, for example when states like courage or pride or magnanimity are at stake. What is supererogatory for reason in such conditions may be the elemental staging ground for establishing one's claim to honor a particular ethos. And there are many conditions where regulatory reason simply cannot get a hold on the conative stakes involved in our affective lives. These conditions are generated at one pole by investments that cultivate personal or cultural differences and so cannot be brought into any scheme allowing commensurate principles to be brought to bear. At the other pole, we find situations where our investments themselves are not based on reason yet have enormous importance for us. The paradigm case is our choices about whom to love and to honor precisely because the relevant considerations cannot be generalized. But this same logic applies even in quite casual modes when we find ourselves pursuing states simply because they seem to fulfill some basic interest or drive or mode of attention that gives the world distinctive qualities.

In these cases all we can do as social beings is display why we care about how the affects move us. What we value depends on our conative investments and on what can be mediated through the manners of acting that enable us to express those investments. We can seek recognition from others and offer them the same opportunities, but we have no terms by which to compel agreement about these values.[6] Or, to put the case more paradoxically, we can imagine our long-term interests requiring us not to bind ourselves too severely to analytic frameworks and modes of assessment that are often insensitive to what makes situations unique and behaviors compelling. Many possible values for us depend on our being able to pursue interests to find out where they lead, in part because our judgments may be quite different once we have let ourselves explore who we become *as* we develop new attitudes. Suppose for example that I "waste" a good part of the family fortune trying to become an opera singer, if only to win the love of another opera singer. This is clearly imprudent, but the imprudence is part of the conditions that make me feel satisfied by my passion: the passion must have some nobility if I am willing to take such risks. And the imprudence might lead me to very good reasons why the life of an opera singer is preferable to that of a tycoon. From such considerations it is not a large leap to the many forms of heroism and virtue that depend on repudiating prudence. One might say that Kantian morality is sublime precisely because it depends on a passion for reason that makes no sense to instrumental versions of rationality.

## II. Why Nussbaum? Why Now?

Now I have to stop promising and start developing arguments. And so to Nussbaum's *Upheavals of Thought*. There is just no escaping the importance of this book, so one might as well stand and fight. I almost did get away with ignoring it, since it was only when I invited a friend to lunch in order to celebrate finishing a draft of chapter 4 that I was told, with considerable suppressed glee, that Martha Nussbaum had just published a seven-hundred-page book on the emotions. My own emotions at that point seemed as complex as any I have been discussing, so they afford an initial test case for where my doubts about reason might make an appropriate entrance. Apprehension and anger and self-pity had to share the stage with an odd sense of delight and expectation because I knew enough of Nussbaum's work to realize that I would want to contend with virtually every claim she made. And I knew enough of

Nussbaum's abilities to recognize that all my own conative drives would be sorely tested. But I did not realize until reading the book what a fortunate fall my friend had prepared for me (or how useful my negative emotions might turn out to be).

A simple sense of obligation would require my taking up at length both the specifics of her analyses and her general efforts to redo cognitivist theory so as to show how it can correlate with Aristotelian eudaimonic thinking. But I found too much pleasure in the endeavor to allow me to speak only of obligation. I think Nussbaum is gloriously and influentially and usefully wrong on almost everything she says about the emotions, especially when she uses them as a means of gaining access to the power of individual works of art. So her book provides an almost ideal contrast to the claims I will be making. Not only does she attempt to open cognitivism to the complexities inherent in intentionality, she also makes a bold effort to provide strong normative assessments by bringing into play as background for these intentional states the framework of developmental psychology. This psychology provides grounds that reason can bring to bear in establishing which affective states are and are not in our interest. However, I will argue that this new framework for her teleological thinking only intensifies old problems in the enterprise of pursuing teleological accounts because it still insists on a fundamentally moralist perspective keeping intentionality subject to the authority of reason.

Because I want to root out the various ways that unwarranted idealization proves crucial in the development of Nussbaum's teleological thinking, I will have to work patiently through how she establishes the building blocks of her case. Then I will try to develop an alternative expressivist model for the values constituted within affective life because her model simply will not suffice for the texts she deals with. In my view her impatience with particularity and eagerness to find wisdom in literary texts often lead her to distort probable authorial intentions, to ignore the work style does, and to force concrete affective complexities into thematic frameworks that she can formulate in her philosophical terms. So I imagine literary texts crying out that there must be some other way to be taken seriously for philosophical discourse. And I envision myself using contrasts with her readings to formulate two arguments that I hope can serve that purpose. I will try to show that for ambitious literary texts, and not only for ambitious literary texts, many of the values the emotions constitute have to be appreciated simply in terms of what they make manifest as manners of being that individuals pursue. And I will try to show that art matters for a culture largely because particular works exemplify ways of coming to terms with the tensions and contradictions that reason passionately tries to resolve.

Finally, I want to extend the contrasts I draw to take up concerns fundamental to how we distribute authority in Western intellectual culture. My concrete claim will be that Nussbaum systematically fails to distinguish values characteristic of emotional forces from values that derive their authority from a standard generated by argument and then applied to affective particulars. But I hope to raise issues that apply to all efforts to establish normative contexts within which to judge how people act out their affective investments. Even though Nussbaum's specific views of rationality are distinctive, they share with more traditional perspectives a desire that reason retain the power to determine what is and what is not good in such activity. And, unlike most philosophers who simply assume the authority of reason, Nussbaum works very hard to establish the grounds for this overall stance. That work makes it possible for a critic to isolate specific conceptual moves that may be necessary for that task, but also that may involve serious problems in bringing the power of reason to bear. On the most general level Nussbaum seems to me so ingenious in correlating the cognitive and the psychological that just tracking this ingenuity may provide the most persuasive case I can make against the enterprise of making the emotions safe for philosophical habitation and control.

One advantage in dealing with a writer of Nussbaum's clarity, intensity, and earnestness is that one can be reasonably sure one grasps both her argument and the implications she develops from the argument. This is her characteristically strong description of how her general project will adapt the basic analysis of the emotions provided by the Greek Stoics:

> This view holds that emotions are appraisals or value judgments, which ascribe to things and persons outside the person's own control great importance for that person's own flourishing. It thus contains three salient ideas: the idea of a *cognitive appraisal or evaluation*; the idea of *one's own flourishing* or *one's important goals or projects*; and the idea of the *salience of external objects as the elements in one's own scheme of goals*. (*Upheavals of Thought*, 4)

Nussbaum is committed to making the theory of emotion much more sensitive than traditional cognitivism is to complex features of intentionality and to the qualities of turbulence fundamental to the emotions. But she also wants to preserve the roles that epistemic functions play in cognitivist accounts, so that her revised cognitivism can still explain emotions in terms of belief, establish norms for what constitutes healthy emotions, and offer therapy when necessary. By relying on Aristotelian notions of reason, she hopes to be able to criticize the excesses of modern epistemic commitments but still secure reason's authority. Because I want to challenge her use of that authority, I feel I have to work through four features of the argument that she develops to sustain these ideas—her effort to reconcile complex psychology with conventional cognitivism so that she can preserve the idea that emotions involve truth values, her use of the concept of "flourishing," her effort to back up that concept by invoking developmental psychology, and her practice in extending her normative thinking to the work of literary criticism. In each case opposing Nussbaum provides a useful means of clarifying by contrast the possible significance of the positions that I have been developing.

Nussbaum characterizes her own perspective as a "cognitive-evaluative" view because that perspective allows her "to substitute a broader and more capacious account of cognition for the original Stoic emphasis on the grasp of linguistically formulable propositions" (23). She still needs to link emotions to beliefs, but she cannot accept the cognitivist practice of treating the beliefs involved as simply thoughts about the object that cause our affective response. She wants to show instead how the relevant beliefs combine that interpretive focus "with thought of the object's salience or importance; in that sense they always involve appraisal or evaluation" (23). This cognitive-evaluative view does not require the "presence of elaborate calculation, of computation, or even of reflective self-awareness" (23). By "cognitive" she tells us she means "nothing more than 'concerned with receiving and processing information'" (23). That claim suffices for her to clarify why four basic properties of judgment make possible these evaluative appraisals. (1) The judgments we make in forming emotions are about something: they have an object or target (27). (2) The "object is an intentional object" (27): the emotion does not just point to an object but embodies an interpretation or "way of seeing" by "the person whose emotion it is" (27). (3) These emotions embody beliefs, often quite complex ones about the object. For example, anger requires beliefs about possible damage to the subject and about the state of mind of the person doing the damage. (4) The "beliefs characteristic of the emotions" are typically "concerned with value." "They see their object as invested with value or importance" (30). And "the value perceived in the object appears to be of a particular sort. It appears to make reference to a person's own flourishing" (30).

Nussbaum's basic example is the fear and grief she experienced in relation to her mother's own death. Her emotions would not have been possible without a strong sense of the value of the life her mother led. But they also would not have had the intensity they did if they did not involve her own sense of her capacities for flourishing in her own life. The values concerned with flourishing then "appear to be eudaimonistic" (31) and so to invite links with Greek eudaimonistic ethical theories:

> A conception of *eudaimonia* is taken to be inclusive of all to which the agent ascribes intrinsic value: if one can show someone that she has omitted something without which she would not think her life complete, then that is a sufficient argument for the addition of the item in question. . . . For example, an Aristotelian really pursues social justice as a good in its own right: that is why she has put it into her conception of eudaimonia. She doesn't want just any old conception, she wants the one that values things aright, in the way that a human being ought to. (32)

The connections Nussbaum forms establish a very attractive model, substantially different from the cognitivist views that I addressed earlier in this book. Now we see the possibility that cognitivist values can sustain a much more complex model of intentionality and so can show how the entire person comes into play in the experiencing of emotion. Now a refurbished cognitivism need not treat emotions as isolated, atomistic states of mind: emotions present orientations toward the world that involve agents' overall capacities for making value judgments. And now the valuing involves modes of judging that bring to bear the agent's sense of who he or she becomes by virtue of pursuing such values. Impressive as this project is, however, it seems to me to suffer from one large problem with several consequences. Nussbaum wants to make cognitivism more humane by shifting the emphasis from a reliance on propositional beliefs to the presence of evaluative beliefs, beliefs that are embodied and so fundamental to the person. This move gives her a strong basis for showing how reason should enter the picture as the vehicle by which we best carry out the evaluative processes.

Nusssbaum cannot accept treating emotions as "propositional attitudes in the classical sense" because "a crucial core" is not "detachable" from the specific situation (52n). This core involves the qualities of intentionality that make this emotional turbulence significant for a particular agent. Conventional cognitivism can deal with my anger as a judgment that someone has done me wrong and as an orientation toward acting in relation to that belief. But, as I have also been arguing, cognitivism cannot assess the various ways that I might hold that anger. It is to keep a conceptual space for such ways of holding emotions that Nussbaum insists on this "crucial core" of the emotion not detachable from specific situations. But this effort to maintain access to such intentional states and still make cognitive claims about their relations to their objects requires her to take a step backward from the conventional cognitivist position. Unable to base the cognitive aspect of emotions in the kind of belief that shapes them, she has to redefine "cognitive" so that it refers to "nothing more than" being " 'concerned with receiving and processing information' " (23). Then she tries to recoup what might be lost through this move by casting emotion as a "function of the cognitive faculties (of thought in its most general sense) rather than a non-rational movement produced in some way by cognition" (44).

This link to thought then satisfies the basic cognitivist commitment that emotions function primarily as means of understanding "what really is the case in the world." Complex intentional states need not pull against the straightforward assertiveness of belief because they manifest a kind of evaluation that has to be interpreted in the language of belief. We no longer have to treat the emotion as a conclusion from a premise. Rather we are free to make the condition of "upheaval" the agent's recognition of the emotion's relation to its object. Nussbaum's grief about her mother's death is not the result of a specific belief about her mother so much as a specific realization of the many ways that what was of great value to her is no longer available. In fact we can even claim that the "recognition is the upheaval" (45). Analogously, Nussbaum makes it possible to treat a state like anger as taking quite different shapes when one shifts from the position of righteous judge to the position of frustrated complicitor to the position of one suddenly realizing one has been betrayed, even if the relevant propositions remain pretty much the same. And she can show how conflicts among emotions are not "the battles of unthinking forces" (86) but processes of "oscillation and shifting perspective" (86) as we try to understand "what is really the case in the world" (86).

In other words, Nussbaum seems on the verge of a marvelous synthesis in which we can honor the full complexity of intentional states while preserving the access to rationality that talk of belief and cognition allows, now with rationality freed from reductive versions of believing and judging. But does the synthesis work? Will it suffice to locate the cognitive dimension of the emotion simply in its processing of information? Will linking that processing to "thought in it most general sense" secure for the emotions close affiliation with rationality? And can it suffice for a renewed cognitivism to replace propositional beliefs by the idea of "embodied evaluative beliefs"?

Ironically the best way to see where the problems lie is to treat conventional cognitivism with more respect than Nussbaum does. When conventional cognitivism treats belief as giving propositional form to affective turbulence, it provides narrow but consistent and useful ways of identifying emotions and of specifying what must be true for the emotion to be well formed. In rejecting this fundamental building block for traditional cognitive claims, Nussbaum puts the entire enterprise at risk. Her device of turning to "embodied beliefs" will not get the cognitive work done.

Nussbaum says that once we can regard the agent as bringing the cognitive into play just by processing the information, there need be no explicit belief that gives the emotion its identity. Rather, the processing itself must somehow carry the belief—hence her tight connection between attitude and belief. And once we emphasize processing information by attitudes, we can no longer quite say what the agent might actually posit as the determining existential belief. We have to locate the belief within the attitude rather than dealing with it as a specifiable conscious assertion. The relevant belief has to be embodied because it is not necessarily present in the agent's intentional stance. We even learn later in her book that the agent may not recognize what the operating operational belief is because the agent may be developmentally barred from knowing what he or she is actually feeling. Yet if one cannot locate some kind of explicit and self-conscious believing, I do not see how one can make cognitive claims for the agent or bring rationality to bear within the agent's activity. One can always bring rationality and truth concerns to bear on what an agent does, yet Nussbaum wants those concerns to be somehow aspects of the agency and hence part of flourishing. But I do not think the concept of embodied beliefs sufficiently clear to do the job. Who is to tell which are the embodied beliefs and to what degree they are embodied?

This is one of those moments in philosophy where the more sharply we perceive the need for a given concept to solve internal problems, the more wary we should be of its adequacy for addressing external realities. And the more wary I at least become of any enterprise that promises to be able to link cognitivist priorities with the complex textures of our intentional states. It seems to me more accurate to maintain a position that cognitive concerns have to emphasize how the emotion connects to the world, while intentionalist ones focus on the subject rather than the object. That position is in keeping with how conventional cognitivist theory gets its power: it is willing to subordinate subjectivity to belief so that it can emphasize only those aspects of the emotion that attach it to cognitive judgments. Then it can justify its emphases because it establishes clear cognitive links between these particular aspects of the emotion and the world. If an intentional state is heavily involved in fantasy, then a cognitivist would have to say either that the emotion fails at its cognitive chore or that it is non-sense because no proposition can be formed.

Nussbaum rightly finds this stance psychologically impoverished. But a richer psychology may well not produce a more effective cognitivism. Consider now the basic move that enables Nussbaum in effect to expand the field of the cognitive so that it contains psychological intricacy. As we have seen, she argues that one can be cognitivist simply by emphasizing how emotions process information without imposing on that information the shape that beliefs provide. Is this true? I think the processing of information cannot be significantly cognitive unless we can connect the input to some kind of output device whose activity we can assess. We also have to know what shape the processing gives to the information and how we can relate the representation to the actual conditions. Even in the simple case of fear, there must emerge some kind of representation that can provide a picture of states of affairs (however loosely one takes "states of affairs"). Dreams too process information but are difficult to treat as cognitive (unless we say that they too embody beliefs).

So Nussbaum is left with a dilemma, both halves of which she tries to occupy. Either she has to admit there are significant aspects of our emotional lives where there is too much imagining for there to be cognizing, or she has to take back with her cognitivist hand what she gave away with her phenomenologist's one. The cognitivist in her tries to blur this distinction by arguing that there is no significant difference between the attitudes that give shape to people's emotions and the beliefs they hold. But how can she then also keep foregrounded the complexity of these attitudes? Her basic response is that it suffices to talk about embodied beliefs rather than intentionally situated ones. So while the agent's attitude can differ from the agent's formulated beliefs, the attitude will express the embodied belief. However, even if one is willing to grant that such beliefs are structurally fundamental to emotions, there remains a crucial problem in how we identify their place in the emotion and the possible force they can have.

For the difficulty in such identification we need only turn to Nussbaum's effort to establish a sharp distinction between those feelings "with rich intentional content" that "do not contrast with our cognitive words perception and judgment" and those feelings "without rich intentionality or cognitive content" like bodily states that merely may accompany an emotion but are not "absolutely necessary for the emotion" (60). If this distinction works, her embodiment claim is justified. For when feelings themselves ally with activities of perception and judgment, the emotional turbulence is fundamentally part of the epistemic effort to know what is really the case in the world. To make this argument succeed, however, Nussbaum has to be able to provide some specifiable means of determining which feelings playing a part in our emotional turbulence have rich informational content and which are merely accompanying bodily states. Otherwise one cannot identify the attitude with the work of cognition. Yet it seems to me that we have to know what the emotion is before we can identify what feelings matter and which are mere accompaniments. But how do we know what the emotion is without heeding the full range of feelings involved?[7]

Conventional cognitivism could make the necessary distinction because the only feelings that matter are those connected to the identifying belief. But without such beliefs, without relying on that narrow form of intentionality, it is very difficult to make distinctions about what does and does not matter as information within intentional states. The whole point of honoring the complexity of intentionality seems to me to be acknowledging the interplay of complex levels of feeling. Nussbaum, though, claims both the transparency of clear hierarchical identifying conditions and the complexity of dense interwoven feelings. After all, since the beliefs are only embodied, they do not shape the attitude but are only revealed by it. But what then is the relation of the embodied beliefs to the feelings? I think her treatment of the feelings shows that the only way to generate even embodied beliefs is to return to the fundamental hierarchy between reason and affect that she inherits from conventional cognitivism. Either feelings are an aspect of the attitude embodying the evaluative belief, or they are banished to the status of mere accompaniment. Yet it is never clear why it is the embodied belief that trumps all the other intentional features that go into exploring feelings and shaping attitudes.

Nussbaum does not face the possibility that often what matters about feelings is the resistance they give to the terms belief provides. There is no room in her binary opposition between the essential and the merely accompanying for any significant unruliness or inchoateness to emerge. She simply cannot handle the imaginary dimension of affects that can make images as important as thoughts and projections—and defenses as fundamental as perceptions. Instead she has to know which feelings fit and which do not—otherwise the embodied belief may not be the driving force. But the more closely we look at her case, the more likely it seems that we cannot separate what is cognitive from what is projected unless we either accept propositional beliefs or turn away from intentionality to examine the emotion from the outside. In the latter case we can isolate what has cognitive possibilities within the emotion, but we do so by judging the agent's intentions, not by inhabiting what it feels like to engage the world in a certain manner. Manner is the matter lacking in Nussbaum's account of how attitudes bring values into play.

## III. The Basic Normative Arguments Posed by *Upheavals of Thought*: A Eudaimonics for the Emotions

There is a good reason why manner is lacking in Nussbaum's account. She cannot be satisfied with the complex ways intentionality is expressed because that emphasis would not produce the mode of ethical consciousness that she desires. For her the only values that seem to matter are those that are clearly presentable in the form of beliefs. Always eager to make philosophy an edifying instrument, she finds the emotions an ideal topic for elaborating such beliefs because the emotions manifestly involve energies and commitments that have no place in versions of the good developed by any kind of prudential or empirical reason. Emotions seem to involve kinds of desiring that cannot be treated simply as interests, and they seem to shape values that have no place in an empiricist psychology. Love is not just a kind of desire, and grief is not just a perturbation to be brought under control in as efficient a manner as possible. So for philosophy to appreciate the values involved, it needs something like an Aristotelian principle of reasoning that can bind our most significant experiences as subjects to the normative concerns that characterize our identities as citizens in the public sphere.

Nussbaum's distinctively normative arguments begin with the plausible claim that emotions "see their object as invested with value or importance" (30). Then she goes swiftly to the notion that the value is "of a particular sort"; she interprets that particular sort as a concern with "a person's own flourishing" (30); and she fleshes out the concept of "flourishing" by arguing that the values involved do not just produce happiness but involve eudaimonistic concerns for the goods involved (32). Emotions are linked to eudaimonistic ethics because they involve us in the pursuit of valuing "things aright, in the way that a human being ought to" (32).

A great deal hangs on this notion that emotions develop values "of a particular sort." It would be easier to claim that there are a range of values, of particular sorts, that arise because emotions do not frame situations in the same way that prudential reasoning does. For then we could rest with a series of potential phenomenological distinctions. But that approach will not get us to a strong version of normative reasoning. To reach that goal Nussbaum has to sustain two claims—that there is one significant particular feature of values distinctive to how emotions operate, and that there can be one particular preferred means of establishing and testing these values. The first task requires demonstrating that the values involved prove intractable within analytic philosophy's preferred models of reason; the second requires showing that there is in fact a feasible alternative model of reasoning enabling us to clarify how the emotions bring into play eudaimonic principles of assessment.[8] Just as she tries to have both cognition and embodiment, now she pursues linking "upheaval" by emotions with ultimately ethical modes of judgment.[9]

Nussbaum's key operator in this grand enterprise is the concept of flourishing. Emotional excitement invites our reflecting on what kind of an agent a person becomes by virtue of how he or she builds on that excitement. Moreover, because there can be a common sense of how such emotions contribute to flourishing, our understanding of that concept proves inseparable from recognizing how the relevant values can be ends in themselves. Talk of "flourishing" brings Aristotelian naturalism into the core of our emotional experience. And once there is room to talk of "flourishing," there has to be something like a eudaimonistic ethics for working out what will count as the "oughts" intrinsic to this flourishing.

But talk of "flourishing" within philosophy also requires our being able to say clearly just what flourishing consists in when emotions make possible these values of a particular sort. Nussbaum proceeds as if there were no doubt that the person as a whole flourishes. That is why the sense of flourishing makes the agent attentive to eudaimonistic imperatives to live up to our potential. Yet I distrust this connection. Nussbaum's confident move from the emotion to the person as a whole seems to me to depend on a move not unlike Descartes's derivation of the *ego* from the *cogito*. As many philosophers have pointed out, "cogito ergo sum" is true only as an assertion that cogitating takes place and so some cogitating process exists. That it is an "I" who cogitates and that this "I" somehow exists because of the cogitating are not valid inferences from the evidence. Analogously, when a person has a sense of flourishing in relation to an emotion, or in relation to the values it makes present, all one can confidently say is that the emotion flourishes or that the emotion is accompanied by a sense of flourishing. If my anger seems to fit its object, then the anger takes on an intensity and even a dignity that ennoble it. Or my love flourishes when my beloved shines in a particular way or when my attentions are reciprocated.

In both cases it is by no means clear that "I" flourish. The anger could dispose me to ignore other possible ways of dealing with the agent, and the love could trap me in a relationship that is destructive in relation to my own interests and the interests of those to whom I have obligations. Or we might say that while the conative "I" will flourish for those moments when the emotion can expand into the world, we cannot extend the welfare of that "I" to the "I" who lives by reasons and plans. And even if we could get from the flourishing of the emotion to the flourishing of particular ego states, we still would have no clear warrant to extend that sense of self so that it recognizes and responds to eudaimonistic "oughts." Instead the "oughts" have to be derived by reasoning from the experience of flourishing and then adapted to specific narratives and projections about the self. The quality of our emotions may be a reason for pursuing certain ideals of flourishing. But there is nothing within the actual flourishing that calls for such ethical conclusions. By leaping so quickly to the ethical, Nussbaum tends to ignore the range of investments we make in and through emotions, especially investments in various aspects of agency that may have very little to do with ethics. Consequently, she subordinates the expressive aspects of our manners of expression to the self-justifying stories we can tell about ourselves.

## IV. Some Basic Problems in Using a Developmental Psychology for Establishing Normative Models of Emotional Activity

This difficulty of getting from the particular intensities of emotions to the idealized roles they might play in some grand scheme of human flourishing seems to me to haunt Nussbaum's entire account. She has to reject Enlightenment ideals of reason as the grounds for such idealizations because these rely on instrumental judgments that do not sufficiently distinguish among the qualities of lives that individuals pursue. Aristotelian reasoning proves much more congenial because it can establish models of virtue and hence indicate why certain values sustain flourishing and others diminish human potential. However, one has to be wary of adapting Aristotle for contemporary culture because he relies on very general predicates about human nature that ignore our emphases on the factors making for individuation. Nussbaum faces up to this difficulty brilliantly. Rather than just speculating about human nature, she seeks the modern discipline best equipped to make reasoned conclusions about norms of flourishing for human beings. And she finds the relevant teleological framework afforded by the developmental perspective elaborated within object-relations psychology.

This perspective provides quite clear and concrete models of why certain emotions make it impossible for us to flourish, and it therefore also establishes a cogent means of determining what emotional structures are best for our welfare. Developmental psychology directly engages "normative questions" because it finds itself asking "whether there are features of the typical human child's history that make its emotions intrinsically problematic from the ethical viewpoint, and more generally from the point of view of practical rationality" (179). When we pursue this inquiry, we discover how our emotional lives are formed in large part by our having to negotiate the contrary pulls of infantile fantasies of omnipotence on the one hand and, on the other, the vulnerabilities that stem from the years we have to depend on others for virtually all of our gratifications.[10] Our emotions often express both the projection of imaginary power and the aggression and defensiveness that stem from resentment of those dependencies. Recognizing such tendencies enables us to isolate these destructive traits and encourage their opposites. Understanding factors that block development also provides a strong sense of how there can be a normative model of flourishing.

This extension of Aristotle is obviously an exciting shift in contemporary theory. But, in my view, it is also a dangerous one that brings to the surface what I find disturbing in Nussbaum's effort to build reason's functions into our affective lives. For we find her once again fudging the difference between what the emotion pursues and what might be good for the agent. She never even considers the possibility of a significant difference between recognizing what is good in and for our emotions and concluding that the emotions themselves are structured so as to pursue that good. And, more important, we find her insufficiently engaging the difference between having normative ideas about the emotions and having grounds for persuading others that the normative ideas hold for them. Civilization has by now clearly developed considerable general wisdom about what is and is not good for most human beings. But there is a huge gap between general wisdom and specific eudaimonic imperatives. General wisdom allows us to point out to someone that there are strong precedents indicating that a certain path is foolish or dangerous. But if the person gives decent reasons for pursuing that path, or if the person's manner of acting characterizes that path in a certain way, I doubt we can treat the agent as somehow at fault because he or she fails to satisfy the overall norm. The very idea of normative assessment in relation to reason tends to blind us to what individuals achieve as they work out their own quite particular ways of negotiating long-standing problematic orientations toward the world.

The best way that I can clarify my objections is to turn directly to Nussbaum's own engagement with questions about judging emotions as she works through her vexed relation to Stoicism. She wants to defend Stoic interpretations of how the emotions create values, but then she also has to repudiate the conclusions that the Stoics drew. They insisted that because the values so created are products of the imagination and not of reason, the emotions have to be distrusted and ultimately conquered. Nussbaum argues instead that reason is not antithetical to these constructions of value but can provide a normative foundation for how we adapt such judgments. Normative models of anger foster a sense of what might count as a good reason for getting excited. And these models can establish rationales for how one might then conduct oneself. Reason need not destroy the anger because it can build on the information that the emotion produces and guide it to the forms of behavior most conducive to flourishing in relation to what causes the emotion in the first place.

Reason has the necessary power because it has developmental psychology on its side. Developmental psychology shows that the Stoics were often right about our irrationality, not because it is fundamental to how emotions are constituted, but because developmental processes often skew our sensibilities:

> When these emotions manifest themselves, or when their motivating activity is made clear, the person may well feel as if forces of a non-cognitive kind were pushing her around: for the cognitive content of these emotions may not be available to *her,* and even to the extent that it is available it may have an archaic and infantile form. (230)

Such persons may even have "very strong interest in not identifying those needs" as aspects of their characters because they may be ashamed of them (231).

When certain developmental patterns take hold, we can experience emotions while being "quite ignorant of what our emotion-cognitions are." Indeed "we may have a lot invested in not changing them" (233). This is especially true of the negative emotions because their roots lie very deep in "our ambivalent relation to our lack of control over objects and the helplessness of our own bodies" (234).

Nussbaum puts a good deal of faith in this power to diagnose the workings of the imaginary dimension, even though for the Stoics that dimension so pervaded the emotions that in their grip we could not trust any diagnostic tool. In her view, a framework that can clarify the probable causes of irrational behavior can also clarify how the emotions can be part of our flourishing. By examining "sources of variation in development, individual and social," we can ask "to what extent it is possible to encourage developmental patterns that are more supportive and less subversive of ethical norms." So this time it seems as if Nussbaum can have it both ways, can claim that a "cognitive view, by including a developmental dimension, makes room for the mysterious and ungoverned aspects of the emotional life in a way that many such views do not," while also imagining reason as "extending all the way down into the personality, enlightening it through and through" (232). One can clarify why emotions remain opaque or resistant to reason by ascribing "the difficulty of emotional change to habit and the early roots of the relevant cognitions." And by understanding such difficulties one can at least point the person in a healthier direction.

Now I have to ask myself why I get so upset at this line of thinking. Could it be that my aggression indicates my own malformed emotion and sustains the need for envisioning a reasoned normativity in relation to such emotions? Or could it be that my own deviance makes me especially sensitive to aspects of the tone and the language here that there is good reason to find disturbing? Clearly Nussbaum's developmentalism offers a position in which the individual has to heed the therapist: everything we think we know may be a result of our inability to handle developmental issues, so we need someone with a richer relation to reason to set us straight. But how can we know that the analyst in fact possesses the appropriate reason? The analyst may know the norms and have mastered a diagnostic method. The Stoics never doubted that there could be diagnostic methods. They doubted only that agents in the throes of the emotions were in a position to heed those methods or even to see how they might apply. Analogously, those of us who want to defend the significance of the role of imagination in these emotions can point to the positive side of this same conceptual move. It is extremely difficult to apply a language of norms as any kind of imperative in a domain where what matters are particular distributions of energy and attention that bring their own satisfactions. Because the manner of our acting can carry its own expression of responsibility, and because individuals treat expression as a mode of taking responsibility without invoking norms, Nussbaum has to do considerably more work to show not only that the norms exist but that they have significant force for the agents involved. However, Nussbaum has trouble showing how her norms might have actual authority because she does not resolve basic tensions that haunt the effort. Conventional cognitivism does not correlate well with developmental psychology because it tries to isolate the individual belief as much as possible from any historical background— then in particular cases one is not trapped in intentional states but can look directly at how information is being processed and conclusions are being formulated. If one were to bring to bear developmental concerns about family history and the dispositions it produces, the emotions involved would be likely to appear malformed and agents blind to what produces the beliefs shaping their appraisals. And then it becomes likely that the cognitive component of the emotion is either ineffective or itself contaminated by projections and defenses.

On one occasion Nussbaum admits that "the cognitive content" of some emotions may "not be available" to the agent. But she never worries about any systematic conflict between a stance devoted to how emotions sort information and a stance devoted to how historical circumstances shape the very possibility of sorting information. In fact, she never shows how to get beyond the fact that while some cognitive sortings mislead, others seem to work. When she is thinking developmentally she cannot provide a theory of what kind of cognitions regularly characterize the emotions. If the cognitive content is not available to the agent, how can we speak of knowledge at all? We could say that the emotion knows what the agent has to figure out, but this seems rather far-fetched. Or we could say that the analyst is now the one in the position to know, or that the analyst potential in each of us is in that position. But then further problems emerge. We become dependent on the authority of theories about our development in order to get access to our own emotions. And in order to secure the authority of the theory, one has to let most emotions seem driven by the playing out of needs that have psychological reality but no distinctive access to usable information.[11] Yet it seems to me that this is just what cognitivism has to deny.

Faced with these difficulties, Nussbaum turns to what I think is a revealing equivocation on two possible meanings of "cognitive." She shifts from emphasizing the cognitions that emotions afford in relation to objects and situations to a concern with cognizing what specific emotion one is experiencing. Developmental theory cannot tell us anything about how cognition does or does not take place in particular cases. It is a theory not of how we engage the world but of how we are disposed toward it. But developmental theory can tell us a good deal about what we know or do not know, or can know but fail to know, about the particular emotion we are feeling. Any emotion lacking such knowledge is likely to be malformed and will thus invite a developmental analysis of what has gone wrong. If I cannot recognize love, or if I act out aggression as my way of defending myself from vulnerability, I have made cognitive mistakes and I need therapy. An analyst can see clearly where reason would lie in such situations because he or she has an object to know and a path to identify from which the agent has wandered.

I emphasize this shift in Nussbaum's perspective because it marks a crucial difference in how we attribute values to the emotions. For Nussbaum the cognitivist in sense 1, the emotions produce values by establishing appraisals of the world more subtle and better connected to the person's sense of welfare than an instrumental reason could establish. The very dynamics of appraisal even allow us to postulate a norm of flourishing as the end that reason perceives in such activity. And the flourishing is specific to these appraisals. Nussbaum the cognitivist in sense 2 shifts attention from how agents pursue value within the emotions to how analysts assess these emotions (or at least to how the analyst within us should assess them). Now the dynamic forces organized within emotions matter far less than the dynamic forces organized by how dispositions have been formulated over time. The drama provided by the emotions centers in the reflexive processes we bring to bear on them.

This altering of focus is especially significant because it reinforces what I take to be the most serious and dangerous aspect of Nussbaum's arguments. Once identifying the emotion becomes primary, the agents who count are those who have mastered interpretive strategies and can develop norms on the basis of those strategies. Therapists and philosophers turn out to understand much better than the agent does what the appropriate values are: "The virtuous agent will be the one who chooses *and desires* to lie in the sun at the right time, for the right reasons, and so forth" (235). Consequently, theory can proceed as if there were no significant differences between the imaginative activity involved in establishing what deserves to count as values within our emotions and the reasoning activity that enables virtuous persons and only virtuous persons to have flourishing emotional lives.[12] And those who are not virtuous seem condemned to a world in which their emotions warrant only the kind of interpretations the Stoics produce, despite what began as an effort to provide an alternative to Stoicism. Agents can trust the values developed by individual emotions only after they submit themselves to those who are virtuous, or—worse—to those who claim to know what the virtuous would know.

Perhaps Nussbaum's most egregious imperialism in the name of virtue comes when she argues that Donald Winnicott's "perspective on human beings may be more illuminating, ultimately, than that of Proust, whatever his genius, because Winnicott is simply a saner and more responsive person, more genuinely interested in human variety and interaction" (181). While I might quarrel a little about what kinds of responsiveness have to be assessed here, I have no doubt that Winnicott is the saner person and is more responsive to moral concerns. So too is my barber, a marvelous philosopher in his own right. But there are illuminating and wise ideas and then there are kinds of illumination that a writer like Proust can establish. Winnicott simply does not in his writing climb the mountains and valleys that Baron Charlus does; nor does he quite walk the lanes of Combray as does the young Marcel. Yet Nussbaum will not give any normative significance to Proust's claim that such processes are enriched by the very agitations that they produce. Despite his upheavals, or, better, because of them, Charlus compels Proust's respect to the end, even though there emerge revelations that damn him from a perspective based on normative ideas of flourishing. For Proust the role of imagination is not to establish norms but to develop passions and compassions that make predicates like "saner and "more responsive" seem painfully inadequate. Ideals of "variety" and "responsiveness" have to involve sympathy with any kind of nobility that struggles for its realization, whatever the prevailing norms. We have to be careful not to confuse judgments we might make about the emotions from the outside as assessments of their place in a social situation with judgments whose shape and authority are based on forces internal to the energies and the perspectives that the emotions make available. For if we do not honor that difference, we end up reducing art's intensities to philosophy's forms of projecting and assessing wisdom.

I do not want to disparage developmental accounts of the emotions or deny that these accounts help explain some of the forms of irrationality that the Stoics identified. But I think one can acknowledge the importance of developmental concerns when we examine emotions without building developmental norms into our basic theory of the values that matter within our emotional experiences. Nussbaum refuses to make that distinction because she wants to bring the analysis of emotions directly into the sphere of ethics. For her there is ultimately no gap between how we are to value emotions and how we make ethical judgments about these emotions in relation to developmental norms. Where there is tension between the two arenas, we have to treat the tension as the result of pathology. Consequently, she seems to me unable to adapt judgment sufficiently to particular contexts, as her comments on Proust painfully demonstrate. And, correspondingly, she has no compunction about deciding what is rational from a position not the agent's and then attributing that judgment to the normative structure she claims to locate within the emotion. Invoking developmental patterns in this way involves telling the agent from the outside what it is right not only to do but also to feel. There is no room for recognizing why the agent might refuse the dictates of even the most enlightened reason. From my perspective Nussbaum's approach is bad psychology and bad morality because the approach cannot sufficiently engage the tensions we often experience between feeling and thinking. And it cannot sufficiently honor the adjustments we often make in order to bring the two into momentary conjunctions. What moves the person to adapt certain attitudes need not be the same set of concerns that take hold when persons are confronted with issues of justification and responsibility. So rather than assume that there is a "right time" and "right reason" for the emotion, we are likely to do better if we let the emotion play out its claims while we also recognize that practical reason may have competing claims based on more comprehensive, but often less powerful, models of value than those driving the emotion.

## V. A Case for Dramatistic Individualism: The Example of James Joyce

Ultimately Nussbaum matters so much to me because her thinking enables me to develop by contrast the claim that a dramatistic individualism provides the richest model for recognizing how emotions constitute values. For her there are normative patterns that guide our adaption of rationality to specific cases. Where there seems some kind of failure to approximate the norm, she looks to generalized developmental contexts for an explanation and for a judgment. She insists she is a philosopher, not a psychologist, so she does not apply specific developmental analyses (except to poor Proust), but she uses ideas about flourishing based on what developmental theory provides. This means that philosophy establishes the relevant ideals and gives us the means of showing both why we fail to accomplish those ideals and how we might better pursue them. I want to suggest instead that we treat the entire process of evaluating emotions as a matter of individual economies. Whatever our theory of how emotions are constituted, its ultimate test is the degree to which it can handle the variations demanded if we are to appreciate the stakes individuals establish for their investments and the modifications their actions establish as they pursue these investments.

Suppose we grant the developmental stories elaborated by object-relations psychology. I think we then have to admit that, in their processes of coping with their own vulnerability, agents work out certain patterns of adjustment that do not and often cannot fit normative images of emotional flourishing. This limited condition stems in part from the fact that adjusting to developmental pressures takes its toll on our eudaimonistic orientations. People rarely have clear ideas of how they might flourish. And when they do pursue such ideas, they have to do so from within developmental difficulties, leaving them at considerable odds with the forms of reasoning about the self idealized by philosophers like Nussbaum. This does not mean that people cannot at times be rational or even deontological in relation to their actions. It does mean that they are not likely to be Aristotelian in their approach to their own specific ways of making and satisfying emotional investments. Idealization seems too much like the projection of childhood omnipotence, so that it continually reminds us of our vulnerabilities. So, instead, we make adjustments. We develop patterns allowing us as much control over our most destructive traits as we can muster, and we then develop the kinds of attitudes that will enable our emotions to bring us more satisfaction than suffering.

Take for example James Joyce's rendering of Stephen Dedalus. Joyce could be the poster child of developmental malformation. His father left him with a nagging void at the point where there might have been a symbolic exemplar providing the child an identity approved by his society. And Joyce tells us he was haunted by the thought of having abandoned his mother because her unquestioning love seemed to him one more crippling feature of Irish life from which he had to defend himself. Should we point out to Joyce how he might find ways of flourishing by acknowledging these vulnerabilities and making himself what his father failed to become? Well, we might, but any helpful response would have to be far more fine-tuned. For one thing, Joyce might have been right in his interpretation of the crushing effects of Ireland and the roles that mothers played in reproducing those effects. Adaptive behavior that might fit a developmental norm in one context can in another involve submitting to oppression. And for Joyce the best path may have been the economy he managed to produce for himself as a writer, seeking in a concrete imaginary world adequate stances toward what he felt could destroy him. In his situation, any norm that might be invoked could be doubly contaminated—by the culture that endorsed it and by the personal psychology that had to embrace it.

*Ulysses* engages just these issues (among many others). Clearly Stephen is as responsive as he is to Bloom and to the idea of Molly in large part because these characters provide him in imagination what he lacks in his actual parents. But he cannot simply embrace them or identify with the emotions it would take to embrace them, even in imagination. His developmental history makes him far too wary for that. Instead he shares with the other Dubliners a slightly suspicious distance from Bloom's perennial good will. And he is careful to distance himself from any reading of Molly that is not sensitive to the possibility that her final affirmations have much less to do with Bloom the individual than with the continual excitement she finds in the world of male desire that he momentarily exemplifies for her. Joyce had read his Nietzsche, and so was keenly aware that the essence of Dionysian affirmation is its utter indifference to particularity.

The only way Stephen felt he could handle all of these pressures is to become the author of the novel. This is by no means an ideal resolution, and it does not realize any clear norm for the emotions at play. For we cannot quite know where Joyce stands in relation to his creations except insofar as he is committed to a certain kind of writing. We see that he keeps a wary distance from all his characters even as he milks identifications with their emotions—irony becomes for him a form of sensitivity, but also a means of avoiding commitment to what he comes to understand and even to appreciate. If he is to identify with the feelings that make him an imaginary son to Bloom, he will do so only in the guise of an endless Telemachian voyaging. For Stephen there can be no homecoming and no final battle in which he allies with father and grandfather. And ultimately there cannot be any fully vibrant woman who does not elicit substantial terror. Yet what choices does he actually have? Would it make sense to ask him to eliminate his tendencies to bring all sorts of theatrical qualities to his imagining of other persons so that he could distance himself from what he composes? And should we wish on him greater efforts to establish personal intimacies? Well, yes, we can have such wishes, but I doubt we should let them take on normative force. What ultimately matters are the attitudes Joyce develops to the life made possible by his decision to become a modernist writer. We have to ask what he made of the emotions that elicit that decision and then are enabled by it.[13]

## VI. Nussbaum on Joyce's *Ulysses,* or Losing One's Ethical Way because of the Desire to Gain Ethical Wisdom from Literary Texts

Nussbaum too is interested in *Ulysses.* But, as we will see, her perspective gives her virtually nothing to say about Stephen. She can find exemplary norms in Bloom and in Molly, but she cannot adapt to the rich and disturbing particularity of the emotions that circulate around the making of those characters. Nor can she sufficiently appreciate the difficulties Joyce saw in identifying completely with the more positive features that these characters come to represent. Such an omission is not an accident. I think it stems directly from limitations in the project of using narrative art as a means of illustrating teleological visions for how emotions mediate values. I want to conclude this account of Nussbaum by showing how her way of seeking ethical wisdom from the arts cannot but prove reductive in relation to how the arts foster the intricacy and mobility of our emotional lives.[14] For I think her view and mine are bound together as are the two cones in a Yeatsian gyre. The more problematic her quest for generalized ethical wisdom becomes, the stronger the case for my own emphasis on embodying and testing the representative force embedded in individual attitudes.

*Upheavals of Thought* does not offer itself as literary criticism. Nussbaum admits from the start that she is not offering "an exhaustive account of texts" but is concerned only with "a philosophical meditation with my own normative questions in mind" (15). So she models a literary education for a young woman, named A in honor of Proust's Albertine, who is eager to learn what authors of major narrative texts have to teach her about the ladder of love. This ladder is essentially an affective one because she must distinguish four basic "level and types of emotions": "emotions toward characters," "emotions toward the 'implied author,'" "emotions toward one's own possibilities," and "emotions of exhilaration and delight at coming to understand something about life or about oneself" (272). In each case these emotions can involve either identification or reaction and consequent critical distance. But whatever way we become engaged, we then find these texts showing "us general plausible patterns of action, 'things such as might happen' in human life. When we grasp the patterns of salience offered by the work we are also grasping our own possibilities" (243). Indeed "these experiences would lack power if we were not investigating our own psychology and the possibilities it contains." Art generalizes through specificity precisely by bringing us to awareness of how these possibilities implicate our lives within what the text dramatizes. For example, when we watch Janet Leigh's shower in Hitchcock's *Psycho,* "we both wish Leigh well and want to see her slashed, both identify with her and persecute her. In the process we become aware of our own aggression toward cherished objects" (247). Even noneudaimonistic emotions become states we can take to be valuable in art because these emotions can make "what would otherwise be painful wonderful and delightful" (278). A's most important task is to develop a rich appreciation of how literary texts embody and energize ethical ideals. From Proust's purgatory, A's philosophical path of "love's ascent to the clear sight of understanding" will lead her through three models of love (Dante, Brontë, and Mahler), past Whitman's hymn to democratic desire, to the climactic sense of possibility afforded by Joyce's *Ulysses. Ulysses* takes the exalted position because it manages to honor the ascent tradition while simultaneously reversing it, perhaps as Hegel does when he makes comedy the spirit's access to the full force of religion. Joyce proves necessary to A's education because he avoids the tendency to have the ascent of soul "repudiate daily life" and so create a wide gap between the implied reader and the real-life reader. Indeed, thanks to Joyce, we can now see Dante's allegory as rooted in infantile and narcissistic conceptions of love because the entire text seems shaped by the child's desire for omnipotence sustained by faith in an adult (681–82).[15] Joyce's love of the concrete can provide a plausible ethical alternative to the benighted idealism of the ascent tradition by carrying out "a holy sacrament of Aristotelian purgation, in which the censorious metaphysics of the Irish

Catholic Church will be carried away by the cleansing sewer-pipes of Joycean literary frankness" (683).

In Nussbaum's account Joyce offers a bold reconciliation of philosophy with a literary realism usually seen as spurning philosophical idealization. The ethical power of this realism proves especially significant in the three chapters that for her best dramatize Joyce's critical relation to the ascent traditions she has surveyed. "Nausicaa" brings the world of fantasy into social relations; "Ithaca" presents Bloom becoming and failing to become Spinoza; and "Penelope" offers A a model of adult female sexuality in all its materiality, contingency, and "incongruity." These chapters present us with a Bloom who realizes in his simple kindnesses and his ways of loving Molly "whatever is real in heroism," and "whatever is generous and genuine in the spiritual life" (691). Through Bloom the text "appears to argue that love is the great hope for public life as well, the great opposite to the 'insult and hatred' that are themselves 'the opposite of that that is really life'" (692). And Joyce manages to develop a moral import to Molly's "yes" that is not sentimental. Molly comes to embody "a mercy and tenderness that really do embrace the inconstancy and imperfection of the real-life reader and real-life love" in terms of "comic realizations of that longing" (707). Finally, on the basis of these private realizations the novel carries "political significance":

> Focus on the body's universal needs is an essential step on the way to the repudiation of localism, therefore of ethnic hatred. Second, by showing Molly Bloom as the one character in the novel who never entertains thoughts of revenge . . . the novel suggests, again with Whitman, that the root of hatred is not erotic need. . . . It is, rather, the refusal to accept erotic neediness and unpredictability as a fact of human life. Saying yes to sexuality is saying yes to all in life that defies control. (709)

I was tempted to criticize Nussbaum because she dwells only on Joyce the realist and not Joyce the ironist or Joyce the constructivist or Joyce the "Nighttown" surrealist, or Joyce the author projected into the various moments of self-hatred that pervade Stephen's moments on stage. But it is more important and more revealing to emphasize how selective Nussbaum is in her realism. For then we capture the forces of philosophical imperialism at their most invasive and perhaps at their most vulnerable. In her account, realism stops at the points where it can be transformed into ethical value. She sees no realism in "Nighttown," despite what we know about Joyce's ambitions. And she sees precious little realism in those moments when we see the pathos of Bloom's impotence—not only sexually but also as a decent man in a corrupt social order. Similarly, Nussbaum sees Molly as treated realistically insofar as she is shown directly asserting her values and interests. It apparently never dawns on Nussbaum that a twentieth-century author might also flirt with a very different anthropological and structural realism that distrusts what characters say and tries to locate in the actions signs of more comprehensive impersonal forces. In other words, Joyce may be a realist because he equates Molly with a Dionysiac indifference to particularity eventually to be fully articulated in the "mind" of Anna Livia Plurabelle.[16] Finally, Nussbaum has to ignore the novel's efforts to be realistic about the investments and engagements characterizing the presence of its maker. Yet Joyce's realism is ultimately not philosophical; it is writerly. Realism does not build toward generalization but explores the constant deforming and reforming effect of an intelligence that attempts to take responsibility for the slipperiness and excessiveness of his own passions, including the passions that lead him to construct a Molly and a Poldy who will taunt him with the desirable but inadequate realisms shaping the values by which they think they live. From Joyce's authorial extension of Stephen's position, the paths taken by Leopold and Molly are not parallel to his, but intricately and painfully tangential.

Nussbaum wants to praise the descent that opens as love's ladder reaches toward its transcendental home. But what kind of a descent can she idealize for A when her criticism virtually ignores the dark realism pervading Stephen's presence in the novel—as character and as figure for the needs of the authoring? What kind of descent can refuse even to consider how the presence in the novel of Dedalus as an earlier state of the implied author might require reading all the characters as problematic projections of the author's own needs and desires? Clearly, while Poldy and Molly are attractive to Joyce and to Stephen, they are not normative for either figure. Nussbaum has shown on other occasions that she is quite capable of providing rich interpretations of texts as intricate as this one. So her limitations as a reader here lead us beyond the person of the critic to the nature of her methodological commitments. In that light, her effort to idealize Joycean passions seems a doomed enterprise, faring even less well than the idealizing of anti-idealization that one finds in Derrida's writing on Joyce. Joycean passions involve constant concrete negotiations with the world as specific attitudes get tested and adjusted and explored in terms of what they help mobilize and resist. The very idea of "flourishing" would set Joyce to etymological fantasies that he would then try to weave into his realistic texture.

This attitude may not be as healthy as the ones Nussbaum proposes. But it may be the one Joyce had to adopt in order to free himself from what he saw as the horrors shaping his development. Rather than make normative judgments about the range of attitudes he elaborates, we do better to examine what worlds Joyce could realize given the plausible options available to him. But how can we correlate such attention to particulars with the ambitions that drive philosophers like Nussbaum?

If there is a moral here, it must take the form of an ethical judgment of the ethical roles Nussbaum claims for philosophically oriented literary criticism. Simply on empirical grounds, her philosophical stance does not come out looking very good because of the gulf between its idealizations and Joyce's fascination with concrete tones and intricate interrelations among specific affective states. By ignoring Stephen Dedalus because he does not play a role in her own search for wisdom, Nussbaum ends up dismissing not only a character but a figure for the author's own investments in this text. She then desperately needs philosophy because she is not in dialogue with an author and so has to locate the authority for her reading somewhere else. But this puts philosophy in an ironic position that may need a Joyce for its unfolding. In the pursuit of ethical ideals Nussbaum comes close to indulging in what for Joyce's world and for mine is the one manifestly unethical practice—ignoring or sacrificing particularity in order to support the fantasies of importance one gains by taking on the power to identify with ethical ideals. If it takes such impositions to define "flourishing," we have a very strong case for letting the values emotions produce find their way without the sustenance of philosophy and its demands for rationality in our affective lives. And we have what I think is a strong challenge to all philosophy that it be very careful how it authorizes the model of rationality that it brings to bear in making assessments about these affectively constituted values.

# 6 Emotions, Values, and the Claims of Reason, Part 2: Conativity and Its Consequences

> It isn't an accident, as I sit in the yard reading poems
> Under the hemlock, that I'm drawn to Basho.
> It's clear that his blood runs in my veins,
>
> Clear he's my father or else my twin
> Misplaced at birth in a shorthanded village hospital.
> How else explain that a poem of his
> Is nearer to me than the proverbs of seven uncles?
>
> Witness the first haiku in the new translation
> I bought this morning at Niagara Books:
> "Even in Kyoto, hearing the cuckoo's cry,
> I long for Kyoto."
>
> Carl Dennis, "Basho"

## I. Toward an Expressivist Model for Values Made Possible by the Affects

Now I have to switch from the pleasures of identifying with art against philosophical moralizing to the pains of trying to bring the two domains into some accord with each other. So I will try to show that my expressivist perspective provides a substantial alternative to perspectives that rely on reason to establish norms or determine value by calculations about interests and welfare—at least for dealing with axiological aspects of our affective lives. I do not like talk of "ends in themselves" since this expression claims a metaphysical purity unnecessary for practical purposes. But it is important to be able to show how the emotions establish and pursue significant values that cannot be characterized or assessed from within any normative model relying on principles of reasoning. These values are too closely woven into particular subjective states to be amenable to the forms of generalization reason requires. And the forms of responsibility they involve have much less to do with reasoning than with how agents place their relevance for specific subjective ends and for connections with other people that matter because of the immediate satisfactions they afford.

Elaborating my case will require weaving together four basic lines of argument. First, I want once again to bring aesthetic theory to bear on how we characterize basic affective states. This time my focus will be on adapting to the affects Kant's demonstration of how there can be forms of judgment that do not rely on categories of the understanding but are responsive to how particular activities unfold, thereby establishing a focus for our investments. Then I have to fill out the conceptual space Kant establishes by specifying concrete modes of affective investment that establish their own conditions of satisfaction and so develop aspects of judgment without relying on generalizations reason can process.[1] As examples of these investments I will concentrate on states of intensity, of involvedness, and of plasticity because these establish value within a wide range of emotions. My third step will shift from particular qualities of emotions to overall structures or complexes in affective life that determine judgment without being bound to rational criteria. Here I am most interested in the possibility of demonstrating how an emphasis on conative states is compatible with immediate and sustained attention to the situations of other human beings. Finally, I will return to a question that I treated superficially in my introduction, the question of how my arguments can address current emphases on the social construction of the values the affects pursue. I will argue that while most of the values that matter for our emotions are constituted through cultural life, it does not follow that these values take quite distinctive forms that depend on the working of social units whose determining force can be clearly established. One does not have to believe in cultural universals in order to rely on the notion that societies with complex histories produce values that bring to bear several strands of the culture and so involve complex overlaps with other cultural units. Here aesthetic experience is especially useful because the arts clearly reach across apparent cultural boundaries to test what can be shared among those dwelling within quite different mores.

I find contemporary support for my effort to resist reason-based accounts of the values in the exemplary analyses developed by Simon Blackburn in his *Ruling Passions*. Inspired by Hume, Blackburn seeks an ethics fully responsive to "the polymorphous nature of our emotional and motivational natures" (14). Therefore rather than elaborating principles, he concentrates on practices, or, more precisely, on what we can say the moral capacities are that we bring to attributing ethical praise and ethical blame in specific situations:

> Amongst the activities involved in ethics are these: valuing, grading, forbidding, permitting, forming resolves, backing off, communicating emotion such as anger

or resentment, embarrassment or shame, voicing attitudes such as admiration, or disdain, or contempt, or even disgust, querying conduct, pressing attack, warding it off. When I say that these are involved in ethics, I mean . . . that by describing the contours of a character in terms of doings like these, a narrator can tell us all that is important about a character's ethics, regardless of the words said. (51)[2]

Values then can be seen as depending on "the full dynamic range of our practical natures" (13). And moral analysis becomes the effort to find out how we can reach agreement on approving or disapproving how these natures establish values in particular circumstances. Rather than seek agreement in terms of general principles and propositions, we work "within a moral scheme," connecting what people accept with how they behave (302).[3]

My concern is with conative capacities rather than with ethical ones. Yet I think I can develop useful analogues with Blackburn's emphases—both in terms of clarifying what behaviors involve and in terms of specifying how judgments remain sensitive to particular agent situations. His emphasis on capacities for participating in value-laden activities leads me to suggest that a conative perspective can help us address three important questions. What forms of behavior characterize my treating affects as sustaining some value? What forms of behavior characterize my caring about such caring? And what processes of regulation or adjustment emerge when we do make judgments in relation to these affect-based values? I hope that putting the issues this way will allow me to finesse the need for a lengthy catalogue specifying how different emotions involve different values. I have no doubt that there are such differences. But my concern is with what might be common within the range of affective values we experience.[4] By taking this perspective, we separate ourselves from concerns about the beliefs underlying the specific emotions so that we can concentrate on the sense we have of ourselves as subjects putting various affective states to work.


## II. Kant's Aesthetics and the Possibility of Judgment without Rational Criteria

As much as I admire Hume, Kant remains my inspiration, so I will begin with a level of abstraction not acceptable to Blackburn. For in my view Kant's ability to use reason against itself is the most important contribution of Enlightenment thought to contemporary theory. Kant's ways of dwelling on the limits of reason make it both necessary and possible to emphasize the roles that expressive processes play in establishing our value commitments. If we cannot successfully interpret values when we deal with the emotions as objects of knowledge, we have good reason to turn instead to how values operate from the first-person perspective of the agents assessing their significance.[5]

Thinkers like Hegel then took Kant's subtle analyses and expanded them so that rather than opposing subjectivity to reason, they treated reason as if it had the same properties as first-person expressive efforts. Reason was given the power to negate fixed boundaries, to establish new expressive possibilities for spirit, and to gather what these expressions established within an overall dynamic sense of emerging systematic relationships. This is not the place for such ambitious arguments. But it can be useful to attempt giving life again to those aspects of Kant's aesthetics that made it seem feasible to try such a recasting of reason. By doing that I hope to clarify the conceptual grounds for relying on expressive models as our means of elaborating and assessing values. For Kant makes a powerful case that some of the more resonant satisfactions we find in spontaneous subjective acts are due to the modes of judgment these states bring to bear. To appreciate these we have only to recognize the limitations of the interpretive frameworks developed by the understanding to deal with objects, since these simply do not hold for those situations where subjects foreground their constitutive powers.

Kant's *Critique of Judgment* posits as its basic antagonist the Enlightenment tendency to rely on forms of reason that sought laws subsuming individuals under the categories enabling hypotheses to be formed and tested. In aesthetics proper he had to deal with Leibnitz's theory of beauty: if beauty is a kind of perfection, then it is a judgment issuing from the understanding as it exercises its capacity to appreciate essential truths. Appreciating a work of art depends on knowing its relation to the appropriate cognitive categories. And on the issue of how judgment extended into the domain of ethics, Kant had to resist various forms of empirical and prudential judgment that subordinated the subject to the situation, a sense of spontaneity to a sense of abstract justification. In both ethics and aesthetics, then, he confronted a situation where emphasizing objective conditions located all intellectual authority in the discipline of understanding, the discipline where how we reason lucidly about the object determines what we can say about the subject. But for Kant, judging "objects merely in terms of concepts" loses "all presentation of beauty" (59) because such an approach eliminates both the concreteness that imagination produces for its ideas and the spontaneity by which agents are free to specify their own engagement. Analogously, emphasizing the understanding makes ethics a matter of processing maxims and laws with no attention to how agents might act as legislators. So Kant turned to aesthetic experience to develop two major shifts that help us establish richer roles for subjective agency. And in doing that he prepared the way for the range of expressivist theories that were to build on his example.

First, Kant proposed a sharp distinction between "determinative judgment" and "reflective judgment" because he wanted a domain where the subject's self-awareness might be granted powers not subordinated to practical rationality.[6] Determinative judgments operate under the "laws given by the understanding" and so are "only subsumptive." They make decisions by bringing a particular under the rubric provided by some kind of generalization. One determines what is true by including a particular event under a rule, and one determines what is good by showing that a particular maxim makes sense for this situation. Reflective judgments are quite different because they do not depend on generalizations. Rather, they operate by bringing unity to particular cases even when we cannot know the relevant principle. Imagine having to make a decision about where one is traveling when one has no map. One organizes the space in whatever provisional way enables one to feel one is moving forward. Or imagine what artists do in creating characters we take as significant individuals. In such cases, it makes sense to say that with reflective judgment we do not derive law from experience, but produce an imaginative model refined by the particular situation and enabling us to engage its complexities.

In order to put this distinction between kinds of judgment to work, Kant then proposes a second contrast between the attribution of purposes and the attribution of purposiveness: "Now insofar as the concept of an object also contains the basis for the object's actuality, the concept is called the thing's *purpose,* and a thing's harmony with the character of things which is possible only through purposes is called the *purposiveness of its form.*" When we treat an object or an act in terms of the relevant purposes, we see how general laws take on practical applications. Chairs have actuality for us because the concept of chair tells us what purpose chairs play in our lives. And food has actuality because in effect it fits with the concept of the needs that the body has to sustain itself. But there is no purpose that establishes our sense of how the chair or the food might be "in harmony with the character of things." For we have no concept enabling us to make the relevant distinctions. We are dealing with the projection of possible unities among "what is diverse in nature's empirical laws." Consequently, we are not instantiating laws that unify various particular instances but we are producing a sense of relationship specific to the occasion.

For Kant the ultimate such occasion is our sense of a harmony enabling us to see all of creation as having purposive unity even though reason cannot produce the laws responsible for that unity. For me such observations matter less for their metaphysics than for psychology. Kant helps us show how art works can be exemplary for providing a sense of visible purposive unity that we cannot adequately characterize in the terms either the reason or the understanding provides. The purposiveness has no objective existence apart from the audience's sense that it is engaging many possible ideas that interact powerfully yet cannot be characterized in conceptual terms. But this audience engagement in the intricate play of internal relations proves for Kant sufficient grounds for attributing to the maker a power of genius that composes as if it were producing laws for nature rather than imitating them or instantiating them.

Kant's genius produces works of art. But I think the same principles of activity can be attributed to any kind of expressive activity that we take as warranting talk about purposiveness. On the most fundamental level, Kant helps us see how we might attribute specific intentional qualities to certain aspects of conative behavior without having to project the agent as acting in accord with specific reasons. Conative activities take on purposiveness when concerns for unity and for the manner of acting make the kind of impression that cannot be reduced to irrationality, even though the activity also cannot be subsumed under rationality. One might even say that this sense of purposiveness also characterizes our own sense of direction as subjective agents. Expressive behavior then is the fleshing out of such agency by giving qualities to the unities we establish without subsuming them under the forms of articulation and assessment that reason provides. Some of these qualities will be immediate to the manner of acting. Others will involve second-order aspects of these unities. So we can see how concerns for satisfaction and for responsibility can circulate around this expressive purposiveness. Taking responsibility is a form of identification and a bid for recognition marking one's investment in what the expression makes articulate. And the very fact that such purposiveness can produce recognitions indicates aspects of public judgment that do not quite depend on concepts deployed by practical understanding.

## III. Intensity as the First of Three Basic Aspects of Affective States that Constitute Ends in Themselves: The Example of Yeats's Lyrics

Kant shows how it is possible to locate significant values within the active states subjects develop so that we can interpret purposive expressive behavior as a manifestation of our investments in those values. But we still have to show in practice how these capacities for establishing values actually work. So now I will turn to the analysis of three basic subjective states that I think afford significant affective satisfactions in relation to the manners by which we pursue investments even though the values involved are very difficult to fix or to assess in the terms provided by the practical understanding. These states are the experience of how intensity modifies subjectivity, the experience of an involvedness within which we feel our personal boundaries expanding to engage other lives on the most intimate possible levels, and the experience of the psyche's plasticity as it adapts itself to various competing imaginative demands. I am sure there are many other plausible candidates for this kind of analysis. But I have chosen these three modes of valuing because they dramatize purposive features of actions that also give us access to important features of aesthetic experience so often subordinated to the kinds of allegorizing and thematizing represented by Nussbaum's work. In order to demonstrate these close links between art and life I will base my accounts of these values on lyric poems. And I will

*[handwritten marginalia: Beloved is all affective state — expression without verbal medium]*

try to show how many of the judgments we make as we develop these values are closer to how artists make adjustments in their craft than to how we process beliefs and arguments.

For a state so enticing to modern consciousness, intensity has not elicited much theoretical discourse.[7] Perhaps this is because intensity seems to be possible within virtually every emotion and so seems a little odd, or naked, when it is isolated for attention. Moreover, intensity does not necessarily involve elaborate modes of imagination or specific acts of self-reflection. I do not have to tell myself that sporting events or human encounters are intense in order to respond intensely. Yet this very range makes intensity central to any value story we are likely to tell that attempts to bracket the authority of reason. So it is crucial that we try to be as specific as we can on how and why intensities matter to us.

Theodor Adorno sets the stage by defining intensity as "the mimesis achieved through unity and ceded by the multiplicity to the totality. . . . The power accumulated in the totality is, so to speak, restored to the detail" (187). Intensity gives the appearance that "the whole . . . exists only for the sake of its parts." The greater the pressure of the whole on the particular, the richer the intensity. Think of the difference between hearing Lear's "never, never, never" speech the first time one sees the play and hearing it with an awareness of the forces at work in the play as a whole. Or think of everything that comes to bear on Oedipus's blinding himself. (Intensity may be the intricacy of purposiveness experienced sensually.)

Adorno seems to me exactly right about what produces our sense of intensity. We can even use his attention to the distinctive way intensity absorbs contexts in order to suggest that moments of intensity can be described in terms of three basic dimensions. There are dimensions of magnitude established by the kind of elements brought together, dimensions of compression established by the forces of resistance engaged by the act, and dimensions of sharpness established by how the act comes to appear distinctive in its particularity. Lear and Oedipus can turn suffering into sublimity largely because all three dimensions work so seamlessly and fully together.

However, here I have to turn to a question that Adorno does not address directly: Given how often intense experiences are painful and resistant to reason, why do they produce such deep satisfactions? I do not have a very good answer, but I hope I can point in the direction of what might eventually be a good answer. In my view, we take satisfaction in intensity because it makes available a sense of our own vitality in relation to the present tense that we rarely experience any other way. At one pole, there emerges a vivid awareness of particulars; at the other, the will is called into some kind of decisive action, if only to persist in what is extraordinary or to turn from that to the comfort of more habitual behaviors. Usually this act of will has very little to do with choosing or refusing to act. The will involved has to do with affirming or escaping the version of the self emerging in this distinctive present. Intensity may be the most compelling conative value.

Because of this sense of the vivid present, intensity often pulls us away from descriptive languages into metaphoric registers: description seems inadequate to the influx of realizations about power and need that suddenly come to occupy the stage. On the simplest level, this sense of the present is distinctive because, as Adorno indicates, whatever constitutes the present seems to expand to incorporate the impact of complex background situations and forces—whether agents produce the synthesis or have it foisted upon them. Consequently, the sense of the present that emerges is not merely a moment of enhanced attention. Rather, intensity renders the "here" and "now" as sharply distinct from the "there" and "then" constituting its boundaries, and it makes this sense of the "here" seem woven into the agent's sense of its own possibilities. As T. S. Eliot might have said, only those whose "heres" keep wandering into "theres" and whose "nows" are undone by nagging "thens" are likely to appreciate fully what this concentrative centering can involve.

This strong sense of contrast gives the present an aura and a resonance quite different from the force it has when we are concerned primarily with questions about knowledge. Following Hegel, Derrida made a compelling case that an insistence on immediacy cannot provide reliable knowledge claims. For when we are focused on epistemic concerns, we have to concentrate on the forms of mediation that link immediacy to specific practices of inquiry. How I perceive counts only in relation to the framework of understanding into which the perception can be encoded, and the code itself will always place us at a remove from what we claim to know. But intensity is decidedly not epistemic. Intensity has the force it does because it leads us to posit our present state as set over against ordinary epistemic practices. Intensity has to be measured in terms of the degree to which it allows us to engage the world differently from the practices we adapt when we are operating on the same practical plane as those around us. Consciousness is often not even content with producing metaphors that characterize the engagement as different; it also wants to dwell in the metaphors to see how they transform self-awareness. That is why Shakespeare loves to have metaphors actually promise new states of being at those moments when his tragedies tie their various knots together. Consider Lear's "We two will sing alone like birds i' th' cage" (5.3.9), where his madness may in fact also provide a transcendental state of awareness. And then there is Othello's realization of how the magnitude of his crime swallows up subjective being: "Oh heavy hour! / Methinks it should be now a huge eclipse / Of sun and moon, and that th' affrighted globe / Did yawn at alteration" (5.2.97–101).

If this sounds mystical, the reader will understand why I am turning to poetry, for me the domain where the mystical and the ordinary often seem continuous with one another. The best self-conscious explorations of intensity I can find occur in the lyrics of W. B. Yeats, the modern poet most obsessed by this topic. We see embodied in his poems not just ideas about intensity but a sharp realization of why intensity can make such a difference in our lives. These differences take two sharply opposed forms. One mode of intensity involves centering all consciousness on the self's triumphant will; the other mode produces a sense of actively yielding all individual will to the absorptive pull of forces far more powerful than the self. Consider first how Yeats's brief poem "He and She" stages the affirmation of self as the locus of an expanding present that becomes sharply resistant to the pull imposed by the "there" and the "then":

> As the moon sidles up
> Must she sidle up,
> As trips the scared moon
> Away must she trip:
> 'His light had struck me blind
> Dared I stop.'
>
> She sings as the moon sings:
> 'I am I, am I;
> The greater grows my light
> The further that I fly.'
> All creation shivers
> With that sweet cry.
> *(Poems, 286–87)*

The first stanza offers the self at its most unstable. Drawn by the gravitational pull of the other person, the woman cannot even speak for herself except for the one moment when she gets to utter her dilemma. Her being absorbed by the moon makes it necessary to describe her state from the point of view of some remote witness. In the second stanza we find just the opposite process. As she finds the strength to push against the person or forces to which she remains bound, her cry of panic gets transformed into a song that is ultimately about her capacity to sing. And as the self turns away from the moon, it actually manages to share what gives the moon its song—the sense of pure affirmation of its own singular situation. Consequently, when the third-person voice returns here, it does not present itself simply in the mode of impassive description. Instead, the third-person voice now registers the full sexual force of the interaction created by the opposing wills. When she manages to experience her voice as intensely hers, the singing brings the entire scene within its own self-celebration. There seems no distance between the subject singing and the objective state that is the song made physical, so that even the observer is caught up in the metaphoric register necessary to describe what is happening.

Technically speaking, the assertion "I am I" cannot be trusted. Only God can experience the complete coincidence of subjectivity and objectivity. (For other beings, change in the subject as it realizes something about the object cannot be an aspect of what is objectified.) But the poem is less interested in the truth of its assertion than in the energies and desires that it can make visible by the effort to purify song of everything but the "I." The singer's present tense becomes inseparable from the singing, as if this at least could establish a pure coincidence of subject and object. In this state the framing "there" and "then" lose their hold on consciousness.

While we cannot empirically test the truth of the poem's assertions, one can point to considerable formal features that at least give a kind of substance to the desire itself and so provide concrete articulation for the process of bringing the world into the sphere of the will. The utter simplicity of the situation, for example, shaped only by a contrast to the dependency of the first stanza, gives us a world in which there might be nothing but the singing, with all impurities driven away by the need to separate oneself from what the moon dominates. Here lyric seems to approach its own inner possibilities— presenting not any one role, one version of ethos, but the essence of what any role becomes when it can be entirely the matter of song. And, as song, the poem's physical qualities deepen the all-absorbing nature of the "I am I." Long *I* sounds literally take the poem over, spreading the light produced by and as the "I" of the singing. That intensity in turn becomes so great that self-absorption cannot rest in narcissistic states. Just as the "she" of the first stanza is bound to the ways of the moon, the "I" of the second must return to its own setting. But now the setting consists only of one's place in the whole of creation. And what a place it is! The singer's self-absorption constitutes a fantasy lover who draws out of the created order its deepest sexual pleasure because finally creation has an opposite active enough to make its own presence felt. Resistance to the force of the moon enables the second stanza to treat creation itself as once again something to be loved and not merely feared or respected or moralized.

Clearly, too clearly, we do not wake in the morning singing such songs. Poetry is not reality. But we can learn from examples like these to want to approximate singing such songs. And, perhaps more important, we can learn from these examples not to flee from or defend ourselves against those moments that do approximate such singing. In the interest of dispensing further nuggets of wisdom, I would love to go on to poems that explore the same level of narcissistic intensity attached to quite different emotional orientations.[8] Yeats's "Lullaby," for example, completely absorbs the ego within that traditional folk form, using literary self-consciousness as its vehicle for becoming much more absorbed within the state of care than may be developmentally prudent.. This poem uses the context of a domestic situation in order to show how self-consciousness becomes identified with the very core of what people can experience within the mode of lullaby. But I will have to let my one extended example suffice to show how what is normative or exemplary in these lyric states is not their eudaimonic reasoning but their ability to invite possible identifications with the states of mind they make present. By responding to such invitations, we find out if we can affirm them as our songs. When such expansive excess lies down with this extreme, precise care, it should be no wonder that all creation shivers.

Yeats's other basic mode of intensity brings us to quite the opposite process of finding the self absorbed by the present. He has several poems in which the will finds itself overwhelmed by forces that cannot be incorporated as features of the "I" but establish a shape for the "now" and the "this" that exceeds anything the mind can treat in its own categories. We see these forces most clearly when Yeats gives the form of the refrain a distinctive ontological task to perform. Traditionally, the refrain serves primarily musical purposes. But Yeats makes its synthetic force a figure for the imagination's capacity to dwell in intensive states that reach well beyond domains where the ego can assume any control. Take for example his "Long-Legged Fly," a poem that beautifully supplements Adorno's vision of intensity as bringing all the composing powers of the whole to bear on particular situations:

> That civilization may not sink,
> Its great battle lost,
> Quiet the dog, tether the pony
> To a distant post;
> Our master Caesar is in the tent
> Where the maps are spread,
> His eyes fixed upon nothing,
> A hand under his head.
> *Like a long-legged fly upon the stream*
> *His mind moves upon silence.*
>
> That the topless towers be burnt
> And men recall that face,
> Move most gently if move you must
> In this lonely place.
> She thinks, part woman, three parts a child,
> That nobody looks; her feet
> Practice a tinker shuffle
> Picked up on a street.
> *Like a long-legged fly upon the stream*
> *Her mind moves upon silence.*
>
> That girls at puberty may find
> The first Adam in their thoughts,
> Shut the door of the pope's chapel,
> Keep those children out.
> There on the scaffolding reclines
> Michael Angelo.
> With no more sound than the mice make

His hand moves to and fro.
*Like a long-legged fly upon the stream*
*His mind moves upon silence.*

(*Poems*, 339)

Each individual unit renders a moment of intensity so keen that it can be fully appreciated only by forcing a substantial leap between what description can present and what the refrain can evoke. Where the description is fascinated by world-historical moments seen from the outside, the refrain reaches for a psychological reality apparently realized as a limit condition of historical consciousness. It seems as if even the most ecstatic efforts to represent the situation have to acknowledge that they cannot quite render the force that gives the moment its significance. We need the space that the refrain opens up, and we need to appreciate how the refrain gives a kind of reality to what the three moments share. Without the refrain, the three moments would be discreet cases; with it, they all seem to participate in some single transcendental domain realized only when persons can so sacrifice themselves to the necessities that their genius enables them to enter. That is why the agents' body parts seem relatively independent of consciousness, even though these agents seem at the same time to realize levels of consciousness not possible for ordinary mortals. The force that drives history becomes manifest only on these most intimate and elemental of levels. These minds do not move within silence but upon it, so their task is not to interpret silence but to extend it even as they rely on the strange mode of support that the silence provides. Perhaps such pure concentration leads them beyond the cognitive functions of consciousness to some fundamental reality knowable only to the degree that one can feel its constitutive force.[9] The refrain is the poem's means of acknowledging that force and of seeking identification with it. For it not only points to the silence but also offers a mode of circling back on one's own states so that one might be able to glimpse what evades all our practical orientations. And this circling with increasing intensity is the best response lyric can offer to the history that always threatens to reduce it to irrelevance. If we dwell on moments of crisis for consciousness, we may be able to isolate an imaginative force enabling us to treat what history imposes as if it were a challenge rather than a sentence.

Yeats's poem is sustained by imperatives—imperatives from within history and imperatives for characters and readers that open possible paths of response to historical knowledge. But because the imperatives are repeated, we cannot dwell simply on each isolated moment of utter concentration. We have to ask what form of concentration the poem asks of us if we are to raise ourselves to the modes of intensity that bring the various moments into conjunction. What do we have to do as readers to flesh out why three moments form this particular sequence? When we pose the question this way, we are in position to understand why Michael Angelo's hand moving to and fro constitutes the poem's climax. In one sense the final moment is the least imposing because its public stakes are on the face of it considerably less grand than the other two states. Caesar's concentration is ultimately for the sake of civilization, Helen's for a particular battle and perhaps for the power of women to incite violence, and Michael Angelo's only for the shaping of individual imaginations. But if we dwell on how physical details are emphasized, there is a significant progression toward Michael Angelo. The poem leads us from eyes fixed upon nothing to feet that practice a tinker shuffle, to a hand silently moving to and fro. The first two cases present the hero as developing from within the psyche some way of having an influence on events. Michael Angelo's hand, in contrast, moves in just the same way that the fly moves—not addressing history but absorbing it into an image that ultimately pulls against the entire historical order. So we can consider his mode of consciousness as a power capable of synthesizing and expressing what drives all three moments. The artist not only participates in this underlying force but also has the means of actually entering consciously in the elemental silence that is at the core of all these acts of concentration. His moving mind is inseparable from the stillness and so can participate self-reflexively in the forces that impose history upon us.

We cannot leave Yeats without turning to a more melodramatic and problematic aspect of intensity fundamental to his understanding of life and of lyric. At stake here is one limit condition that arises when we set passion against reason. Yeats insists on casting intensity as a force that draws consciousness toward and often beyond basic boundaries of civility. Just as "Hatred of God may bring the soul to God" ("Ribh Considers Christian Love Insufficient" 284), intense involvement in our own heightening energies positions us at boundaries where we are not sure whether we are god or beast or god demanding its own beastliness as a sacrifice so as to confirm the possibility that there is something beyond us compelling our service. "Hound Voice" is Yeats's effort to speak for everything in the psyche that resists "boredom of the desk or of the spade." To hear those voices is ultimately to face hours of terror that "test the soul" and "waken images in the blood."

"Hound Voice" is spoken in the first-person plural by a band of characters renewing their choice to reject this boredom in favor of "bare hills and stunted trees" and the sharp call of "Hound Voice." The poem's third and final stanza has the task of giving a compelling reality to this fantasized identity, so that its difference from the civic order becomes as appealing as it is definitive:

> Some day we shall get up before the dawn
> And find our ancient hounds before the door,
> And wide awake know the hunt is on;
> Stumbling upon the blood-dark track once more,

Then stumbling to the kill beside the shore;
Then cleaning out and bandaging of wounds,
And chants of victory among the encircling hounds.

(331)

Here even the syntax functions to make demands that normal civility cannot handle. The subject-predicate structure of the first lines of this last stanza modulates beautifully through adjective modification ("wide awake") to a series of participles and finally to a world where only noun phrases define the action. The participles compel consciousness to a pure present within the fantasmatic. And the last line then celebrates a world in which even images are almost erased by chants so triumphant that it is they, not the agents, who have control. The event reaches completeness only when the chants themselves establish the only agency possible in this perversely transcendental domain. At its most absorbed, consciousness puts itself in the proximity of absolute conditions in relation to which the fiction of selfhood seems a mask to be torn aside by even greater powers.

## IV. Involvedness as a Value: The Example of C. K. Williams, George Oppen, and William Wordsworth

Few of us are likely to have quite this reaction to hound voices. But many of us are likely to experience the pull between intensity and civility, and for a moment at least long for the sense of release that the intensity affords. In contrast, the impact of involvedness, my second basic value within the emotions, seems much more benign. This value has its genesis in just the opposite mode of self-consciousness from the one fostering intensity, and it involves just the opposite challenge to the ego's boundaries. For not all concentration turns back on triumphs and limitations of the individual will. The self's concentrative powers also provide means of appreciating how we are modified by our connections with other people and with the natural world. In order to characterize this second basic condition of affective value, I will rely on examples of the lyric's capacity to sharpen our awareness of the intricate ways we feel our attention and care becoming contoured to other existences. This awareness can be cultivated as a direct identification with a dramatic situation, or it can depend on second-order investments in how the text asks us to envision our relationship to other readers.

Ideals approximating what I am calling "involvedness" seem quite widely shared among contemporary thinkers. At one pole, we have Richard Rorty's claims about solidarity; at the other there are numerous contemporary Heideggerian proclamations about singularity and letting the other be because we appreciate some aspects of what otherness entails. Even the Republican party tried for a while to cloak its economic positions in a psychology of compassionate conservatism, although being actually in power seems to have precipitously curbed that enthusiasm. But, as the Heideggerians insist, we have to be careful not to turn this sense of involvedness into a basis for making claims that we understand these others and so have the right to impose norms upon them or make them objects of our self-congratulatory sympathies. So theory faces the challenge of having to work out what roles the emotions might play in helping to satisfy both desires—for better understanding and for using that understanding as a means of honoring what gives others their claims to independence and to singularity.

Lyric poetry proves very useful in this theoretical enterprise because it need not generalize about the senses of other lives that it makes vital for us. And, more important, lyrics actually establish quite complex modes of identification through which we manage to feel more strongly what we share with other people while simultaneously intensifying our awareness of the particular locale from which the call for identification emerges. I am not talking about basic sympathy, an important value in its own right and a topic I will briefly address later. Now I want to concentrate on those senses of involvedness that depend on consciousness of how we are positioned in the process—in part because these are the kind of cases where poetry offers distinctive news, and in part because this perspective on identification keeps in focus how the self finds satisfaction by virtue of the terms establishing its relationship with others.

Consider for example lyrics that invite us to speak in voices not our own. Here we have a paradigm case of using self-consciousness as a means of extending beyond the self. When we participate in such texts, we find ourselves literally enacting how these agents engage their worlds while we use our own responses as a measure of their situation. Taking on other voices is of course not unique to poetry—if it were, the poetry would be the less valuable. But I dwell on the poetry because lyrics call attention to a range of satisfying involvements with others that have very little to do with moral abstractions and the accompanying self-congratulations.[10] These poems sharpen our awareness of how and why we take pleasure in using self-awareness as a means of appreciating what creates significance and shapes dispositions in other lives.

I want to specify here three kinds of lyric states that indicate various forms of involvedness and bring to consciousness the sources of our satisfaction in pursuing those forms. First, there are what we might call acts of existential  sympathy like the one we find in C. K. Williams's "Reading: The Cop," where a full knowledge of the cop's life depends on our first understanding our reaction to him, then projecting his having to face such reactions all the time. A second mode of involvedness takes Cézannian form. In poets like  W. C. Williams and George Oppen, for example, the central affective force of the texts consists in their ability to connect our appreciation of what we observe to an intense awareness of the constructive energies at work in how the texts organize our seeing. Finally, one could use Wordsworth's grand rhetorical passages like the crescendo in "Tintern Abbey" to illustrate having poetic rhetoric build its sense of involvedness on its awareness of its participation in general forces and situations that extend beyond its control.

One of the advantages of dealing with C. K. Williams's poetry is that his long line provides a powerful example of processes of judgment taking place because of the flow of emotional energies rather than because of rules of understanding brought to bear on particulars. For "Reading: The Cop" the judgments offer a process of coming to recognize the inwardness of another person through self-reflection:

> Usually a large-caliber, dull-black, stockless
>     machine gun hangs from a sling at his hip
> where a heavily laden cartridge belt in the same blue as
>     his special-forces uniform cinches his waist,
> and usually he stands directly in the doorway, so that
>     people have to edge their way around him—
> there was some sort of bombing in the building, and
>     presumably this is part of his function.
> He often seems ill at ease and seems to want to have but
>     doesn't quite because he's so young
> that menacingly vacant expression policemen assume when
>     they're unsure of themselves or lonely,
> but still, today, when I noticed him back in the hallway
>     reading what looked like a political pamphlet,
> I was curious and thought I'd just stop, go back, peek
>     in, but then I thought, no, not.
>
> (55)

The first four long lines establish considerable distance between the observer and the policeman. We progress slowly through elaborate particular details, to a sense of his position as an obstacle for other people, to a vague understanding of the purposes governing his activity. And the repeated "usually" gives him the indifferent duration of a thing, a regular feature of this environment that seems not to have a significant present tense. Then after a vague purpose is attributed to the cop, the second half of the poem shifts to providing him with just this present tense. The speaker speculates on the cop's state of mind, and in the process of doing that has to make qualifications that better attune him to what his description actually reveals. This policeman in effect cannot quite be the generalized policeman that the speaker initially posits. For he is not sufficiently menacing and hence not sufficiently self-protected. Perhaps then the more "nots" the poem can muster, the closer it will get to his specific situation.

Then the poem offers its last twist or set of twists. For it manages to shift

attention very quickly back to the speaker and through that self-consciousness back to what I think is a marvelous act of sympathy with the ambiva-
lences we have been led to see in the policeman. Now the policeman has a
present because he is doing something not expected as part of his role. Rather
than enforcing a political order, he seems to be inquiring into it. No wonder
the speaker is attracted to a possible humanity he has not before recognized.
But he does not take up the gambit, and the poem insists we ask why. In fact
it insists we not only ask why the refusal but why the double negative, "No,
not," as a way of rendering the emotions of that refusal. The only hypothesis that makes sense to me is to assume that ultimately the speaker cannot
bridge the boundary between the policeman and the citizen. He is moved
more by his alienation than by his possible sympathy.

Williams as poet can now put the limitations of his speaker to powerful
use in projecting a possible understanding of the policeman's fundamental
social identity. For the speaker's double negative rejecting the possibility of
connection makes visible the fundamental plight the policeman faces. He has
to bear the burden of almost everyone's narrative "not," since very few of us
can see beyond the uniform, especially those of us likely to have very different politics from those the cop has. To be this policeman is to be on the other
side of such refusals, indeed to have a life of uncertainty or, for more experienced policemen, lives of vacant menace, because they have to internalize
the fact that other people will not find ways of breaking through the appearances. Involvedness here comes in negative form, but it is the more compelling because that negative form so fully brings with it what life must be
like on the other side. The policeman has to internalize the fact that in society he will always be the cop, never the person who is also a cop. He has to
internalize the presumed refusal by others to grant him any other form of humanity. The poet, on the other hand, has to offer this realization while avoiding the temptation to treat the policeman as simply an object of pity through
whom the poet types among us can stage their own delicate sensibilities.
Williams stops with the negatives so that he can preserve for the policeman
the dignity of remaining unapproachable even as his situation becomes more
intelligible and sympathetic.

My second mode of involvedness is more abstract, but I think it embodies
one of the most effective ways that art makes a difference in how we see life.
Here the sense of involvedness depends on our recognizing that the form of
our affective engagement derives from structures we share with other agents.
The most dramatic examples I know of such emotions are prompted by
Cézanne's paintings. His still lives and landscapes derive much of their power
from showing that the dynamic realization of the object depends on making
articulate the forces brought to bear in our activity as viewers. We not only
see each individual fruit, we also see how modeling by what he called an "api-
cal point" establishes that sense of presence.[11] This drastically shifts the

kinds of values involved in our appreciating the work. For we are not quite occupying the position of empirical subjects attending to how a scene unfolds. Rather, we become something like Kantian aesthetic subjects who respond to how the very dynamics of subjectivity take objective form, making them available for any agent willing to take up the access that the painter provides.

Cézanne's experiments specify two distinctive possibilities for dealing with how we experience our involvedness with other people. First, by trusting the powers of mind that his painting can bring into visual focus in direct relation to its objects, Cézanne can modify how we take satisfaction in social relationships. The objects of attention no longer depend on narratives and arguments for the power they wield as persons. This power stems directly from how they hold the eye and keep the mind engaged in how it is positioned because of this visual relationship. For example, Cézanne's mature portrait figures, especially his large *Card Players,* make affective connections with us simply because we cannot not recognize the dignity in how they present themselves. We do not need to project any particular role or produce any pathos in order to care about them because the painting in effect substitutes for social plots direct visual structures that compel our respect. The second possibility consists in the qualities of self-consciousness mediated by this way of seeing. Because of how our seeing keeps the mind involved, we recognize how the very structure of our seeing binds us to other people. By putting that looping pine branch in the frontal plane when he paints Mt. Sainte Victoire, Cézanne develops gorgeously intricate and intimate relations between the place from which we see and the distant object brought in effect within what becomes a figure for the eye.[12] The painting then seems to embody the very process of seeing as a feeling of internalizing distance, and it does so in a way that immediately implicates anyone who can reflect on what is involved in being able to look.

For a brief thematic development of this point it helps to shift to the impact Cézanne had on cubism and then on noniconic abstract painters like Piet Mondrian and Kasimir Malevich. Painters working within this historical trajectory realized that they could provide an alternative to what Mondrian called the tragic nature of our investments in individuality if they could make immediately visible and affectively compelling a sense of what we share with other agents simply by virtue of how we are led to process visual information. Mondrian's dynamic balances or Malevich's various tilts offer themselves as intense affective states that appeal directly to what is interpersonal in our most intimate capacities. To participate in their work is to recognize that what we feel about what our vision is doing links us directly to how other viewers must be processing these objective structures.

In my *Painterly Abstraction in Modernist American Poetry* I tried to tell a story of how writers took advantage of these experiments. Here I will content myself with two lyric examples from George Oppen. My first example may be somewhat awkward because I have to cite two sections from a longer poem. But I indulge myself because the example also brings us back to contrasts between how reason pursues interpersonal values and how emotional involvedness pursues those same ends. In the first quoted section, Oppen builds a path of feeling and of thinking that produces considerable force for the shift to the rich sense of involvedness in the brief four-line segment that constitutes the second quoted section:

> 32
> Only that it should be beautiful,
> Only that it should be beautiful,
>
> O, beautiful
>
> Red green blue—the wet lips
> Laughing . . .
>
> And the beauty of women, the perfect tendons
> Under the skin, the perfect life
>
> That can twist in a flood
> Of desire
>
> Not truth but each other
>
> The bright, bright skin, her hands wavering
> In her incredible need
>
> 33
> Which is ours, which is ourselves,
> This is our jubilation
> Exalted and as old as that truthfulness
> Which illumines speech.
>
> (183–84)

The first of these sections works out an ecstatic response to its own demand for beauty. The initial abstraction yields to a dazzling series of particulars, each apparently self-sufficient until the last line introduces a surprising twist. Apparently, the woman's very capacity to elicit praise for beauty generates an "incredible need." Perhaps the need is incredible because she cannot quite believe what others say about her. And the need also probably stems from the fear that she will not be able always to elicit the kind of responses that seem fundamental to the narrator.

Section 33 then provides a powerful alternative to the ecstasies produced by projections about beauty. Because beauty is an idealization, the one idealized can never be quite sure what is being praised or whether the respondent actually understands what he praises. Need on the other hand seems not to invite illusion and not to depend on the frenzied attention to surfaces characterizing this quest for beauty. So this sense of need provides quite different grounds for appreciating what people might hold in common and for escaping the anxieties that idealization produces throughout the social order. But in putting the case this abstractly I evade what matters most for Oppen about this sense of need. The poetry can make the realization of commonness something other than pure speculation. It can test the possibility that the shift in section 33 to simple syntax and direct affirmation can provide a distinctive sense of peace. The poem can offer a plausible second-order investment made possible by the sense of sharing that the poem asserts. In this section there is no more wandering about and no need for supplemental explanations. Having located a domain where need can be acknowledged, the poem can quickly develop what seems an inherently social emotion.

There is jubilation because what cannot be satisfied by beauty can at least open a world in which that very frustration comes to constitute what the agents can share. And the jubilation can be concretely paralleled to the uneasy ecstasy established by the search for beauty. Oppen does not simply assert a resolution. He gives the reader a strong contrast in modes of experience, especially in relation to time. Beauty demands the present and is tormented because of that. But for "need" to produce jubilation the reading must literally fold time back on itself. Reflection must build on her sense of need to appreciate how it links audience and character. And this particular unfolding of need seems to lead us from the present back to the very origins of speech. For the final lines invite us to speculate on why truthfulness illumines speech. Perhaps we need the desire for truthfulness because it provides affective grounds for refusing to be satisfied by everything that beauty offers. Truthfulness is what binds speech to need—on the level of sympathy with the woman and on the level of how readers are invited to focus on their own capacities to identify with her and with each other. Then it makes sense to link jubilation to such speech rather than to beauty. Reflecting on our sympathy with the woman's sense of need provides something like a sense of form to that sympathy. We do not merely understand the woman's plight; we live through its social implications as the poem tries to provide a way of appreciating the struggle we go through to bring that need within the domain of speech.

Oppen is often this abstract. But he also constantly tries to work out concrete social forms for this sense of collective selves that his abstractness affords him. So I cannot leave his work, or leave this notion of involvedness, without turning to a poem like "Street":

> Ah these are the poor,
> These are the poor—
>
> Bergen Street.
>
> Humiliation,
> Hardship . . . ,

Nor are they very good to each other;
It is not that. I want

An end of poverty
As much as anyone

For the sake of intelligence,
'The conquest of existence'—

It has been said, and is true—

And this is real pain,
Moreover. It is terrible to see the children,

The righteous little girls;
So good, they expect to be so good . . .

(127)

Here the tone seems to me quite complex, establishing a suppleness of voice necessary for the kind of involvedness that the emotion eventually composes. From the beginning the speaker has to try different modes of expression—I think because that is the only way the poem can recognize that, as Fitzgerald said of the rich, they are different from the rest of us. So what can one say that is not mere tautology, or the heaping of names and of adjectives that only objectifies what it tries to pity? If one has the temerity to resist these attributions and look at the actual lives led by the poor, one risks losing even the sense of sympathy that the abstractions bring. The poor are probably not very good to each other. Realizing that, the speaker stops looking entirely. He shifts to trying out for himself the postures that compose the middle of the poem. He even makes himself the focus of the "real pain," only to be led by that gesture back to the source of pain in the poverty. Even in fleeing the reality of poverty, the speaker stumbles on the sense of pain that reopens the doors of possible sympathy.

And then he makes a remarkably apt observation about the poor: "The righteous little girls; / So good, they expect to be so good." Here he recognizes that their plight in the present is not likely to change in the future, and he recognizes the deeper heartbreak in store for the girls when they can no longer maintain their expectations. The children of the poor share with the better-off the dream that they can be good and that the goodness will somehow be rewarded. This is the mark of their irreducible humanity. But this optimism is doomed to fail—that is the mark of their existence under capitalism, a mark so visible that the poem need not even mention it.

The poet's problem is to produce a form of speakable sympathy that does not ignore the reality and does not settle for piety. Somehow the observing audience has to be made participants so that they do not merely recognize the girls' situation but share an awareness of their future that the girls themselves have not arrived at. To deal with this problem Oppen makes distinctive use of a basic strategy in modernist visual art. He makes us cut through the level of illusion or scene, the level in this poem of trying to find a way to speak, so that we feel ourselves identifying not with characters but with forces inherent in the ways that the mind deploys its constructive energies. His first step is to invite us to realize that we can identify with the girls only because in fact in our distance we know what they do not know. We know their fate. And we are asked to call upon our understanding of the society to appreciate details such as the poem's focusing entirely on girls. The older people have already internalized the despair that the reader comes to feel. So the more we let ourselves explore what our own understanding of expectations brings to this poem, the richer our sense of its political urgency.

Calling on this understanding foregrounds the fact that we are reaching out to occupy the position of a fully social agent. But that realization is not sufficient to exhaust the poem's power. For Oppen wants not just that recognition but a relation of our will to what the recognition makes possible. He wants us to realize that saying more about the girls would risk returning to the world where their concrete differences from us dispel sympathy or allow us to be patronizing. More speech here would cover over the poem's painful realization of the gulf between how easy it is to sympathize with the girls and how hard it is to turn that sympathy into any kind of political action. And more speech would risk repeating social pieties and producing a self-congratulation that blinds us to the realities. The other alternative is to make the refusal of more speech itself a highly self-conscious empowering activity. For by feeling the limitations of speech the audience is in a position to take on a kind of responsibility for the painful knowledge the girls encounter. Our constrained speech is less painful than their total impotence. But it is the beginning of actual sympathy with the kinds of constraints inescapable in a warped social order. And because the poem provides terms for understanding the very situation the reading produces, we have the consolation of hoping that in sharing the intricate form of frustrated sympathy produced by the reading we are at least glimpsing the prospect of a social group that might not hide from the reality as the speaker initially tried to do.

A third type of involvedness shifts from finding shared identity in particular forms of experience to discovering modifications in subjectivity as we extend ourselves to participate in quite general reflections that lead us beyond our empirical selves. These reflections can be sponsored by religious visions—Gary Snyder's vision of connectedness is a good example—or they can derive from the power created by eloquent rhetorical performances. Since Wordsworth's lyric poetry combines both vehicles, I will use as my example this grand crescendo from "Tintern Abbey":

> For I have learned
> To look on nature, not as in the hour
> Of thoughtless youth; but hearing oftentimes
> The still, sad music of humanity,
> Nor harsh nor grating, though of ample power
> To chasten and subdue. And I have felt
> A presence that disturbs me with the joy
> Of elevated thoughts, a sense sublime
> Whose dwelling is the light of setting suns,
> And the round ocean and the living air,
> And the blue sky, and in the mind of man:
> A motion and a spirit, that impels
> All thinking things, all objects of all thought,
> And rolls through all things. Therefore am I still
> A lover of the meadows and the woods
> And mountains; and of all that we behold
> . . . well pleased to recognize
> In nature and the language of the sense
> The anchor of my purest thoughts, the nurse,
> The guide, the guardian of my heart, and soul
> Of all my moral being.
>
> (I: 360)

Wordsworth faces a considerable problem here. He wants to make his individual situation stand as potentially a representative one demonstrating quite general values, yet he wants also to repudiate the modes of reasoning that usually are required if we are to take such generalizing seriously. How can the appeal to what he has "felt" and continues to feel take on sufficient weight to do the work usually done by reasoning? Wordsworth's response is focused on what syntax can establish as a visible locus for affective processes set in motion by this mode of reflection. In effect syntax proves to be the locus of involvedness, with apposition and conjunction serving as the heroes of this little drama. These foregrounded syntactic activities define the intricate relations that emerge as affects elicited by memory elicit the mind's most expansive acts of self-reflection. Apposition and conjunction become vehicles that allow feeling to modulate into thinking and thinking into the mode of willing that brings the poem back to its magnificent climactic assertion "Therefore am I still. . . ." Consequently, the poem does not have to make arguments about its representative status. It can invite the audience to try out its own speaking of the language, in the hope that the audience will recognize how its sense of its own capacities and dependencies changes as it participates in this syntax. The mode of speaking becomes representative by being exemplary and demonstrating what a particular style of involvement makes possible.

Initially the passage I have quoted simply fixes the speaker in the present by stating clearly how he has learned to reconfigure his relations to nature.

But the reconfiguring cannot stop with the objects of thought. These objects were, and are, so pervaded by feeling that thinking about the past modulates swiftly into caring about the present: "And I have felt a presence that disturbs me with the joy of elevated thoughts, a sense sublime. . . ." The rush of feeling in turn drives the mind to rapid associations as it tries to come to terms with all that is implicit in its situation. Remembering a felt presence swiftly modulates into the present joy of elevated thoughts, which then immediately becomes a *sense sublime*. And as thought becomes sense, syntax becomes its own almost physical force of cadenced conjunctions heaping up on one another. How could one not find spirit in these motions?

Yet motion in itself cannot suffice as the principle by which we identify spirit. Motion displays the complex involvedness that this poem celebrates, but display will not suffice. Wordsworth wants the sense of involvedness to have consequences, so the poem has to manifest a concern for how the will gets deployed because of this mode of thinking. Wordsworth handles this need by bringing all the poem's motion to a triumphant stasis in the climactic assertion "Therefore am I still. . . ." Thinking that can move so fluidly and so expansively manifests its full power when it brings these energies to a moment of coming to rest in a simple and expansive assertion. This "still" is in personal time what the "all" is in reflective space, and it provides a locus for combining both modes of generalization. In order to measure the power stemming from this sense of arrival, the poem then reaches for an even greater crescendo. And through this crescendo the celebratory "I am" comes to seem less a matter of being William Wordsworth than of being this particular locus organizing such involvedness within what remains a vivid present moment. The "I am still" is a matter not of belief but of responding to the eddying in self-reflection of all this expansive turbulence.

Neither the "still" nor the "all" could have this resonance if one had to rely on the resources of rationality or a sense of self as an established character. The language able to meet the demands posed by these "motions" seems to require as its correlate a form of self-consciousness quite different from the one that produces our usual defensive and needy images of selfhood. The "I" that emerges here does not fight for its imaginary sustenance by opposing itself to other people's identifications. Rather, this "I" depends on its ability to adapt itself to the various forces of perception and memory and reflection that in effect call it into existence. Paradoxically, it is only the work of establishing identity that can bring to bear sufficient synthetic capacity to allow the will to embrace this reach of imagination. When the imagination moves so fluidly and so intensely among perception, apposition, and conjunction, "motion" and "spirit" and "all things" and a "sense sublime" all seem necessary correlates of the "I." No wonder then that Wordsworth's "I" can slide quickly and easily into "all that we behold." The ultimate point of the passage is that sufficiently appreciating the "all" that memory initiates entails this "we." Moral being and perceptive being and imaginative being form an expressive whole because they exhibit what it takes for all of us to be able to say "Therefore am I still" and not close off much of what matters to our imaginative investments. The involvedness making the ego sublime also establishes for it a substantial social framework for appreciating what it takes for all subjects to live fully the syntaxes of which they are capable.

## V. The Value of Plasticity as an Attribute of States of Mind: The Example of Wallace Stevens's "Sunday Morning"

Intensity and involvedness account for the two basic directions in which the psyche moves in its experience of affective values—toward increased participation in the present moment and towards a more expansive sense of how those moments lead us beyond the confines of our egos. My third aspect of affective value returns us to states of subjective intensity, but now the states take on value because of how they handle those pressures from beyond the ego. This aspect consists in the values we experience because of the plasticity that our psyches are capable of producing as we encounter various tensions that emerge in trying to realize our desires. I mean by the term "plasticity" the capacity of a psyche or work of art to establish satisfaction in holding together without collapsing diverse aspects of experience which all have substantial claims upon us. My basic examples come from modernist art. Consider the range of sexual tensions and threats held in a single structure by the shallow space of Picasso's *Les Demoiselles d'Avignon* or the capacity of still lives like Braque's *Violin and Candlestick* to keep in dynamic relation the pull of gravity and the decentering forces released by the contours of shadow and *passage* moving out toward the edges of the canvas. There are also many powerful sculptural examples ranging from Michelangelo's late *Pietà* to the play of void and angle against the sexual intensities of Gaudier-Brzska's *Red Stone Dancer*. In all these cases, the distinguishing plasticity arises because containment is treated as a relation generated from within the work rather than from without. Containment becomes a purposive matter of how tensions achieve balance and of how oppositions interpenetrate and strengthen each other, often in ways that allow the interacting forces to seem open to attracting further aspects of experience.

Wallace Stevens's "Sunday Morning" provides the best condensed literary example I can discover of plasticity as a direct mode of satisfaction. The poem's speaker faces a basic problem that is as elemental as it once seemed intractable. He focuses his imagination on a woman who seems torn between two apparently contradictory sets of possible affective satisfactions, so he finds himself trying to imagine how one might satisfy the demands of both worlds. One world demands honoring Sunday as a memorial to religion, since her Christianity offers what seems the only feasible alternative to despair at human mortality. The other world seems capable of forgetting mor-

tality, if not of overcoming it, simply by reveling in the plenitude of immanent sensual satisfactions. Dialectical reconciliation seems impossible because there is no mediating principle. So Stevens tries another kind of
reconciliation—not by resolving the tension into some third term, but by letting the tension itself expand sufficiently to hold the opposites as dynamic
interrelationships that come to include one another's basic concerns. Resolution must be a matter not of producing a new answer to the questions but
of establishing powerful instruments for dwelling emotionally within what
the oppositions help unfold.

Here I have to concentrate on the poem's concluding stanza. The stage for
it is set by a process in which each time the speaker proposes eloquent arguments insisting that the second world of sensual satisfactions should
suffice, the woman manages to invoke needs and desires that his schema cannot encompass. So the poem's final reflections try to expand the affective field
into an elastic space that is given its contours by the poet's efforts to invest
fully in the intricate imaginative process required to engage these conflicts:

> She hears upon that water without sound,
> A voice that cries, "The tomb in Palestine
> Is not the porch of spirits lingering.
> It is the grave of Jesus where he lay."
> We live in an old chaos of the sun,
> Or old dependency of day and night,
> Or island solitude, unsponsored, free,
> Of that wide water inescapable.
> Deer walk upon our mountains, and the quail
> Whistle about us their spontaneous cries;
> Sweet berries ripen in the wilderness;
> And in the isolation of the sky,
> At evening, casual flocks of pigeons make
> Ambiguous undulations as they sink
> Downward to darkness, on extended wings.
>
> (70)

The woman's sense of mortality frames the imaginative labors and will not
be dispelled by what Stevens elsewhere calls "the intricate evasions of as."
The most the speaker's reflective stance can do is turn the fact of death into
a renewed awareness of the chaos that faces the living and that forces upon
them a freedom haunted by its need to face this mortality. Yet as he explores
metaphors for this unsponsored condition, his imagination is increasingly
drawn into the specific sensual details, now made especially resonant by the
backdrop of inescapable doom. Deer introduce motion and bring the mind
into the very world that it seems to avoid when it seeks abstract interpretations. Then this concrete world flourishes in a range of balancing attributes.
The quail's spontaneous cries complement the much more enduring tempo-

ral aspect of the ripening berries. And all of these particulars spread out against the isolation of the sky—each framing the other while linking echoes of the death motif with powerful figures of fertility. No wonder that now the stanza can move from being the property of one perspective or the other to the collective presence of an encompassing "we" given substance by what it can see in the scene composed for it.

Then there is the amazing last figure of the pigeons sinking "downward to darkness, on extended wings." Note first the physical plasticity. The pigeons stretch out this isolated sky (like a photograph by Felix Gonzalez-Torres), and their "ambiguous undulations" also slow down the time framed by that sky. The darkness is everywhere, but the living creatures refuse quite to submit to it without drawing it out and stretching themselves into it. This may be all the bliss we can know. Sound and syntax also work to slow down the sentence by suspending clauses and by playing long vowels and lush n and d sounds against the temporal flow of the sentence. Syntax and sound here function as the poet's extended wings, allowing the speaker's affective investments to dwell fully in what nonetheless he knows must pass.

Finally we must note the direct psychological work plasticity accomplishes. At first the poem could not reconcile in one space the idea of religious value and the fact of mortality. But now we can see that the problem may have been caused by the effort to seek resolution in argumentative terms. Resolution may be possible if we can simply approach consciousness as if it could treat its own embodiment as closely allied to the force of these extended wings. Religion fails for modernity when it has to be grounded in vertical relations creating an order superimposed on the secular one. But perhaps the imagination can produce analogous satisfactions by composing horizontal space so that its folds come to contain the flow of time.

Plasticity in conceiving space also establishes a remarkable comprehensiveness of will because it manages to embrace this isolated sky, as if understanding our failures to transcend the world enabled us to accommodate ourselves slowly and lovingly to the space we have available to inhabit.


## VI. From the Importance of Intentionality in the Affects to the Elemental Grammar of Four Basic Emotion Complexes

I have emphasized affect in aesthetic experience because there complex intentional states are especially important, and, correspondingly, there belief-centered models of the emotions cannot suffice. The values of intensity, involvedness, and plasticity flow directly from the enacting of stances that often do not require any kind of propositional judgment. But these are by no means the only central affective experiences in our lives. Much as I might want it to be the case, aesthetics is not life. An aesthetic orientation by itself will not sustain an adequate account of how we connect individual agency to many basic social structures, in large part because it also does not adequately handle the variety of investments supported by our conative drives.

One way to make the necessary adjustment is to take two perspectives on what goes into constituting the values fundamental to affective experience. One pole is the emphasis on complex states of subjectivity that we have pursued. The other pole calls for switching from an emphasis on individual subjects to the grammars that bind subjects because of expectations or desires they hold in common. By grammar here I mean Wittgenstein's concept of how education into our culture takes place. We learn a language by exploring possible uses of linguistic expressions. I think part of that grammar is affective. We learn what is possible or feasible to expect by observing how others imagine satisfactory affective experience, and we learn by exploring what elemental concepts like love and pain and joy can mean for us. Therefore I want for a few pages to explore these cultural expectations because they constitute fundamental building blocks for our emotional lives. I here will have to argue on the level of the adjectival—because we are talking not about individuals but about common expectations. And I might even have to swallow a little normativity in our developmental patterns. Yet I repeat my resistance to making normative claims about individuals because a grammatical learning does not decide adult practices. People are free to modify that grammar if they feel it suits them and does not harm others. And they typically vary in particular experiences of what they nonetheless in general terms treat as the same emotion.

I see two useful purposes to developing this argument. First, one can enrich our image of our conative impulses by stressing powerful basic emotions. And, second, we can point out that cultural particularists or cultural relativists often speak with unwarranted confidence. No doubt there are major cultural differences about affect experienced even in the modern West, and no doubt that the more microscopically we examine affects the more we can emphasize the cultural differences. But I suspect that now there tends to be an idealizing of difference without sufficient attention to what is common about our expectations and much of our practices. So I will emphasize the opposite case. I want at least to suggest the degree of cultural overlap there is even when there are justified claims to differences in how individuals experience affective bonds. It is true that grammars of expectation migrate and are affected by migrations. But it also ought not be forgotten how affective ties are asked to negotiate situations basic to almost any form of culture. Therefore significant conjunctions are possible even when cultures differ substantially in beliefs and customs.

Addressing these issues could easily elicit a separate book. But I mercifully do not have very much to say that is not already obvious from my previous arguments. So I will be as brief as possible in getting to what I think are the consequences of looking at the case this way. Because I have neither the ability nor the space to develop an extensive taxonomy of how different emotions bring values into play, I am going to take the opposite tack. Rather than focus on particular emotions, I will pursue a taxonomy bringing together large families of emotions. Obviously this emphasis makes it easier to show how certain affective states are legible across cultures because all one has to demonstrate is that the overall paradigm seems to apply in comparative cases. But making a process of explanation easier does not necessarily mean one is stacking the deck. It may be the case that even when our grammars for specific emotions produces significant differences across cultures, our grammar for sets of emotions makes the adjustments necessary for negotiating cultural borders. We will be testing that even as we explore whether my brief descriptions are adequate and whether they cogently represent the values that are typically at stake for those experiencing these emotions.

My taxonomy consists in grouping paradigmatic emotion types into four basic complexes distinguished from one another by the orientations toward values that direct how we project satisfactions for the emotions.[13] The first two complexes consist of fundamentally self-regarding values. In the first complex, the emotions are oriented toward immediate investments projected by auto-affective interests; in the second they are oriented toward how the self can stage itself over time in relation to various versions of a public gaze. The other two complexes involve our investments in values that draw us out of the self into "the things of this world" (as Richard Wilbur put it). I call the first of these an "engagement-attention" complex because many emotions either constitute values or call our attention to values because they position us in distinctive ways toward what unfolds in immediate situations. Then what we can call a "care-connection" complex gathers those emotions where our attention to the present develops significant commitments that extend over time. Although I put each complex in positive terms, we could easily tilt the picture to cover negative versions of the same orientations: frustrations in pursuing pride generate shame, and frustrated care becomes anger or jealousy. (Conversely we could see the "positive" states as overcoming latent "negative" states.)

This simply taxonomy of complexes becomes somewhat dynamic if we represent it in the form of a matrix:

|  | Self-focused | Other focused |
|---|---|---|
| Event-oriented | auto-affection complex | engagement-attention complex |
| Duration-oriented | public recognition complex | care-connection complex |

The basic components of the auto-affection complex are those attitudes that pursue values directly in our ways of experiencing ourselves as enhanced subjective agents. Here we usually deal with feelings rather than well-defined emotions. So it should suffice to say that at the core of the auto-affection complex we find the values of intensity and plasticity that most directly satisfy our conative desires. The public recognition complex, on the other hand, presents a very different version of self-regard. Here the values the self seeks depend on the identities others will, or will not, confer. Pride is a good test case here because it can appear in either complex. Hume speaks of pride as the fundamental emotion because it gives us the sense of self without which we lack the conative energies to pursue any value at all. Then there is the form of pride that is the other side of shame. Pride here is the identification of the self with a particular image that, in imagination at least, one earns from one's community. And pride admits of infinite adjustments and internal tensions depending on how much one allows the others to matter at any given moment and on how they actually offer or withhold what is desired.

When we turn to the emotion complexes based on our responsiveness to the world, we clearly need to distinguish values that depend on the intensifying of immediate interests from those that enter into enduring states and so persist through a variety of shifting particular modifications. The first of these complexes provides a striking illustration of why we ought not to be too intellectual in our treatment of values. Emotions like sexual passion or anger substantially modify our attention to details even when we do not make considered judgments to attend or to keep on attending. And, more important, casual shifts in attention can suddenly fascinate us with how something appears, so that we make intricate psychological adjustments. Consider again impressionist paintings. These works demand and celebrate processes of attunement to what we see that clearly cannot be derived from or adjusted by standard intellectual practices. The attachment itself is the work of feeling. But we can make investments based on those feelings that then take the form of full-scale emotional attitudes. We organize memories and direct desires in accord with how certain places and even certain moments sponsor affective responses. Analogously, portraits remind us of how the intricacy of faces can take hold in our affective lives. And then it is not a large leap to recognize how quickly anger or envy can emerge from the details we observe, at times in ways that remain in tension with the justifying beliefs that the agent offers.

The second complex does involve beliefs because it points us to emotional states that cast subjects as pursuing relatively long-term concerns about their objects. The obvious paradigms here are love and hatred, but in fact many emotions involve similar ways of building duration into their structures of concern. Think for example of the many different ways we forge social relations by emotions of loyalty and by emotions based on sympathy or responsiveness to what seem possibilities in other persons. And then there are important emotions devoted to how we regard our overall relationship to the world. What wonder does as part of the engagement-attention complex, joy does as a more enduring form of care (or at least as a form of care that projects itself over time even though it rarely lasts).

These other-focused complexes are especially important to my argument because they at least gesture toward two sets of concerns on which my account has been woefully inadequate. They get us out of the constant self-regard that has been central to my version of an aesthetics of the affects. And they allow us then to pursue a more complex model of how our investments form and develop. We can appreciate how some aspects of our values derive from the energies of consciousness pushing out into the world while others seem to be responses to how the world pulls us or solicits our capacities for caring.[14] If I had the time and the patience, I would now spell out how these kinds of values differ and what place each kind occupies in our typical practices. But I have nothing to add to an account of the particular manifestations of these values that is not already visible in our grammar for the specific emotions I have grouped under these complexes.[15] So in the place of extended analysis, I am going to move immediately to two quite general theoretical consequences that follow if my taxonomy is at all feasible.

The first consequence can be handled by simple assertion because it just extends what I have been arguing. At core many of the arguments about the relation of reason to passion derive from this basic dichotomy: are the values constituted within our affective lives fundamentally fictions, projected by egos or imposed by cultural formations, or is there sense in treating our emotions as significant because they help us attach ourselves to qualities the objects in fact possess?[16] I don't think we can make arguments at this level of generalization that will convince anyone not already disposed to accept a particular view. But we can use the two object-oriented complexes I isolate in order to help clarify what each option involves and to show that it can make sense to dwell on those attributes that solicit our involvement. When philosophers stress the fictive qualities of emotions, they enter quite strange alliances. Traditional rationalists join existentialists like Sartre and cultural constructionists like Rom Harré in distrusting any sense that we are so wired that the emotions are in fact responses to value-conferring properties in the world. Imaginations project values on an indifferent world. So we have to seek some stance outside the emotion as the only trustworthy means of assessing the values. Any more sympathetic mode of consciousness is likely to be seduced by what it must govern. It is no accident then that Louis Althusser makes more ambitious claims for analytic reason than Derek Parfit does; nor is it an accident that Sartre could justify existential despair because he thought there was no faculty that could have both the lucidity to make the necessary judgments and the interest necessary to will any particular form of life.

At the other pole, we find strange conjunctions between Dantean Catholicism, Whitehead's cosmology, the phenomenological perspective developed by Maurice Merleau-Ponty, and Deleuze's rhizomatic expressivism. From these perspectives, we do not begin with dichotomies between what can be demonstrated objectively and what is fundamentally fictive. We have to realize that it is this very hunger for sharp distinctions between what the agent contributes and what the world solicits that leads philosophers and social planners to rely on the fiction story as their default position. At least the default position does not require intricate patience adapted to particular cases, and it affords a much more transparent and workable overall model. But the very reasons for accepting this position are also reasons for wondering if we are choosing the easy way out. So it may be worth our while to see if theorizing about the emotions can help us at least keep the second option alive for approaching particular cases. We can begin by suggesting that the concept of fictiveness has important but quite limited uses. That concept makes good sense only when we are trying to separate what can be objectively demonstrated about existence from what cannot. Then the relevant concerns engage matters of epistemic stability. How values emerge is a very different domain: not being objective in an epistemic sense does not entail being only subjective in the domain of psychology. This negative argument will not in itself warrant claiming that there is some other kind of nondiscursive objectivity that values possess. However, it may help indicate the limits of theory on such matters, so that we remain free to explore whether in particular cases the agents can be represented as discovering values that are not simply projections.

Two of my obsessive themes can be helpful in establishing this freedom. If emotions depend on a wide range of intentional states that often cannot be treated as the projection of beliefs, then it is also more difficult to impose the model of fictionality. Where we cannot point to beliefs, it is not easy to speak of fictions. Then if we can put these modes of intentionality within large complexes that stress the frameworks for our emotions rather than the specific events of their formation, we are not reduced to the small range of psychological predicates provided by epistemic perspectives. For there to be fictions, there have to be expectations about truths. But if emotions are primarily ways of coping with the needs and desires characterizing particular situations, then we can adapt psychological vocabularies that stress the kinds of adjustments we make in our senses of self and senses of the world. Value need not be either a discovery or a fiction; it can emerge as a relationship between structures of concern and the details forming specific situations. In such cases, it can be a mistake to assume that the emotion inheres in particular fantasized objects. Instead, our sense of the entire situation can elicit and even organize our investments. (That is one way lust turns to love, or what we think of as love becomes manifest as wanting the world of the other person more than we want that person.)

If these observations are defensible, we can say that what begins as conative push can yield to the pulling force of particular qualities. As observers, we are in a position to recognize the force exercised by our interests in being certain kinds of persons, even with respect to how we care for others. But recognizing that force need not preclude our also registering what plausibly reaches out to that interest and provides a soil in which it might flourish. Moreover, since we are dealing with overall structures of need and desire, we have good reason not to see the pursuit of value in terms of isolated decisions. By stressing how overall dispositions can frame situations, we make it possible to realize the various roles time can play in shaping what comes to count as value. Over time I have grounds for appreciating differences among those in whose gaze I seek my pride or face my shame. And I have ways of testing the degree to which what first captures my attention has the capacity to engage and modify it. What might have seemed largely a fictive construction can eventually lead me to discover actual features that continue to engage my attention and elicit my commitments.

## VII. Social Bonds without Subjection: A Hegelian Critique of Judith Butler's Version of Cultural Constructionist Theory

My second consequence depends on pretty much the same line of argument I have just been developing. But now the issue is not the fictive dimension of our values but their relation to the sociocultural conditions within which they are formulated. In some ways the logical form of this issue has significant affinities with the question of fictions. We inherit a quite similar governing binary opposition—this time one that sets an ideal of lucid freedom aware of the partiality of our constructions against the likelihood that our affective investments bind us to particular cultural ideologies.

But developing the necessary alternative takes us through more contentious territory. Ideally we could get a much better grasp on the issue of just what is cultural about cultural constitution if we patiently submitted ourselves to extensive phenomenological descriptions studying the affects in different cultural frameworks. But now we do not have that phenomenology and we do not have the luxury of waiting for it before we take our stand on questions of cultural constitution. All sorts of personal and pedagogical decisions depend on whether we think the emotions mediate and strengthen the hold that given ideological structures have upon us or whether we think they provide some orientation that can actually challenge that cultural hegemony. And my position is complicated by my rejections of cognitivist models that bring rationality to bear because then it seems as if I have no grounds for denying the prevailing culturalist claims. If emotions are not rational or allied with reason, then it seems they have to get their force from what is now called "the cultural imaginary."[17] Affective values become prime examples of how agents are interpellated into cultures and of how their senses of subjectivity are in fact subjected to prevailing cultural fantasies. But I hope I can show that a sufficiently rich psychology engages levels of our attention and care and conative intensity that cannot be accommodated within a strong culturalist account.

Clearly, all values that are available for self-reflection depend on some kind of cultural framework. Otherwise they would not be intelligible. The challenge is to establish this intelligibility within culture without insisting that the value depends on any set of cultural determinants that bind agents to specific local social units and so blind them to how other social groups constitute values. To handle this challenge I treat the cultural framework as a range of grammars at different levels of generality, some of which are embedded in each other. We might share with another culture a vision of what counts as an expression of jealousy and still have somewhat different ways of assessing whether the jealousy is warranted or wise. Just as the feelings often prove resistant to our efforts to impose representations upon them, our affective investments often produce modes of expression that pull against or substantially modify the standard predicates that make the effort at modification intelligible. So if we can show that our grammars and the emotional complexes they mediate have embedded levels that allow us to make judgments about specific prevailing systems, we can appreciate how to use terms like inventiveness or sensitivity or complexity in relation to something capable of binding cultures rather than cultivating differences. And we can treat an expression of an investment in a particular value as a testing of how agents can manipulate the available resources to be responsive to various kinds of pressure put upon that value.

I could cite as evidence for my claims how the various modern art objects we have examined try to express states that are not predictable from within their culture's standard repertoire. But my strongest case goes back to the concluding action of the *Iliad,* because there, at virtually the beginning of our recorded tales of cultural conflict, we find agents coming to appreciate how there might be a structure of affects and related values that requires reaching beyond what have been compelling cultural convictions. The scene presents two absolute enemies, Priam and Achilles, who come to identify with one another because each person's grief enables him to understand what the other is suffering. Within Priam's culture there was no category for forgiving someone who had killed his favorite son. And even when he was not in a vengeful rage over the death of his beloved friend, Achilles was committed to destroying enemies, not to letting them live because he could appreciate their pain and the nobility it took to meet with him. Yet the story presents both characters' individual suffering as so intense it enables them to form a mutual bond that from the point of view of either culture would be virtually unimaginable. They find their links to each other as creatures who mourn loved ones much more important than the many traits that manifest their differences and constitute them as enemies. In fact, they find this likeness precisely within their emotional states. It seems as if the ways in which they are moved require that they explore latent aspects of what their culture affords them as forms for grief. In that exploration they discover resources providing alternative paths that they can learn to negotiate by reflecting on what they find themselves expressing.

Examples, however, cannot carry much theoretical weight. They can prevent certain conclusions. But to take full advantage of them we have to propose a conceptual structure that clarifies the factors making it possible to read the example in a particular way. For this theoretical model in relation to values constituted within our affective lives, I want to propose a Hegelian way of thinking (although without making any claims about *Geist*), then apply it to Judith Butler's influential claims about the cultural constitution of values. Hegel enters my picture because any effort to deal with cultural constitution has to begin with a basic opposition between cultural practices and what is at least initially other to those practices. There are needs, drives, and felt modes of attentive interest, connection, and satisfaction that seem inchoate and inarticulate and so not dependent on the forms of understanding provided by a specific culture. How then do we explain the roles these inchoate factors play in cultural life? One option is to treat the social forms as oppressive and alienating clothing that disciplines and distorts the originating conditions. Or the forms can be more seductive, implicitly promising us identities and recognitions so long as we adhere to the structure of roles that preserves their power to make determinations and preserve social hierarchies: to be subjects, we have to undergo subjection to the prevailing grammatical and social frameworks. Social structures interpellate the subject by offering terms by which it can be called and then recognized for having been so called. Consider what mothers offer their children or teachers their students or the police to those whom they sort as innocent and guilty.

In both models of social constitution, the opposition between culture and its "others" takes the form of a sharp dichotomy between what enters dominant and dominating forms and what manages somehow to resist the forms of articulation that produce that subjection. But Hegel's interest in dialectical negation enables us to recast this dichotomy into a variety of small but significant interactions between the individual event and the work done by the social order. Hegel sees spirit and substance as mutually dependent. What lives by negating form and what secures existence by embodying form require each other. While there seems to be something always other or negative in relation to cultural representations, this otherness comes into active play only against the backdrop of the practices and grammars that provide what intelligibility is possible. The sharper our sense of how intelligibility is formed, the richer our appreciation of what puts pressure on that intelligibility. Conversely, the more fully we feel that pressure, the better we are likely to understand what that intelligibility makes possible. For we know the difference between the inherited cultural form and the needs for a more adequate expression of one's particular state. And once the cause of the limitation is seen as the overall constraints of a social grammar, it becomes impossible to determine from the outside who can and cannot participate in the new form of expression.

So far I am offering a very tepid Hegel. I have been dealing with one aspect of Hegel on the expressive process, but I have so far ignored an important second aspect of how he understands dialectic. For Hegel it cannot suffice just to point out how the opposites depend on one another, as if we could find some comfortable position from which to observe history's blend of the comic and the tragic. We have to see the internal dynamic as a distinctive process by which the forces involved are in fact continually modifying each other. The dialectic is not only for observers. It is an actual matter of how what appears as negative and what becomes articulate live one another's life and die one another's death. Each pole is literally folded into its opposite and in constant flux. What emerges as other, as the world of needs and drives and felt connections, does so because this otherness is in effect continually spun off from the processes by which experiences become articulate. I could not feel alienation if I were not interpellated into a culture and encountering its limitations. There is no "other" without the desire of there being a "same." And that desire in turn is inseparable from at least a potential sense that the fabric providing for sameness is unraveling. But that unraveling is not the end of the story. The agent has the possibility of taking up a stance in relation to that unraveling and so opening paths for new modes of mutual recognition within the society.

Hegel is so abstract that we probably can make almost any situation fit his model so long as agents feel themselves struggling against limitations. But it is important to see that ultimately he is not making only an empirical assertion. True child of Kant, he is making a transcendental claim about the structure necessary if we are to treat culture as a dynamic framework rather than a static one. We cannot understand the possible force of particular social practices without appreciating how individuals depend on them. And we cannot develop a concept of significant individuality without locating the individuality as establishing some negative push against dominant practices. Every judgment we make that confers individual expressiveness indicates either a plasticity within the culture or a pressing limitation in its overall authority. The better we sense the limitations of any cultural scheme, the more we also have terms for appreciating just what it provides for us that enables us to articulate this particular limit condition.

To illustrate my version of Hegel I think it appropriate to shift from the *Iliad* to a garden variety example like those we find in contemporary philosophy. The example has to demonstrate that by treating the emotion as the developing of an attitude we can correlate its negativity, its insistence on its own particular density, and the frameworks that make it possible to articulate its complexities. These frameworks consist in the cultural grammar explicit for the society and the implicit structures that emerge when we expand the context to include more general complexes extending beyond the confines of particular cultures. In reacting to something Jim did, I find myself taking on one of the standard forms of anger that my culture makes available. But as I elaborate that anger I also find myself feeling somewhat uneasy—perhaps I had offended Jim or forced him into the corner from which he inflicted pain on me. Now I begin to experience a subjectivity not fully at home with the roles that my culture provides. I still need the cultural frameworks in order to recognize where the limitations occur. But a strange transformation has occurred. I cannot be as secure as I have been in my assessment of myself: to be other to the culture is also to be in part other to one's self-image. That in turn means that the culture is incapable of providing what I want, so my presumed place within it becomes considerably less secure.

However, this sense of weakness at both poles is accompanied by a more vivid sense of specific existence at each pole. My anxiety is inseparable from a sharper awareness of myself as an individual, since when the culture loses authority I have to compensate for the sense of identity it provided. And as my sense of the "I" wobbles, the cultural order seems paradoxically both weaker and much more imposing. The terms it does provide for expressing anger now seem limited and perhaps shaped by ideological needs I now might be in a position to grasp. But seeing that also makes me feel more strongly the need that there be some culture with which I can identify. As I am thrown back on this sense of ungrounded subjectivity, I am also forced to see how much my needs for expression bind me to what may underlie those very cultural grammars that fail me. Now I am forced to attempt reimagining the culture in more abstract terms—in part so that I can at least develop terms for sharing with others the sense of dissatisfaction involved, and in part because I might then find new grounds for recognizing what is being expressed. I can discover that there have been similar struggles in other circumstances where people with analogous confusions have pushed against the limits of their cultural repertoires. What was a negativity in relation to the specific cultural framework on which I originally relied may turn out to be a positive force in terms of establishing possible identity with those who share my need for an affective grammar responsive to such tensions.

One reason Judith Butler has been so influential is that she has developed a model of cultural constitution honoring some central Hegelian concerns. (She has written a fine book on Hegel.) But we have very different approaches to the role negation plays, and hence to how dialectic functions. Butler is deeply suspicious of talk about social structures that gives any place at all to the "fiction of the ego as master of circumstance" (*Bodies That Matter*, 124). When she talks about identity and identification, she refuses to allow any distinctive agency for the ego—it can create negativity but not transform that negativity for its own purposes. Identification is simply a social process, although a necessarily incomplete and unstable one because of that negativity. Identifications are formed by two basic factors that enable culture to reproduce itself through the investments it solicits from agents. Culture provides the stable names we need to be able to refer to experiences and substances, and it establishes incentives for our identifying with those categorical terms. Consider a topic dear to Butler's heart, the process of gender identification. There must be a specific name allowing us to be called repeatedly by the culture so that we can describe ourselves as particular kinds of agents occupying roles within it. And there must be a set of incentives and prohibitions which prevent our realizing just how unstable these foundational names might be. Once one is identified as a girl, many institutions within the culture reinforce that call so that one is heavily rewarded for answering without hesitation or doubt. Hence concepts of normalcy are established and specific cultures can develop practices that depend on agents' accepting that notion of normalcy. But the very urgency of efforts to establish heterosexual models for these norms suggests that the culture's "effort to become its own idealizations can never be finally or fully achieved." It will be haunted by the need to exclude other sexual possibilities (125). Those possibilities are its ever-present negative energies.

This instability creates the possibility for change—not because we also internalize alternative cultural possibilities, but because there can never be a fully adequate version of the binary division of boy from girl on which the call depends. Some of this instability is evident in the room culture gives to try playful variants on its basic binaries. But such play merely relieves pressure without constituting significant differences. Substantial change comes because the established prohibitions will not be accepted with the same degree of satisfaction by all agents. Where there is dissatisfaction, there are incentives to see the prohibitions not just as negatives but also as instigations, as sources of possible fascination. The child made intensely curious by what he or she is told not to touch is the father of the man and woman who find society's "no's" enticements to experiment with the dominant code. [18]

Butler's central concern then becomes how we can give force and substance to these enticements: "If one comes into discursive life through being hailed or called in injurious terms, how might one occupy the interpellation by which one is already occupied so as to direct the possibility of resignification against the aims of violation?" (123). Butler's answer converts what had seemed an individualist notion of performativity into much more social terms. Resignification is performativity that appropriates the master language in order to make it over. And if the resignification can be repeated regularly, it has the power to create "the discursive and social space for community" (137). The transsexuals in Jenny Livingstone's *Is Paris Burning?* resignify not just sexuality but also the very language of family. And by constantly repeating these resignifications in their lives, they actually open new ways of living as family.

Butler's model offers compelling accounts of the pressure on marginalized social groups, and it makes it possible for us to appreciate just what Livingstone and those she represents establish by their interventions. Butler's model makes good sense of how gender prescriptions work because there the temptation to establish binary oppositions is so strong. But, contra Saussure, the model based on binaries will not encompass the full range of relevant needs and desires and modes of adjustment that the theory of cultural change must address. Accounts of language that causes injury and that constrains gender and kinship possibilities are not particularly appropriate for situations where language simply fails to articulate people's investments or even where agents struggle to shift from the parameters of a local culture to some more general model of affective possibilities. And treating all positive emotions as based on enforced identifications ignores by fiat the possibility that we are actually responding to features of the world that might elicit pretty much the same emotion under a wide variety of cultural frameworks. It is unlikely that all sympathy exists only because agents pursue the identity of sympathetic persons. Emphasizing identity needs is simply not sufficiently dynamic to handle either what subjects want or what the many levels of culture provide. So an adequate account of socialization requires more supple means of elaborating both the inchoate dimension of our sense of self and the resources available by which that inchoateness can take satisfying forms.

Probably the best way to meet Butler's challenge is to explore the possibility that resignification may well not be the most appropriate label for such struggles with expression and communication. Perhaps the problem is less with the specific language we use in evoking identity than with the frameworks that we bring to bear in appreciating what force language can have. Therefore my Hegelian leanings lead me to prefer "recontextualization" to "resignification" as a term for the dynamics of cultural change. Recontextualization does not entail making it new or forcing parodic relations on the dominant language. It simply entails finding alternative modes of expression and grounds for associations within available cultural resources. Consequently recontextualization does not force us into binary oppositions, and it allows us to treat concerns about manner and quality as basic to these efforts to form adequate expressions.

Even more important, the modified Hegelian view I am proposing does not require always setting one form of life against another or treating dissatisfaction as a form of negativity requiring political resistance. If we move the cultural frameworks around sufficiently, there might be space to find a framework of values that can be shared by those with quite different initial understandings of call and response.[19] And we need not treat the inchoate as caused by some kind of suppression. Rather the inchoate is often directly proportional to modes of desire eager to celebrate what makes them seem aspects of the subject's deepest investments. We struggle to find satisfying expressions based on forms of caring that are not easily translated into identity terms. And we can mine our emotions to find out what lies at their core that might not be bound only to one specific culture or structure of call and response. Culture may be the very resource by which we find models and analogues of our struggles or examples of what seems to reach beyond particular cultural formations. Theory honors how that culture works when it locates the possibility of values that go beyond the structure of call and response.

## VIII. Joyce's *Dubliners* as Test Case for Developing a Partial Alternative to the Constructivist Case: How Emotions Cross Cultural Boundaries

The best way I know to thicken the difference between recontextualization and resignification in relation to emotions and values is to turn to James Joyce's *Dubliners,* the literary text that I think most intensely grapples with the logic of cultural constitution in relation to affective values. If Dublin is not a character in the text, it is at the least the source of a pervasive condition that seems to doom everyone who encounters it.[20] To be a subject in this world is to find oneself internalizing both the values Dublin produces and the affective strategies that enable its inhabitants to protect themselves from the destructive consequences of those values. So the text posits for itself the challenge of rendering this condition accurately and still establishing some alternative position from which judgment is possible and release thinkable.[21] Or, better, Joyce wants to make the very effort to render the condition accurately carry with it possible means of breaking away from it, if one is willing and able to pay the prices involved.

Joyce's particular rendering of how cultures interpellate subjects perfectly matches contemporary theory. In *Dubliners* the culture's values are not imposed on agents but actively embraced by them as the means by which they can establish identities and feel their actions having meaning. Ironically, the frustrations built into these values turn out to intensify their power because the pain makes people have even greater needs for imaginary identifications. Joyce elaborates these powers by turning his stories into a dark bildungsroman tracing the various life stages of typical Dublin denizens. The first three stories offer first-person tales that render a range of childhood hopes all destroyed by the interactions with the adults the children encounter. As the stories move out to young adults and then adults, we realize in retrospect why the children in their disappointment become the adults who disappoint. The apparent progression in the sequence betrays an endless cycle of failure and recrimination calling for its Dante. The very factors that block the children's dreams lead them eventually to take on the psychological dispositions of the adults who cause the problems in the first place. Disappointment generates frustration and despair, and those states produce a range of aggressive and self-deluding strategies that make it possible to survive the omnipresence of abject failure. Increases in wealth and status make the oppressive behavior less overtly brutal, but the blindness necessary to preserve status creates an even more oppressive ideological smugness. Even when Mr. Duffy in "A Painful Case" wants to be different from all the drunks and whiners in his culture, the blind righteousness created by his need to be different produces perhaps the collection's most painful betrayal of possibilities.

If Joyce had relied on naturalist principles, he would have been able to posit substantial authority for his interpretive position. His task would have become clarifying the relevant cultural determinants by calling attention to how very general historical and biological forces do their work. But by refusing naturalism, Joyce gave himself the much more difficult task of rendering the ways agents actively imbricate themselves in these cultural forces. That is why the opening stories begin with the first person. There can be a first person for the children because their imaginations are not yet reduced to self-protective fantasies and compensatory aggression. By the fourth story, the collection begins to shift from inviting identification with characters to emphasizing how the characters are destroyed by what they take to be their possibilities for heeding calls and establishing identities. So the narrative needs the distance of a primarily third-person perspective. But Joyce cannot be content with that distance—in part because it assumes there can be a clear bird's-eye view and in part because that distance risks losing the level of intimacy one has to maintain if one is to understand why the distortions take hold (rather than just note that they take hold). So he relies frequently on free indirect discourse, thus gaining that distanced perspective while developing access to the intimate levels on which people represent themselves to themselves. By so manipulating point of view, Joyce can show how values prove inseparable from the ways in which characters speak, and he can render these speeches so that they reveal how the agents are spoken through by what keeps Dublin Dublin. Chandler offers little but the language of the failed poet, Jimmy the language of social hanger-on, and Maria the internalizing of spinster fussiness.

Joyce seems to have offered one way out of this gloom when he insisted that his stories produced moments of epiphany in which we recognize a situation as "that thing which it is. Its soul." "Its whatness leaps to us from the vestment of its appearance." An epiphany is the moment when the spiritual eye manages to adjust its vision to an exact focus.[22] Just as Dante's *Inferno* tries to help us see the justice of each character's punishment as part of the eternal logic of sinful character, Joyce wants his reader to see the totality of a life in a gesture. But the Dante analogue also indicates the dark side of how this aesthetic principle works in Joyce's text. For having a life subject to epiphany is not likely to be a desirable state. Epiphanies are possible here because these are lives that can be summarized in a moment of illumination. We can know them because they are so fixed within the culture that they cannot change. Or if there is change, it is only the work of time intensifying the deleterious effects of Dublin life as the person gets further away from youthful hope. Thus Maria in "Clay" is only a more desperate version of Evelyn's finding freedom so terrifying she cannot leave Ireland. And Farrington in "Counterparts" is only a more desperate version of the two gallants, now letting all the repressions of lower-class life boil up into aimless, self-destructive anger.

The crucial questions then become, To whom can these epiphanies matter and for what purposes? Who can understand the actual values driving this society without becoming subjected by it, and what powers and costs go along with the capacity for such understanding? It seems that the epiphanies cannot be for his characters because they are so trapped in defensive postures that they are incapable of lucidity. So Joyce has to develop two other sites where the resonance of their situations can reverberate. Both sites require being able to stand at least partially outside the specific culture one is engaging. One site involves the projection of an authorial role somewhat different from traditional ones; the other a complex set of demands on the reader made possible because of the authorial activity. Joycean authorship is pronouncedly a process of resignification. The author does not occupy some reflective promontory but clearly gets sucked into his material. Writing becomes a direct challenge that tests whether he can find ways to "occupy the interpellation by which he is already occupied."

Yet if we rely on Butler's version of resignification, I don't think we can adequately characterize the author position in *Dubliners*. On the one hand, Joycean resignification seems not directed at how others might come along and by repetition form community. For him resignification is intensely personal and momentary. His text engages language at its most enslaving in order to make clear how personal agency might reinhabit it as a field of play. By making writing fundamental to hearing how voices are constituted, Joyce makes available for himself a range of auto-affective values based on his power to revalue Dublin within his own textual medium. If the writer cannot live freely in Dublin, he can make his elaborate architecture and capacity to take on his characters' most intimate concerns the substance of a Nietzschean revel. But the Nietzschean revel may be inseparable from Nietzschean pathos. For we find that this authorial presence takes on power precisely because it cannot quite successfully resignify what it encounters. Play as he can, this author keeps returning to the trap that is Dublin. He cannot not pity what Dublin makes of its inhabitants, and so he cannot enter fully into any alternative community. And his realist heritage insists that any resignification that matters cannot just reweave those aspects of the cultural fabric that intensify victimage. If an author is to have the right to assert the freedom distance and artifice can bring, parody will not suffice. The author must be able to identify intimately with every situation he wants to overcome or escape. To resignify successfully depends on being able also to reproduce the forces of oppression and the dispositions that embrace those forces. The author as subject must live and die with the cultural structures that make visible the need for this opposing stance.

Joyce handles these problems in large part by introducing a modernist version of the second person to complement his shifting third-person stances. The entire text seems to me a massive appeal for an audience to be willing to try out the form of reading Joyce is modeling for it. He cannot be content with projecting an authorial wisdom able to interpret the actions it represents; nor can it suffice to rest in awe at the artist's brilliant compositional accomplishment. Joyce wants his audience to use the understanding of Dublin he affords them in order to attempt identifying provisionally with the struggles that he takes on as he tries to find some way not to be destroyed by the conditions he anatomizes. Even if the characters are doomed, there remain options for taking particular attitudes toward their plight. And a readership able to share the author's own sense of struggle might make it possible to envision a social order not quite trapped by Dublin, not even by the temptation to stop with the effort to elicit sympathy. There can at least be an imaginative community formed by identifying with the complex emotions driving this author to this mode of writing as his means of coming to terms with coming to culture through Dublin's forms of life.

In other words, Joyce could revel in his powers as a writer only if he could also fully dramatize the powers he wanted to make available for his readers. What resignifying could not accomplish, recontextualizing might. So if I can trace the novelist's efforts to show what this recontextualizing involves, I may be able to demonstrate how the values constituted by the emotions need not be confined to the culture that both elicits them and gives them their initial means of expression. Because distance and sympathy are so fully conjoined in this constructed reader position, Joyce's readers are given the opportunity to find a site where they can share with the characters (and with other readers) the intimate texture of frustration that shapes their experiences of value. Only by pursuing such powers will these readers be able to work their way through the traps pathos sets for the psyche and still manage to find ways of continuing to engage in the pain and anger created when one cares about those who have succumbed to those traps. And only this project will allow the hope that the novelist can construct readers capable of a sympathy that is not complicity and a sense of freedom that is not merely a pleasure in escaping the sufferings Dublin produces.

I would love now to indulge in a comparative analysis of what becomes available through the reader positions established by Joyce and by Proust, each of whom has a whole lot of interpellation to work through. But it will be much more efficient if I turn directly to "The Dead," the last story in *Dubliners*, because there Joyce offers a powerful and complex dramatic situation that both illustrates and tests his version of exemplary reading. The story's main character, Gabriel Conroy, has much in common with the implied and with the actual author of this volume. We encounter Gabriel as his life reaches a crisis that requires him to wonder about the cost of having developed strategies enabling him to negotiate a social order from which he feels thoroughly alienated. Gabriel's frustrations are not those of the other Dubliners we meet. Rather they stem from his labors to retain a distance from the lives of Irish working people and to take on for himself the manners and skills of the British professional classes.[23] But this effort at opposition may well turn out to be part of the trap Dublin prepares for its citizens: it seems one can avoid the corruptions of the colonized only by aping the manners of the colonizers. Being Irish, Gabriel cannot entirely accept the alternative identities, and so he turns out to lack any stable place in his society, while he also fails to establish any workable imaginative version of how he might stand outside that society. Even early in the story we find him forced to become an uneasy reader of his own situation:

> The indelicate clacking of the men's heels and the shuffling of their soles reminded him that their grade of culture differed from his. He would only make himself ridiculous by quoting poetry to them which they could not understand. They would think that he was airing his superior education. He would fail with them just as he had failed with the girl in the pantry. He had taken up a wrong tone. His whole speech was a mistake from the first to the last, an utter failure. (163)

Two features of this passage seem to me especially important for this study. First, Gabriel's reading position is a complicated one. His very care for the Dubliners at the party proves inseparable from contempt for their submission to a life that narrows their imaginations and corrupts their sensibilities. Yet his sense of alienation is also no comfort. The pose of alienation seems part of one's birthright as an Irish intellectual—even resisting the pathos may require becoming bound to the overall pathetic situation. Second, I think it is significant that for most of the story the demands on Gabriel as a reader are matched by his commitment to his role as author of a toast that he gives each Christmas. He tries by subtle resignification to honor both the Dublin values of his audience and his own sense of the difference his cultivation makes. But by identifying with the author position, he intensifies his own uneasiness about his differences from his audience. And, worse, his fantasies about his power as the speechmaker carry over into his fantasies about his sexual power over his wife—a very vulnerable self-projection in which to indulge. Susceptibility to such investments may be why writers need (and fear) readers whom they cannot control.

The climax of "The Dead" occurs when Gabriel is forced to shift from his role as author to a kind of reading quite unfamiliar to him. And it is here that Joyce most emphatically seeks, through the figure of Gabriel reading, his own capacity to engage the Dublin he has rendered without being destroyed by the sympathy and rage that his engagement elicits. If he could identify with a reading position, he might be able to gain some distance from his own fantasies and so open himself to what he can neither invent nor control nor subsume under his writerly stance. He might then learn to appreciate values that are not trapped within the Dublin destiny.

The climactic sequence begins as Gabriel leaves the party and looks up at his wife Gretta, who is listening to someone singing. He feels intense desire for her—partially because she seems suddenly transfigured by the intensity of her attention, and partially as the extension of his own sense that she should be impressed by his being the central figure of the party. The conquering hero wants to be desired. So as they arrive at their hotel, he sees possibilities for erotic romance that offer a world where he need no longer feel the guilt and incompleteness that accompany his social role:

> But now after the kindling again of so many memories, the first touch of her body musical and strange and perfumed, sent through him a keen pang of lust. . . . as they stood at the hotel door, he felt that they had escaped from home and friends and run away together with wild and radiant hearts to a new adventure. (196)

Joyce's prose is so sensitive to Gabriel's emotional intensity that it allows Gabriel's ways of formulating desire to enter the third-person narrative— Joyce would not allow himself phrases like "radiant hearts."[24] So it is no surprise that Gabriel is thrilled that Gretta seems to share his sexual arousal. But even with all his investments in romantic "escape," Gabriel's sharpened senses also lead him to notice that she is intently thinking about something and so he asks what it is. Her response surprises him. She is thinking of a boy who was in love with her when she lived in Galway. Gabriel pursues the topic and is told that the boy actually died because he risked his health to see her.

This is not the kind of information with which Gabriel regularly deals, especially when he is full of sexual desire and self-satisfaction. And the Ireland whose music she hears is not the one for which he can maintain the kind of contempt one develops by identifying with the colonizer. (Nor is the music comparable to the performances at the bourgeois party.) So having let himself attempt to read her, he now has to become once more a reader of his own situation. But this time there can be no illusion of his own importance. He seems to himself not an object of someone else's desire but a poor second or substitute for the kind of man who can elicit full romantic feelings:

> Gabriel felt humiliated by the failure of his irony. . . . While he had been full of memories of their secret life together, full of tenderness and joy and desire, she had been comparing him in her mind with another. . . . He saw himself as a ludicrous figure, acting as a pennyboy for his aunts, a nervous wellmeaning sentimentalist, orating to vulgarians and idealizing his own clownish lusts, the pitiable fatuous fellow he had caught a glimpse of in the mirror. (200)

There is much more in this great passage than I can elaborate here, especially Gabriel's painful and also self-righteous effort to reduce the Irish boy to "another," so this all too accurate self-description calls up the figure of a mirror that catches the self rather than stages it. But for my purposes, the crucial part of the scene occurs when Gretta falls off to sleep and he shifts from this slightly melodramatic self-contempt to rapt attention to her sleeping body. As he stares, all the dark lucidity of his new state of self-awareness gravitates to thoughts about mortality, and then to a much more desperate version of his, and Dublin's, fantasies of escape: "One by one they were becoming shades. Better pass boldly into that other world, in the full glory of some passion, than fade and wither dismally with age" (203).

But Gabriel does not escape into this other world. His new lucidity allies him closely with the author of the other stories in the volume and forces him to recognize that this life of passion is not for him: "Generous tears filled Gabriel's eyes. He had never felt like that himself toward any woman but he knew that such a feeling must be love" (203). Even Joyce's writer figure has to succumb to a Dublin that triumphs over all romantic dreams. Yet this writer as reader seems also to have come to a point where he can make a major adjustment not made by the other Dublin characters. He can really pay careful attention to what Gretta has experienced, so that he ends up imaginatively engaging an aspect of her that is not primarily a figure of his own desire for her or his demand for her response to that desire. In making that effort he finds a strange identification between his own sense of failure and her sense of loss. And from that conjunction he develops a relatively unsentimental vision of mortality. So he manages to shed "generous tears" that express what is for Dubliners a rare and distinctive emotional state. Then in his final gesture Gabriel turns his attention to the west of Ireland until it spreads over the entire country, brought together here by the snow and by the sense of mortality that the snow comes to represent. Challenged by the narrative of Gretta's lost love, Gabriel feels his thwarted passion finding release in this strangely compelling sublimation of his long-sought orgasm into a comprehensive sympathy linking the realist author with what has been the objects of his contempt:

> [Snow] was falling, too, upon every part of the lonely churchyard on the hill where Michael Furey lay buried. It lay thickly drifted on the crooked crosses and headstones, on the spears of the little gate, on the barren thorns. His soul swooned slowly as he heard the snow falling faintly through the universe and faintly falling, like the descent of their last end, upon all the living and the dead. (204)

Perhaps I am too influenced by the affinities of this passage with the last scene in the *Iliad*, even though Joyce's post-Enlightenment sensibility replaces a conflict between two actual cultures with the struggle to get out of the grips of one particular one. But I think it fair to say that none of the now prevailing theoretical perspectives on how emotions constitute values can produce an adequate account of what happens to and through Gabriel in these concluding pages of *Dubliners*. What he feels is not quite contrary to reason, nor quite supported by it, nor derived from any kind of norm. Rather, the story plays out as the interchange between Gabriel's conative projections and constant pressure coming both from the world he encounters and from his own habits formed by that world. The resulting frustration leads not to careful reasoning but to somewhat desperate efforts to make what adjustments he can. And the adjustments in turn require further adjustments— some to preserve his conative investments and others to adapt to properties of other persons who become actual for him precisely because they do not fit his projections.

Resignification would fail to meet the challenge here. For what shift in valuing he realizes takes place less because of how the author finds new paths than because he finds the objects of his attention blocking the paths he would like to take. Some of the time it is these objects that elicit emotions even when he intends something else; at other times, new aspects emerge out of the care-connection complex because he is forced in effect to mine the available resources in order to find his way. This sense of resources within the emotions also helps account for the fact that, while all the emotions here are deeply dependent on Irish cultural motifs, they also clearly require continually pushing against those motifs—first as the basis of Gabriel's fresh attention to Gretta and to himself, and then for his elaborate reaching out to bring within the affective sphere the most generalized frame of consciousness he can develop. Gabriel's Irish situation is the basic cause of his alienation and neediness. Handling that situation requires coming to recognize his own complicity in that alienation—not only in the elaborate closing rhetoric but also, more powerfully, in his mining his own limitations as a lover in order to appreciate what Gretta once experienced.

In all these cases, authoring and reading engage in increasingly dense interactions. Conative desires drive Gabriel, but his self-scrutiny and his growing awareness of who he cannot be keep these desires open to possibilities in persons and in the emotion complexes themselves that push against his initial efforts at satisfaction. Conativity seems sufficiently capacious to find its way through these detours and, indeed, to find within them forms of attachment that help him avoid yielding to the cult of shame and defensive aggressiveness that to Joyce constituted his national heritage. But in order to honor what these detours make available, these conative energies have to turn abstract. Increasing disgust with himself opens him to thinking about what love might involve, even if he has to be satisfied only with the knowledge of what he cannot possess. This is not resignifying because it is not the codes that must change, but Gabriel who must change in order to get beyond the codes to forces and structures that they substantially oversimplify.

Gabriel does not so much create new meaning as learn to dwell more attentively at the edges of meaning, where he can begin to see why his sense of self-importance cannot suffice. This shift in perspective does not provide an impetus capable of moving beyond a resigned sense of shared mortality. But given how much Dublin seduces its inhabitants into repression, this constitutes a major step toward accepting his own limitations as well as those of his fellow citizens.

## IX. A Plea for "Generous Irony" in Interpreting Affective Experience

I would like to be able to end on this positive note. But even the hope for such success might make me too much like Gabriel, too tied to the demand for a rhetoric that is ultimately inseparable from self-congratulation. So I am almost happy that the reading of reading that I have been developing ignores two important problematic features of this ending. On the concrete level, Joyce's play on first- and third-person relations invites us to recognize Gabriel's self-delusion even at these moments of proclaimed insight. The talk about becoming shades and wandering the other world is clearly a melodramatic projection on Gabriel's part. And the last sentence of the text (cited above) is embarrassingly florid in its chiasmus and the alliterative excess of "his soul swooned slowly." This is not the rhetoric of someone ready to engage seriously in what western Ireland might teach an anglicized Dubliner. The second problematic feature is more general. No rhetoric of mine about the powers of reading will obscure the obvious fact that there is immense critical disagreement about the force of this ending. As John Paul Riquelme puts it in a superb essay on this topic, while some readers think Gabriel has "begun to disburden himself in a painful but salutary way of illusions that had kept him from accepting those around him . . . on terms of equality," others think he "just gives up" and becomes "one of the dead" (Schwartz, 220).

Perhaps this disagreement stems not from indeterminacy within the text but from indeterminacy about the range of contexts that one can invoke as frameworks for understanding how intentionality is positioned in any given case. If that is the case, we can admit indeterminacy without leaving it the final word (which of course in theory it cannot seek). Perhaps indeterminacy is itself something that can be framed and appreciated for the kinds of emotions it elicits and rewards. In the case of Joyce's text, I think the potential for indeterminacy is less a conclusion than a challenge to the reader. For how we understand Gabriel depends on two things—on how we come to terms with his continuing reliance on inflated rhetorical stages for his sensibility and on the degree to which this expansiveness at the end of the story brings with it significant changes in his emotional economy. Is Gabriel now open to the world his self-image closed off? Or, better, is Gabriel more open than he was to that world because he recognizes the limits of his own cultural framework?

The crucial issue is how Joyce's text leads us to dispose our emotions and our will. Joyce asks whether the one occupying the position of the reader can find a way to produce some equivalent of Gabriel's "generous tears" even while recognizing how difficult genuine change will be for him. A positive response to this challenge requires first sharing Gabriel's commitments to lucidity and then attuning ourselves to the limitations of that lucidity. But rather than resting in irony, we have to sympathize with Gabriel's realization about his own limitations. Then we can bring that sympathy to bear also on Gabriel's own efforts to make a limited rhetoric extend beyond the cultural grammars that formed it. For *Dubliners stresses* the fact that it cannot offer a more assertive ending, even as it still hopes to get beyond a mandarin ironic distance from a Dublin that in fact will not let go. Were Joyce to offer strong grounds for believing that Gabriel is transformed, he would trap himself within Gabriel-like idealizations and in effect evade the haunting sense that his critical sensibility and hatred might have led him to miss something crucial about Ireland. But were he to distance himself entirely from Gabriel, there would be no alternative to the vicious irony and consequent utter alienation that characterize all the other stories. Joyce would be left with a dream of his own freedom, a dream that invites an ironic response to all his fantasies.

An ideal of "generous tears," however, seems to me too close to "swooning souls" to provide an adequate register of the emotional values Joyce projects for his readers. We can do better with a slight adjustment that gives us somewhat more distance from Gabriel but still profits from his example. As we pursue that distance but still keep some sympathy with Gabriel's dilemma, we find ourselves taking on what we might call an attitude of generous irony. This attitude provides us affective access to the factors that pull us toward competing readings, and it helps us avoid the other available alternatives. We do not have to repudiate all the intimacies that the text establishes in order to approximate the forms of freedom provided by more bitter ironic stances. And we are not trapped in the essentially epistemic aporias that also leave deconstruction without sufficient access to what these intimacies make available. Moreover, a readerly stance based on generous irony may manage, although just barely, to avoid the self-congratulation that comes when we decide that our way of reading realizes some kind of ethical ideal. For generous irony shares with its more bitter counterparts a refusal to trust any single version of the self, although it also needs to repudiate those counterparts because they too submit ultimately to the desire for philosophical authority.

As I understand Joyce, generous irony retains the distance necessary to recognize how easily we make a mess of our conative needs and how readily we make the imagination do the work of reason—nowhere more than in our quest to claim ethical identities for ourselves. But, at the same time, generous irony will not yield to the authority of the "lucid" intellect. It will not let the ideal of clear seeing block out the emotions elicited by our attention and demanded by our awareness of our own investments. Rather, it will insist that this intellect attend to the passions mediated by its rhetoric of lucidity. And it will not allow the attitude it sponsors to become a principle or a normative demand. The call for generous irony can only be a plea made appealing by exhausting the alternatives.

Finally, an ideal of generous irony provides a framework within which I can bring this book to a close. This ideal goes a long way toward summarizing how engaging aesthetic aspects of our affective lives can bring us a potentially richer account of the values governing these lives than we find in more epistemically oriented analyses. We need the irony because we are never entirely in control of our conative drives or our propensity to be moved by what we cannot rationalize. And we need irony even more desperately because expression is an inexact art, where what is symptomatic lies down with what agents manage to give a distinctive shape. Yet inexactness is not indeterminacy, and the effort at expression need not be simply an effort to evade the self or seduce the other. Once we recognize the limitations inherent in our powers and in the resources we have for expressing our investments, we can project a wary trust that keeps us attentive to particular expressions and the contexts they elicit. And once our expectations are chastened, we can make provisional identifications and share understandings precisely because we do not have to depend on problematic assertions about the force of reason. Even authors of books like this one can imagine entering a community with readers willing to explore the models of agency it proposes, the values that it asserts, and the satisfactions it might make possible.

# Appendix

## *Reading Feelings in Literature and Painting*

This overwhelming of the immediate consciousness is nowhere so striking as in the case of our feelings. A violent love or a deep melancholy takes possession of our soul: here we feel a thousand different elements which dissolve into and permeate one another without any precise outlines, without the least tendency to externalize themselves in relation to one another; hence their originality. We distort them as soon as we distinguish a numerical multiplicity in their confused mass: . . . A moment ago each of them was borrowing an indefinable colour from its surroundings: now we have it colourless and ready to accept a name. The feeling itself is a being which lives and develops and is therefore constantly changing. . . . by separating these moments from each other, by spreading out time in space, we have caused this feeling to lose its life and its colour. Hence we are now standing before our own shadow: we believe we have analyzed our feeling, while we really replaced it by a juxtaposition of lifeless states that can be translated into words.

Henri Bergson

## I. Toward a Practical Grammar for Isolating How Feelings Take on Force within the Arts

In the body of this book I have concentrated on how we characterize affects and how those characterizations have consequences for the values we attribute to our experiences. But I am unwilling to leave this book without explicitly taking up the question of how one might adapt the account I give of feeling for practical criticism in the arts. This book has taken the time to draw close parallels between attitudes that express emotions in practical life and those that do so in poetry. But when I focused specifically on feelings, most of my efforts went toward establishing their intricate relation to sensation. I made no attempt in the body of this book to provide any typology for

231

complexes of feeling, and I avoided close readings devoted to the various ways these feelings bring intensity, complexity, and precision to individual works of art. Although I did use works of visual art as examples, I concentrated on their rendering ideas about feeling rather than on how they actually deployed feelings. Getting involved in how the feelings worked within art objects might have distracted from the continuities I wanted to develop among the various kinds of affect.

My decision may have been the right one with regard to the shaping of a theoretical argument on the affects. But it also might have proved costly in relation to the possibility of this book's actually making a difference in how people read—especially since criticism now is more comfortable with emotion-attitudes than with the work feelings do in developing the internal dynamics of art works and so intensifying what the work makes available as experience. Many of the modes of valuing created by feeling are more subtle than those typically generated by the plots that emotions establish, in part because they do not readily fit into an account of how actions are sponsored and responsibilities assumed or evaded. So now I take the opportunity an appendix affords to outline an elementary practical grammar for isolating how feelings take on force within the arts. Then I can begin exploring how criticism can be responsive to the work these feelings do within particular art objects, and I can demonstrate some of the values that emerge when we put our emphasis on this dimension of affective life.

## II. The Modernist Contrast between Emotion and Feeling Revisited: The Example of W. C. Williams

In a few moments I will sort feeling in the arts under four general complexes that roughly parallel the complexes of emotions that I develop in chapter 6. This structure will enable me to develop extended examples of how criticism can engage the modes of intensity and engagement that these feelings produce. But first I want to set the stage by dramatizing the challenge that theory faces in this domain. By engaging William Carlos Williams's short lyric "The Young Housewife," we can quickly recognize why philosophers like Bergson are so leery about approaching the feelings through our conceptual structures, and we can then specify some of the difficulties that theory faces in this regard—all the while finding that theory in its stumbling phases offers one powerful contrast by which to set off what artists can accomplish by foregrounding a difference between feeling and emotion. "The Young Housewife" gathers most of its power by inviting us to share its efforts to prevent any large dramatic emotion from imposing its form of coherence on the relations between sensation and feeling that charge a particular scene. Responding to this scene requires foregoing the temptation to project attitudes upon the characters or seeing them as acting in accord with considered motives. What matters is the interplay of feelings giving this moment its particular strangeness and its evocative tensions.

The poem's basic situation makes us think of several standard emotional scenarios, but it does so primarily to call attention to how actively this simple rendering of the event manages to avoid those scenarios. We have to keep our attention dancing among the particulars:

> At ten A.M. the young housewife
> moves about in negligee behind
> the wooden walls of her husband's house.
> I pass solitary in my car.
>
> Then again she comes to the curb
> to call the ice-man, fish-man, and stands
> shy, uncorseted, tucking in
> stray ends of hair, and I compare her
> to a fallen leaf.
>
> The noiseless wheels of my car
> rush with a crackling sound over
> dried leaves as I bow and pass smiling.
>
> (1:57)

The wife is obviously a figure of pathos. Mention of "her husband's house" somewhat melodramatically sets the stage and leads us to expect more contextualizing about her alienation. But instead Williams wants us to see that by avoiding narrative and by avoiding giving her a speaking presence he can deflect that pathos to a considerable degree. The result creates new possibilities of respecting what she makes of her world. For the housewife's basic problem may be how easily she is forgotten or repressed in a world where power and attention go to those who can stage themselves as enacting grand attitudes. The housewife does not emote for us; she only carries out what her day requires of her. Consequently, we are not given any dramatic content that provides access to her emotional life. We have to approach her only in terms of what glimpses provide, and we have to understand her as the kind of person who can offer to others only this access.

Williams's speaker handles the situation by dwelling on concrete details, to be appreciated in terms of the specific qualities of sensation and the relations they produce. Affective engagement will have to emerge within the scene, not as aspects of an attitude the speaker articulates about the scene. In the first stanza, the details present an aura of everything being arranged, almost ceremonious, as if she did the same performance of her play every day. The second stanza then shifts to quite particular feelings gathering around the ways that her body contrasts with that order. Each detail complicates the picture. Her shyness makes us think of her as powerless; her uncorseted fleshiness indicates a simple voluptuousness; and her stray ends of hair mark a minimal rebelliousness or at least freedom to be something other than her husband's possession. Yet her freedom is severely limited and not internalized at all. One might say it is the freedom of a fallen leaf, attractive in its pure contingency and marginality.

Such details give the woman a believable form of presence that I think she would lose were there more effort to narrate her condition. Then she would be an instance illuminating some general condition; here her traits are too evanescent to carry such weight, so she has to be appreciated for how she specifically occupies the speaker's attention. Perhaps her richest sense of her own subjective agency resides in how she holds her body and interacts with the traders who come by.

The poem is not concerned only with this woman. It is also "about" the quality of relationship that the observer can develop through this way of engaging the woman. Williams tells us that he smiles, then leaves that smile as one more detail in the scene that occupies the reader's attention. So we have to ask what are we to make of the smile, and of the fact that this is all we know of what he makes of this moment. Because she is so much within these details, the speaker has to recognize that whatever desire might be elicited in him by what he sees will not be returned—indeed, will not even be recognized. So he positions himself not to project desire. Hence his smile, his expression of accepting all the limitations of his situation and adapting himself to the restrained but intriguing forms of attention that define that situation. He does not turn her into a forlorn woman needing his consolation. He does not even quite turn her into a *"figlia che piange"* whom he can fix in photographic detail. His reaction has to be as concise and minimal as the modes of expression to which he is responding. So his smile cuts both ways. It acknowledges that a fleeting link has been made with the woman, but a link on which nothing can be built or even imaginatively elaborated. And the smile allows him to come to some self-reflexive terms with his own contingent and frustrated freedom. Like the woman, the speaker cannot be said to have a full emotional response to what he sees. Rather he registers the scene and registers too the significance of his own irreducible distance from it. Beyond looking at the essentially static scene, the only movements that engage the situation as it emerges are when he smiles and when he drives away over the dead leaves, ruefully recognizing their link to her metaphoric status as a fallen leaf.

The reader sees more than the speaker does. The reader is in a position to recognize how much the two persons have in common in their isolated worlds and how little they can do about that. And the reader can make articulate what the speaker's smile simply registers. Any stronger reaction by the speaker might bring with it a mind-set assuming that something can be done about such situations. That would conceal the full impact of the forms of contingency and alienation fundamental to both lives. For this alienation is not a matter of frustrated social ambitions or existential angst. It is simply the fact of their isolation and the endless chores that both mask and reproduce their senses of being without significant substance. Alienation is the stuff not of dramatic outburst but of resigned adaption. So when the speaker smiles, that smile almost links him to the dead leaves that litter the street and figuratively absorb what might be individual about the woman. Smiling is adapting to all these limitations. But the adapting is not entirely a surrender to contingency. The speaker can appreciate the pure momentariness of his vision and his ability to accept just passing on, leaving her to her plight. The smile may ultimately constitute a slim bond with the equally slim potential of her uncorseted presence. At the least, he has not substituted metaphor for perception or pity for a more intimate sense of this shared frustrated contingency. He is in a position to realize that by refusing to impose meaning or rhetoricize sympathy he does not impose the husband's rules of ownership. Fleeting sympathy tinged with self-mockery can be its own celebration of the only form of freedom these agents have available.

## III. Four Basic Complexes of Feelings Outlined

Because feelings are so closely woven into sensations, one might say that there are as many feelings as there are sensations. Or, more accurately, one might have to say there are as many feelings as there are ways of attributing "asness" to sensations. Faced with that diversity it seems ridiculous to attempt any kind of taxonomy. Yet I think it is possible to isolate four basic complexes of sensation that seem especially significant in providing modes of affective investment central to aesthetic experience. So I am going to spell out these four complexes and then attempt to show how we can foreground each one in our approach to relevant works of art.

1. Many feelings take on significance because they bring attention to bear on qualities that can be attributed directly to how specific sensations occur— for example, color tones or voice tones or the quality of brush strokes or rhythmic shifts or pure aural patterns that become part of the sense of presence we attribute to the artists or to a figure within a work.
2. The arts rely heavily on feelings that emphasize the expressive quality of spatial relations. The most obvious of these are feelings organized by a sense of scale (as we saw in Munch's *Street Musicians*), along with related concerns for proportion and fit—both positively and negatively. Analogously, spatial fit or configuration draws immediate conjunctions among details and foregrounds the significance of the linked features, as we saw in Giorgione's *Holy Family*. But probably the most intense and intricate spatial feelings occur in relation to how boundaries and frames work. This is partially a matter of how separations can be rendered forcefully. But it also involves the qualities of potential and frustrated transition that circulate around the space charged by forming boundaries in the first place. Boundaries can repel connection or

seem invitingly porous. They can activate contact all along the line of division, or they can seem continuously on the verge of collapsing—into new unities or into anxious indeterminacy. On a more abstract level, boundaries between the literal and the metaphoric can themselves take on all of these relationships—and they do so with respect to all four complexes of feeling.

3. Where there is space there will be time. And where there is time there will a range of qualities of movement that also can take on charged significance within works of art. If painting provides the basic vocabulary for the spatial relations, dance provides it for these qualities of movement. The most fundamental affective qualities of movement seem to me organized around literal and figurative aspects of pacing and of how gathering and releasing take on presence. Within these general parameters, many different registers of adjustment take place, for example in terms of specific lines of flow and the blockages they encounter; in terms of specific qualities of interaction, coordination, and resistance in relation to an environment or a collectivity; and in terms of modifications in rhythm, pace, and timing. Analogously, the lyric modulates pace and intensity and urgency (or their contraries); narrative arts control time by stretching scenes or making them compact; and painting like Jackson Pollock's can give basic expressive force to how line gathers thickness, thins out, takes various turns and dalliances in relation to the directions it initiates, and enters into relations with the forms that it passes through. Other arts in turn can develop figurative parallels to what takes place literally in a Pollock drip painting. One could argue for example that the best way to read John Ashbery's poetry is to follow its thickenings and thinnings and wanderings and gatherings much as if one were exploring a Pollock.

4. Finally we have to deal with a more abstract set of concrete feelings that involve how our intentional states project coherence and encounter various permutations in the process. The best way to view this set of feelings may be to treat them as a broad range of proprioceptive adjustments. But proprioception is not just a matter of how the body adjusts to particular situations. It involves how all of the instruments the organism employs become involved in making the kind of adjustments that produce senses of fittingness or belonging or coherence. In other words, this version of proprioception includes the feelings of relation isolated in William James's famous argument: "There is not a conjunction or a proposition, and hardly an adverbial phrase, syntactic form or inflection of voice, in human speech, that does not express some shading or other of relation which we at some moment actually feel to exist between the larger objects of our thought. . . . We ought to say a feeling of *and,* a feeling of *if,* a feeling of *but,* and a feeling of *by,* quite as readily as we say a feeling of *blue* or a feeling of *cold*" (*Psychology,* 29). From James it is not a large leap to Nietzsche on the will as a particular kind of sensation.[1] So I want to add to this list those feelings that attend to the degree to which we can project ourselves as actively taking responsibility for what we are doing or expressing.

## IV. The Foregrounding of Sensual Qualities

I cannot say much about my first complex of feelings. But I can try to say something about why I cannot say much about this complex. Feelings directly connected to the specifics of sensory experience are our most fundamental registers of how art works give distinctive affective shape to experience—literally of how artists manipulate their medium to produce specific effects, and figuratively of how they manipulate representations that invite our engagement in the imagined worlds of landscapes, still lives, and dramatic situations. Art cannot be treated as primarily a discursive practice precisely because questions of significance arise in relation to the constant process by which sensation seems charged with affect. Feelings provide an "asness" that pervades every level of the work, from its ability to elicit specific investments to its stance as at once within the world of objects and apart from it in a world of felt meanings. On the most elemental of these levels the charged sensations are not figurative. Artists work hard to efface the signs of their interpretive interests so that the audience will take the sensuous properties themselves as the expressive register rather than treating them as only a mediation of what the artist "wants to say." But there are also levels within the work where the awareness of affectively charged sensations does involve a relation to the artist's purposive activity: the asness has to be attached to a will.

Think of how we orient ourselves to subtle changes in hue or in the intensity of brush strokes or the turns of rhythm in poetry or the modulations of tone in speaking voices. The "asness" is there because we align ourselves with an intelligence that has produced the sensations as aspects of an intentional labor. So the sensations are charged with possibility and with a kind of purpose. Yet at the same time they constitute a triumph over our standard desires for treating expressions of will as signs that are to be interpreted in the expressive register we adapt for dealing with human actions. Therefore, if we can make the adjustments that the artists ask, we put ourselves in a position to pursue two basic rewards. We develop an expanded sense of how rich the concrete world can become. And we develop a feel for how these sensed features of the world can carry expressive energies—in themselves, and as they enter into complex conjunctions with other elements.

My own insistence on sensation as an alternative to the semantic register makes it difficult for me to give any extended interpretation of how this complex takes on force in particular works. In the place of such interpretive labors, I want to spend a few moments speculating on how criticism and teaching can bring more attention to these features of the arts than it now tends to provide. Dealing with charged sensation in art may be a matter less of providing verbal analogues for the expressive act than of developing much more elaborate mechanisms than we now have for the critical art of judicious pointing. Wittgenstein repeatedly argued that the ultimate measure of appreciation in art is not what we can say but what we can point to as worth honoring or as requiring that the work be performed in a particular way. I want to be more accommodating to interpretive practices (for obvious reasons), but I also want to be as clear as possible on why this pointing is called for and, more important, on the resources we have available for honoring this dimension of aesthetic experience.

The now conventional distinction between knowledge by statement and knowledge by acquaintance provides a useful framework within which to explore criticism as a kind of pointing. Dealing with charged sensations is one domain where how we negotiate acquaintance proves absolutely crucial. Rather than offer specific interpretations for many of the sensuous effects art provides, I think we do much better simply to establish comparative contexts through which different material properties and processes can begin to take on significance. Critics and teachers have to reproduce some of the powers for making distinctions that artists develop as they learn their crafts. It is very difficult to find words for characterizing the effects of a Titian brush stroke or a red in Rauschenberg or a cadence in Wordsworth or the lineation in Creeley. But we can begin to establish the expressive force of such materials by surrounding the particular with concrete contrasts, with a brush stroke by Bellini and by Mantegna or cadence in Milton and in Yeats. Criticism of this kind of affect requires developing practices of concrete comparison that highlight qualities and at least suggest what expressive range might be mobilized in a given use of the medium. We might even try imagining the critic as a speculative eye doctor trying out which lenses are best suited to our vision in particular circumstances.

Comparison need not stop with purely sensuous detail. In fact comparative contexts for these sensuous details go a long way toward linking them directly to the ways that individual artists work and to the investments these artists have in doing things particular ways. Comparison keeps the sensuous closely linked to the purposive. Consider, for example, a story Robert Hass tells of an artist colleague who once heard him interpreting Cézanne and took him back to his studio. "Here are some paints," the artist said. "Make me a green that shimmers the way Cézanne's green shimmers and I will listen to your interpretations." At the least, criticism ought to make us see that shimmering green and the effect it has on related colors and shapes. And the theory of criticism ought to recognize the roles that vividness of material qualities plays in cultivating precise, yet indescribable feelings in an audience. Then it can move outward to more intricate kinds of figural play that inhabit our sensations. Many works of art ask us to imagine ourselves responding sensually to the world. Wordsworth is always staging listening, Caravaggio touching, and Rembrandt the sense of what can be involved in just looking out from the canvas.[2]

As we engage these concrete orientations, we also can develop feelings that attach to the specific ways that the artists use their ability as craftspeople to give the medium its own sensuous distinction. Audiences do not only observe the meticulous care that goes into a Vermeer window; they align themselves affectively with the inferred activity creating such a distinctive presence. Analogously, van Gogh is a powerful artist less because of the energy that he represents somewhat melodramatically than because of how the dynamics of his brushwork give a tangible force to the processes of seeing. Somewhat more abstract forms of elemental feelings arise in relation to sculpture, for example in the sense of pure skilled forming ability and finish that one encounters in a typical piece by Constantin Brancusi or Martin Puryear. And then it is not a large leap to the metaphorical sensuality involved in responding to the gravity of Wallace Stevens's lines or the edge Jane Austen gives to conversation.

## V. Three Aspects of Feelings Involving Spatial Relations

I have argued that every feeling is based in sensation, so it might seem odd that I then isolate one specific complex for sensations and try to develop three additional complexes. I do this because while every feeling is based in sensation, not every feeling is primarily concerned with the immediate quality of the sensation involved. As we have seen, the qualities can take on metaphoric registers because they give concreteness to a range of imaginative properties. My other three complexes all emphasize these imaginative implications developing from how the sensual world emerges for consciousness. "Asness" proves more important than "whatness." For we dwell from the start on the role that the sensation can play within an overall signifying structure, a structure framed by both the agent's activity and the dramatic world that the work establishes. Yet for us still to speak of feeling, the material of sensation cannot be simply translated into a sign representing some meaning. Criticism has to find ways of holding onto the power that the embodiment establishes, without settling for the inarticulate pointing that I have just been performing.

When we turn specifically to the complex of feelings that gather force because of the deployment of spatial relations, I think we can further distinguish three basic modes by which these relations take on significance. The most elemental is the force established by how spatial configurations form patterns and so emphasize specific aspects of the details presented. We noticed this force of patterning when discussing Giorgione's *Holy Family* and Caravaggio's *The Fortune Teller*. In Caravaggio's painting the spatial relations were largely a matter of comparable shapes and weights of the heads and bodies of the two protagonists, along with the rhythms of how the bodies are rendered in intricate circular forms. Giorgione puts much more emphasis on the spatial configurations that line establishes. He wants us to feel the many ways in which this family creates a single unit, brought together by the very bounding lines that also distinguish them as individual persons.

The second important mode of spatial feelings is scale, a factor rarely addressed in critical writing. Scale is most visible as a measure of ambition—whether it takes the form of celebrating a political regime, defining human capability, or establishing exemplary values. I think for example of Rubens's historical paintings, Michelangelo's frescoes for the Sistine Chapel, and Barnett Newman's immense and imposing monochromatic fields comprehensive enough to insist on the spiritual reality color can be said to compose. But other uses can be even more striking. In his *Farewell to an Idea* T. J. Clark offers a brilliant analysis of the role that the scale of the human body plays in Pollock's art. When the paintings connect the life of the hand and arm to a form coextensive with the human body, the work carries out a powerful set of experiments in "self-risk and self-realization" (358). But when Pollock turns to work in a more than human scale (as in the 1950 works like *Autumn Rhythm*), the paintings risk losing their core sexual drive and becoming decorative. In effect these grand paintings have to be held together by design rather than by desire.[3]

At the other pole there are many great examples of the force of compression, not the least of which is Williams' "They Young Housewife." I immediately think also of Vermeer's *Lace-maker,* a painting whose diminutive scale parallels the painter's concentration to that of his subject. And I think of the amazing relation of scale to foreshortening that makes Mantegna's *Dead Christ* so bleak and pathos-laden a rendering of the dead god. But for me the two most interesting uses of visual compression in Western painting are works that have no human presences, so that all the forces of habitation have to be controlled by formal dimensions of the work. The first is Vermeer's *Street in Delft*. This endlessly fascinating painting gets much of its force from a remarkable sense of capacious reduction. The eye struggles to find the human forms, each framed by a pronounced architectural space. And each of these spaces is so confined that it cannot be seen from distance. The spaces have to be felt as forces. Once this sense of force begins to register, we realize how many different forms of architectural life the painting brings into a steady focus apparently giving them all equal emphasis. Arches give way to windows which echo bricks while also setting off by contrast the colors and forms of shutters. All this is in the foreground. In the background, pushed toward the front by the sky and by the different heights of the buildings, we find bricks modulating into smokestacks that seem almost visual parallels to the more detailed foreground. Finally all these rough equivalences seem continuous with a much more comprehensive framing set of relations that intricate shapes of the buildings establish with the sky. These shapes divide this sky, bring it into the foregrounded dance of textures, and give the atmosphere itself a sense of substantial dwelling within the scene. In effect this coexistence of so many diverse perceptual domains composes a glorious abstract community out of pure visual detail.

The second experiment in scale I want to discuss is Braque's *Houses at Estaque,* a work that offers intriguing comparisons with Vermeer's. Compression in Vermeer makes material presences dance with each other while celebrating the intricate composed dwelling these presences establish. Braque wants to move from how material composes a dwelling place to how the idea of being an inhabitant can be pictured as a purely visual state. This painting offers a compressed version of a hill village with no persons in it. But there are multiple perspectives called up within the painting, perspectives that are very closely tied to the façade of the houses because they are pushed toward the front and heaped on each other with very little intervening space. In my view, Braque uses the compression to force on us the vitality of these multiple perspectives. We see the village as if it were being created for the many ways of seeing that it contained and that give it visual vitality. The plasticity of the work then becomes a concrete way of dramatizing how one might visually inhabit a dwelling place. Estaque need not be pictured as having inhabitants because the force of vision within the painting gives us what it feels like to see this place as one of its inhabitants.[4]

Developing critical accounts of scale in literary works is a more difficult and so quite rare project. There are obvious uses of scale that are inseparable from epic ambitions on the one hand and condensed lyricism on the other, just as scale is a crucial factor in a novelist's decision about the most important ways to render action. *Ulysses* is so great a text in part because it combines utter magnitude of epic scale with utter commitment to small detail, so that the text claims as its own the very capacity to remake what counts as scale. But scale also organizes a wide variety of local intensities. Yeats's "Long-Legged Fly" plays three scale frameworks against each other—the local focus on the agent's body part, the reach out into history, and the even more specific attention evoked in the refrain. Analogously, the ending of "Sunday Morning" moves brilliantly among the expanse of sky, the detail of the pigeon's wings, and the activity of extended wings that seems to combine both perspectives into a third, encompassing metaphysical perspective. And then there are Shakespeare's sonnets which often make dazzling moves between registers of scale. One of the most striking examples is Sonnet 73, "That time of year thou may'st in me behold." The first quatrain links the psyche to the overall landscape where the autumn's "bare ruined choirs" offer the only traces of "where late the sweet birds sang." The second quatrain moves out to the twilight, figured as "Death's second self" sealing all at rest. Then the poem turns to a very close focus on the glowing ashes from a spent fire "Consum'd with that which it was nourished by." In effect the full reach of imagination is itself forced into this close focus because no matter how grand the rhetoric, the pain of dying comes down to this utterly local residue of failing desire.

The third aspect of spatially organized feelings is more overtly involved in metaphoric possibilities. These are feelings based upon how we experience the presence of boundaries and the force of the relational fields that these boundaries activate. As we saw in discussing Judith Butler, every boundary can also be a source of fascination or permission, every "no" a "what if" or a means of sliding into a possible yes. In visual terms, what outlines a shape also activates the margin between forms so that we can become engaged by how one refuses another, how one bleeds into another, how one modifies the boundaries of the shape that in return gives it definition, or even how the border itself can tremble with possibility or with fear or with pleasure. And the same issues of boundaries function metaphorically in relation to how we negotiate the relation between what appears in a work and what we take to be the overall impact of that appearance. Part of the pleasure of abstract painting is the sense that its insistence on refusing all verbally inflected content invites our projecting onto that boundary all sorts of psychological and philosophical implications.

Few painters have been more insistent than Frank Stella that you get only what you see—the paintings have no metaphoric intent. Yet when attending to the work in his *Protractor Series,* I cannot but find boundary formation and crossing an exciting adventure. The form of the paintings is quite simple, several protractor circles in different flat colors cross each other so that no one band has continuity. Even though Stella deliberately prevents any local activity where the forms interact, both the protractor forms and the play of colors take on fascinating modes of appearance and disappearance and recombination. What we infer behind shapes and colors becomes almost as important as what is present. And colors that in themselves are only standard house paints become vital because of the spaces they have to share and the interactions that occur for the eye and for the mind projecting beyond the boundaries the eye has to respect.

Paul Cézanne's interest in *passage* offers an almost diametrically opposed way of activating the spaces that boundaries form. Cézanne likes to call attention to what happens to paint at the precise moment when two objects come together. Painting has conventions that allow us to treat the objects as independent, with one passing below or above or beside the other even though the painter has to make complex choices about how to create transitions on a flat surface where everything is continuous. Cézanne refuses to honor those conventions. He has rocks bleed into trees, trees into an atmosphere that suddenly becomes inseparable from other modes of substance, and trunks or branches become continuous with body parts like the legs and shoulders of those who lean against them.

These treatments of transition activate a wide range of affective investments. On the most elemental level, Cézanne wants us to feel what the painter feels as he or she confronts the tension between the two-dimensional surface where color and shape create these forms and the illusory third dimension where each individual shape has its own mass and so sets its own boundary conditions. Even the simplest rendering of an image involves pulls among the life of sight, which is bound only to how things appear, the life of painting, which is committed to making visual events out of that appearance, and the life in the world beyond the painting, where we expect to deal with mass and so with individuals. Consequently we encounter feelings basic to

*individuation*
*&* *Beloved*

the relational processes on which this sense of individuation depends. And we are invited to feel this individuation as a continual event established by how color and form migrate, yet also seem always on the verge of disappearing as sight turns to new permutations. Finally, this framing of individuation opens out to bring to self-consciousness the range of affective investments possible within the process of representation. If what we see is continually metamorphosing, why should we assume that what we desire is any more stable? If we let painting show us possible forms of desire, we have to adapt ourselves to how the psyche might find its own truth in its power to invest in the distortions *passage* affords. Rather than locating the object of desire as a single shape, we might project it in a metamorphic moment when what we see is still woven into its background. There is no better way to make us aware of the mobility of desire and the immense suppression that occurs when we deal only with fixed forms as sufficient causes of our fascination.[5]

Poetry is an art that almost equals painting's interest in boundaries, if only because every line of verse faces several adventures in transition, culminating in decisions one makes about how one line will connect to the following one. Will the line be end-stopped or enjambed, and what degree of emphasis will be put on the kind of pause that is produced? For my extended example of the affects circulating around boundaries, I have chosen a poem that relies on a visual example to bring to consciousness all these little unremembered acts of decision-making. This is Elizabeth Bishop's "The Map."

> Land lies in water; it is shadowed green.
> Shadows, or are they shallows at its edges
> showing the line of long sea-weeded ledges
> where weeds hang to the simple blue from green.
> Or does the land lean down to lift the sea from under,
> drawing it unperturbed around itself?
> Along the fine tan sandy shape
> is the land tugging at the sea from under?
>
> The shadow of Newfoundland lies flat and still.
> Labrador's yellow, where the moony Eskimo
> has oiled it. We can stroke these lovely bays,
> under a glass as if they were expected to blossom,
> or as if to provide a clean cage for invisible fish.
> The names of the seashore towns run out to sea,
> the names of cities across the neighboring mountains
> —the printer here experiencing the same excitement
> as when emotion too far exceeds its cause.
> These peninsulas take the water between thumb and finger
> like women feeling for the smoothness of yard goods.
>
> Mapped waters are more quiet than the land is,
> lending the land their waves' own confirmation;

And Norway's hare runs south in agitation,
Profiles investigate the sea, where land is.
Are they assigned or can the countries pick their colors?
—What suits the character or the native waters best.
Topography displays no favorites; North's as near as West.
More delicate than the historians are the map-maker's colors.

(3)

The basic affective logic of the poem is established in the opening four lines. The first line provides a simple and unqualified description that perfectly fits an end-stopped line. But the second line introduces a very different order of being. Here we see the map not from the perspective convention provides but from one more attentive to the visual detail. That perspective brings options into play. Then the fact of the options seems to anchor attention so that rather than rely on end-stopped lines Bishop introduces a gorgeous drive of enjambed, heavily monosyllabic long lines pushing against quite strong rhymes. Once the shadows step partially free of their color-coding, once shadows might be shallows, it seems as if all the signifying conventions begin to wobble. Consequently, transitions become more engaging than the specific territories defined by the map. And the mind begins to see the map as constant mapping, the world as constantly open for repartitioning. Where the map seemed merely an instrument before, now it seems to participate in the same active focusing of consciousness that we find in works of art.

As art, the map foregrounds two kinds of boundaries, each made emphatic by the possibility of transgression. The more immediate boundaries are attributed to how the printer's compositional energies produce distinctions. The second set of boundaries is more abstract. These boundaries have to do with what the mind can negotiate by holding off conventional, task-oriented associations sponsored by the sensations. Once boundaries appear as drawn and colored shapes, the imagination begins to feel its own capacities to treat boundaries not as existing borders but as themselves compositions charged with affect. And once affect enters, lines seem to create their own expansive possibilities and questions become invitations to see just how many transformations the boundary-setting process can instigate. (Bishop's elaborate sound play provides an aural analogue to the play of colors within the map, and her emphasis on sound provides a further invitation to treat the boundary between the art of writing and the truth of writing as itself a source of endless transitional possibilities.)

All of this seems to me suggested by the opening stanza. Bishop then has to work out a way of intensifying what can be at stake once description fuses with composition. So she makes the second stanza an extended encounter with quite specific features of the map, features proximate to her own childhood life in Nova Scotia but not explicitly referring to them.

Close focus also generates sympathy with the position of the printer. We are told that in letting his words cover the colored spaces, the printer must have experienced "the same excitement / as when emotion too far exceeds its cause." So as the poem focuses on the actual ways the map signifies, it also brings a sharper attention to what is released by attending to the compositional force accompanying these signifiers. But it is not easy to feel sure one is getting the full resonance of this observation. Is the excitement a simple pleasure in the capacity to develop excess by projecting meanings, as with the analogue to the women that concludes the second stanza? Or is there something more painful and more profound to be negotiated about the pressure of boundaries in relation to the pleasures of composition and transgression?

I think the last stanza chooses the second option, but I cannot be confident in my reading. (The desire for such confidence may just reflect my desire to turn criticism into mapmaking in black and white.) I see here a set of reminders that compositional freedom also has its limits. To lose the mapmaker's discipline, and hence to lose his or her worry about what is appropriate, is to forgo the basic source of the excitement that comes as one plays on the boundaries that one finds imposed on one's mapping. So this stanza calls us first to the appeal of the area of the map which is quiet, which has none of the writing that gambols through the mountains. Perhaps allowing the water its quiet allows it to retain the power to shape what remains the ultimate boundary in the poem—that between a domain that is habitable, and one where there are only natural and unconscious forces never to be articulate.

A lesser writer would organize these feelings into an overall dramatic attitude responding to this immanent darkness. Bishop refuses that temptation, perhaps because such an attitude would only become another writing on the land side that loses touch with the water necessitating the boundaries in the first place. Better to stay with the flow of feelings because they do not have to take sides. In this respect the feelings are significantly unlike the historian's colors. Historians have to bind colors to specific social and temporal locales, and so their topography will also display favorites. The mapmaker's colors have to be more delicate because they have to register the pathos of history. They have to pursue the strange combination of greater disinterest and greater affective fluidity that is necessary to negotiate between a sense that boundaries are necessary and an awareness of how arbitrary and fluid they come to seem in retrospect. Part of the mapmaker's task is to project the limitations that emerge when historians try to maintain differences by making certain colors too vivid, others almost indistinct. The mapmaker has nothing to work with but what the historians give him or her. But that very constraint also brings out his or her capacity to move around within the given materials. The mapmaker can dwell on how the very forming of boundaries transgresses and transcends them. And at the same time the task of fitting everything in demands the recognition that so long as the quiet of the sea pushes against the land there will always be the need for new maps.

## VI. Feelings of Movement and Qualities of Transition in Time: Sylvia Plath's "Cut"

Dance most intricately articulates feelings grounded in how movement is sensed or engaged. But since my emphasis is on feelings that can be given verbal significance, I will have to play somewhat metaphorically on only certain elements that take on significance within the dance medium. Feelings based on movement involve qualities that can be attributed to how sensations and actions unfold. We make affective investments attached to whether a movement is fluid or jerky, nervous or assured, self-contained or requiring related movements before balance or resolution is accomplished. And sensibilities shift depending on whether the movement gravitates toward other elements in its environment or resists accommodation, whether it shares the rhythms that surround it or establishes some new sense of tempo within that field, whether the movement becomes weary or tentative or blocked, or whether it speeds up in excitement or grows anxious in its unstable pushing against the forms giving definition to the path it is taking. And when there seems to be change in speed or the specific density and texture of the flow, our response will alter depending on whether the change seems roughly continuous with previous adjustments or whether there is a struggle for a new beginning, or even whether the movement can manage a dialectical reinterpretation of territory it has traversed.

However if we become too enamored of these physical analogues for psychological states, we will block ourselves from interpreting how movement also takes place as a condition of signification. We do not have to approach works as if they were all Pollock paintings. I think we do learn a great deal from interpretive stances that resist thematic and allegorical emphases on what works of art can be said to "mean." But on many occasions we do not have to accept this dichotomy. It becomes possible to treat the affects involved in how a work moves as fundamental to the overall drama it is presenting. Such feelings cannot be reduced to language, but we can elaborate their possible significance by articulating how they depend upon or solicit interpretive frameworks. Here I cannot take up the most challenging and probably the most important instances where concerns with quite specific qualities of movement carry overall semantic significance. For these cases usually emerge in longer works, especially serial poems, that are consistently taking off from possibilities or senses of entrapment created by previous moments in the series.[6] However, Sylvia Plath's "Cut" provides a pretty good substitute because the poem emphasizes several kinds of motion and provides an ending substantially intensified when we see how it relates to these dynamic processes:

What a thrill—
My thumb instead of an onion.
The top quite gone
Except for a sort of a hinge

Of skin,
A flap like a hat,
Dead white.
Then that red plush

Little pilgrim,
The Indian's axed your scalp.
Your turkey wattle
Carpet rolls

Straight from the heart.
I step on it.
Clutching my bottle
Of pink fizz.

A celebration, this is.
Out of a gap
A million soldiers run,
Redcoats, every one.

Whose side are they on?
Oh my
Homunculus, I am ill.
I have taken a pill to kill

The thin
Papery feeling.
Saboteur,
Kamikaze man—

The stain on your
Gauze Ku Klux Klan
Babushka
Darkens and tarnishes and when

The balled
Pulp of your heart
Confronts its small
Mills of silence

How you jump—
Trepanned veteran,
Dirty girl,
Thumb stump.

(235–36)

The short lines and the exaggerated enjambment between stanzas are the first indications that how this poem moves is crucial to its expressive force.

But the situation is extraordinarily static. The speaker simply observes her cut thumb, from a position that seems so far away from the event that it is almost disconnected from her body. The only motion is the proliferation of metaphors that seem to gush out almost as fast as the blood does, and with perhaps a similar relation to the range of pains she is feeling. Indeed, the metaphors move so easily that one has to wonder about their source. How does the flow of metaphor connect to the static distance of the observing position? And why would someone modulate from such annoying cuteness to the barely concealed desperation suggested by how the blood becomes a champagne fizz?

A partial answer emerges in the two stanzas that constitute the midpoint of this ten-stanza poem. The two stanzas seem each to lurch in an opposing direction. The call for celebration seems excessively self-ironic, as if the distanced reflective consciousness could, or had to, absorb the physical event completely into the world the metaphors make possible. But then the movement of metaphor seems to betray her and to make the call for celebration seem perhaps too literal, too indicative of how few resources for pleasure she in fact possesses. When the blood becomes the redcoats, the metaphor raises questions about allegiances and governing purposes. Or so we have to assume because of the next large shift in attitude. When the speaker asks "Whose side are they on?" she reveals fears and anxieties that probably influenced the choice of metaphors making this realization possible. Where all the motion has been in the metaphors, now it is in the attitudes that the speaker assumes. The quasi-playful celebration gives way to the deadly serious sequence of revelations that come to the fore through the reference to redcoats.

We still have to explore why her first thought about the redcoats is "whose side are they on." Literally she refers to the fact that the blood is running out not in, and so flees from where it is needed. But when this metaphor calls up the thin papery feeling that is not just located at the thumb, and when taking a pill gets connected to an imposing rhymed and enjambed "kill," we are invited to understand this fear of betrayal as connected to her own deep insecurities. Identity itself seems at stake in which way the blood flows, perhaps because this "thin papery feeling" may be the only effective conative drive she experiences. And even that experience seems haunted by an awareness of its own insufficiency in helping her stabilize her affective condition.

At this point Plath makes a marvelous shift. When the poem turns to the stained gauze now on her finger, what began as a series of metaphors enacting and proclaiming the dispersal of energy and blood is transformed into slow focus on the thumb as static object, then on the pressure that this bandage puts on the raw wound opened by the cut. The chain of metaphors no longer transforms the wound but demands that we focus our attention on it, until by the last stanza the speaker can actually address the thumb as a surrogate self. From producing metaphors, consciousness has to take a position sufficiently distanced to be able to read them. Consequently, the metaphors no longer address the event of the cut. They are driven to the self-reflexive level where she must come to terms with what the metaphors have been revealing.

We see this shift most vividly when the bandage elicits particular identifications with the Ku Klux Klan and with the culture of babushkas. It seems as if she has taken a step back and asked what it will take to bring this object back to being her thumb, so that the thumb can reflect an identity beyond the papery feeling. But the results are not encouraging. When she turns to address the bandaged cut, she encounters a psychological state where all motion is spent and consciousness has to face directly its own self-revulsion. Even the speaker's immense linguistic gifts now condense into the two magisterial half-rhymed monosyllables "thumb stump." Where all was metaphoric fluidity, now there is only this completely static and objectified metonymic mask that has to bear the pain for whatever is the cause and locus of her illness.

I have to convince myself as well as others that attention to feelings of movement brings something distinctive to the poem that would not emerge in readings focused by more thematic concerns. So I will try to show that this emphasis on movement highlights three aspects of the poem that would not play much of a role in thematic readings. First, my emphasis calls attention to the shifts in focus and in tone that occur in those middle stanzas of the poem. The modes of intentionality change and the poem asks that we understand the speaker by sharing as much as we can in her effort to adjust to what her own metaphors produce. We cannot be satisfied with the semantic work the metaphors perform because we also have to find ways of engaging the pains and pressures that the poem gradually reveals as calling up these metaphors.

This emphasis on the time of the poem then also establishes the basis for my second claim. While one aspect of the poem's motion is contained in how the speaker's views of herself change, another is projected by the way the poem opens itself to the forces only partially expressed by the metaphors. Movement in this poem is backward as well as forward because we have to read through the metaphors to appreciate how the psyche is driven by the forces that generate them. More important, we have to be responsive to a beautiful shift in the poem from the production of half-playful metaphors to its own effort to name without adornment the "papery feeling" which refers both to the thumb and to whatever makes her give "kill" so pronounced a place in its line. This section of the poem charges the movement with the pressures of the unconscious and so severely slows down the metaphors and thins out the sound. By the closing stanzas this slowing down adds something like a viscous quality to the texture of metaphor because what began as free play seems increasingly burdened by wounds that have nothing to do with her thumb. As questions of identity and identification enter the poem, free movement takes on qualities of desperate escape, so the features of the scene that cannot escape come to seem imposingly intractable.

Finally, attending to the qualities of motion is the only way we can respond fully to the terrifying way that the concluding stanza imposes a kind of stability on the situation. Here metaphors do not generate further metaphors. Each metaphor stands as a way of fixating on overdetermined features that the thumb has taken on. The only actual motion is the poet's intense internal sound play that adds to the sense of these figures as the only forms of identification capable of expressing her self-disgust. The internal assonance of "Dirty girl" has the force of chiding herself for revealing all the shame menstruation can bring, but it also insists that she is at least that person and can bear that name. Then "thumb stump" marvelously extends this naming process. I experience the inner rhyme and strong pair of monosyllables as something close to nails binding her to this self-image—in part as a total embodiment of powerlessness, and in part as a means of stopping a flight to an even more desperate lack of substance.

## VII. Proprioceptive Adjustments: Elizabeth Bishop's "Sonnet" and the Force of Exclamation

My final complex of feelings is the most difficult to discuss because the instances tend to be very subtle—often mere matters of momentary attunements to changing situations. But I think much of our mental life is lived in just such quiet proprioceptive adjustments. And much of our art depends in large part on exploring the degree of intensity these adjustments can bear. I came to this awareness by thinking about modernist abstraction: Mondrian and Malevich are each in his own way painters of the infinite subtlety of our capacities for registering the sense of fit that emerges as we adapt ourselves to the emerging of various kinds of balances. And the modern long poem provides an example of a sense of structure keenly resistant to predictable or argumentative frameworks and so dependent on constant small recognitions about fit and balance. But thinking about modernist abstraction need not restrict us to twentieth-century art. Modernism gives us powerful ways of recuperating the past—in part to recognize how deeply rooted the modernists' emphases are in orientations basic to elemental features of aesthetic experience in general, and in part to test how their own making can modify what we make of this heritage. Walter Pater's *Studies in the Renaissance* is a hymn to the complex sensations afforded by the intricate modes of fit pursued by Italian painting of this period. Analogously, it was no accident that the late nineteenth century came to take Vermeer very seriously. The play of light in Vermeer's interiors provides a beautifully intricate dance emphasizing how the figures within his scenes come to balance one another. In literature, emphasis on proprioceptive feelings enables us to recognize the amazing achievement of Shakespeare's sonnets, which on every level from versification to argument continually keep us poised between a sense of balances being formed and a sense of expectations thwarted so that we have to try new paths. His greatness consists in large part in providing such constant pleasure of recognition that we take the frustrations less as disappointments than as promises of further pleasure in the offing.[7]

In my view the most interesting proprioceptive adjustments occur in the register of feelings articulated in the famous statement I quoted from William James on our awareness of linguistic operators as affective forces. So I have chosen Elizabeth Bishop's "Sonnet" as an extended example of how art foregrounds those forces. This choice risks destroying the symmetry of my own argument because this will be my second use of her work in this appendix, while I ignore many other possibilities. But because Bishop was so intensely resistant to explicit argument as well as to melodramatic versions of self-expression, she puts extraordinary emphasis on the powers of feeling cut free from anchoring large-scale emotional attitudes. That makes her perfect for my concerns here. And her poem is simply too fine an example to ignore of how poetry can both manipulate and satisfy our investments in small adjustments and balances. I am especially interested in how she brings the exclamation mark within the parameters of concerns basic to William James:

> Caught—the bubble
> in the spirit level,
> a creature divided;
> and the compass needle
> wobbling and wavering,
> undecided.
> Freed—the broken thermometer's mercury
> running away;
> and the rainbow-bird
> from the narrow bevel
> of the empty mirror,
> flying wherever
> it feels like, gay!

> (192)

We might start with the fact that this sonnet is only thirteen lines in length. So even the most fundamental adjustments we make to form will require recalibrating. However, before we can talk about adjustments, we have to have an image of what the overall situation is. Therefore I am going to rely on a classic New Critical strategy of beginning with a paraphrase of the poem, then asking what the paraphrase cannot capture. Taken as statement, the poem consists of two contrasting descriptions made with a series of conceits. First, the poem develops a sense of entrapment inseparable from seeking some kind of mirror for projected identities. Both the carpenter's level and the compass needle register states of a subject left divided and undecided because it can only see itself as caught within some containing structure. The second half of the poem then presents the opposite state of mind. Here the conceit compares the effort at self-definition to dealing with a thermometer that is broken so that the mercury runs out. Metaphorically the bird carries the force of spirit becoming gay because it feels it can fly away from the mirror (another instrument for self-measuring) and so is free to go wherever it chooses.

These are not uninteresting ideas. But cast in this paraphrase, the poem's rendering of freedom seems to depend on entirely negative categories. We encounter a clear instance of "freedom from," not "freedom to." And so it is no wonder that from this perspective all the poem can do at the end is name the feeling. From within such a reading, poetry does not transform sensibility. At best it celebrates a fleeting and casual state that can be summarized by the adjective "gay." This picture changes considerably if we treat the poem as making articulate specific affective adjustments that seem fundamental to how the psyche can experience that gaiety. Two basic processes within the poem then come to the foreground. First there is the pronounced effect of enforced then disrupted symmetry that Bishop produces by her elaborate patterning of participles. This aspect of her structure makes central to the poem a realization of the sudden sense of release that seems fundamental to the feeling of gaiety. But if there were only this sense of release, the poem might not manage a sufficiently complex sense of why the gaiety matters. So Bishop complements that sense of release by using syntactic and aural patterns to give a kind of substance to this gaiety. In effect, the gaiety seems to complement abiding intentional structures, and thus provides satisfactions central to a person's sense of his or her own functioning. Ultimately Bishop wants the psychological processes embodied in this poem to establish for the fluidity of gaiety a sense of duration and scope usually attributed to full-scale dramatic emotions and the narratives they elicit. Gaiety becomes comparable to a condition like "joy" even though it is traditionally seen as sharply opposed to joy in not seeming grounded and not persisting in time. Because "gay" in particular relies on multiple modifications within the poem, it comes to modify not just the bird but also the very process of realization that the poem embodies. One might even say that this sudden emergence at the end of the poem carries enough force that it provides the spiritual substance for the inferred but unstated fourteenth line of this sonnet that may only seem to be missing.

Bishop's motto might be "gaiety is what gaiety does"—as an emblem for freedom and perhaps as a term for sexual preference. In this poem gaiety is first of all a matter of negotiating pronounced structural balances. Each of the two main sections of the poem is inaugurated by an imposingly general past participle ("caught" and "freed"), and each half is made up of two closely related physical analogues for feeling. But the apparent rigidity also sets the stage for complex and resonant deviations that realize an active presence not predictable by the structure. Each section relies on present participles to interpret the condition registered by the initial past participle: "wobbling and wavering" balances the "running" and "flying" in the second part of the poem. Yet there is an important difference between the parts. The two present participles in the first half and the initial one in the second simply modify the preceding noun so that they function entirely as adjectives. But "flying" also has the power of a verb to open into an indeterminate future, "wherever it feels like." While the other participles are limited to the role of clarifying what is already determinate, "flying" seems capable of setting its own determinations. It disposes the psyche to very different anticipations of what the parallels will ultimately afford.

These syntactic expectations set off by pattern build to a climax in the concluding assertion. In one sense "gay" is just another piece of description, paralleling "undecided" and modifying "rainbow-bird." Yet "gay" clearly is not confined to that specific modification. "Gay" both names the specific condition of release and serves as an expression for an overall awareness of where the movement of the entire poem leaves us. So there is a sense in which "gay" is not a modifier but a very general condition, even a mode of activity that might take on modifiers if it could be located in any one space. In the opening half of the poem, self-definition was a matter of urgently seeking just such spaces. But here the poem manages to give substance and weight to a space that cannot be tied to particular objective settings. The shifts in orientation seem to have made it possible for the agency within the poem to reject its dependency on the kind of identifications that are constantly threatened by "wobbling and wavering." Now the poem itself seems capable of establishing grounds for identification with the very processes of feeling that it embodies. Identification seems inseparable from pursuing this path of constant inventive variation on established expectations. Identification involves appreciating what gaiety affords.

No wonder then that this poem concludes with what might be the most affectively engaging and expansive exclamation mark in American poetry. The exclamation reaches beyond the stance of observation to a stance of affirmation. The poem's efforts to produce precise emotional description now so fuses with its object that the language cannot be content with description. It relies on the exclamation point in order to attach will and sensibility to the force that the bird suddenly takes on. In effect the exclamation mark aligns reflective consciousness with the affect the bird elicits, and so it helps give gaiety a relation to psychological need not typical of feelings. One might even be tempted to distrust assertions about gaiety, or about freedom, that are not sustained by such exclamation marks. For this exclamation point not only offers a sense of affirmation but literally establishes the presence of will as an affective force. So it creates the possibility that we can articulate states of will without relying on the narratives necessary if we appeal to reflective judgment. Here, at least, the exclamation just is the work of judgment, without problematic dependency on abstractions linking the particular to some value-conferring general criteria. Poetry's strange conjunction of restraint and excess may have something to teach philosophy.

This last claim is not without its own excessiveness. But look at all that Bishop has done to make us experience self-reflexively a force in and value for gaiety without ever losing its mobile contingency. She confers a psychological weightiness on the feeling of weightlessness because the poem locates the sense of freedom in a series of affective adjustments that nonetheless remain so light they keep freedom from depending at all on concerns involving duty or morality. There is no need to reach beyond the poem's intelligence in order to establish ponderous justifications of freedom or to invoke ideological mirrors that the poem shows only destabilize identity. The exclamation mark proves sufficient affirmation because it is more attuned to investments consciousness has been making in these dimensions of gaiety than any more general abstract reasoning might be. Gaiety, like freedom, may have to be utterly simple, something inseparable from the mind's most elemental forms for investing in its capacities to make sense of its world.

At the risk of imposing a ponderous period, I want to add the moral that our most important task as critics, and perhaps as theorists, may be to keep available the possibilities for exclamation built into our affective capacities that are given expression in the arts. Gaiety does not require appendices, but appendices might help us recognize why it matters when it emerges.

# Notes

## 1. INTRODUCTION

1. I take up the issue of definition more thoroughly in section 4 of chapter 2.

2. For a statement representing the dominant concerns of philosophers in relation to affect in the arts, I cite the introduction of Hjort and Laver, *Emotion and the Arts*: "Although most readers will be inclined to see the contributions to *Emotion and the Arts* as so many exemplifications of the cognitive approach, it is important to note that some of the contributions reveal a social constructivist bent, while others clearly support the idea that constructivist and cognitivist insights can be mutually supportive" (9). For the editors there simply are no other respectable ways of approaching the topic.

3. I also became painfully aware that my talk about the arts would have to be confined to arts with a strong representational dimension—in part because I lack the expertise necessary to talk intelligently about music and in part because it helps to have readily available dramatic contexts for one's analyses.

4. For a good example of this emphasis on emotions as preparation for action I offer the following passage from Keith Oatley:

> The normal function of an emotion is to change goal priorities and to load into readiness a small suite of plans for action. At the same time information is inserted into consciousness, prompting interpretations of the event that caused the emotion, and sustaining attempts at problem solving in planning. Emotions have a consciousness-raising function in allowing us to infer goals that might have been obscure, and hence to build models of our own goal structures. (89)

The person then seems equated with goal structures, to me a highly reductive notion because it ignores manner and style and tentative exploration and immediate desire. Other theorists are less extreme but almost equally reductive. Aaron Ben-Zeev, for example, insists that "Emotions are not theoretical states; they involve a practical concern, associated with a readiness to act" (61). But why is practical concern the only alternative to "theoretical states"? Some emotions do involve that readiness, like anger or fear, but others like love or anxiety are much more connected to self-reflexive states. And even when there is readiness for action there is also a strong propensity to make investments in the attitude the action allows rather than in its practical results. So my argument is not that cognitivism is entirely wrong but that its emphases do not fit important features of the affective lives modeled by the arts. I find useful support for my position in Jon Elster's argument that there are two major roles the emotions play in our psychological lives: they generate behavior and they generate other mental states (137). And I find substantial sustenance in the criticism of the belief model developed in the first lecture of Richard Wollheim's *On the Emotions*. Wollheim shows how the cognitivist account assumes that "what any desire is directed toward is something that can be expressed in a complete sentence," on the model of propositional attitudes (19). But in fact this emphasis on belief in propositional form ignores the role the imagination plays in our desires, in part because the imagination can take multiple ideas as significant and positive at once, even though for reason these are incompatible. Paul Griffiths (37–41 and chap. 4) also offers a useful critique of the belief model based on processes of modularity and encapsulation driven by evolutionary adaptions. And Jack Katz is terrific on the forces and pressures within emotional life that are within one's subjective control. Katz also provides good analyses of how subjects can "exercise a nuanced sensitivity to the aesthetic possibilities in their bodily resources" (341–42).

5. At the risk of one more lengthy endnote fleshing out these introductory remarks, I want to take a few moments to distinguish my approach from two contemporary theorists whose work explicitly offers a parallel concern for treating affects aesthetically. In many respects I share the basic commitments of Robert Solomon's *The Passions: The Myth and Nature of Human Emotion*, but these similarities intensify my sense of our differences. Solomon seems to me importantly right in his insistence that what matters most about the emotions is the sense of self-reflexive agency that they establish. Solomon conceives emotions as "our own *judgments*, with which we structure the world to our purposes, carve out a universe in our own terms, measure the facts of Reality, and ultimately 'constitute' not only our world but ourselves" (xix). Correspondingly our interest in the emotions is in their capacity to maximize "personal dignity and self-esteem." And "self-esteem is often better served through the retention and intensification of an emotion rather than its satisfaction" (279). Self-esteem derives from the capacity of emotions to "bestow meaning to the circumstances of our lives" (133), a process that makes them "welded together into a single unit" with reason (14). Emotions are our best vehicles for those comprehensive judgments that make self-esteem possible.

The full force of my differences from Solomon will only emerge later, but I want to make clear from the start my three basic objections. First, Solomon remains concerned primarily with the meanings emotions produce rather than with the qualities of experience they make possible. Feeling is prelude to thinking and the world prelude to a kind of self-knowledge. Second, because he deals only with meanings, the only state of the self that Solomon can fully honor is one of self-esteem, that is, of the self's reflection on itself as a bestower of meanings. I will argue later that we do much better to treat the self's interest in its affective states in terms of the power and disposition frameworks made possible by Spinoza's treatment of conative energies. Value lies in how selves inhabit the affects more than in how they interpret them. Finally, Solomon is so thoroughly a cultural constructivist that for him we are always the creator of our emotions, so that all claims about passivity are acts of Sartrean bad faith (e.g., 430). Analogously, Solomon insists that subjectivity is "always a projection into the future" (71) because the facts of reality are never enough for it. This cultural constructivism weakens the dramatic challenges posed by the emotions because it evades the kinds of experiences where we are mastered or moved and have to adapt ourselves to compelling forces. For example, Solomon takes guilt as "extreme self-indulgence" because it maximizes self-esteem (321). Guilt is a creative solution, not a curse. Would that this were always the case, or blessed is the person who can always get guilt to produce self-esteem because it produces excessive self-consciousness. More important, Solomon's emphasis on the future ignores his master Nietzsche's insistence that letting subjectivity dwell in futurity is a sign of ultimate spiritual weakness because in so doing one avoids one's own relation to the eternal return.

The second book I feel I have to engage at length is Philip Fisher's *The Vehement Passions,* which was published after this book had been submitted to Cornell Press. In addition to the many shrewd judgments it makes, this book matters because it proposes a powerful case for how "each of the strong emotions or passions designs for us an intelligible world and does so by means of horizon lines that we can come to know only in experiences that begin with impassioned or vehement states within ourselves" (2). These formings of worlds occur in two basic ways. Fisher's fundamental claim is that "It is by means of the vehement states and their causal power that we derive a clear model of what 'having an experience' looks like" (21). These models are independent of reason and the appetites, the two basic other forms of our models for the world, though they can intersect, and passion can have strange but intelligible forms of rationality in its own right (93–94). But he is also committed to specifying how the passions enable us "to know the periphery and characteristics of what we call 'my world' as opposed to 'the world' " (175). "The passions concern two quite different peripheries that they both mark and reveal: first, the radius of my will; and second, the census of my world along with the exact contour of the phrase 'me and mine' " (175).

But as much as I respect this book, I find two serious problems with it. The first is largely a matter of emphasis, but with substantial historical and pyschological consequences for our appreciation of the range of affect. For the good part of eleven chapters the passions for him consist primarily of grief and anger and fear, the passions that deepen our sense of mortality. Then in his last chapter he announces that there is a second fundamental feature of the passions, their spiritedness and capacity to arouse the soul. But seven pages into the chapter we arrive at Kant's dispiritedness, and the discussion of Kant concludes the chapter (234–45). This may be the economy of tragic literature. But it is not the economy of aesthetic experience in general or classical literature and art in particular.

Fisher's use of Kant also dramatizes the second, more serious problem. I think Fisher cannot resolve a tension between the ambition to develop a "sustained core account of human nature" (7) and the desire to tell a historical narrative about what changes when the language of passions gives way to a language of emotions and feelings in figures like Hume and Rousseau and Darwin and their heirs. So when he does make historical claims, the tendency to reveal human nature in extreme states generates extreme claims about history that strike me as certainly not adequately grounded by Fisher's examples because these examples come only from the domain of high art and philosophy. Consequently it is impossible to demonstrate how these examples could be representative for specific cultures. Equally important, Fisher fails to observe the complex ways that cultures compensate for changes in philosophical vocabularies. Classical tragedy, for example, selects situations limited to a heroic world, and classical philosophy is so frequently torn between describing emotions and regulating them that its representative status for a society is very difficult to establish. And, as Fisher notices but does not sufficiently elaborate, the passions have everyday forms as well as high art ones—not only in simple states like anger and love but also in the versions of the elaborate cases Fisher dwells on where grief and fear intensify our sense of mortality.

Let me cite three examples of what I find problematic about Fisher's way of doing history. The first can be stated succinctly. In saving Kant for his climactic example of dispiritedness (Kant allowed only the passion for a good will), Fisher achieves a rhetorical triumph, but at the cost of ignoring just how unrepresentative Kant was of his culture. Fisher is not wrong about Kant. But he is wrong to give Kant the status of a historical exemplar, even in the limited domain of philosophy. Kant knows he is running against the grain in his argument for the absoluteness of moral concerns and in his critique of the domain of maxims. One can read him as being more interested in the possibility of a coherent case than in the practical consequences of his thinking. And even if one does not compromise Kant in this way, one has to admit that Kant never took hold on the level of his society's culture's grammar for affects. Certainly the main lines of Anglo-American philosophy never followed Kant, and even German idealism broke with him on his ignoring history and hence ignoring the domain where the moral must be tempered by pragmatic concerns.

My other two problems involve Fisher's specific historical claims about the differences between a culture where passions are fundamental and one that has replaced this emphasis on the language of emotions, feelings, and moods. Fisher claims at one point that "the historical dismantling of singularity [the mark of states of vehemence] into privacy means that the authority of each person's state of being, which was once absolute, now reappears as a cautious island within a more and more universalized and pervasive social existence" (63). Clearly there are many more communities that claim one's loyalties today, but that does not entail there being a more pervasive social existence. Life for the Greeks at Troy for ten years had to be an intensely social existence. One has to admit that there were classical ideals of singularity despite this social existence. But they are marked and strange and not representative—that is how Lear and Achilles gain their dramatic authority. And while Fisher dwells at length on Achilles suffering because of the death of Patroclos, he does not even mention what for me is the most important feature of the *Iliad* (discussed in chapter 6)—the renunciation of singularity by Achilles and Priam because the shared sense of mortality comes to outweigh any individuating passion. Similarly, while Fisher is terrific on the ways that "emotions" is a middle-class category seeking rationality and moderation against the "exceptional" vehement feelings (45), I think one has to recognize that while the classical heroes are caught up in the passions, their supporting cast, the representatives of plausible social lives, sound very much as contemporaries do in seeking moderation— Cordelia is a model of moderation, as is Banquo and even Macbeth until he falls under the spell of his Lady.

Finally, this bias against the emotions as moderating forces becomes especially costly when Fisher discusses "feelings." From his perspective, "In the vocabulary and grammar of the 'feelings' we see a mechanism for a controlled fading out of the passions, a subordination of them to the self that in earlier vocabularies they had flooded and eclipsed" (43). Ultimately we arrive at a sense of modern culture as absorbed by "moods" such as boredom and fear that "are states rather than motions of the soul," and so "conditions from which the spirit needs to be rescued" (153–54). But I will emphasize those modernists bored with boredom and hungry for the possibility of satisfying experience. And I will do so by showing how for the modernists "feeling" provides a way of exploring the boundaries of a self that they perceived as otherwise locked into grand dramatic categories such as the passions. I fantasize, in short, this book as a defense of modernity against Fisher's dream of a world elsewhere.

6. I can illustrate the insidious power of the cognitivist perspective, or, better, of the ideals of philosophy that generated the cognitivist perspective, by pointing to two examples of how its fundamentally epistemic values take over despite the author's stated commitments to provide a more complex story. Consider first the opening chapter of Ronald de Sousa's *The Rationality of Emotions*. There we find a powerful rendering of seven antinomies that occur when philosophy tries to get a grasp on the affective dimension of life. But then de Sousa's individual chapters resolve all the antinomies by praising the capacity of our emotions to play the roles of helpful spouse to reason's powers for pursuing human welfare, despite the fact that one of his seven antinomies includes their problematic

relation to rationality. My second example occurs at the conclusion of Paul E. Griffiths' very useful *What Emotions Really Are*. After providing in his second chapter a telling critique of cognitivism, Griffiths eventually bases his claims on a sharp distinction between "affect programs" and "higher cognitive emotions," each requiring quite different modes of analysis. Where affect programs are driven by basic psychological mechanisms that depend very little on the agent's distinguishing input, the higher emotions do depend on specific self-reflexive processing that involves correlating beliefs and desires. For Griffiths, then, it is a mistake to treat "emotion" as a workable category since it contains these incompatible processes. He may well be right in this conclusion. But I think his formulation of the differences is flawed because it relies on such sharp dichotomies between kinds of emotion, rather than between kinds of activities possible in relation to most emotions. What he calls mechanical emotions like anger or fear can be stylized and engaged by consciousness, while higher-order states can involve all kinds of dialogical relations with other people and so ought not to be reduced to cognitive functioning. Yet for Griffiths, as for most Anglo-American philosophers, "higher" and "cognitive" seem necessary cognates. These philosophers continue to treat the person having the emotion as concerned primarily with understanding and judging how he or she is placed within an ongoing narrative. There is almost no attention paid to the strange identifications and disruptions or extensions of what we mean by person that can occur if we attune ourselves to the intricate contours of affective situations within which consciousness comes to awareness of its own possibilities.

After such examples it may come as no surprise that with the exception of Sue Campbell and Richard Moran (as well as the sociologist Jack Katz), the only influential American philosophers I know who fully repudiate cognitivism are those with psychoanalytic orientations like John Deigh and Richard Wollheim. And Moran is the only one of the philosophers who does not go on to bring to bear a somewhat different epistemic regime. Wollheim for example is bound by his psychoanalytic perspective to connect the emotions intimately to fantasy and to repudiate their cognitive functions in the name of psychoanalytic knowledge about the psyche. And while Campbell stresses expression rather than belief, she nonetheless remains concerned primarily with determining what is expressed and what kind of knowledge is possible in relation to the expression. (I will argue that how the expression occurs and allows identifications is a more useful question than "What does the expression mean or communicate?") There are other philosophers, like Sue Cataldi and Quentin Smith, who work directly on the affects rather than the emotions and hence are not at all cognitivist. But their work is very rarely cited, probably for the obvious reason that such work has no role to play in enterprises shaped by cognitivist ideals.

7. In focusing on work in Anglo-American philosophical traditions I will for the most part ignore discourse on the emotions developed in poststructuralist theory. When dealing with that work I find myself either intimidated, as is the case with the work of Gilles Deleuze, or underwhelmed, as is the case for me with Derrida on this topic. Analogously, I simply cannot engage the neo-Heideggerians who develop various aspects of Derrida's emphasis on the event qualities of the affects that keep them distinguished from any concept or from any clear lines of identification. This work leaps much too quickly to the ontological level, and its emphasis on what cannot be conceptualized prevents it from developing usable models for interpreting and evaluating specific emotions. There is one quite fine and intricately concrete adaption of poststructural theory on this topic—Rei Terrada's *Feeling in Theory: Emotion after the Death of the Subject*. But rather than attempt to engage this book here, I have to hope the reader will consult my review of it, "Constructing Emotion in Deconstruction." My basic argument is that Terada's superb emphasis on the event qualities of emotions has to be connected to the roles they play as aspects of articulate attitudes.

8. I am painfully aware of the problem of writing about affects as if they could be treated as universals even though the author is obviously bound to quite limited social contexts. I can only say in my defense that for me the best heuristic strategy is to seek as much generalization as possible because then there will be a clear target for working out how individual cultures might differ from the models I propose. Getting straight on what one can say on the basis of various Western examples should help prepare the way for decent comparative analysis, and it may even produce some theoretical terms that might apply to a wide variety of cultural formations.

9. Ronald de Sousa isolates seven aspects basic to describing an emotion, as does Jon Elster, albeit a different seven. Paul Griffiths proposes six aspects, Aaron Ben-Zeev four, and the list could obviously go on. Other theorists like Herman Parret and Robert Plutchik provide highly suggestive but somewhat arbitrary intricate maps of relations among emotion types.

10. The simplest definition of intentionality may be the most useful: intentionality is what it takes to turn *a* situation into *this* situation. Put more philosophically, "intentionality" refers to those orientations of consciousness that give it directedness and so make it possible for the activity of mind to engage a concrete world. Intentional states are those through which we make possible the offering of descriptions and the motivating of actions. For a clear treatment of some of the complexities that I evade, see Richard Wollheim's contrast in *On the Emotions* between his own position and the traditional one most fully formulated by Franz Brentano. For Wollheim, "Intentionality is the thought-content of a mental phenomenon, and it is intentionality that secures the directedness alike of mental states and mental dispositions" (6). Brentano, on the other hand, treats intentionality as the "directedness of mental phenomena," which then requires an additional claim about the contents developed by that directedness (7). Wollheim also makes two very useful complementary distinctions. "Subjectivity" differs from "intentionality" because subjectivity is a property of mental states but not of dispositions. Subjectivity is "the feel of a mental state," or it is what it is like "for the person whose state it is to be in that state"(6–7). "Phenomenology" then is the "fusion of intentionality and subjectivity," and so it "attaches only to mental states" (8).

11. See for example Keith Oatley, who argues that jealousy is an example of a complex emotion that denotes a mental state and implies a context including the self in which the emotion arose: "It is anomalous to say 'I feel jealous, but I do not know why,' . . . To talk of being jealous refers to a control state in relation to a sense of outrage for the self because of a second person on whom one has some claim and in relation to a third person who could supplant one in the affections of that second person" (76–77). But while the passage is quite reasonable, it also affords a good example of how philosophy can produce an appropriate definition that nonetheless simply ignores how agents might configure this awareness in distinctive and expressive ways.

12. Antonio Damasio, *Descartes' Error*, offers the most influential concrete scientific account of these bodily dimensions, and Jack Katz provides probably the richest access to how the emotions take on performative complexity as conscious enactments through our bodies.

13. Jon Elster (56) notices this close relation between cognitivist accounts of emotions and the promise of making available a powerful perspective from which therapeutic efforts can be organized.

14. In my *Subjective Agency* I elaborate a rationale for crossing Kant's treatment of judgment with the treatment of exemplarity developed by Nelson Goodman's *The Languages of Art*. Goodman shows that art works typically have a different referential status than propositions do. Art works are not pictures of facts but labels facilitating the forma-

tion of complex semantic units. We do not check the accuracy of such works in relation to a determinate reality but rather use them to make discriminations in what comes to count as reality. As Goodman puts it, we do not take a red swatch to see if it matches the red of a sweater but use the swatch to see if there are more that are like it in some situation.

15. In chapter 6 I offer a more careful explanation of why Kant on purposiveness is central to my account.

16. Analogously, when we interpret emotions we often do not base our judgments on normative criteria. Instead we circle around the case, bringing to bear roughly parallel cases and exploring how the particular case seems to be continuous with a projected context. We convince others that we are dealing with a specific emotion not by specifying which criteria are met but by elaborating possible fits among the details and then in the relation between the details and the situations.

17. Elster himself is not so sanguine about the possibility that affects can be amenable to rational argument, but he shows how they often have an unexpected rationality that we can learn to appreciate.

18. As Charles Taylor's work on multiculturalism shows, this link of the expressive and the cognitive seems especially appealing for politically oriented contemporary theory. Expressivism keeps identity issues in the foreground and so foregrounds the possibility that agents can "know" what makes their situation different and requires their pursuing distinctive cultural identities. From this perspective it is irresponsible to pursue expression as an individual end without attending to the political factors that might go into shaping that expressive activity.

19. Susan Feagin seems to me the philosopher most attentive to the need for connecting aesthetics to models of human agency and interest. Her last chapter points out for example that the arts not only indicate how complex and fluid affective life can be but also call our attention to "a capacity for affective flexibility" that we can come to see characterizing our own responsiveness to those elements.

20. Michael Stöcker devotes an entire chapter to the Greek view of anger as a state to be valued. And Philip Fisher has a convincing account of anger in heroic culture as a positive value (171–86).

21. Ironically, in *The Feeling of What Happens* (22), Antonio Damasio, perhaps the scientist most sensitive to the phenomenology of affect, comes very close to Spinoza when he speculates on how affect also involves a sense of self: "The deep roots for the self . . . are to be found in the ensemble of brain devices which continuously and *non-consciously* maintain the body state within the narrow range and relative stability required for survival. These devices continually represent, *non-consciously,* the state of the living body along its many dimensions. Damasio elaborates his case for Spinoza in his *Looking for Spinoza: Joy, Sorrow, and the Feeling Brain.*

22. In his fine book in progress, *Literary Emotion: Performing and Judging What We Know,* Donald Wesling claims that with literature "a phenomenology of feeling is just what is not possible" and argues instead for a "systems approach" (20). I think he makes this claim because art involves a deliberate medium and hence cannot be treated as an immediate relationship to the world. However, we can also treat phenomenology as a means of understanding how works of art "realize" certain aspects of the world. The immediacy lies in the experiential work that articulation performs. I should add that Wesling is very good on the limitations of cultural criticism

23. The best way to demonstrate my claims here is to turn to Damasio's *The Feeling of What Happens* because even his sensitivity to the limitations of third-person perspectives on the mind does not allow him to escape both of the problems that I see as basic to seeking practical illumination from neurological models. First, Damasio recognizes but

does not sufficiently confront the difficulties involved in attempting to link what can be mapped by science with what human beings actually experience. He relies on responses to stories and, mostly, on hypotheses made possible by the study of people with neurological damage (see especially 85–86). Consequently his account of the emotions emphasizes generic emotions like fear and anger that link us directly with other animals and that can be equated with distinct aspects of the brain's most elemental functions. This methodology simply will not allow one even to admit into the picture the kinds of emotion like grief tinged with relief that are probably distinctive to humans and require multidimensional maps. One might grant Damasio the benefit of the doubt here and conclude that eventually neurology will be able to map the more complex emotions, at least so long as it attends to phenomenological accounts of what those emotions involve and remains as sensitive as he is to concerns about first-person affective awareness. It is not so easy to be sanguine about the second difficulty that seems to me endemic to this research. This difficulty emerges when he tries to correlate what we know about bodily functions with the domain of purposes and values that also seem to play significant roles in our affective experience. Despite his sensitivity to humane values, Damasio seems forced to rely on elemental evolutionary stories as his model for explaining the functions of what he is trying to map. Thus we find him asserting, "The biological 'purpose' of the emotion is clear and emotions are not a disposable luxury. Emotions are curious adaptions that are part and parcel of the machinery with which organisms regulate survival" (54). This takes place in two basic ways—by producing "specific reactions to inducing situations that might involve danger" or provide pleasure (53), and by regulating "the internal state of the organism so that it might be prepared for the specific reaction" (54). Clearly this is right, but is it sufficient? Can we accept letting pleasure drop out of the picture except insofar as it is a matter of survival? Soon after these theoretical pronouncements, we find Damasio giving this explanation of how emotions attach to pleasure: "in the case of pleasure the problem is to lead an organism to attitudes and behaviors that are conducive to the maintenance of its homeostasis" (77–78). I submit that there is little evidence for such conclusions beyond the fact that they link behavior to a systematic view of evolution, so that we need phenomenology to get clear on the many different value possibilities that circulate through affective experience. For humans, many forms of homeostasis come to seem like death, so that often we have pleasure connected with emotions because the emotions promise momentary disruptions of regularity and even bring a possibility of risk and potential change, or just sheer escape from conforming to any survival instinct. And when that certain look comes into the eyes of my spayed female golden retriever as she humps her male playmate, I have trouble thinking that her basic interest is in homeostasis. She is probably experiencing the excess of life and not its regulation.

24. For a good statement of the limitations of cultural constructivism in relation to these historical grammars, see Richard Freadman, *Threads of Life*, 35–42. For a test case dramatizing these limitations, see Lauren Berlant, ed., *Intimacy*. The entire volume deals with emotions as if they were deeply flawed social constructs to be interpreted and resisted in their current forms. Yet there is no effort to reconstruct what might be desirable or necessary or even changeable in our ways of experiencing these emotions. Distanced righteousness replaces any kind of engaged self-reflection. For the best general criticism of strong constructivist claims, see Ian Hacking, *The Social Construction of What?*

## 2. ENGAGING AFFECT IN PAINTING AND IN POETRY

1. For one striking instance of this tendency to bypass elaborate personal psychology, I want to cite a moment I heard on the radio in August 2001. John Madden, the macho

football announcer, was speaking of the smell of grass at early morning preseason football practice as one of his treasured feelings. The very simplicity of the state makes it possible to use it as the basis for making connections to other people without the agents having to agree on anything except their sharing of the particular feeling, yet nothing seems to be lacking because of that simplicity.

2. I rely here on the Louvre version of this motif. There is another version in the Capitoline Museum in Rome. That Caravaggio attempted two versions of the motif should not be surprising because he seems obsessed with exploring this point of contact where touch produces a sudden transformation of habitual intentional attitudes in forms too swift and too comprehensive to be mediated by mere belief. For his most intense renderings of touch, consider his *Doubting of Saint Thomas,* with Christ forced to take into account what is involved in submitting his divinity to a flesh that can be so rudely probed by someone seeking only proof of his material reality. Then there is at the opposite pole the shocking sense of liberation in *Youth Bitten by a Green Lizard,* with its proleptic sense of everything that can happen when one's fingers are drawn to perfect flowers. (A more radical version of this kind of touch occurs in *Youth with Flower Basket,* where the flowers figuratively embody what it means to feel one's chest taking on the plenitude of a still life.) Both kinds of situations prepare for the more figurative forms of touch that produce the conversion of Paul and the ambivalent yielding we see in Matthew's response to Christ's call.

3. In the version of this painting in Rome this hand does not wear a glove and the sword has a much less obtrusive presence. It seems that Caravaggio here does not want to detract from the boy's meditative face. In the Louvre version the face remains almost successfully cocky, so there remains work to be done by the ironies of hand and sword.

4. There are also at least two closely related versions of Titian's painting—one now in the Dublin National Gallery, the other in Madrid's Prado. I will rely here on the Dublin version.

5. Richard Wollheim's *Painting as an Art* offers a fine treatment of how the activity of painting in Titian involves feelings for flesh as flesh (319–29). But where he sees this emphasis as a matter of style, I see it as a thematic and self-reflexive principle, in *Ecce Homo* at least. For more by Wollheim on feeling, see *On the Emotions,* 119–28.

6. Affect also then has a complex relation to social context. In one sense the boy's feelings depend on his social station and expectations. But they do not simply reinforce what the society constructs. Rather they indicate fault lines within the prevailing social grammar.

7. Jack Katz seems to me the most helpful theorist on the complex relation between clarifying how one is moved and composing or stylizing a self through whom the impact of the affects can be made visible. Katz also adds the important consideration, to which I will return, that the agent who seeks visibility is likely to construct audience figures to whom to be visible. And that construction will affect how the agent presents a self.

8. I will elaborate how I use the concept of expression in the next chapter's engagement with Richard Wollheim's work.

9. Elizabeth Bishop's "Sandpiper" offers a fine example of how affect fuses imagination with perception. Here a responding consciousness initially sees the sandpiper against the backdrop of the ocean beside which it runs. Then that consciousness uses that way of seeing the bird in order to develop a strange empathy:

> The roaring alongside he takes for granted,
> And that every so often the world is bound to shake.
> He runs, he runs to the south, finical, awkward,
> In a state of controlled panic, a student of Blake.

By the end of this five-stanza poem this empathy with the sandpiper's scrutiny of the beach leads the poet beyond a series of analogical feelings to an overall metaphoric emotion. Attention to the bird turns it into an object of meditation because the bird comes to stand for the condition of searching perpetually for what cannot be found, even if one has the power of detailed observation that a sandpiper has.

10. For a good example of minimizing the significance of feeling, we can to turn to Aaron Ben-Zeev's *The Subtlety of Emotions*. In the midst of an otherwise fine and subtle account of the emotions, Ben-Zeev offers an extended discussion of the feelings that confines them to "modes of awareness which express our own state and are not directed at a certain object" (64). It follows then that feelings are simple sensations, while emotions have "intentional components in addition to the feeling component" (65): "Feelings themselves are not intentional; they do not have cognitive content describing a certain state; they are merely an initial expression of our current state" (65). The values that feelings do engage are simply matters of pain and pleasure (66).

Each of these claims seems to me wrong. Consider the feelings that might have been elicited from us in relation to the paintings just discussed, or consider the feelings represented by Caravaggio. Clearly we are aware not just of ourselves but of a relation between our present state and some soliciting condition. More generally, there are feelings like being interested that are primarily object-related, although they admit a second-order response. Analogously, feelings can involve distinctive modes of intentionality, as the Caravaggio painting demonstrates. Ben-Zeev assumes that if there is no belief there is no intentionality, but he can sustain that claim only by begging the question and eliminating states that otherwise have all the attributes of intentionality. In *The Fortune Teller,* the boy focuses on an intentional object and is sufficiently aware of the nature of that focus to have the potential for second-order reflection on the kind of subjectivity he is experiencing. Finally, to claim that feelings have values only as pain and pleasure is again to impose terms based on one's initial assumption that there is no intentionality involved with simple feelings. The boy in the painting has a very complex experience of attraction focused in his feeling, and the terms of the attraction do not resolve into pleasure or pain. For an intellectual framework capable of dealing with feelings like these, see Brian Massumi, *Parables for the Virtual: Movement, Affect, Sensation,* another book that appeared when mine was under consideration at Cornell. And for a magisterial treatment of how art extends the life of the sense see Susan Stewart, *Poetry and the Fate of the Senses.*

11. In order to show how conceptions of feelings are conscripted for romantic purposes, we have to distinguish two quite different stances—one that links feelings to a celebration of the subject and another that makes feelings our richest way beyond the limitations of narcissistic subjectivity. Nancy Chodorow, in *The Power of Feelings: Personal Meanings in Psychoanalysis, Gender, and Culture,* provides a striking example of the first tendency because she simply equates feeling with those aspects of subjective powers and values that cannot be dealt with in discursive terms. Emotions and feelings are the work of processes like projection and introjection that "enable us to create personal meaning" and bring personal resonance to the world (14): "Unconscious fantasy projectively endows the world with personal meaning, filtering the world through an emotionally laden story, and it affects and shapes the introjective construction of an inner object world" (239). But her defense of subjectivity leaves us with a very limited version of psychological life. Her subject composes values but has no way of engaging what we might call demands and invitations from the world, and no reason for being interested in finding out how such demands might be possible. More important, she gives the psyche no flexibility at the subject position; we have feelings and emotions because we foster against a cold objective world the kind of personal investments that have to be tracked in the form of narratives. There are no dense interrelationships between subject and object, and so no sense

of how feelings become structured as intentional stances open to all subjects, as is the case with the art we have been considering.

Quentin Smith and Sue Cataldi provide strikingly different accounts of the feelings that emphasize their close involvement in the world beyond the subject. But even though these philosophers have a great deal to teach us on this topic, they end up making such large claims and relying on such metaphorical language that they place themselves on the margin of contemporary philosophy without offering a sufficient alternative community. Smith is concerned primarily to set against "the metaphysics of reason" a "metaphysics of felt meaning," and in the process he offers lovely observations about the "direction of the flow of energies" brought into play by feelings (44–47). Cataldi aligns herself directly with Maurice Merleau-Ponty and has many good observations on how feelings take on depth by complex foldings of subject-object relationships. But she burdens feelings with such quasi-semantic import that they lose the immediacy and fluidity that Smith highlights. Consider for example a passage that culminates a very good discussion of how changes in affective fields can elicit corresponding changes in intentional stances. Cataldi then wants this discussion to show how this intentional activity demonstrates the work of a single ordering identity. But to secure that claim she has to put the following metaphoric burdens on her language:

> Transformative leaps of perception are related to emotional depth as an alteration in identity in at least the following way. However or whenever these perceptible shifts in the *order-ing* of our perceptual world occur . . . , they tend to require or demand, from us, a similarly "whole" adaptation "in response." They require that we (our "selves") break / brake and change—somehow—that our identity critically shifts itself "in order" to adapt to the changes on this other, perceptible side of our Flesh, because we, our "selves" are, or were, also "blind"-folded into the same fabric of Flesh as its "reverse" or "other side." (161)

In my view talk of blindness and insight only confuses the ways in which affects emerge in relation to shifts in situations. What one comes upon need not be "self" at all; it can be simply one way of investing in how appearances emerge—that is what it means to be free of the world of will and idea. Cataldi's prose is haunted by that world, so it is no wonder she must labor so hard to envision herself on its margins.

Because poetry seems more at home on those margins, I cannot close this without mentioning a tradition in modern literary criticism that asked the feelings to ground similar values. Critics like John Crowe Ransom and Owen Barfield who worked with the values of New Criticism made feeling the psyche's means of adapting the power of metaphor to processes of establishing values. This link of feeling to metaphor then also allowed the theorists to claim they could establish concrete analogies for Christian incarnational principles: metaphor gave concrete feeling a spiritual reality and spiritual hunger a concrete satisfaction. Moreover, metaphor flaunted a refusal to submit to epistemic discursive principles, yet it clearly afforded something like new knowledges of the real—think again of what Bishop could see in the sandpiper. Northrop Frye once said that even if Christianity did not provide an adequate picture of the world, its doctrine of incarnation provided the best poetics the world was likely to see.

12. I face a serious problem here because some of the best theorists of emotion insist that there are only occurrent events of feeling, thereby denying the possibility that feelings as well as emotions can constitute full intentional states. These theorists are content to deal with feeling as simply the bodily locus of the turbulence we identify as an emotion. But I think feeling also involves qualities by which sensation takes on asness and so affords a distinctive stance in relation to the world.

Wollheim and Antonio Damasio offer good reasons for reserving the concept of "feeling" for the first pole. Wollheim is eloquent on the three tasks the concept of feeling must perform: it must show how feeling can "initiate emotion," "manifest emotion properly," and provide evidence for "the specific character of the emotion" (*On the Emotions*, 119). Damasio uses an analogous account to make this sense of occurrence the neurological basis for our awareness of ourselves as individual subjects with a sense of ownership in relation to our experiences. To secure this sense of self he tries to establish a "continuum" within affective life. Emotions emerge first as processes by which the mind finds itself moved by something beyond itself, something public and outward. Then feelings take up that being moved in a direction that is "inwardly directed and private" (*Feeling of What Happens*, 36), marking "those images as ours" and allowing "us to say, in the proper sense of the terms, that we see or hear or touch" (26). This process enables us to explain how the feeling becomes conscious and the self takes on a position as the one having this emotion and feeling. This consciousness in turn "allows emotion to permeate the thought process through the agency of feeling" (56).

Clearly Wollheim and Damasio identify one crucial aspect of feeling. But I think stressing only the immediately occurrent aspect of emotions blocks us from appreciating the subtlety of feelings and the full range of our affective investments within experience. Perhaps we need some separate concept to distinguish the occurrent dimension of an emotion from a range of sensations charged with imaginative resonance. But for now I will be content to argue that at the least we have to keep the concept of feeling closely linked to intricate modes of intentionality that invite self-consciousness about intentional states. Otherwise we end up with one of two problems. In Damasio's scheme feeling is completely identified with emotion and so can only indicate the presence of the emotion: feeling has no other role in psychological lives. Or, to put the same point another way, all emotion becomes only the primitive kind of emotion characterized by Paul Griffiths (16–17). Damasio has no means of elaborating important differences between immediate senses of one's own participation in affects and states where feeling comes as a mode of relation to some phenomenon beyond consciousness. So by working so hard to locate consciousness of self as part of neurological experience, Damasio ironically ignores the intricacies of intentionality within affect that make consciousness so interesting a phenomenon in the first place.

Wollheim presents the second problem. He grants feelings intricate intentionality, but deprives them of any access to the world that is not part of the melodramatic domain of our emotional dispositions. Feelings become entirely means by which emotions take on force in a present moment. In effect dispositional structures become activated. However then we are not a long way from Chodorow. All feeling focuses on the orientation of the subject, with no significant differences allowed for the objects of feeling or the various modes of adjustment to the world that feelings can establish. As I will argue in the next chapter, Wollheim tends to limit our imaginative activity to the fantasy-driven states that stage full dramatic attitudes. And in doing that he ignores the range of possibilities feeling affords for having rich affective lives based on resisting the pull of fantasy. He does not allow for those affects that engage the imagination in elaborating what appears for consciousness. This theoretical position simply cannot attribute value to many of the most significant experiments worked out by modernist artists.

13. See for example T. S. Eliot, "Tradition and the Individual Talent," in *Selected Essays*, 8–11. For Wallace Stevens, see my "Stevens's Ideas of Feeling: Towards an Exponential Poetics." And for a representative statement by a noniconic modernist, I offer Kasimir Malevich in one of his less obscure moments: "The so-called 'materialization' of a feeling in the conscious mind really means a materialization of the *reflection* of that feeling through the medium of some realistic conception. Such a realistic conception is without value in Suprematist art. . . . To the Suprematist, the appropriate means of representation is always the one which gives fullest possible expression to feeling as such and which ignores the fa-

miliar appearance of objects" (Chipp, 341). Later in this essay Malevich draws a sharp contrast between the theatricality of our self-representations and the pure nonobjective representation of feeling as such (344).

14. I am relying on analyses of noniconic painting that I presented in my *Painterly Abstraction in Modernist American Poetry.*

15. I take this description from Popper, 140.

16. For typical analytic discussions of mood, see Elster, 272, and Oatley, 64. Philip Fisher discusses only negative moods like boredom (e.g., 146).

17. Alfred Tennyson's poems like "The Lotus-Eaters" and "Marianna" are probably the best mood poems in English, in part because the author feels the pulls of both the absoluteness of the mood and the need to submit that absoluteness to some kind of judgment. Heidegger's account of mood discussed below has the same duality.

18. I think the stakes in this discussion will be more dramatically present if we keep in the background some concepts developed by Emmanuel Levinas in his speaking about those aspect of subjective life that do not quite seem in the agent's control. Levinas clarifies why it is a severe limitation in philosophy to make the subject the center of epistemic practice without attending to the ways that the subject is first called toward what it tries to master. At those times when the subject does not simply will to know but is called toward knowledge, there is something in that relationship not easily captured within the language of knowledge. For knowledge can tell us what the object is but not why it could have the power to solicit the subject's attention or offer it a call to which the subject responds. And the subject is necessarily incomplete to the extent that its position as mastering subject depends on responding to such calls. Perhaps a full appreciation of subjectivity requires acknowledging that incompleteness and pursuing its implications.

19. I think I have to clarify two basic assumptions in my treatment of affect in the art objects. The first concerns where we locate the affective energies we claim for a text or painting, and the second concerns how we correlate the concept of "aesthetic emotion" with the kinds of worldly affects that I take as fundamental to the power of these works to modify those who participate in them. The concern for locating affective energies requires engaging a long history of commentary on how we respond to works of art. For a general account of how issues of response arise in all the arts, see the essays in part 3 of Hjort and Laver. And for my own position on response in relation to literary criticism, I refer the reader to two of my essays so that here I can just assert my view. These are "The New Criticism" and "Reading for an Image of the Reader." The issue of response seems a simple one: either we have a strong way of showing how words or images in specific deployments lead audiences to mental states mapped by the work or we have to locate the intensities of the work primarily in what the audience brings to the stimuli that the artists provide. Often the second position also sanctions claims that the resulting imaginative activity is a mode of freeing the reader from various kinds of cultural constraints. Where formalism stresses contemplative states, a new response theory would idealize active participation in the construction or "co-creation" of meanings. But in my view the freedom claim has just the opposite effect. It makes clear why we need some version of the first stance. Renouncing the force of the art object as object severely limits what these response theories can say about the subject they want to set free. Once the shape of the art object is not a factor in how we deploy our emotions, and once it no longer makes demands on how subjectivity is constituted, then the theory has as its subject only the consumer shaped by the prevailing marketplace notions of subjective agency. Response theory's efforts to honor the subject's emotional investments also condemn it to prevailing notions of free choice.

Art works themselves then become no more than commodities dependent on subjective preferences but without any significant power to shape how agents make and justify specific investments. Hamlet becomes what Rosencrantz and Guildenstern make of him. And, more generally, this stance undercuts the efforts of the institutions built up around art in the West to establish significant differences between choice in the marketplace and the provisional shaping of identifications that art produces when we learn to submit ourselves to its demands on the imagination. Therefore I value works of art not because they promise to reward my prevailing emotional dispositions but because they promise to modify them. And they promise to modify them in ways that emphasize objective qualities of the work and so encourage me to reflect on who I become by virtue of how the states of mind are rendered.

This task is made much easier if we can preserve the idea of distinctive aesthetic emotions without making these necessarily the primary affective dimension of the art we engage. Let us then define aesthetic emotion as that range of affective states that is focused on those features indicating specific qualities in the making of the work, hence in the workedness that makes it a distinctive work. Aesthetic emotion, or, more properly, aesthetic emotions, gather in relation to how materials are handled and how qualities like elegance and balance and formal cohesiveness shape the overall structure. By so limiting specifically aesthetic emotions we can then explain how these emotions can constitute an end in which we find immediate satisfaction. Yet we can also treat such emotions as a means of fostering our involvement in other kinds of affect, precisely because they free us to take on these affects as purposive and hence framed by the aesthetic context.

When responsiveness to aesthetic emotions serves as an end in itself, it takes the form of engaged admiration enabling the work to produce a sense of transport, of being caught up in the artist's capacities to make this object establish a distinctive experience. But once this transport is established, aesthetic emotions can also become a means of freeing us to dwell imaginatively on why the experience is distinctive and why it matters that certain kinds of distinction have been achieved. When emotions align us with the forming intelligence, they also give us an interest in how other affective energies within the work reach out for the kinds of resonance that extend the work into the world. The work's formal energies become its means of resisting ordinary categories of understanding and of sharply realizing alternative ways of caring about the sense we can make within experience. Workedness establishes the intricacy of affect, and it provides a significant test for what we might take on by virtue of the provisional identification the work proposes—with the situation of the maker if not with the characters and situations represented. So the arts matter for social life primarily because they keep alive the sense that it can be by our objects that we measure our possibilities as subjects—possibilities of response and possibilities of modifying our own priorities. One can hope to identify specific powers conferred by those works that produce new capacities for response or exemplify how agents might take on different forms of self-reflection. And this perspective on response also makes it possible to treat the powers so displayed as themselves open to all subjects (or even open to projecting what it might be like to experience as something other than a subject). What art exemplifies can be shared and can provide terms for the reflexive appreciation of common interests and abilities.

20. For a concrete example of what seem to me quite general traits in Pissarro's landscapes, I suggest *Garden of the Tuileries in Winter* (1900) in the New Orleans Museum of Art. Here trees at each corner of the foreground provide anchors that enable the sky to stretch out actively as an atmospheric container. That effect organizes a constant interchange between the overall play of colors and the distinctive particularity of the Tuileries.

## 3. INTERPRETING EMOTIONS

1. I include passions because I think there are distinctive kinds of emotions in which we find our identities seriously at stake. Once "passions" did the work I am asking the

concept of affects to do: the term referred to all events where the soul seemed moved by something impinging upon it. But at the same time the sense of "passion" that I am using also existed in the work of seventeenth-century theorists like John Dennis. We need a term for those emotions that are the stuff of opera, those emotions that become inseparable from the agent's sense of what makes life worth living. In my definition love and civic pride can be considered passions, anger and lust emotions. Yet anger and lust can become passions when the agent mixes the motives they provide with motives putting a high priority on self-regard. Obviously, questions of how these stakes concerning identity get worked out can become quite complex. But I think we can address those situations in the terms I develop for talking about the emotions. So here I will not take up the passions as a distinctive topic. But I will note that Philip Fisher seems at least on a similar track in his basic notion of the fundamental role the passions play: "The intensity of fear and danger . . . makes clear this negotiation of the radius of the will in which the self remains in a state of alert to any injury to the claims that the will makes on the surrounding world" (117). But I would stress more than Fisher those senses of the ego's stake in the world that are not fundamentally based on fear and injury.

2. Other theorists of the emotions obviously make important contributions to psychologizing the emotions, especially Katz, Ben-Zeev, Elster, and Moran. But Wollheim is distinctive in providing a thorough theoretical model for the roles consciousness plays in enabling the emotions to take on force in our lives.

3. Wollheim characterizes Bernard Williams as writing "in what he would be the first to concede is a depsychologized, or perhaps fairer, a prepsychologized language" (259). But I prefer to think of Williams as attempting to develop postpsychoanalytic ways of honoring what seems most psychologically compelling about the emotions to the agents in the midst of experiencing them.

4. Wollheim shows no awareness of Kenneth Burke's brilliant treatment of the concept of attitude. Yet it is this conceptual parallel with Burke that helps make Wollheim the most useful of analytic philosophers for my aesthetic purposes. However, once I recognize affinity, I cannot prevent giving a Burkean cast to Wollheim's claims about attitudes.

5. These three categories can be seen as a practical analogue to Justin Oakley's insistence that emotions involve three basic components—cognitions, desires, and affectivity (16).

6. All theories of the emotions have to explain this mediating process. But, Wollheim argues, cognitivism does not do a very good job of it. For by stressing how a situation "is thought of or evaluated" (77), rather than how it is perceived and imagined, cognitivist theory loses the dynamic force of how the relation to frustration or satisfaction is affectively and intellectually negotiated. More important, cognitivist theory gives being moved too much direct influence on desire, as if there were no further interpretive processes taking us from being moved to making investments and performing actions. Wollheim's version of mediation through the construction of attitudes offers a positioning of consciousness that is much more subtly attuned to what evokes it and much more complex in its accounting for how actions might emerge or fail to emerge. But in my view Wollheim is not sufficiently sensitive to the ways that many of our attitudes need not be specifically parts within our cultural repertoire for negotiating situations. There is some room for invention, as is demonstrated by the work of Jack Katz.

7. In his overall history of an emotion, Wollheim seems to put the projection of a precipitating factor before the formation of an attitude. But he also argues that this factor is established as part of the formation of an attitude and extroverted as an object of the emotion.

8. Because Goodman is a nominalist he talks only about properties, not about persons.

But for Wollheim both works of art and persons take on expressive force because we engage the presence of embodied agency making articulate a particular attitude. See *On the Emotions,* 250.

9. I am making a link that I do not find explicit in Wollheim but that I think is necessary for the coherence of his argument, or at least for the coherence of my use of his arguments. For a parallel sense of the limitations of judgment, I offer the following passage from Katz: "When they are emotional, people are engaged in bringing previously tacit dimensions into their awareness. *But this self-reflection does not take the form of thought.* Drivers do not *perceive* themselves cut off *and then decide* to construct their anger; rather, it is in seeing themselves cut off that they first find themselves angry" (34). I think expression is the making visible of how agents interpret what precipitates their behavior.

10. Michael Stöcker (169–75) makes a version of this point when he argues that there are two kinds of emotions—those that are means of revealing values we hold and those that constitute values. In the second case—his example is pride—the emotion is internal to the taking of pleasure and pain and not caused by the pleasure and pain.

11. I wish I had the space (and the nerve) to bring to bear the extended engagement with Hegel on force that I take up in my essay "The Concept of Force as Modernist Response to the Authority of Science."

12. In *Philosophical Explanations* (chap. 5), Robert Nozick makes an important distinction between values that emerge from the push of the subject into the world and values that emerge as the pull of the world upon us. I think these distinctions ought to play a much larger role that they do in our discourse about the affects. For obvious methodological and ideological reasons, we tend to treat the subject as the source of all emotional intensities, since that is the locus where the intensities can be located. But an aesthetic approach to the emotions may help us realize how often the emotion is in fact solicited by states of affairs that cannot be readily subsumed into the processes that register them.

13. For a completely different and to me much more plausible speculative account of the origin of moral emotions in terms of how we establish identities, see especially Christine Korsgaard, *The Sources of Normativity,* chap. 3. How we engage this domain of identities constitutes what I would like to call "the theatrical space for psychologization."

14. Wollheim gives a careful distinction between fantasy as a state and fantasy as a dispositional attribute; then he offers four roles or levels of function that fantasy takes on in mental life (140–47). The most elemental role is the "internal representation of desire" in a particularly vivid form. Because the representation can "fall victim to error" it takes on a variety of psychological burdens, culminating in a focus on introjected internal figures. Fantasy depicts a cast of figures in a world of facts "in ways that accord with the attitude that lies at the core of the emotion" (142). But then it is very difficult to see what in attitudes is not ultimately fantasy or how we can avoid moving from the first level, where fantasy just offers an internal representation of desire, to the third and fourth levels where we need the unconscious to deal with the full force of the fantasy. Wollheim himself seems to me to wobble on just how central fantasy is in the forming of attitudes. There are moments when he makes sharp contrasts between successful and fantasized relations to the real. But then when he has to attribute depth or talk about how expressions carry identity he relies entirely on fantasy as his model for attitudes.

15. I suspect Wollheim finds such efforts sentimental or naïve because they rely on ideals of increasingly transparent self-understanding that do not pay sufficient attention to the workings of fantasy. Campbell's expressivism presumes one can read through mental states to the underlying dispositions, while Wollheim is constantly aware of the inadequacy of phenomenological analysis in this regard.

16. In this context "passivity" refers to the emotion being shaped directly by the experience of frustration or satisfaction, while "activity" refers to the degree to which the con-

struction of the precipitating cause brings other aspects of the agent's expressive interests and powers into play. Analogously, I distinguish "imaginative" from "imaginary" by treating the first as an exploratory process of modifying hypotheticals while the second involves fixation on a structure of images not readily susceptible to modification by particular circumstances. But even when agents are active and imaginative, they can be woefully mistaken. So while my version of expression emphasizes the agent's self-consciousness, it does not bind us to accept the agent's terms. We can interpret these terms as we do any other account of actions that agents produce. The attitude establishes how the agent attributes meaning, but the entire act of attribution can be read in relation to what we know about the agent and about human behavior in general. We can always reinterpret interpreters if in an individual case we can give sufficiently strong reasons for our suspicion. What seems active may in fact be passive and governed by external forces.

17. It is worth mentioning two other basic distinctions that prove crucial in our understanding of how attitudes establish agency. The first one involves how emotions negotiate what constitutes the borders of a subject's sense of the relevant identities taken on. Some attitudes generate states of intense concentration: the self becomes the only active force in an indifferent environment. Other attitudes distribute energies and investments so that personality and specific agency seem almost irrelevant. Here the crucial features consist in those qualities of events and appearances that elicit investments in what is happening beyond the self. The power of melodrama is one clear indication of how we can become affectively absorbed without referring that absorption to our own constructive activity. Second, the question of borders leads by analogy to the need to make distinctions between attitudes that are entirely personal and private and those that are fundamentally impersonal. In the first case, the precipitating factor and the orientation the attitude composes seem entirely the product of what is happening to me and through me. But there are also attitudes like those we attribute to religious experience or those that emerge from our responses to nature that seem to move us precisely because they seem available for everyone. For more on this issue of boundaries see chapter 4.

18. I think the most interesting contemporary Hegelian work on the concept of expression is that of Charles Taylor, especially in the first chapter of his *Hegel* and in his "The Politics of Recognition." He does a superb job of clarifying why expressive behavior cannot be understood in the same way that we try to understand representations and propositions. The expression not only points to something else, as a referring picture does to its target. In addition the expression literally becomes something that bears significance because of how it organizes its constituent details. This organization is why we feel the sense that expressions are ways of possessing rather than only ways for referring. Therefore, we can envision the expression as managing to create increasingly richer links between the subject and the object in a process that initially has a good deal left undetermined or inchoate. Being moved by an expression, or into an expressive activity, draws us to want to be able to participate more fully in a certain way of being. However, I criticize Taylor in my *Subjective Agency* because he insists that ultimately expression is linked to "authenticity" (103–10).

19. For an extended discussion of "depth" in relation to feelings (not emotions) that is quite different from both Wollheim's and mine, see Sue Cataldi's application of Merleau-Ponty to this topic (167–75).

20. In chapter 4 I will pay much more attention to issues of manner in relation to the affects.

21. One could make the point about the importance of projected audiences for our expressive activity by relying simply on the work of microsociologists like Erving Goffman. Indeed Jack Katz does just this in very useful ways. But neither theorist engages the question of why we have this dependency. Correspondingly, neither has a very rich account of

expression. Here I think we need a Hegelian sense of how the subject needs to produce substance for itself in order to value fully what expressive activity makes possible.

22. For good discussions of how narratives render important aspects of emotions, see Nussbaum and Dadlez. But also please see my "Lyrical Ethics" for its criticism of philosophers' tendencies to dwell only on narrative fiction as their literary examples. I argue that this emphasis keeps their moral concerns focused on judging actions, rather than on matters of ethos and performative qualities achieved by expressive subjects.

23. I want to be clear about a basic assumption that underlies my approach to the two poems offered in this chapter. I cannot know whether the authors are sincere and so whether we are dealing with anything approximating the real construction of an attitude. But I can be reasonably certain that we are offered a fictive presentation of attitude-formation that claims to be exemplary for our appreciating specific aspects of real world emotions.

24. I deal with both the Victorian situation and the modernist responses in my *Painterly Abstraction in Modernist American Poetry*. In concrete terms my reading of this poem will show how easy it is for Arnold's speaker to become Eliot's Prufrock, forced to confront the displacing force of his own need for primarily imaginary identities. And here we are in a position to appreciate why Eliot saw the need to make sharp distinctions between emotions and feelings, the former dependent on self-staging plots while the latter are closely woven into the rendering of sensations. Because of that closeness to sensation, he thought feelings afforded intensities and attachments much less bound than emotions to the illusory project of constructing individual egos.

25. I am aware that there is something limiting in dealing with a work of art as if it were the experience of a character within the work. My basic defense is that I am interested here primarily in how agency functions as it forms attitudes in intelligible contexts. But it is also worth mentioning the fact that the different emotional strategies in the two poems I deal with reflect quite different authorial positions. I am not at all sure I understand Arnold's position in this poem. I suspect that he is not entirely aware of the ironies that emerge because I see him identifying with the speaker, and hence betraying many of the same blindnesses. But he might have occupied the position of the ideal reader who is aware of all the ironies and seeks a mode of sympathy responsive to them. With Bishop King's poem, on the other hand, there seems little problem in identifying the author's as the state of consciousness the reader wants ultimately to appreciate. One cannot know how rhetorical King is in manipulating tropes of sincerity. But one can be pretty sure that one is asked to reflect on the poem as if sincerity were its driving force.

26. In one of his novels Balzac has a merchant remark that he always stutters when completing deals because then his adversary spends all his energies trying to complete his thoughts rather than focusing on his own interests.

27. On emotions that derive from neither pleasure nor frustration, there are few examples as subtle or precise or suggestive as Wallace Stevens's "Cy Est Pourtraicte, Madame Ste Ursule, Et Les Unze Mille Vierges." The poem presents Ste Ursule offering God a gift of radishes turned into a bouquet, then shifts to God's perspective:

> He heard her low accord,
> Half-prayer and half ditty,
> And he felt a subtle quiver,
> That was not heavenly love,
> Or pity.
>
> (21–22)

28. Although I am very happy with the mixture of theoretical and historical concerns brought into focus by King's poem, I worry that contemporary readers will want something more recent as an example of attitude-formation resistant to the slippages of self-

consciousness and the seductions of imaginary audience figures. So I cite a contrast I make between Robert Lowell's "Skunk Hour" and Sylvia Plath's "Tulips" in my "Contingency as Compositional Principle in Fifties Poetics" (collected in my *Postmodernisms Now*, 82–106). I try to show how imaginary identifications undermine the assertion at the close of Lowell's poem; then I trace how Plath scarily reabsorbs all of those openings to imaginary others back under the pure control of the one forging a comprehensive emotional attitude. And for contemporary elegies that warrant a reading very much like the one I provide for King, see Carl Dennis's "School Days" and "The Fallen."

29. In this respect emotion in traditional lyrics can be contrasted sharply to emotion in traditional painting. Lyrics present the work of forming an attitude; dramatic paintings give the result of that work and invite us to speculate based on what the work gives us as to why the attitude took this particular form. Although painting is the paradigmatic non-narrative art, much of the affective force in these traditional paintings stems from how they direct us to reconstitute what might be causing the attitude we see in its already for-mulated mode. When Fuseli paints a passion, the inferences back to attitude-formation are utterly conventional. But when we move to Caravaggio, we find a very different use of painterly attitudes. My favorite painting of his in this regard is the challenge to traditional versions of the Abraham and Isaac story that he posits when he has Isaac sitting by him-self on the side in what seems pained frustration while Abraham chats with the angel.

We have to infer that Abraham, having stopped the sacrifice, now wants to ingratiate himself with the angel, so he ignores his son at a moment in the child's life when some sympathy would seem called for. The painting becomes even more telling if we see this Old Testament scene as typological of New Testament events.

## 4. WHY MANNER MATTERS

1. Campbell does insist that expressions constitute feelings and do not picture them, so I am using "represent" only to refer to how expressions come to stand for these states. Her underlying "interest" remains in hermeneutic judgments about how expression re-veals to people what is "important" about "the situations and occasions in their lives" (11). Solomon's emphasis on self-esteem comes closer to the performative perspective on expression that I prefer, since he addresses the agent's relation to its own qualities in car-rying out the emotion. But Solomon confines these relations to that one picture of motive, and he makes the only arbiter of value the agent's own imaginary states. I think there are much richer dramatistic ways to focus on agent activity. Katz in fact offers a better, more performative one, but in my view his model of interest is too public, too much concerned with modifying what audiences see rather than appreciating what agents accomplish.

2. In their introduction to their Oxford reader *Aesthetics,* Susan Feagin and Patrick Maynard do a good job of surveying the various interests theorists might have in expres-sion: "Ideas about self-expression are significant because they involve concepts of self-understanding and also cultural identity, the ways one would like to play a role in one's culture, and the relationships among personal freedom, cultural reality, and political ne-cessity" (3–4). But they do not try to clarify what the relevant sense of "freedom" is or how one might play a role in one's culture. Instead, the only aspects of this they develop are self-understanding and the expression of cultural traits.

3. Initially I tried to organize this chapter as a response to Jon Elster's statement that "one outstanding unsolved problem is that of the relation between emotion and interest" (416). I abandoned the idea because I could not feel confident that I was dealing sufficiently with his framework for understanding "interest." However, I do want at least to mention the line of argument I would have pursued. We need an aesthetic approach to the emo-tions because the other available approaches simply cannot adequately explain fully why

the emotions are in our interest. If we confine our analyses of the human interests fundamental in any given phenomenon to measures of practical results, then the emotions seem
just too unstable and too caught up in the imaginary to be reliable guides to action (despite cognitivist efforts to argue the contrary). The emotions *can* produce useful salience
and *may* structure our attention in productive ways, but they also often distort situations
along the lines we observed in dealing with "Isolation: To Marguerite." If we want stable
and materially satisfying lives, we might well be better off without them, or at least without many of them.

Any account capable of making a wide variety of emotions fundamental to our interests as human beings will probably have to build a teleology into its fundamental principles of analysis—as we see for example in the reliance of virtue theorists on Aristotelian
versions of "human nature." Once the teleological principle is assumed, then emotions
like loyalty and sympathy turn out to be important interests not because of what they produce as results in particular situations, but because of what they enable as dispositional
traits. However, while I cannot deny that virtue ethics provides a plausible account of our
possible interests in some emotions, I cannot find it very satisfying on the whole, for reasons developed in my next chapter. The range of emotions it sanctions is quite narrow,
and the values attributed to the emotions have very little to do with their distinctive workings as emotions. For virtue theory, the emotions matter because of what they mediate
rather than what they provoke, and their value can be subsumed into those mediated principles. Emotions become moral instruments, a result that is fine for morality but devas-
tating for our overall affective lives. This approach reduces self-consciousness to what
Arnold dramatized as the oppressive need to think well of ourselves as virtuous beings. I
propose instead that we emphasize the interests we have in the theatrical conditions that
the emotions produce—for our own construction of identities and for our engagements
with other people.

4. Jon Elster comes close to my concerns when he makes the following distinction:
"Emotions by and large are passively undergone rather than actively chosen or enacted,"
but emotions are under our voluntary control in the sense that we can let the emotion happen, "amplify it by giving full rein to its expression, or try to limit it, for example by directing attention elsewhere" (311). In one sense I am simply trying to give cash value to
the idea of giving full rein to its expression, but with the emphasis on the agent rather than
on the emotion per se.

5. I use this early work by Moran in my *Subjective Agency*, 37–38. His arguments are
clearly summarized in his "Making up Your Mind: Self-interpretation and Self-Constitution." After I completed this book manuscript, I encountered Moran's magisterial *Authority and Estrangement: An Essay on Self-Knowledge*. This work does not return to his
concerns with manner, but it is superb in developing significant asymmetries between first-
and third-person stances in relation to our own behavior. These asymmetries are crucial
for understanding the work expression has to do in getting at aspects of behavior not governed by belief and in understanding the mode of relation we enter into with other people
precisely because we cannot treat our response as simply a response to beliefs. In "The Expression of Feeling in Imagination" Moran offers a long concluding argument to this effect that is based on the question of how might we reject or resist a world offered by a
fictional text. The simplest way to reject the fictional text is to assert that the world offered by the text depends on assumptions or descriptions that are incoherent or so vague
as to prevent sharp affective engagement. In these cases, we base the judgment on what
we take to be demonstrable features of the object, and we assume that these features hold
for virtually all subjects because the relevant details are elemental building blocks determining whether the fictional world can cogently take on further predicates enabling an audience to bring life to its properties. There is no need to rely on one's own deeply felt values.

However, there are also occasions when we want to resist a text not because it is false but because we cannot abide the manner of its ways of making investments in characters or ways of seeing and of thinking. Consider the example of Céline. These cases require a personal accounting. For one is not just repudiating an opinion. One is repudiating a mode of personal action that seeks from us intimate participation. And because of that appeal, there is a good deal of urgency in the repudiation: we are not merely saying "No"; rather we are warding off what tries to compel identification. In such cases what counts as value depends on how the agent makes investments in being a certain kind of person and then on how those investments find expression. We cannot repudiate that expression on the basis of its objective limitations as a failed proposition. We have to locate the failure in the agent, and we have to base the repudiation on what sympathies and adjustments our own personal priorities do and do not allow. Considerations of identity and identification replace epistemic frameworks.

6. Unfortunately, I cannot base any of my arguments explicitly on Deleuze because I simply do not know how to translate what I understand of his work into a theoretical language capable of engaging the other thinkers I address. To adapt Deleuze would require engaging and translating his entire vocabulary. Deleuze requires not only that we turn away from the priority of belief but that we adapt a complex and fluid spatial vocabulary for the work affects do. They enable passages in relation to boundaries, have different degrees of thickness and fluidity, and produce different forms and levels of contact and penetration and resistance or reaction among surfaces. So all I can do here is mention my deep regard, recommend Brian Massumi's new book *Parables for the Virtual* because it extends Deleuze, and recall the second epigraph to this chapter as one measure of what Moran's emphasis on the vividness of manner might sound like in French.

7. Walton's basic arguments are offered in his *Mimesis as Make-Believe*. But it is also important to note that in his essay "Spelunking, Simulation, and Slime: On Being Moved by Fiction," in Hjort and Laver, 44–46, Walton accuses Moran of not recognizing the degree to which Walton sees mimesis as dealing with imaginings that "reflect actual attitudes." Moran's point, however, is not that fictions *reflect* actual attitudes but that they present actual processes that we are invited to engage as such. I want to add to this the suggestion that all epistemic thinking is likely to have trouble on issues of fictionality because it cannot easily shift from talking about objects to talking about processes. For the very idea of demonstrable knowledge depends on separating what is real from what is fictive—often a necessary task but not the primary one where emotions are at stake. We see the limitations of this perspective most dramatically when we realize how epistemic realism in relation to the emotions also provides the basic model for those who are skeptical of their having any truth-value at all. Where Walton sees emotions within fictions as problematic, Sartre and Lacan put fictionality within the emotion itself so that it can never have a stable place in rational judgments. They differ from Walton only in their insistence that all emotions, not just those in fiction, are pervaded by imaginary qualities and so cannot have any place in the lucid analysis of real world situations. And it is not a great leap to bring Wollheim into the picture. He too treats the psychological reality of the emotions as a displacement of the empirical world: because belief cannot get to what is real about emotions, one has to locate that reality entirely within the psyche. All of these thinkers seem to me trapped into having to choose one side of an intractable binary opposition: either they have to ignore why emotions thrive in the vividness fictions bring or they have to treat emotions as doomed to irrationality because they cannot be satisfyingly attached to the world with which reason deals. In both cases, we get at best rational agents who think about emotions rather than imaginative agents whose humanity is wound into producing and responding to the vividness that the emotions afford.

8. Moran's reasoning tempts me to take the opposite pole from Walton: perhaps most

great art achieves that greatness because it is deeply unsatisfied by direct equations with our real, practical worlds. The art wants us to consider what it might take to engage an imaginative intensity possible only in a world to which we must aspire. I once had a student who told the class that Dante's love for Beatrice was like her boyfriend's for her. She was learning how to read actively but had not quite appreciated the difference between realism and allegory.

9. Moran offers this concise version of his argument while criticizing Walton's inability to deal with phenomena like Shakespearean language: "Such expressive qualities of a work, and their central role in engaging the emotional life of a reader or audience, don't seem to find a natural place within the theory of make-believe, or the original problem to which it is a solution" (84).

10. Now another problem arises. My proposal fits the ways that most professional critics read, since they treat texts as filtered through authors. That however is not the case for most nonprofessional readers. They tend to ignore authors and take the world offered by the text as the focus for their imaginative participation. So I think we have to admit that there are different uses of the imagination that come into play when we read. When we deal with the speeches as aspects of make-believe worlds, their vividness is directed toward intensifying the imaginary reality. Yet this does not mean we have to accept Walton's account of that reality. E. M. Dadlez, *What's Hecuba to Him: Fictional Events and Actual Emotions,* seems to me to provide a better account than Walton's because she sees the fictive world not as illusionary but as inviting efforts at imaginative construal. We do not make believe the fictive world is a real one, but from the start we devote ourselves to construing how it can engage our real world concerns. Having learned from Moran, she treats our participation in the text as a matter of active construal in relation to the reader's real world concerns. We bring characters to life by construing the differences their forms of vividness might make for us as readers in our worlds. And by stressing construal, she does not have to insist on consciousness of the self as part of our emotional involvement: we are focused not on how our beliefs get deployed but directly on how what the character is doing might matter for us. Yet while I admire this argument and obviously find it useful in dealing with characters, I think it important to point out that Dadlez does not extend her model to our relationship with authors. Consequently, she is good on how we engage the particular world created by a text, but not on how we might treat it as somehow exemplary in its specific manners for dealing with situations. Her model then will not travel well to modes like the lyric or to fictiveness in visual art, although I think the necessary adjustments would not be too hard to make.

11. I should engage briefly two theorists who show the way toward an adverbial view of the affects. John Deigh's superb essay "Cognitivism in the Theory of Emotions" opens significant possibilities by first making a very useful historical distinction between "traditional cognitivism" and "contemporary cognitivism," then building on that to recuperate the intricacy of intentionality within affective states. Traditional cognitivism sees emotions as "mental states in which the subject is cognizant of some object" but the cognizance need not involve a judgment by the intellect (828). Contemporary cognitivism turns from the study of intentionality to the study of the concepts that intentionality might bring to bear in formulating specific beliefs about the target of the emotion. To feel pity is to believe that a person is in some distress (831). For traditional cognitivism, on the other hand, one might feel pity simply because of what one registers in the person's appearance or gestures. This distinction enables Deigh to return to work of C. D. Broad that elaborates complex versions of intentionality compatible with traditional cognitivism but not with the contemporary version. Broad had to emphasize intentionality in order to resist William James's contention that emotions are defined by specific modifications in our bodies. But

Broad was not willing to give up on the ways that affective dimensions of the emotions take on psychological reality. He argued that emotions "are cognitions that have a felt quality or tone." "Crudely put, he conceives of anger, when one is angry at P, as thinking angrily about P rather than, as James would put it, feeling hot and angry in response to some thought about P" (829). This view of intentionality then lays the groundwork for what is in essence an adverbial view of emotions based on how intentionality is deployed in particular situations. But, Deigh points out, Broad's effort to break with James was vulnerable to exactly the same criticisms as those that philosophers used to reject James. Broad, too, had no clear way to distinguish one emotion from another and so could not sponsor significant empirical studies. He could only claim that different kinds of emotions could be distinguished by "their characteristic emotional tone" (831). Because "emotional tone" sounds all too much like Jamesian "correspondences," philosophers could point to such vagueness as a justification for concentrating on aspects of intentionality that could provide stable interpretive terms for a wide range of emotions. Hence the eventual primacy of belief as the one basic intentional orientation.

Deigh's essay leads us to the question of how we can locate the "feeling tones" that enable us to deal with emotions as adverbial modifiers of subjects. His own project uses this opening as a means of bringing psychoanalysis into play. Since I am not eager to take up that option, or to rely on neurological models as presently constituted, the only feasible alternative for identifying emotions without emphasizing belief seems to me to adapt a Wittgensteinian stance and point to the dense grammars we learn as we develop abilities to make distinctions in forms of affective behavior. Dadlez offers one quite useful precedent for taking on this task. Building on Moran, she uses the concept of "an adverbial approach" (8) and connects that to the readerly work of fleshing out fictional worlds. But her emphasis is on reading well, not on living well. So she does not take up the topic of expression. Instead she concentrates only on how thinking about emotions in terms of manner can clarify audiences' real emotions about imaginary worlds: we care not for the illusion itself but for the modes of activity foregrounded within it. Then, because she is concerned primarily with participating in the emotions of others rather than with understanding expression, she treats the adverbial state as necessarily a relation to a thought: "Instead of an emotion being characterized as an attitude held toward a certain thought's content, the emotion is reconstrued as a way of having, holding, or entertaining that particular thought" (102). Now, though, we are again dangerously close to cognitivism, because Dadlez still holds that the values within our affective states depend on beliefs. In so confining her analysis, she also runs the risk of collapsing all affect types into those driven by ideas. That prevents her from developing adequate conceptual terms for the many ways that the force of the affect lies in how something is done rather than in how some belief is put into action. Adverbs become only manners of entertaining and adapting those beliefs. In contrast I am trying to establish manner as a general feature of expression that helps us explain why people are invested in their emotions and how we have to adjust in interpreting those investments. So I argue that the adverbs directly modify how we see the agent and how we then are positioned in relation to carrying out some interaction with that agent.

12. Where Moran and Dadlez deal with specific activities that take place within fictions, I deal here with manners of dealing with fictionality as itself a mode of affective activity.

13. I think one has to separate Spinoza's overall ontological distinction between the active and the passive from his practical ways of distinguishing between active and passive emotions. In his practical analyses, the determination that a state is active seems to derive more from the absence of external determining causes than from the full presence of ade-

quate ideas. Later in this chapter I will rely on his looser practical model, in part because it is compatible with the second-order perspective that I propose.

14. This is not to say that it is has not been attempted. Stuart Hampshire's *Spinoza* offers the richest account I know of the relevance of Spinozan views of freedom for contemporary culture. And Jerome Neu makes an elaborate case for preferring Spinoza to Hume because Spinoza's emphasis on understanding seems to fit so well with cognitivist concerns. But the problems arise when we ask what kind of understanding we can produce in relation to the affects. "Understanding" human activities involves much more ambitious claims in Spinoza's system that it does for most contemporaries.

15. Kant's response to Spinoza offers an interesting example of how attitudes to necessity have shifted. I think it fair to say that Kant's fundamental moral distinction between heteronomy and autonomy derives directly from Spinozan ideas of active causality. But in Kant the necessity is conceptual, not quasi-empirical. Autonomy is not a relation to the power to see one's life as part of a causal nexus but a relation to the power of reason to act directly on its own necessities. Reason in Kant freely wills to bind itself to universal laws because the universals manifest reason's own constructive powers. And because reason can live actively in relation to its own constructive powers, it demonstrates the fundamental structure of what we have a right to call "spirit." Spirit is what lives for itself in itself, as opposed to nature, since nature follows laws it cannot formulate or identify with. Hence it is wrong to tell a lie, not because the lie will lead to bad consequences, but because in submitting to the need for the lie one submits to the rule of nature and denies the possibility of living in accord with principles internal to reason.

16. When one speaks about plausibility in areas where no rigorous testing is possible, one has to rely on some hypothesis about competent observers. My competent observer here would be a projected audience sympathetic enough to appreciate why someone acts in a particular way but impersonal enough not to base the decision on any special relationship to the agent.

17. For Creeley on the interplay of subjective and objective see his *Quick Graph*, 18–19.

18. Maurice Merleau-Ponty once argued that Cézanne differed from his fellow painters because rather than painting what the eye sees he wanted to capture the feelings associated with a sense of "the visibility of the visible." Think for example of his interest in framing the view of Mt. Sainte Victoire between pine branches that seem strangely like eyes. In effect, he plays with a completely psychologized sense of the eye's activity without repudiating the sense of nature as the active source of all the visual relations. Analogously, one can speak of Creeley's poetry as obsessed with "the desirability of the desirable." His poetry does not simply track subjective energies as they engage particular situations. Rather it tracks itself attending to those energies as they work "'toward a perception that is the mind's peace.'" I cite Creeley citing Louis Zukofsky in Creeley's *Quick Graph*, 37. See also p. 39: "Again and again I find myself saved, in words—helped, allowed, returned to possibility and hope. In the dilemma of some literal context a way is found in the words which may speak of it."

19. I like to think that my account of identification in my *Subjective Agency* roughly parallels Kamler's, except for the fact that I pay more attention to how identification is involved with notions of expression. But Kamler gives a much better concrete sense of how identification works than I did. Also important to this discussion is Michael Stöcker, *Valuing Emotions*, a text I will discuss in the next chapter. And I should note that Stanley Cavell's discussions of owning oneself offer a more dramatic and complex version of identification than do Kamler's. However, Cavell seems so involved in the drama that he does not try to account for the building blocks in the way that Kamler attempts.

20. Kamler establishes his position by pushing against the two dominant alternatives— one emphasizing the causal forces that identification would be seen as recognizing, the

other locating selfhood in the forming of what Charles Taylor calls "strong evaluations." Causal explanations of identification cannot suffice because they cannot explain how we become modified within the very process of forging the identification. Identification is not a matter only of clarifying how one's past produces the traits that dominate the present. It is also a matter of how one's activities in the present modify and are modified by projections about future selves. (One day we will have causal explanations for that as well, but probably not along the lines of how we now apply concepts of cause to the work of defining one's values.) On the other hand, the evaluationist models developed by Taylor and by Harry Frankfurt prove problematic for just the opposite reason. Their basic claim is that we have to make a sharp distinction between the kinds of choices that do not affect identity because they are merely practical decisions and those that involve "strong evaluations." If I am choosing whether to go to Paris or to London tomorrow, the only thing that stops me from doing both is the physical difficulty involved. But if I am choosing between acting as a coward and acting courageously, I cannot base the choice simply on preference but have to see the choice as continuous with deciding to be a certain kind of self. Choosing a cowardly act is not just choosing something to do; it is choosing to take on specific traits as a person. One can modify the meanings of the terms, but one will have to seek an identity in relation to the meanings chosen. (I may for example try to convince an imagined other that what seems cowardice is really courage.)

Kamler sees himself having substantial affinities with the strong evaluation model because it shows how identities can be constituted by modes of judgment. Yet he insists that there are two closely related ways in which the Taylor version leads us astray. This model makes identification a matter of reasoning and choosing among meanings when there is a more fundamental question about valuing. And it makes our moral beings the fundamental source of identification. But our identifications have their core in the "brute evaluations" by which we set up the values to which we are committed. These evaluations in effect put the person in the world as determiner of values by specifying the communal terms that will be appropriate for assessing what counts as significant identifications for him or for her (Kamler, 10–13). And the more radical the constituting of identities, the less we can be content with purely moral vocabularies. Where Taylor sees strong evaluations as also a process of discovering identities already formulated by our personal and cultural histories, Kamler treats fundamental valuings as continually open to determining the vocabularies within which they can be judged.

21. Marx Wartofsky puts a similar desire much more eloquently. After pointing out some problems with Spinoza's thinking he adds, "Yet the towering attempt at a system, and the power of his monistic imperative still provide, to my mind, one of the most valuable heuristic guidelines in the formation of a contemporary science of psychology." See his "Action and Passion," in Green, 334.

22. When I speak about satisfactions I am referring only to the experience of the affective states themselves. Clearly very different satisfaction stories enter when we attend to the actions that the emotions might help generate.

23. I take this formulation of the mind as idea of the body from Marx Wartofsky (Green, 336). One can also find the idea stated explicitly by Spinoza, for example in this statement: "This idea of the mind [the idea of God] is united to the mind in the same way as the mind is united to the body" (80; see also the scholium to part 2, proposition 17). And my reference to "becoming" is homage to Deleuze's great book on Spinoza which I engage at length in my *Subjective Agency*.

24. Spinoza is very good on imagination, in part because he sees it as conatively connected to the body's relation to its environment and not as a faculty that abstractly produces a certain kind of content, like fantasy. Specifically, imagining is the developing of an idea by which

the mind regards something as present, with emphasis on the state of the body as it organizes its attention (220). Imagination dwells on something outside the self, but with a primary focus on the condition of the subject as it yields or withholds certain qualities of participation and investment in the images it brings before itself. So when I imagine a landscape I don't just see its details but see its details as if I were present and engaged modally within it.

25. There are actually two problematic ways of dealing with the will to individuation. We have to distinguish those philosophers who idealize the will to power from those like Schopenhauer and Sartre who are much more negative about our dependency on that will because it generates endless meaningless striving for what remain only imaginary projections about selfhood. For clarification of these issues see Henry Staten's *Nietzsche's Voice* and his book in process, "Lines of Force: Victorian Novels, Nietzschean Poststructuralism," that takes Victorian novels as efforts to work out viable versions of that will in relation to an oppressive moral order.

26. After developing a very suggestive account of multiple modes of individuation in Spinoza, Etienne Balibar takes the case in the opposite direction from the one I take by emphasizing the ways that individuals can bond together without all the problems of boundaries that plague rigid substantialist notions of individuation. See his published lecture *Spinoza: From Individuality to Transindividuality*. See also Wartofsky (in Green, 346–47).

27. In my *Painterly Abstraction in Modernist American Poetry* I have elaborated at some length what I take to be the four basic modalities that the "as" governs (343–55). (In a terrific recent unpublished lecture, "Figuring Out," Lyn Hejinian elaborates eight different senses of "as.") Here I hope to supplement that treatment by showing how these modalities are not simply semantic operators to be appreciated for the abstract self-reflexiveness they allow. We must see the "as" as fundamental to a relational model of feeling, and therefore we have a good example of the ways in which for Stevens the most abstract reflections engage us in the most concrete and intimate emotional dispositions.

28. For an important prose rendering of the same ideal, we have to turn to Stevens's remarkable essay "A Collect of Philosophy":
The philosopher's world is intended to be a world, which yet remains to be discovered and which, at bottom, the philosophers probably hope will always remain to be discovered and that the poet's world is intended to be a world, which yet remains to be celebrated. If the philosopher's world is this present world plus thought, then the poet's world is this present world plus imagination. If we think of the philosopher and the poet as raised to their highest exponents and made competent to realize everything that the figures of the philosopher and the poet, as projected in the mind of their creator, were capable, or, in other words, if we magnify them, what would they compose, by way of fulfilling not only themselves but also by way of fulfilling the aims of their creator? (*Opus Posthumous* 199)

29. I also discuss this passage in my *Painterly Abstraction in Modernist American Poetry*, 339–40. There I emphasize how the poem makes good on its own assertions and so can be considered testimonial rather than representational because it demonstrates the actual presence of the values that it asserts. Here I am interested in how that testimonial work not only demonstrates what it claims but produces an interweaving of feelings that seems inseparable from the thinking process.

## 5. EMOTIONS, VALUES, AND THE CLAIMS OF REASON, PART 1

1. I can only accept a notion of "rationality" that is limited to the ideal of giving reasons for one's actions and attempting to make decisions that can be defended because one has followed an appropriate discipline for assessing these reasons.

2. Contemporary philosophers tend to be much more comfortable with concepts of incommensurability than traditional thinkers were. In ethics that way of thinking generates what we can call a particularism very sensitive to the limitations of abstract reason. So while only Robert Solomon among theorists of the emotions seems to approach the position I will be taking, the underlying logic of my concern for incommensurable values seems to me consistent with the thinking of both Richard Rorty and Bernard Williams (neither of whom would like to be aligned with the other). But I should also point out that despite my affinities with the arguments of Rorty's *Contingency, Irony, and Solidarity,* I do not agree that the only way to resist applying public criteria to private matters is to call on the resources of irony. For a good critique of this emphasis from a very useful expressivist approach to ethics, see Blackburn, 291.

3. Let me cite some useful contemporary philosophical criticisms of economic choice models of rationality, of traditional and teleological ideals of reason, and of general normative rationality applied to the emotions. Consider first Jon Elster's work on the limits of applying rational models for decision making to the emotions. Despite a career devoted largely to indicating how often behavior is in fact governed by economic rationality even when it seems irrational to many, Elster concludes that we cannot use a cost-benefit model to weigh incentives related to emotions. Emotions do not simply postulate rewards; they shape "choices as well as rewards" and so establish the frameworks by which we have to understand the rewards as rewards (413; see 303–6). This means that we cannot assume there will be clear trade-offs between the domain established by emotions and the domain of material incentives. Our models of rational calculation then run into substantial tension with the ways that emotions establish values:

> We may conclude . . . that the interaction between emotion and interest cannot be modeled in terms of competing costs and benefits. Concerning the short-lived emotions, the model correctly predicts that there will be a trade-off between emotional rewards and other rewards, but it fails to incorporate the fact that the trade-off itself may be shaped by emotion. Concerning the durable emotions, the model ignores that the pursuit of emotional satisfaction may be so fundamental to a person's life that all the other considerations become secondary. In brief summary, the short-lived passions undermine the theory of the rational actor, whereas the durable ones undermine the theory of *homo economicus.* (306)

To rely on reason to establish models of either the actor or the basic calculi is to impose one practice or one aspect of the psyche on another with no clear justification for the domination and no clear path for how it might produce the appropriate mode of judgment. Instead Elster calls for a "historical psychology" that may be capable of providing a common platform enabling connections between objectifiable incentives and affective investments. And Elizabeth Anderson provides a powerful supplement to this case by spelling out the many various personal incentives that enter into valuations and require what she calls an "expressive theory of rational action."

I am most impressed with the arguments made by Bernard Williams against teleological ideals of reason. First, there are the brute facts of sharp and significant differences among cultures and even among human dispositions that make any single normative vision have to risk becoming so abstract in its pursuit of representativeness that it becomes ineffectual as practical guidance. Second, teleological thinking about the emotions has to rely on a picture of how emotions establish values that is easy to find highly idealized. For such thinking has to evade or sanitize the concrete powers that many philosophers suggest make it possible for the emotions to construct values in the first place. So long as values are not laden with associations and projections but seem the direct consequence of how we bring thought to bear in making appraisals, there can be clear normative versions of how these appraisals might best take place. Yet we have seen that the psyche rarely works with such clarity and directness. Instead, values are mediated by the complex states persons occupy as they engage specific situations. States like pride or hope or anger or love do not so much appraise facts as bring to those facts the possibility of entering certain stories and states and interpersonal relationships that emerge as we develop attitudes toward situations. Moreover, attitudes are not transparent. They involve fantasies about personal needs and about possible identities that audiences can confer.

When we turn specifically to the role of emotions in relation to moral thinking, Aaron Ben-Zeev seems to strike the right note. He argues that even though the emotions have important roles to play in the moral domain, these roles are limited to certain circumstances. One must integrate the tendency to think as a particular agent when confronted with moral decisions with the more "general intellectual perspective" (261) characteristic of other forms of rationality. And more impressive yet is the powerful critique of using reason for the production of normative principles that one finds in the expressivist arguments of Simon Blackburn's *Ruling Passions*. Basing his analyses on a Humean empiricism, Blackburn argues that reason is an input device, a means of sorting the world, and not an output device that produces compelling principles: "Reason determines our understanding of our situation, which means the inputs, not the way inputs are transformed into outputs" (261). For Blackburn, then, it is only when desires are taken as objects that we can imagine their fitting into one normative framework based on the question "Why must I do that?" When we look at the actual circumstances within which choices are made, we find a wide range of available perspectives, each with its own justificatory standards. To assess choices we do not need some general principle but some highly specific information about the specific motivating concerns of the individual involved. And it is simply not predictable whether specific agents will be motivated by the forms of self-reflection that for a philosopher make the idea of practical identity so compelling. See pp. 258–60, as well as 233–37 where Blackburn takes up the question of the "sensible knave" who does not lack reason, but lacks the sentiments binding him to standard forms of moral reasoning.

4. Michael Stöcker offers many very useful remarks that apply to two aspects of my arguments. His entire book is devoted to showing how emotions not only respond to values but also play a role in constituting them. And his closing remarks are very good on how we make use of emotions in assessing emotions, especially with regard to concerns about "the lives they [these emotions] foster or hinder" (325). Emotions, in other words, have their own normative dimension that has very little to do with reasoning. However, I suspect Stöcker would not be happy with my emphasis on conative orientations.

5. I have to admit from the start that my emphases will not hold for all emotions. At the least, we have to make a basic distinction (developed by Ben-Zeev, 263) between holding a value emotionally and having a value because of an emotional state. Believing passionately in gun control is quite different from loving one's guns or having pride in one's belief. In the first case, the value is held because of what one believes and the emotion is a relation to oneself as the believer. Therefore, to modify or assess the value, we have to deal directly with the belief as well as with associated beliefs about why this belief matters so much for the person. But in cases like loving one's guns, the value resides in how the emotional state engages our interests and manages to unfold over time. In such instances, the role of belief is considerably reduced, and the other aspects of the agent's intentionality correspondingly become more central. As belief recedes from our account, we have to interpret the emotional investment by examining the specific distributions of psychological energies that emerge and directions of attention that they make possible.

6. Richard Eldridge suggests that we can understand Romanticism as a widespread effort by writers and philosophers to "make sense of ourselves as having something to live

up to" ("Reading For and Against the Plot" 180) when the cultural and civic orders seem to have betrayed the idealizations shaping our sense of such responsibilities. I find this reliance on what he calls "poesis" or the composing of ways of life for which there seem no longer prevailing external sanctions to be a fairly close parallel to my sense of why emotions become increasingly the locus for testing what might count as feasible ideals. For the most succinct account of Eldridge's position, see his "Kant, Hölderlin, and the Experience of Longing," in *Beyond Representation*, 175–96. I also find some of Eldridge's recent work the richest examples of how one might bring close reading of literary texts into discourses within which most American philosophers participate. See especially *Leading a Human Life: Wittgenstein, Intentionality, and Romanticism*.

7. Nussbaum tries to handle this difficulty by what seems to me unwarranted assertion: "So we appear to have type-identities between emotions and judgments—or to put it more elastically, looking ahead, between emotions and value-laden cognitive states. Emotions can be defined in terms of those evaluative cognitions alone, although we must recognize that some feelings of tumult or 'arousal' will often accompany them, and sometimes feelings of a more type-specific kind" (64). I think we can usually give adjectival interpretations offering labels for emotions based on the evaluative projections, if not cognitions, that agents produce. But such interpretations do not go a long way toward appreciating the complexities of intentionality or allowing the feelings any significance in distinguishing the agent's situation. I submit that my own emotions in hearing about Nussbaum's book clearly do not fit the model that it affords.

8. Nussbaum has on many occasions aligned her view of reason with Aristotle's, so I treat it that way in my arguments. But when one uses her index to see what she means specifically by "reason," one gets very disappointing results. Rather than providing any positive definition of "reason," all three passages cited seem content to defeat the assumption that emotions have to be irrational. We see clearly the basic logic of her position in the following footnote from her book. She cites a sentence by Alan Gewirtz asserting that "while the nonrational emotions can distort, delude, or blaze uncontrollably, they have worth in themselves and can also open, clarify, and enrich understanding." Then she comments, "It is hard to see why Gewirtz should call an element that can open, clarify, and enrich understanding 'nonrational,' unless he is using the language of rationality in a purely descriptive and non-normative sense, meaning by it something like 'not concerned with the maximizing of individual satisfactions' " (355–56). It seems to me that many things that can clarify and enrich understanding are nonrational. That is why we have concepts like "desirable but dangerous." I take Gewirtz's point to be that there is no clear means of determining on the level of theory whether these emotions will delude or will clarify.

9. I hope I am not the only one to whom it sounds strange to speak of "supporting the ethical worth of a life rich in personal emotion" (459). On the one hand, I wonder why a life rich in personal emotion needs the additional value claim that it is somehow also ethically flourishing. On the other hand, if a life rich in personal emotion needs also a claim for ethical goodness, there must be something in this richness that otherwise might resist the ethical. Given these difficulties with Nussbaum's formulation, it seems to me much more prudent to dwell on quite particular reasons why we consider certain emotions rich and envision people taking satisfaction in them than to seek ends that require treating the emotions as means to those ends. For an argument similar to the one I am making here, see Blackburn's discussion of cases where concerns about ethics introduce "one thought too many": "In a personal relationship, for example with one's partner or children, the last thing one wants is that people are acting with an eye to behaving well, or out of a sense of duty" (21).

10. Page 190 provides a summary of Nussbaum's understanding of developmental theory.

11. Bringing developmental theory to bear also creates a serious problem for cognitivism in determining just where the emotions reside as they extend from childhood into adulthood. Straight psychoanalysis has no problem here because it can invoke the unconscious or some notion of disposition. We have seen Wollheim make a strong case for the role dispositions play in giving psychological reality to the long-term states that influence particular episodes or occurrent emotions. But Nussbaum rejects Wollheim on this point. She tells us she prefers to speak of a distinction between "background" and "situational" "emotion-judgments." This distinction allows for more of a continuum than Wollheim's does, since "a background emotion is one that persists through situations of different types" without having to be substantially different from the momentary state (69n). And her distinction "does not perfectly map on to the conscious-unconscious distinction" (70n). "A persisting love or joy may have a distinctive phenomenology, without transforming itself into a situational emotion" (70). For "the central form of a background emotion is always love or attachment to some thing or person, seen as very important for one's own flourishing—in combination with some general belief to the effect that the well-being of this thing or person is not fully under one's own control" (74).

This view, however, asks a lot from what remains in the background. Yet Nussbaum seems trapped. She wants the emotion to be governed by thinking, but she does not want the thinking to be propositional and so a process independent of the emotion itself. So she uses the background emotion to postulate a place where this nonpropositional thinking can take place. Background emotions play explanatory roles as long-term judgments about flourishing and as short-term means of connecting these beliefs to what does occur in experience. Hence we find her claiming that background emotions have the power to "explain patterns of action" "even when no specific incident gives rise to an awareness" of the emotion (70n). This in turn means that "cognitive appraisals need not all be objects of reflexive self-consciousness" (126). Even though nothing in a situation has caused us to "register our emotion," "it is often right to say that the emotion remains there, explaining what we do, just as the belief that two plus two equals four" is "present" even though we are not always aware of it (126). This rather desperate ontologizing demonstrates by contrast why philosophers like Wollheim and Michael Stöcker want to keep dispositions distinct from emotions, yet do not want to postulate ideal entities. Dispositions are behaviorally manifest, and they do not entail any mysterious forms of judgment or commitments to flourishing. Some dispositions, like irascibility, hardly aid in our flourishing. But Nussbaum blithely builds a model of flourishing into the very idea of having long-term emotions, without in any way providing evidence. (And she confuses the system-based background of mathematics with the psychological working of background emotions.)

12. The problem I am working through here seems to me even more pressing and more disturbing when Nussbaum turns to normative judgments of those emotions like compassion which can play central roles in public life. She argues plausibly that compassion can guide reason and hence make the cognitive force of emotions available for political and legal decisions. Here it seems crucial that society emphasize norms that allow society to have some expectations about compassion. But again we have to ask where this norm comes from? Does it come from something we realize within the emotion or from reason's judgments about the emotion? And if it comes from reason, why should we see the emotion itself as performing any significant function that reason itself cannot do? After all, it is reason that tells us when compassion is trustworthy.

For a test case let us turn again to Nussbaum's projected confrontation with Stoic suspicions about compassion as a political force. She forcefully presents three challenges to her own views (challenges that I think hold for all efforts to link reason to emotion): How do we know which instances of compassion we can trust? Why should we honor our feelings for a situation more than our dispassionate reasoning about it? and How can we serve justice while relying on ways some people elicit our compassion while others do not? Her response leads to the following summary:

> By allowing Sophoclean tragedy to be my guide, I have given my imagined society a definite set of judgments in the three areas where judgments can go wrong: seriousness, blame, and the extent of concern. But at this point we must confront these judgments directly. For we want not just any and every type of compassion, but, so to speak, compassion within the limits of reason, compassion allied to a reasonable ethical theory in the three areas of judgment. I have argued that if compassion is there, even in a distorted form, we have an ethical core to work with. (414; see also 392, 399)

We would have that ethical core because we could use our notion of reason to set the compassion straight. We could use the feelings offered by the compassion. Then we could use a rational judgment of the compassion to strengthen its hold, and we could from that possibility of rational judgment determine what is wrong with the distorted forms and show how they might be adjusted to meet reason's norms. However, this presupposes that all the work done to keep the discussion focused on compassion within the limits of reason does not already distort the ways we actually experience compassion. For once reason is given so central a part to play, it seems to me that Nussbaum is providing not a theory of the emotion, but a theory about why it matters to have forms of reasoning that can at once rely on and judge forms of compassion. We are told simultaneously to rely on compassion and to determine from outside compassion—from reason—what count as the kinds of compassion on which we can rely. There is an obvious problem of authority here—compassion counts only when it is approved by reason, yet compassion is trustworthy only when it internalizes that rationality. And there is an even more disturbing psychological problem (one that pervades her normalizing of all the emotions but becomes clearest when she is discussing the public sphere). I think we give compassion the power we do because we assume that, as an emotion, it bypasses reason's reliance on generalization and goes directly to sympathy with an immediate concrete situation. Compassion matters for us precisely because it does not require a language of "oughtness." Compassion is a condition of responsiveness, not a reflective judgment about what a person ought to pursue, although the emotion may lead us to develop a sense of obligation. But once obligation emerges, then it seems to me we have to talk about the agent's egoistic concerns. We are acting not out of compassion but out of our egoistic sense of what obligates us to act. We have introduced a second body of motives that have their force not from how we see the other, but from how we negotiate the modes of self-regard that bind us to being reasonable or "flourishing."

Nussbaum seems to recognize this in a sentence that also seems to wish the problem away: "Compassion is our species' way of hooking the good of others to the fundamentally eudaimonistic (though not egoistic) structure of our imaginations and our most intense cares" (388). Because compassion has to be nonegoistic, she wants our eudaimonistic judgments also to be nonegoistic. But it would be very difficult to characterize our interests in reason and in ethics if we deny all egoistic source, especially if we want reason to be linked with our sense of ourselves and not to function as deontological demand. Conversely, this effort to link compassion and reason in eudaimonistic terms subjects the emotion to what establishes good on grounds that have little to do with how the emotion responds to particulars. The emotions are asked to operate as if they were mini-philosophers. Their concern is no longer primarily with their objects but with the justifications that the self-reflexive subject might make for them. Value then is not in qualities of the states they produce or enable, but in how they do or do not contribute to our virtue. And that involves severe constraints on their capacities to create salience, to generate actions, to put pressure on our reasoning, and to establish close relations with other persons.

For a simpler alternative, we need only recognize that conative drives need not be blind to other people. Rather, part of controlling our environment is having the power to move toward what engages us as interesting or compelling in its own right. And part of pursuing second-order identities involves having to worry about the qualities of our behavior that shape our relations with other persons. Denying the egoism fundamental to our emotional investments does not guarantee any greater sensitivity to others; it only subordinates our powers of making these investments to whatever ideology defines the appropriate "oughts."

13. My colleague John Bishop has pointed out to me that the "Scylla and Charybdis" chapter of *Ulysses* takes up the topic of Shakespeare's authorship in order to interpret Joyce's own involvement in his novel. The interpretation Joyce actually provides has to be interpreted in part in relation to the fact that for Joyce's culture the ideal of being a writer sanctioned all sorts of "genius" behavior that most of us find ourselves unable to approve. He often acted abysmally because he felt justified by his talent. But one can argue that his locating so much of his emotional life within his writing provided a somewhat workable alternative to continually playing at being a genius in his social worlds.

14. In this discussion I will grant Nussbaum her premises and deal only with narrative art. But I will mention again my essay "Lyrical Ethics and Literary Experience" because it offers an extended critique of this tendency to base all her claims about ethics in litera-ture on narrative, hence ignoring the specific ways that lyric modes take up that topic. For a superb general account of what is powerful and what limited in Nussbaum's literary crit-icism, see Richard Eldridge, "Reading For and Against the Plot: On Nussbaum's Integra-tion of Literature and Moral Philosophy" (forthcoming).

15. I have to point out that this psychologizing of the idealization in Dantean allegory and in classical literature in general and the praise of Joyce because he does not deny the reality of daily life are difficult to reconcile with any decent literary history. Different gen-res have different relations to daily life so that it is dangerous to make that concern the ob-ject of ethical judgments. Classical texts might not deny daily life but just bracket its importance in order to perform other tasks. One could also point out that there are spaces in Dante's hell for those who deny the claims of practical life, but Dante's main interest is in salvation, not in good sex.

16. For a concrete example of the level of realism that Nussbaum ignores, consider the following statement by Joyce about Molly in one of his letters: "*Penelope* is the *clou* of the book. The first sentence contains 2500 words. There are eight sentences in the episode. It begins and ends with the female word *yes*. It turns like the huge earth ball slowly surely and evenly round and wound spinning, its four cardinal points being the female breasts, arse, womb and cunt expressed by the words *because, bottom* (in all senses bottom but-ton bottom of the class, bottom of the sea, bottom of his heart), *woman, yes*. Though prob-ably more obscene than any preceding episode it seems to me to be perfectly sane full amoral fertilisable untrustworthy engaging shrewd limited prudent indifferent *Weib, Ich bin der [sic] Fleisch der stets bejaht*." See *Letters*, 1:170.

## 6. Emotions, Values, and the Claims of Reason, Part 2

1. When I speak of judgment not based on concepts, I am thinking of thinkers from Stephen Toulmin to Hubert Dreyfus who emphasize tacit knowledge and the ways we are

guided by skills rather than by principles. The best analogue for how the relevant internal adjustments take place is probably the way works of art produce correspondences and provide a sense of purposive coherence for them.

2. Blackburn's practical example is also worth citing: "To understand the value of a piece of money it is no good staring at it. It is necessary to understand the processes of human economic behavior. You need to approach the token not with a microscope and a scalpel, but with an eye for the large patterns of human interactions. Similarly, to understand the ethical proposition, it is no good looking for a 'concept' or 'truth condition.' We need the same eye for whole processes of human action and interaction. We need synthesis not analysis" (50).

3. Ben-Zeev provides a useful discussion along similar lines of how we take responsibility for emotions (246–65). And he helps isolate the domain where expressive behavior is relevant by distinguishing between cases where agents display powers for regulating the emotion itself and cases where they regulate the manifestation of the emotion (222). I will be concerned only with those cases where the activity involves investments in the emotion itself.

4. When I speak about shareable qualities I am emphasizing what we might call the state-dimension of emotions. Some emotions have their rationale primarily in relation to objects—hope and jealousy would be paradigms. Others are closer to illocutionary states than to perlocutionary projections. Take for example joy, trust, pride, and solidarity as well as their negative counterparts. In these states, value resides directly in the specific states of mind made possible by a mode of caring. Indeed, the states could almost be intransitive. Immanent qualities are what elicit the subject's investments.

5. As long as one's valuing depends on something to be known, there is a strong case for relying on the instruments reason affords. If my anger at John can be seen as a proposition about John's place in my life, I ought to be able to judge accurately what my options are and adjust my attitude accordingly. The adjustment may entail overriding the emotion so that judgment can prevail, or it may entail pursuing a richer version of the emotion because I come to appreciate its normative possibilities. In either case, the crucial factor is that we call upon judgment to stand apart from the specific intensities and felt contradictions within the experience of anger. If we can establish the appropriate proposition, we do not have to worry about other aspects of the immediate intentional state. But in pursuing this line of thinking we can also see what is involved when we are not satisfied by the appropriate proposition or are not satisfied by it. Then the intentionality itself becomes the focus of attention. We shift from dealing with values as depending on specific judgments about objects to dealing with valuing as a subjective process whose significance resides in how the subject deploys its energies.

6. My comments and citations below pertain to section 4 of Kant's *Critique of Judgment*, pp. 18–20 in the Pluhar translation. My use of this passage depends in part on my treatment of Kantian purposiveness in my *Subjective Agency*.

7. I do know two terrific philosophical discussions of intensity—one provided by Henri Bergson in *Time and Free Will*, and a second, influenced by Bergson, by Gilles Deleuze in his *Difference and Repetition*, 222–46, which has been reworked in interesting ways by Brian Massumi, *Parables for the Virtual*, 24–34. Ironically, there are close parallels to all three philosophers in the best discussion I know of intensity in relation to literary texts, Allen Tate's quite old-fashioned essay "Tension in Poetry." In all four texts tension becomes a juncture where the extensional folds into the intensional, with each pulling against the other. Ben-Zeev is also useful because he treats intensity as a measure of the significance of emotions. He begins by breaking down the variables that determine how we experience it. Intensity depends on partiality so that there is strong momentary magnitude. The nature of

the intensity will then be shaped by two basic sets of variables—those affecting "the impact of the event," and those constituting the "background circumstances." The impact variables are the "strength, reality and relevance of the event," while the background circumstances vary in terms of "controllability, readiness, and deservingness" (118–50).

8. I propose a sharp distinction between self-reflexive narcissism and pathological narcissism. Pathological narcissism binds the subject to its material image and to all the detritus of memory that gives this image the power to be the focal point for identity concerns, relegating the lives of other people to stage props in this drama. Self-reflexive satisfactions, on the other hand, seem to me necessary to most forms of locating values within the life of consciousness. As Yeats's poem indicates, this form of narcissism may even be basic to our appreciating how other people fully invest in their values. I offer a more elaborate version of finding the other within one's own self-absorption in my essay "Spectacular Antispectacle: Ecstasy and Nationality in Whitman and His Heirs."

9. It is worth noting that "He and She" may itself move beyond the "I am I" to a similar impersonal site. The poem as poem invites us to share the position of a synthetic consciousness putting into one thought both the passive moon terrified of losing itself and this assertive sexual self-absorption.

10. These dangers of self-congratulation are not simply psychological and aesthetic. As Michael Oakeshott and many others have argued, the deep problem in welfare societies is maintaining full human respect for those who become the objects of our abstract kindness.

11. This entire discussion severely abbreviates the argument I develop in chapter 6 of my *Painterly Abstraction in Modernist American Poetry*.

12. Actually there are at least two renderings of this image painted in the late 1880s, one at the Courtauld Gallery in London and one at the Phillips Gallery in Washington, D.C.

13. Silvan Tomkins offers exemplary applications of the idea of complexes with respect to affective investments.

14. I take the notion of push and pull from Robert Nozick's *Anarchy, State, and Utopia*. Nozick does not discuss the emotions per se, but applies these terms in a much more general discussion of values.

15. See Ben-Zeev for good contemporary characterizations of a wide range of specific emotions.

16. De Sousa's brilliant opening chapter is quite good on this dichotomy.

17. I have to distinguish two quite different kinds of theoretical models for interpreting how cultures can be said to constitute the values we attribute to and through emotional states. One kind dominates the social sciences. Here it typically suffices to clarify how we learn emotions by developing a repertoire of social roles that we then adapt in specific situations. "Sophisticated" literary criticism pursues more speculative, psychology-based versions of cultural constitution that rely on the concept of subjection developed by Louis Althusser in his thinking about an "imaginary" order of identifications. For such criticism the crucial element is not the social role, but the processes by which we internalize these roles as the means of asserting identities and seeking recognition for those assertions. Below I will engage Judith Butler as probably the most influential contemporary proponent of the Althusserian heritage, which she crosses with a poststructuralist sense of how cultural institutions establish systematic codes framing those possibilities for identification. For a good critical summary of the first kind of model that dominates social psychology, see Paul Griffiths' superb sixth chapter. Griffiths is somewhat sympathetic to a limited version of this approach because he thinks it is important to view the emotions from a "psycho-evolutionary" perspective. But he offers keen criticisms of the am-

bitious culturalist claims posed by philosophers like Rom Harré. I cite other criticisms of cultural constructivism in my first chapter.

18. I want to give the flavor of incisive precision that Butler's prose gives these ideas. First, on fictiveness: "Does the name, understood as a linguistic token, which designates sex, only work to *cover over* its fictiveness, or are there occasions in which *the fictive and unstable status of that bodily ego trouble* the name, expose the name as a crisis in referentiality?" (*Bodies that Matter,* 139). Then on what this crisis enables: "It is this constitutive failure of the performative, this slippage between discursive command and its appropriated effect, which provides the linguistic occasion and index for a conventional disobedience" (122).

19. I think the basic source of my differences from Butler is her distrust of giving the ego any role in her psychology because she thinks that where the ego is, there we find subjection and fantasies of mastery. But if one rejects the ego, one has only the operations of language or of material forces. Then one cannot deal with conative adjustments or with the kinds of experiences that lead the ego out of itself. Consequently her complex sense of cultural content is matched by a very narrow model of cultural process.

20. For a parallel account of *Dubliners* as social text, see Joseph Valente, "Between Resistance and Complicity: Metro-Colonial Tactics in Joyce's Dubliners."

21. It is always possible to claim, as many New Historicists do, that any effort to struggle against a structure is part of the structure since the terms used in resistance are shaped by what they have to oppose. But precisely because this logic is always available, there are reasons to suspect its relevance in any given particular case. One has to judge concretely whether the alternatives are so contaminated by what they resist as to constitute alternative versions of subjection. On some occasions the effort to resist can open ways of thinking that no longer function simply as bound opposites trapped within the same structure.

22. There is a good account of epiphany and the relevant sources for what I quote in Schwarz, 66–67.

23. Joyce goes to great lengths to dramatize the many ways that Gabriel does not fit even his own upper-bourgeois milieu. In the opening of "The Dead" all the females eagerly await two males, who are the opposite poles of Irish maleness—Gabriel the cultivated unionist and Freddy Malins, the representative of romantic, irresponsible Irish dispositions. Gabriel then proceeds to behave insensitively to all the females because of his uneasy self-absorption. In giving a coin to the serving girl, he even takes on the role of other males in the story who betray significant trusts. When he ultimately tells a joke about being the victim of his aunts, he reveals the anxiety that may lie behind his awkwardness, especially since this comes right after a story about monks sleeping in their coffins.

24. This letting the first person pervade the third is common in Joyce, as Hugh Kenner (*Joyce's Voices*) pointed out in postulating his famous Uncle Charlie principle. The general effect of this device is a pervasive ambiguity within the text about whether we are seeing the characters from the outside or living the world from within their language and so sharing their inability ever to escape imaginary projections onto the world. Yet on some of these linguistic occasions—I hope at least the one I am discussing—we can glimpse a higher-level authorial consciousness that wants to put both possibilities together. Then we have a position from which to acknowledge how the emotion-complex takes on particular force for a given character while also understanding that character's strengths and limitations.

## APPENDIX

1. The best statement I know of in Nietzsche about will as sensation is in section 19 of *Beyond Good and Evil.*

2. Derrida's *Memoirs of the Blind: The Self-Portrait and Other Ruins* offers many brilliant readings of how representations of blindness invite the audience to experience the terrors and excitements of pure touch, and hence of encountering something like the pure quality of event without representation.

3. I think it is also possible to treat the change in scale positively as Pollock's effort to find something larger than the self to which to commit his energies—hence the explicit invocations of nature in the large 1950 paintings. From this perspective, Pollock's turn from abstraction would indicate that even succeeding in this vein could not sufficiently engage the self that he wanted to overcome.

4. I give an extended account of this painting in my *Painterly Abstraction in Modernist American Poetry*, 195–98.

5. T. J. Clark offers brilliant connections between the use of *passage* in Cézanne's late Bather paintings and Freud and Lacan. The core of his argument is that Freud and Cézanne seek "a fully and simply physical account of the imagination." So they show bodies "thoroughly subject . . . to the play of fantasy," then let them "appear as they would in a world where all the key terms of our endless debate—imagination, body, mind, phantasy, and so on—would be grasped, by the bodies and imaginations themselves, as descriptions of matter in various states" (147). Then Clark goes on to tell an elaborate tale of "imagining the imagining" of a phallic scenario in material terms (151).

6. The best examples of work based on these associational linkages are Wordsworth's *Prelude*, Stevens's long poems, and the sequence poems pursued by a wide range of poets writing after 1950. My essay "Reading for Affect in the Lyric: From Modern to Contemporary" addresses the ways shifts in affect structure extended contemporary texts.

7. Although he does not use this language, my colleague Stephen Booth offers compelling examples of the modes of motion and adjustment demanded by Shakespeare's sonnets. I love the fantasy of providing a theoretical framework for his intensely antitheoretical sensibility.

# Bibliography

Adorno, Theodor. *Aesthetic Theory*. Minneapolis: University of Minnesota Press, 1997.

Altieri, Charles. *Act and Quality: A Theory of Literary Meaning*. Amherst: University of Massachusetts Press, 1981.

———. "Affect and Intention in Robert Creeley's Poetry during the 1960s." *Open Letter: A Canadian Journal of Writing and Theory* 11 (2001): 16–38.

———. "The Concept of Force as Modernist Response to the Authority of Science." *Modernism / Modernity* 5 (April 1998): 77–93.

———. "Constructing Emotion in Deconstruction." *Contemporary Literature* 43 (2002): 606–14.

———. "Lyrical Ethics and Literary Experience." *Style* 32 (1998): 272–97.

———. "The New Criticism." In *The Edinburgh Encyclopedia of Modern Criticism and Theory*, ed. Julian Wolfrey, 436–44. Edinburgh: Edinburgh University Press, 2002.

———. *Painterly Abstraction in Modernist American Poetry: The Contemporaneity of Modernism*. New York: Cambridge University Press, 1989.

———. "Poetry in a Prose World: Robert Lowell's Life Studies." *Modern Poetry Studies* 1 (1970): 182–98.

———. *Postmodernism Now: Essays on Contemporaneity in the Arts*. University Park: Pennsylvania State University Press, 1998.

———. "Reading for Affect in the Lyric: From Modern to Contemporary." In Joan Retallack and Juliana Spahr, ed., *Poetry and Pedagogy*. Tuscaloosa: University of Alabama Press, 2004.

———. "Reading for an Image of the Reader: A Response to Block, Caraher, and Mykyta." *Reader*, no. 9 (1983): 38–44.

———. "Spectacular Anti-spectacle: Ecstasy and Nationality in Whitman and His Heirs." *American Literary History* 11 (spring 1999): 34–62.

———. "Stevens's Ideas of Feeling: Towards an Exponential Poetics." *Centennial Review* 36 (1992): 139–74.

———. *Subjective Agency: A Theory of First-Person Expressivity and Its Social Implications*. Oxford: Blackwell, 1994.

Anderson, Elizabeth. *Value in Ethics and Economics*. Cambridge: Harvard University Press, 1993.

Arnold, Matthew. *The Poems of Matthew Arnold*. Edited by Miriam Allott and Robert H. Super. New York: Oxford University Press, 1986.

Balibar, Etienne. *Spinoza: From Individuality to Transindividuality*. Delft: Eburan, 1997.

Ben-Zeev, Aaron. *The Subtlety of Emotions*. Cambridge: MIT Press, 2000.

Bergson, Henri. *Time and Free Will: An Essay on the Immediate Data of Consciousness*. Translated by F. L. Pogson. New York: Harper and Row, 1960.

Berlant, Lauren, ed. *Intimacy*. Chicago: University of Chicago Press, 2000.

Bishop, Elizabeth. *The Complete Poems, 1927–1979*. New York: Noonday, 1983.

Blackburn, Simon. *Ruling Passions: A Theory of Practical Reasoning*. Oxford: Clarendon Press, 1998.

Booth, Stephen, ed. *Shakespeare's Sonnets*. New Haven: Yale University Press, 1977.

Butler, Judith. *Bodies That Matter: On the Discursive Limits of Sex*. New York: Routledge, 1993.

——. *Subjects of Desire: Hegelian Reflections in Twentieth-Century France*. New York: Columbia University Press, 1987.

Campbell, Sue. *Interpreting the Personal: Expression and the Formation of Feelings*. Ithaca: Cornell University Press, 1997.

Cataldi, Sue. *Emotion, Depth, and Flesh: A Study of Sensitive Space: Reflections on Merleau-Ponty's Philosophy of Embodiment*. Albany: State University of New York Press, 1993.

Cavell, Marcia. *The Psychoanalytic Mind: From Freud to Philosophy*. Cambridge: Harvard University Press, 1993.

Cavell, Stanley. *Conditions Handsome and Unhandsome: The Constitution of Emersonian Perfectionism*. Chicago: University of Chicago Press, 1990.

Chipp, Herschel Browning, ed. *Theories of Modern Art; a Source Book by Artists and Critics*. Berkeley: University of California Press, 1968.

Chodorow, Nancy. *The Power of Feelings: Personal Meanings in Psychoanalysis, Gender, and Culture*. New Haven: Yale University Press, 1999.

Clark, T. J. *Farewell to an Idea: Episodes from a History of Modernism*. New Haven: Yale University Press, 1999.

Creeley, Robert. *The Collected Poems of Robert Creeley, 1945–75*. Berkeley: University of California Press, 1982.

——. *A Quick Graph: Collected Notes and Essays*. San Francisco: Four Seasons Foundation, 1970.

Dadlez, E. M. *What's Hecuba to Him? Fictional Events and Actual Emotions*. University Park: Pennsylvania State University Press, 1997.

Damasio, Antonio. *Descartes' Error : Emotion, Reason, and the Human Brain*. New York: Putnam, 1995.

——. *The Feeling of What Happens: Body and Emotion in the Making of Consciousness*. New York: Harcourt, 1999.

——. *Looking for Spinoza: Joy, Sorrow, and the Feeling Brain*. Orlando: Harcourt, 2003.

Dancy, Jonathan. *Moral Reasons*. Oxford: Blackwell, 1993.

Deigh, John. "Cognitivism in the Theory of Emotions." *Ethics* 104 (July 1994): 824–54.

Deleuze, Gilles. *Difference and Repetition*. Translated by Paul Patton. New York: Columbia University Press, 1994.

———. *Expressionism in Philosophy: Spinoza*. Translated by Martin Joughin. New York: Zone Books, 1990.

Deleuze, Gilles, and Felix Guattari. *A Thousand Plateaus*. Translated by Brian Massumi. Minneapolis: University of Minnesota Press, 1987.

Dennis, Carl. *Practical Gods*. New York: Penguin Books, 2001.

Derrida, Jacques. *Memoirs of the Blind: The Self-Portrait and Other Ruins*. Translated by Pascale-Anne Brault and Michael Naas. Chicago: University of Chicago Press, 1993.

De Sousa, Ronald. *The Rationality of Emotion*. Cambridge: MIT Press, 1987.

Eldridge, Richard. *Leading a Human Life: Wittgenstein, Intentionality, and Romanticism*. Chicago: University of Chicago Press, 1997.

———. "Reading For and Against the Plot: On Nussbaum's Integration of Literature and Moral Philosophy." Circulated manuscript.

———, ed. *Beyond Representation: Philosophy and Poetic Imagination*. New York: Cambridge University Press, 1996.

Eliot, T. S. "Poetry and Propaganda." *Bookman* 70, no. 6 (February 1933): 595–602.

———. *Selected Essays*. London: Faber and Faber, 1961.

Elster, Jon. *Alchemies of the Mind: Rationality and the Emotions*. New York: Cambridge University Press, 1999.

Feagin, Susan. *Reading with Feeling: The Aesthetics of Appreciation*. Ithaca: Cornell University Press, 1996.

Feagin, Susan, and Patrick Maynard, eds. *Aesthetics*. New York: Oxford University Press, 1997.

Frank, Robert. *Passions within Reason: The Strategic Role of Emotions*. New York: Norton, 1988.

Frankfurt, Harry. *The Importance of What We Care About: Philosophical Essays*. Cambridge: Cambridge University Press, 1988.

Freadman, Richard. *Threads of Life: Autobiography and the Will*. Chicago: University of Chicago Press, 2001.

Goodman, Nelson. *The Languages of Art: An Approach to a Theory of Symbols*. Indianapolis: Bobbs-Merrill, 1968.

Gordon, Robert M. *The Structure of Emotions: Investigations in Cognitive Philosophy*. Cambridge: Cambridge University Press, 1987.

Green, Marjorie, ed. *Spinoza: A Collection of Critical Essays*. South Bend: University of Notre Dame Press, 1979.

Greenspan, Patricia. *Emotions and Reasons: An Inquiry into Emotional Justification*. New York: Routledge, 1988.

Greimas, Algirdas Julien, and Jacques Fontanille. *The Semiotics of Passions: From States of Affairs to States of Feeling*. Translated by Paul Perron and Frank Collins. Minneapolis: University of Minnesota Press, 1993.

Griffiths, Paul. *What Emotions Really Are*. Chicago: University of Chicago Press, 1997.

Hacking, Ian. *The Social Construction of What?* Cambridge: Harvard University Press, 1999.

Hampshire, Stuart. *Spinoza*. Baltimore: Penguin Books, 1973.

Harré, Rom, ed. *The Social Construction of Emotions*. Oxford: Oxford University Press, 1986.

Heidegger, Martin. *Being and Time*. Translated by John Macquarrie and Edward Robinson. New York: Harper and Row, 1962.

Hejinian, Lyn. "Figuring Out." Unpublished lecture.

Hjort, Mette, and Sue Laver, eds. *Emotion and the Arts*. New York: Oxford University Press, 1997.

Holland, Norman. *The Dynamics of Literary Response*. New York: Columbia University Press, 1989.

Hume, David. *A Treatise of Human Nature*. London: Penguin Books, 1969.

James, Henry. *The Sacred Fount*. New York: Grove Press, 1953.

James, William. *Psychology: The Briefer Course*. Edited by Gordon Allport. New York: Harper Torchbooks, 1961.

——. "What Is an Emotion?" *Mind* 9 (1884): 188–205.

Joyce, James. *Dubliners*. New York: Vintage, 1993.

——. *Letters of James Joyce*, vol. 1. Edited by Stuart Gilbert. New York: Viking, 1957.

——. *Ulysses*. New York: Modern Library, 1961.

Kamler, Howard. *Identification and Character: A Book on Psychological Development*. Albany: State University of New York Press, 1994.

Kant, Immanuel. *Critique of Judgment*. Translated by Werner Pluhar. Indianapolis: Hackett, 1987.

Katz, Jack. *How Emotions Work*. Chicago: University of Chicago Press, 1999.

Keats, John. *The Collected Letters of John Keats*. Edited by Maurice Buxton Forman. Oxford: Oxford University Press, 1935.

Kenner, Hugh. *Joyce's Voices*. Berkeley: University of California Press, 1978.

King, Bishop Henry. *Poems*. Edited by Margaret Crum. Oxford: Clarendon Press, 1965.

Knapp, Steven. *Literary Interest: The Limits of Anti-formalism*. Cambridge: Harvard University Press, 1993.

Korsgaard, Christine. *The Sources of Normativity*. Cambridge: Cambridge University Press, 1996.

Langer, Susanne. *Feeling and Form: A Theory of Art*. New York: Scribner, 1953.

Lear, Jonathan. *Love and Its Place in Nature: A Philosophical Interpretation of Freudian Psychoanalysis*. New York: Farrar, Straus and Giroux, 1990.

Levinas, Emmanuel. *The Levinas Reader*. Edited by Sean Hand. Cambridge, Mass.: Blackwell, 1989.

Levinson, Jerrold. *The Pleasures of Aesthetics: Philosophical Essays*. Ithaca: Cornell University Press, 1996.

Lingis, Alphonse. "Bestiality." *Symplokē* 6 (1998): 56–71.

Luhmann, Nikolas. *Love as Passion: The Codification of Intimacy*. Cambridge: Harvard University Press, 1986.

Massumi, Brian. *Parables for the Virtual: Movement, Affect, Sensation*. Durham: Duke University Press, 2002.

Meyer, Leonard B. *Emotion and Meaning in Music*. Chicago: University of Chicago Press, 1957.

Mohanty, J. N. *Transcendental Phenomenology*. Oxford: Blackwell, 1989.

Moran, Richard. *Authority and Estrangement: An Essay on Self-Knowledge*. Princeton: Princeton University Press, 2002.

——. "The Expression of Feeling in Imagination." *Philosophical Review* 101 (1994): 75–106.

——. "Making Up Your Mind: Self-Interpretation and Self-Constitution." *Ratio* 1, n.s. (1988): 135–51.

Neu, Jerome. *Emotion, Thought, and Therapy: A Study of Hume and Spinoza.* Berkeley: University of California Press, 1977.

Nietzsche, Friedrich. *Beyond Good and Evil: Prelude to a Philosophy of the Future.* Translated by Walter Kaufmann. New York: Vintage, 1966.

Nozick, Robert. *Anarchy, State, and Utopia.* New York: Basic Books, 1974.

——. *Philosophical Explanations.* Cambridge: Harvard University Press, 1981.

Nussbaum, Martha. *Therapy of Desire: Theory and Practice in Hellenistic Ethics.* Princeton: Princeton University Press, 1994.

——. *Upheavals of Thought: The Intelligence of the Emotions.* New York: Cambridge University Press, 2001.

Oakeshott, Michael. *On Human Conduct.* Oxford: Clarendon Press, 1975.

Oakley, Justin. *Morality and the Emotions.* New York: Routledge, 1992.

Oatley, Keith. *Best Laid Schemes: The Psychology of the Emotions.* New York: Cambridge University Press, 1992.

Oppen, George. *New Collected Poems.* Edited by Michael Davidson. New York: New Directions, 2002.

Parfit, Derek. *Reasons and Persons.* Oxford: Clarendon Press, 1984.

Parret, Herman. *Les passions: essai sur la mise en discours de la subjectivité.* Brussels: Pierre Mardaga, 1986.

Plath, Sylvia. *The Collected Poems.* New York: Harper and Row, 1981.

Plutchik, Robert. *Emotions and Their Vicissitudes.* In *Handbook of Emotions,* ed. Michael Lewis and Jeannette M. Haviland. New York: Guilford Press, 1993.

Popper, Frank. *Origins and Development of Kinetic Art.* Translated by Stephen Bann. Greenwich, Conn.: New York Graphic Society, 1968.

Ridley, Aaron. *Music, Value, and the Passions.* Ithaca: Cornell University Press, 1995.

Rorty, Amélie Oksenberg, ed. *Explaining Emotions.* Berkeley: University of California Press, 1995.

Rorty, Richard. *Contingency, Irony, and Solidarity.* New York: Cambridge University Press, 1989.

Sartre, Jean-Paul. *The Emotions: Outline of a Theory.* Translated by Bernard Frechtman. New York: Philosophical Library, 1948.

Schwarz, Daniel, ed. *James Joyce: "The Dead."* Boston: Bedford Books, 1994.

Searle, John. *Speech Acts: An Essay in the Philosophy of Language.* Cambridge: Cambridge University Press, 1969.

Smith, Quentin. *The Felt Meanings of the World: A Metaphysics of Feeling.* West Lafayette, Ind.: Purdue University Press, 1986.

Smithson, Robert. *The Collected Writings.* Edited by Jack Flam. Berkeley: University of California Press, 1996.

Solomon, Robert. *The Passions: The Myth and Nature of Human Emotion.* South Bend: University of Notre Dame Press, 1976.

Spinoza, Baruch. *Ethics.* Indianapolis: Hackett, 1982.

Staten, Henry. *Nietzsche's Voice.* Ithaca: Cornell University Press, 1990.

Stearns, Carol Z., and Peter N. Stearns, eds. *Emotion and Social Change: Toward a New Psychohistory.* New York: Holmes and Meier, 1988.

Stevens, Wallace. *Collected Poems.* New York: Knopf, 1955.

——. *Letters of Wallace Stevens.* Edited by Holly Stevens. New York: Alfred A. Knopf, 1972.

———. *Opus Posthumous*. New York: Alfred A. Knopf, 1969.

Stewart, Susan. *Poetry and the Fate of the Senses*. Chicago: University of Chicago Press, 2002.

Stöcker, Michael. *Valuing Emotions*. New York: Cambridge University Press, 1996.

Tangney, June Price, and Kurt W. Fisher, eds. *Self-conscious Emotions: The Psychology of Shame, Guilt, Embarrassment, and Pride*. New York: Guildford Press, 1995.

Tate, Allen. "Tension in Poetry." *Collected Essays*. Denver: Alan Swallow, 1959.

Taylor, Charles. *Hegel*. New York: Cambridge University Press, 1975.

———. "The Politics of Recognition." In *Multiculturalism,* ed. Amy Guttman, 25–74. Princeton: Princeton University Press, 1994.

———. *Sources of the Self: The Making of a Modern Identity*. Cambridge: Harvard University Press, 1989.

Taylor, Gabriele. *Pride, Shame, and Guilt: Emotions of Self-Assessment*. Oxford: Clarendon Press, 1985.

Taylor, Gordon. *The Structure of Emotions*. Cambridge: Cambridge University Press, 1987.

Terrada, Rei. *Feeling in Theory: Emotion after the Death of the Subject*. Cambridge: Harvard University Press, 2001.

Tomkins, Silvan. *Shame and Its Sisters: A Silvan Tomkins Reader*. Edited by Eve Kosofsky Sedgwick and Adam Frank. Durham: Duke University Press, 1995.

Toulmin, Stephen. *Human Understanding*. Princeton: Princeton University Press, 1972.

Valente, Joseph. "Between Resistance and Complicity: Metro-Colonial Tactics in Joyce's Dubliners." *Narrative* 6 (1998): 325–40.

Walton, Kendall. *Mimesis as Make-Believe: On the Foundations of the Representational Arts*. Cambridge: Harvard University Press, 1990.

Wesling, Donald. *Literary Faction: Performing and Judging What We Know*. Manuscript in process.

Williams, Bernard. *Ethics and the Limits of Philosophy*. Cambridge: Harvard University Press, 1985.

———. *Shame and Necessity*. Berkeley: University of California Press, 1993.

Williams, C. K. *Flesh and Blood*. New York: Farrar, Straus and Giroux, 1987.

Williams, William Carlos. *The Collected Poems of William Carlos Williams,* vol. 1. Edited by Walton Litz and Christopher MacGowan. New York: New Directions, 1986.

Wittgenstein, Ludwig. *Philosophical Investigations*. Edited by and trans. G. E. M. Anscombe. New York: Macmillan, 1958.

———. *Remarks on Color*. Berkeley: University of California Press, 1977.

———. *Tractatus Logico-Philosophicus*. London: Routledge and Kegan Paul, 1961.

Wollheim, Richard. *The Mind and Its Depths*. Cambridge: Harvard University Press, 1993.

———. *On the Emotions*. New Haven: Yale University Press, 1999.

———. *Painting as an Art*. Princeton: Princeton University Press, 1987.

———. *The Thread of Life*. Cambridge: Harvard University Press, 1984.

Wordsworth, William. *Poems by William Wordsworth*. Edited by John O. Hayden. Harmondsworth: Penguin, 1977.

Yeats, William Butler. *Essays and Introductions*. New York: Macmillan, 1961.

———. *Poems of W. B. Yeats*. Edited by Richard J. Finneran. New York: Macmillan, 1983.

# Index